THE HOLY THURSDAY REVOLUTION

Beatrice Bruteau

ORBIS BOOKS

Maryknoll, New York 10545

Library of Congress Cataloging-in-Publication Data

Bruteau, Beatrice, 1930–
   The Holy Thursday revolution / Beatrice Bruteau.
      p. cm.
   Includes bibliographical references and index.
   ISBN 1-57075-576-0 (pbk.)
   1. Maundy Thursday. 2. Last Supper. 3. Lord's Supper. 4. Foot
washing (Rite). 5. Christian sociology. I. Title.
   BV94.B78 2005
   232.9'57—dc22

                                                    2004020070

For Jim

Contents

Part II
Person as the Basis for the New Paradigm

Part III
Human Nature

Part IV
The Covenant Community

Preface

This book has had a long history. The fundamental idea of the social paradigm shift, which appears here under the figures of foot-washing and Holy Communion, was first treated in terms of "partiality" and "wholeness" in an address to the American Teilhard Association in 1975.[1] That occasion led to invitations to do something in the area of feminism, which was a lively topic at that time. "Partiality" and "wholeness" were reworked as "masculinism" and "feminism," but the latter was subdivided into "paleo-feminism" and "neo-feminism."[2] These pieces in turn led to an invitation to help prepare Episcopal male clergy for the expected vote to extend ordination to women, and I developed the same structural theme finally in terms of the great diptych of Holy Thursday. In calling this form "The Holy Thursday Revolution," I had some vague feeling of making it sound like a political remembrance. (I might add here that I call this day "Holy" Thursday, rather than "Maundy" Thursday, because the former is what the Roman Catholic Church calls Thursday in Holy Week.) From that time on I have told the story and worked out the implications of "I will no longer call you servants . . . but . . . friends"[3] (John 15:15) until gradually it seemed possible to attempt a book-length treatment.

I do not pretend to be giving an alternative interpretation of the Last Supper. All great teaching stories are susceptible of endless retelling in different contexts with different emphases and lessons drawn. I am working rather the other way around: not starting with Holy Thursday and looking for its lessons, but starting with an idea of the kind of experiential/conceptual/social shift that is needed and finding that these stories offer a very effective way to dramatize and present the idea. That there was historically a consciously anticipated Last Supper seems to me unlikely. But that there were suppers, lots of them, and that they were used as the Jesus Movement's principal instrument of teaching and implementation seem to me quite likely. And, having begun to make use of New Testament material in this way, I have gone on to build in the baptismal vision, Nathanael and the fig tree, and various words and events that support and display what I want to say. I do think that a shift in consciousness and behavior of this sort was what the Jesus Movement was proclaiming, explaining, and demonstrating. However, even if none of this was historically the case, the thesis would still stand on its own social, psychological, and metaphysical terms.

Readers may note that there is a good deal of Jewish material in this book. Insofar as the thesis of the book is related to the Jesus Movement antecedent to Christianity, this is appropriate, because that was a Jewish movement in its time and place. But the contemporary movement of Jewish Renewal also has appropriate contributions to make, for it is advocating many of the same points that I have been making in regard to the union of mysticism and social transformation.

I want to thank my publisher Mike Leach (first at Crossroad and now at Orbis), for his steadfast support, advice, and encouragement ever since the publication of *Radical Optimism* in 1993.

I want to express deep appreciation also for all the work and frustration my husband, James Somerville, has generously endured in putting this text on disk. He has also been invaluable in sharing knowledge, taste, scripture scholarship, and language skills. I couldn't have done it without him, and to him this book is gratefully and lovingly dedicated.

The ills of the world continue in abundance, but efforts to counter them are also vigorous. We still need to go to the root of the trouble in the way we perceive one another and at the same time work out economic and political arrangements that will give relief to oppressed and commodified people. We all need to learn on every level that everything people do must be for the welfare of all people. *People are the bottom line.* We need to commit ourselves to this and work toward this end.

Beatrice Bruteau
Winston-Salem, NC
Thanksgiving, 2004

Acknowledgments

The author and publisher gratefully acknowledge permission to quote the following material:

Aronson (Northvale, N.J.): Zalman Schachter-Shalomi, *Paradigm Shift,* ed. Ellen Singer (1993); Rodger Kamenetz, *The Jew in the Lotus* (1994).

Guilford Publications (New York): Paul Gilbert, *Human Nature and Suffering* (1992).

Jewish Lights (Woodstock, Vt.): Excerpt from *Honey from the Rock: An Introduction to Jewish Mysticism—Special Anniversary Edition* © 2000 by Lawrence Kushner. Permission granted by Jewish Lights Publishing, P.O. Box 237, Woodstock, VT 05091 www.jewishlights.com. Excerpt from *The River of Light—Special Anniversary Edition: Jewish Mystical Awareness* © 2000 by Lawrence Kushner. Permission granted by Jewish Lights Publishing, P.O. Box 237, Woodstock, VT 05091 www. jewishlights. com.

Oxford University Press (Oxford, UK): J. Z. Young, *Programs of the Brain* (1978).

Penguin Group (New York): Robert J. Russell, *The Lemurs' Legacy* (1993).

Simon & Schuster (New York): *Who Will Tell the People: The Betrayal of American Democracy* by William Greider. Copyright © 1992 by William Greider. Reprinted with permission of Simon & Schuster Adult Publishing Group. All rights reserved.

The author has endeavored to credit all known persons holding copyrights for passages quoted in this book.

A Note on the Notes

There are a lot of notes. They are presented as endnotes at the back of the book rather than as footnotes. They are not merely references. Most of them contain suggestions for further reading, and many of them have whole paragraphs of additional remarks. To spare the reader the nuisance of searching for the right place in the back of the book every few sentences, I have frequently grouped the references and extended material in larger clumps and placed the superscript numbers at what seem to be convenient pausing places in the text. I suggest that you actually read the notes as their numbers come up, because they will usually be commentaries on what you have just read in the text.

PART I

Domination as Worldview

1

The Ills of the World

The Politics of Domination

"Politics," as I shall be using the word, means simply the art of living together in human society. This human society may be as small as a couple or as large as the whole human race. Taken in this very general sense, politics is practically inescapable, for even the hermit has a human consciousness shaped by memories, emotions, and concepts born of interactions with other people. Indeed, it is not possible to be truly human apart from the web of human social connections. Life, for any species, is a matter of interacting with the environment, and for the human species the largest part of that environment consists of humanmade artifacts and other human beings themselves.

"Politics" derives from the Greek word for the typical human society, *polis*, the city. There is a suggestion in this word *polis* of something small and manageable, of dealing with people whom one knows personally, of continuing to be involved all one's life with these people. It suggests real human contact, concern for concrete situations, involvement with things that touch us where we live. It is this sense of real, concrete, human-to-human contact that I want to save as at least an echo, even in the face of complicated, abstracted, bureaucratized, large-scale problems such as war, ecology, and economics. What we are really talking about, what we are really concerned with, underneath all the complications, abstractions, and rhetoric, is the conduct of concrete human-to-human relations. That is what politics is actually about, and it should be about the art of doing it worthily and well.

People are not statistics. Each one is a world and a dynamic set of connections to other person-worlds. Each one is an extremely complex, constantly readjusting, living plasm of experiences, attitudes, relations, and behaviors. We may read in our newspaper, for instance, that there is guerrilla warfare in some foreign country not too well known to most of us and that some number of people have been killed. The news is a number, the issues at stake something we are not familiar with. But seen up close, each victim is a beloved family member irrevocably removed. The actions that caused the death are particular decisions taken by individual persons at certain points in time for particular reasons that at that moment were motivating enough to produce the decision.

There were the decisions on both sides to use force, the decisions to send certain groups of combatants into certain areas at certain times, decisions on the ground to employ certain tactics, and finally the decision to activate at this moment this weapon with intent to kill. These decisions are made by individuals, each person arriving at that position by an enormously complex process, involving heritage, upbringing, the whole cultural milieu, the context of the dispute, considerations of self-image and other personal social needs, and no doubt many other things. It is, for each, a personal process. None of this comes about by some inexorable, faceless machinery, but by a series of decisions made by particular persons in particular circumstances for particular reasons.

Or, we may read that damage to Earth's environment from the practices of certain kinds of industry—pollution of air and water, spread of deserts, loss of forests, destruction of habitat, extinction of species—is of such a magnitude that we can expect qualitative effects on our life and health. The information is hard to grapple with mentally and emotionally because it is expressed in percentages and in probabilities, and because the damage is done by huge, vague entities, such as businesses and governments that also provide us with things that we want.

The effects are very complicated and interact with all the other factors impinging on human life. The effects may be hard to evaluate, some of the consequences being considered advantageous, others disadvantageous. The reasons for taking the actions, the personal backgrounds behind the reasons, the general attitudes, the particular opinions, the local situation in the hour the decision to act was made—all this is extremely complex. But what is important to remember is that the decisions were made and the actions were taken by human persons, not by agencies or companies or other abstract collectives. And those affected are human persons, not markets or ratings or spheres of influence.

It is this fundamental, ultimate, and always implicit person-to-person relation in our political life that I mean to discuss. My approach is to consider that human behavior takes place in a net of interactions and interconnected ideas, feelings, attitudes, and unacknowledged assumptions, which I call a "consciousness-net." This consciousness-net is a *worldview*, the basic human artifact. It is the essentially human world, the world within which all the properly human things take place. It is the background for everything else that we think or feel or do. Only insofar as something falls within the assumptions of this worldview can it be perceived, noticed, and responded to.

Our political life, our living together in our *polis,* small or large, takes place within this milieu of our worldview. If we feel that there is something fundamental that needs to be changed in our political life—in the way we relate to one another as human beings, whether in the family, the workplace, or internationally—we must go all the way to the fundament of our human consciousness, where our human nature is lodged, and to the relevant worldview, and ask whether *that* can be changed, and, if so, how.

Politics Rests on Perception

My thesis, which will be worked out in succeeding chapters, is that our political behavior depends not only on laws and habits, on national or economic interest, or even on emotional prejudices or instinctive drives, but ultimately on very basic views of how the world is constructed. We have tried to alter our political relations in the past by imposition, by negation, or by exhortation, and these methods have produced some results. However, especially in the case of exhortation, which has tried to get to the root of the trouble and persuade people to get along with one another better, we have experienced considerable frustration. Even when people want, on some level, to try to cooperate more peacefully, we find it difficult, and often we do not fully want to do so. We see the world in such a way that we are effectively blocked from changing our feelings and therefore our behavior.

Our ways of seeing the world are so deeply embedded in our consciousness that we do not even know they are there. We presume, without any question arising, that our basic way of perceiving the world is the way the world really is. If we then run into the suggestion that the world is ordered in different terms, we are disoriented. For instance, before the era of modern physics, a person engaged in dividing and subdividing a solid piece of matter to find the smallest parts into which it could be fragmented would have been so sure of finding particles as to be thrown completely off balance by the idea of conducting the analysis in terms of waves. Or, someone who asked "when" something happened would never expect to be told "before X if viewed from A, but after X if viewed from B," and would feel that that was an unreal and nonsensical answer, because obviously the event must have occurred at some definite (absolute) time.

Now, something like this kind of fundamental attack on our presuppositions and the consequent disorientation is what happens when we are told, "Love your neighbor as yourself." This is such a well-known saying among us that we may not realize the profound dissonance involved, but we know that we are not able to live up to this ideal. We have excused ourselves by saying that it is an ideal, after all, and very difficult to attain, and we can only hope to approximate it sometimes and to a certain extent.

But this, according to my thesis, is not the trouble. The difficulty is that this exhortation flies in the face of everything else that our culture encourages and that our worldview sees. *If we cannot love our neighbor as ourself, it is because we do not perceive our neighbor as ourself.* We perceive the neighbor as precisely *not* ourself, but as a potential threat (or potential aid) to ourself. This perception in turn is based on other assumptions and ways of ordering the world that have to do with how reality is differentiated into separate objects and events and how these are organized into groups or unities. It is not a matter of the exhortation being an ideal that is difficult to attain; it is a contradiction of our culture that is strictly *impossible* to realize, so long as we see the world the way we do.

Political relations depend on our view of how the person-world is put together, of how it is possible to put it together. We acknowledge a certain variety within limits; we know that we can have monarchy, democracy, or military dictatorship; majority rule or consensus; equality or privilege. But all of these will still make certain assumptions about the structure of the person-world. These assumptions will be the worldview within which the different political systems can be formed. Anything that does not rest on these assumptions will be impossible.

It is in this sense that politics depends on perception, and if we want to change our political relations at any very profound level, we must first change our perceptions. It is this kind of change that the Holy Thursday Revolution introduces. It undertakes to change our perceptions so that it will become *possible* for us fully to love our neighbors as ourselves.

To show how this can be done, I propose to begin with political relations that seem undesirable among us, pick out what is common to them, trace this back to the worldview on which it rests, and analyze the assumptions of that view. When these assumptions are brought up to consciousness and seen to be assumptions about the structure of reality, it then becomes possible to think about substituting an alternative set of assumptions, that is, another worldview. The shift from one view to the other is the revolution.

One can then speculatively work out what kinds of human relations might result from the perception according to the new view. We will also have to argue the question of whether indeed such a shift is possible, or whether the so-called assumptions of the present view are in fact the way the world is. Further, we will have to debate whether, if change is theoretically possible, it can in fact be made, and whether it would be desirable to try to make it.

Definition of "Domination"

The theme that I believe is basic to many of our political ills is *domination*. We are all familiar with domination. We see it in the way decisions are made in our families; in the way orders are given at work; in the way social life is structured in our city by gender, race, and wealth; in the way our industry or profession relates to its competitors or its market or its clientele; in the way governmental agencies function; and in international relations, economic, political, and military. We speak colloquially of the top-dog and the underdog, of getting top-drawer service and being low man on the totem pole, of who wears the pants and who calls the shots. Psychologically and ethologically we speak of domination/submission relations and of dominance ranking.

A good deal can be said in favor of these ways of arranging personal and social relations. Dominance ranking is useful for animals living in groups; it keeps order, reduces daily decisions to habits, and provides protection. Those who are dominated in these arrangements may benefit from their position in the ranking. Indeed, *dominance* need not be *domination*, it could be argued, in the sense of oppression or disadvantage to those of lower rank. Some people enjoy and prefer being submissive. It relieves them of responsibility, makes them feel secure, and is emotionally satisfying. As for those who endeavor to be dominant, they strengthen themselves by their competitive efforts, keep the other contestants on their toes, weed out the incompetents, and thus benefit the community generally.

All these points will be taken up for consideration in due course. At the moment I merely want to evoke some familiar images and offer a definition. *Domination is an asymmetrical, or nonreciprocal, relation of determination of being: of the fact that a being is, or of what it is, or of how it can act, or of how it is to be valued.* Domination is a relation that does not work the same in both directions. One commands, the other obeys. One shows respect, the other accepts it but does not return it. One gains privileges from which the other is excluded. One acts as a support, aid, or infrastructure to the other, which acts as an end in itself. That is what I mean by being asymmetrical and nonreciprocal. This will later be contrasted with the paradigm of communion relation, which is symmetrical and reciprocal.

Domination determines being. The dominator may be able to determine whether or not the dominated can be at all, or under what limitations the dominated can exist. The dominator may determine what kind of being the dominated may have, by naming, describing the nature of the dominated, socializing the young to their position in life, limiting the activities that will be open to the dominated (such as education or engaging in certain businesses) that might develop their inherent capacities. (This applies to nations as well as to individuals as members of classes.)

The dominator will determine how the dominated will be permitted to act, behave, participate in common life (individuals in the family, classes in the workplace or within the nation, nations or classes of nations in international affairs). Fundamentally, the dominator will determine how the dominated is to be valued. If a certain class is to be put down as of lesser value, then even if no great restriction is put on what that class may do, *whatever* it does will be regarded as of low value and will be more poorly rewarded in the society than the activities of the dominant class. This *determination* of being will be contrasted later with the communion paradigm, which offers an *enhancement* of being in each of these ways.

In saying that the domination/submission paradigm lies at the basis of many of our contemporary ills, I do not say that all our ills can be traced to it, nor do I say that it is productive only of ill.

In fact, I hold that certain versions of it can be useful and appropriate in various limited, specific, functional situations. For instance, in any situation where rapid, efficient transmission of factual information is important, a domination, or hierarchical, model is practical. However, in our culture we have tended to award to the functionally dominant persons and institutions a total value of superiority, privilege, and power that has often led to injustice, damage, and suffering.

I am suggesting that domination is basic to a great many ills from which our particular culture does suffer and that it may be possible to replace it with an alternative paradigm that would afford some improvement. I think that each of these paradigms lies at a sufficiently deep level in our consciousness to be a unifying principle for a great many particular behaviors, and therefore if we could deal with the matter on this deep level, we would thereby effect alterations in the relatively superficial attitudes and actions much more efficiently than by trying to change those feelings and events piecemeal. To see how pervasive the paradigm is, let us survey the several scales of human interaction, beginning with the largest.

Calling to Mind Our Sins: War

War is a distinctly human phenomenon, and always has been. Ancient societies and contemporary primal ones show high rates of destructiveness. Recent estimates for the world as a whole suggest that 59 million persons died between 1820 and 1945 as a result of war, murder, and other forms of humans killing one another. Europe, from 500 BCE to 1925, averaged one year of violence to every four years of peace. Civilian casualties of World War I were 20 percent; of World War II, 50 percent; of Vietnam, 90 percent.[1] War is a central human institution.

War is said to be conducted in a "national interest"—or racial, or ethnic, or religious interest—aimed at removing the threat implied by the presence of those who are unlike "us." Sometimes it takes the form of deliberate genocide, as Nazi Germany killing Jews and gypsies, Hutus slaughtering Tutsis, or Serbs ethnically cleansing themselves of Bosnian Muslims. The Maori, when they came to New Zealand, exterminated the native people there, only to be endangered later by Europeans, and the Europeans have almost entirely destroyed the culture and the native people of the Americas. Sometimes large numbers of people are systematically done away with for narrow political reasons (the "disappeared" in Argentina, by the thousands, and those who rubbed Josef Stalin the wrong way, by the millions).

War and genocide usually involve atrocities. The holocausts conducted by the Nazis and the Stalinists are prime examples, but we can also cite Idi Amin and Pol Pot. The My Lai massacre, which was planned to teach the Vietnamese villagers not to harbor Viet Cong, destroyed 504 civilians—mostly women, children, and old men—and burned the buildings. One of the two survivors is now caretaker of the memorial garden and museum there, which receives small support from the Vietnamese government but never anything from the United States. One American, Lieutenant William Calley, was convicted of murdering twenty-two persons and served three years under house arrest. This was a notorious incident, but the ordinary agents of the war, which included napalm and poisonous defoliants, tortured, killed, and ravaged on a far grander scale.[2]

Behind the wars at the front are the industrial economies, which have a keen interest in the development, testing, and sale of their military products. One of the advantages of the 1991 Gulf War was that it enabled the manufacturers and the military to test their new weapons under real conditions. This industry is a large portion of our economy, and those involved in it could be unwilling to give it up, which may be a basic reason why there is little progress toward disarmament. The threat of job losses at this plant or that military installation is enough to prevent much change. Military hardware—and now software—must be constantly updated, so there is always fresh business, defense contracts amounting to well over a hundred billion dollars in this country alone. This need drives current science, which obtains much of its funding from the federal government's defense budgets (sometimes by concocting a connection to military use in order to support basic research on neutral or beneficial topics).

War preparations of this sort have their own costs and their own dangers. Stockpiles of weapons, especially nuclear weapons, can be unsafe, and burial grounds of wastes are dangerous. Mining uranium has caused health problems, and toxic contamination has made sites of weapons plants permanently unfit for human use. Workers in the plants and families who live nearby are at risk. Accidents can happen; the disasters at Three Mile Island and at Chernobyl not only demonstrate what can happen as a result of error but also what would happen if a weapon were used. Now, in addition to nuclear weapons, we have chemical and biological weapons to worry about.[3]

Tyranny, Oppression, and Slavery

We have only to remember ancient empires, European colonization of Africa, Asia, and the Americas, the Boxer Rebellion, and gunboat diplomacy to see how nations undertake to dominate and oppress other nations. Some of these practices made the dominated people into a despicable underclass in their own countries, ruining their cultures and their self-respect. In other cases, the international affairs of a nation might actually be run by the dominator: consider, for example, the position of the U.S. State Department in many Latin American countries, or the American role in the internal affairs of El Salvador and Chile. The great empires of the past were openly greedy and self-serving; more recent ones have worn a disguise of religious obligation in spreading the gospel or of humanitarian generosity in assuming "the white man's burden" of handling the affairs of people incapable of managing on their own. Even Pierre Teilhard de Chardin, usually so insightful and forward looking, wrote that the British ought not to give India its freedom, for the religiously benumbed Hindus were incapable of self-government. This sort of attitude still colors relations between the former colonies and their erstwhile overlords in the First World. Newly independent colonies are often worse off because they continue to be, in Elisabet Sahtouris's words, "systematically underdeveloped—prevented from proceeding with their own natural development . . . working the land for others . . . often . . . monoculture . . . exporting raw materials . . . importing machine-made products . . . they cannot escape poverty."[4]

Dominated people are still living in a kind of slavery, an institution with a long and massive history. It has lasted for thousands of years and been practiced by all races and most nations. Slaves are totally deprived of human rights and respect. Their "nature," their actions, their relations, their very existence are defined and controlled by their owners. Slavery was originally closely connected with war: people were among the spoils that belonged to the victor. The victor could have killed the people; enslaving them instead meant sparing them. Later, traffic in slaves became profitable, for the slave was an economic asset. People were captured specifically for the slave trade, and slavery became an institutionalized form of labor for large-scale enterprises. The notion that slavery was wrong did not appear in Europe and its cultural derivatives until very late in the 1700s, and the institution disappeared only when it was no longer necessary, being replaced by the machines of the industrial age. Nevertheless, it is still present (more or less) in migrant agricultural labor, prostitution, and manufacturing plants where grossly underpaid workers who have no alternative life.[5]

Oppression of the weaker by the stronger seems to go back as far as we can see into our past: oppression of women by men and of younger people by older apparently are universal. Oppression of adult males by other adult males became widespread only when communities became so large that they could not maintain social cohesion by close kinship ties alone. Simple societies developed into complex ones, characterized by centralized monarchy, political bureaucracy, systematic tax collection, organized priesthood, and hierarchically ordered social systems. Human sacrifice was the centerpiece of many ritual celebrations.

The social ladder created underclasses, and the tyranny that had been practiced in the family was extended to the degraded classes. Conquered peoples were easiest to victimize—or those who differed by race, language, culture, or history—but societies could also oppress their own people. These forms of tyranny and class structure are very hard to change, and they endure for thousands of years in their basic outlines. An important consequence of this is the way it colors people's sense of themselves, making them very conscious of who is in what position, able to dominate whom and subject to domination by whom. Cruelty is implicit and practiced with confidence; there is little or no protection for inferiors abused by superiors.

Tyrannical modern governments, dictatorships, and authoritarian regimes of various types are well known to us; they characterize more nations than do democratic governments, even today. The atrocities visited by these powers upon their own people are monitored by Amnesty International, and some complaints are made, but the cruelty goes on. Sometimes economic considerations make it undesirable for a benefitting nation to complain too much.

In our own country, it can be claimed that ordinary people are being shut out of power in the governing process. William Greider says:

> at the highest levels of government, the power to decide things has instead gravitated from the many to the few . . . ; the government now responds more often to narrow webs of power—the interests of major economic organizations and concentrated wealth and the influential elites surrounding them . . . tacit understandings that determine who has political power and who doesn't . . . some interests are allowed to dominate the government's decision making while others are excluded . . . [some] must be heard . . . and [others] can be safely ignored.[6]

We say we believe that those who govern must be accountable to the governed, but many Americans feel that some aspects of their government are not responsive: laws are passed for citizen protection but not enforced; agencies operate outside the law, keeping their own affairs secret—even from Congress—but terrifying the citizens, sometimes even operating their own governments within the government with their own revenues, military means, and foreign policy (e.g., the Iran-Contra Affair of the CIA).[7]

Those who feel strongly about their powerlessness and the justice of their cause sometimes resort to terrorism. In this way even a very small group can dominate a far larger group, causing much grief, even if they fail to attain their demands. Consider Northern Ireland and the Middle East. Terrorism is also an effective weapon when used by a government against its own people—consider Saddam Hussein—and we have seen some massive examples of that.[8] And when any force attempts to combat terrorism by massive military response, that force inevitably falls into the trap of dominating in its turn.

A whole new form of tyranny and even a kind of slavery has now appeared on the scene in the guise of the world of information. The powerful get the information that enhances their position, while the little people lose their privacy. Having correct information makes those who know more powerful; lacking information leaves people powerless. Being manipulated by crafted information makes people less than powerless to advance or participate; they are actually enslaved in the sense that they are induced to perform in the way their masters desire. Inequality and large-scale movement can often be managed by advertisements, images, emotional appeals, exploitation of celebrity figures, and various other devices.[9]

The most subtle form of oppression is that which enslaves the mind and feelings of the dominated, controlling the psychic powers of the person. Most dominators seek to do this, it being the most efficient way to exact submission. The powerful persons and institutions, their authority, and the media events they control (including entertainments and arts) exert great pressure on their witnesses; peer pressure then usually does the rest. As most people find out fairly early, it's not smart to think differently from the dominant institutions. In this way, quite ordinary people can be induced to do horrible things as the authoritative voice overrides the voice of conscience and declares that the usual restrictions on hurting or injuring others must be set aside in the interests of this higher authority and the needs of the situation. An innate human tendency toward obedience to a powerful authority figure facilitates this, especially as many cultures teach that obedience to established authority is a primary virtue, so that refusal to carry out brutal orders becomes morally wrong. Those who define the moral virtues, who declare what is right or wrong and what the penalties (human and divine, here and hereafter) for transgression are, those who define what is normal or not, natural or not, what "human nature" is—these persons and institutions command the most powerful instrument of social control.[10]

Economic and Ecological Domination

One of the most obvious instances of large-scale domination is the stark difference between rich nations and poor ones. Social scientists of the Third World have concluded that the very dynamics of the world economy lead to greater wealth for the few and greater poverty for the many. The industrialized First World consumes many times more energy than is made available to the Third World. The United States, for instance, with less than 5 percent of the world's population uses 26 percent of the world's oil, 25 percent of its coal, and 27 percent of its natural gas.

Third World countries, seeking loans to jump-start their economies, are often forced into monocultural development as a condition for obtaining the credits. Countries that had previously produced all the kinds of goods that they needed now had to change over to single cash crops, and when the market for these failed, they were left without the means to feed their own people. Some industries are harmful in themselves, yet large sectors of the world economy are dependent on them. For examples, raising beef cattle is a highly inefficient use of grain (to say nothing of the destruction of forest to make range); tobacco contributes to the early deaths of millions every year, but tobacco farmers, manufacturers, and advertisers are unwilling to give it up (somewhat blocked in the United States, they are now turning to the Third World with renewed blandishments); and of course the sale of illegal psychedelic drugs in other nations supports their home economies. Prostitution (including that of children), now known as "sex tourism," is a very large component in the economies of some nations.[11]

Within our own country, money-making considerations override health concerns in a number of industries. Petroleum processing plants and other industries connected to high rates of cancer were required by Congress many years ago to clean up their pollution, but the law was never enforced and the conditions remain unchanged. First World nations are not economic democracies. Wealth tends to concentrate in the hands of a few, and unfortunately these few are in a position to influence the government. Elections are influenced by advertising, especially expensive television ads, so candidates are very dependent on large amounts of money. Thus, the economic consideration dominates the political aspiration of giving all the people an equal voice in their government.

The gap between the rich and the rest of us is great and becoming greater. In the United States the income of the top one percent is comparable to the total income of about half of the rest of the population. The top one percent also hold nearly half of the nation's assets. Particularly distressing are the amounts of money paid to individuals. For instance, the shoe manufacturer Nike paid the basketball star Michael Jordan more money in one year to appear in their commercials than they paid to *all* the workers who actually made the shoes in Indonesia—mostly women and children. The salaries and benefits accorded the CEOs of large corporations are unbelievable in comparison to the pay of the ordinary worker who contributes to the company's production, the former receiving millions per year to the latter's several thousand.

Conservative policy is always to support the economy by reducing taxes on the wealthy, but since the economic dynamic operates by positive feedback rather than negative, this has the effect of increasing the gap between rich and poor. Government subsidies for business also favor large, wealthy enterprises rather than small businesses or family farms. Americans say we dislike hierarchies of power and privilege, but we don't take steps to redistribute the wealth. Preserving income disparities seems to be central to our culture and traditional values. We all hope that someday *we* will be in the top one percent and then we won't want any restrictions on us.[12]

When making money dominates all other concerns, we tend to measure the wrong things. We don't count the costs of consumption in terms of human experience or ecological effects. We're not getting full information. There are health and social costs that we don't figure in and that aren't simply translatable into dollars. For instance, Ralph Nader pointed out that every time there is an automobile accident, the Gross National Product goes up—because ambulances and their attendants have to come; police and maybe firefighters respond; wreckers are needed; hospitals, doctors, nurses, and others are involved—and often funeral directors; lawyers are employed; insurance companies pay; a new car is purchased, and there are ripple effects through many industries. But what of the pain, disability, grief, loss? Why isn't this whole affair counted as a *deficit* instead of a gain?

We are all acquainted with the health hazards of working in many industries, risks of lung ailments, cancer from chemicals or radiation, various sorts of poisoning. But industry fights any attempt to mitigate these ills and risks. Doing so would increase their "costs." The human cost doesn't count. If local laws prohibit exploitation of workers, multinational corporations can easily set up shop elsewhere under more favorable conditions. Then there is the firearms industry, carefully protected by the National Rifle Association's influence with the government, insisting on liberal access to the products it protects, regardless of the resulting high death rate from their accidental or deliberate use.

Economic interests dominate other nonmonetary aspects of our lives. Companies move families around the country, requiring the worker to accept the new location or lose the job, obliging the spouse and children of the family to interrupt their lives, careers, educations, friends, and community connections in order to keep the family "together." Wives of highly placed executives are expected to provide support systems as unpaid assistants and hostesses. Current "downsizing" is imposing extra workloads on workers lucky enough to retain their jobs, causing severe stress on individuals and families. Our lives are being consumed by work instead of work supporting life and being a creative aspect of life.

The economic engine teaches us at every turn that financial success is the overwhelming value of our society. If the company offers enough money, it becomes "an offer he couldn't refuse." Social self-respect has to be purchased for the children in the form of ridiculously priced, stylishly shabby clothes and shoes. Holidays are subverted into occasions of conspicuous display and consumption. Self-images are distorted and no end of psychological problems are set in motion by modish advertising, the new authority that must be believed. Advertisers learn how to manipulate and deceive the public's mind and feelings. The sales chart justifies it. How many people have trouble with their consciences because of the kind of work they do? How many people have learned to bury their consciences because they don't see an alternative that they're willing to accept? If it means taking a cut in income, forget it.

Control over our lives has passed into the hands of such large enterprises that we cannot reach their managers. The elites of the business world run the world among themselves, consulting, buying, litigating, regulating, churning out "information" to support whatever opinion or position is desired by a paying customer. Lobbyists can purchase facts, expert opinions, opinion polls of ordinary people, who are brought to Washington at the expense of the client. What is the legislator supposed to do? The business interest sends its own lawyers to Capitol Hill to write the legislation, and has its political action committee donate to the legislator's next election campaign.

William Greider, detailing this way of doing business/government, concludes that "organized money dominates the action while the unorganized voices of citizens are inhibited from speaking."[13]

One particular area that concerns everyone on the planet is ecology, the web of interactions on the planet itself. Here again money interests outweigh the substance of the situation, the real facts of real life. Our industrial and military projects and our large-population lifestyles are seriously harmful to Earth's self-maintenance system, but few of us are willing to alter what we are doing. In pursuing economic growth (a modest amount of which is healthy), each country tries to secure resources, markets, and strategic locations. But in so doing it arouses anxiety in its competitors, who in turn redouble their own efforts. This puts a heavy strain on the resources themselves, floods the markets, and makes everyone more anxious and tense. Increased production involves more pollution of the atmosphere and water systems, more pesticides and artificial fertilizers, more devices for extending shelf life, more cutting of corners in the quality of goods and commodities, compensated for by increased claims in advertising and fancier packaging.

We need to reevaluate our traditional assumptions about unlimited growth, resources, and competition: what was good in the past, in the days of the "frontier," may no longer be the best way to go. Not only are we running out of land and nonrenewable resources, but we are running out of any place to put our waste. Economic/ecological life can no longer be conceived of as a straight line, open at both ends; it must be seen as a closed circle in which materials are recycled or even as a net in which each participant influences all the rest. The oceans and the atmosphere are not just limitless spaces suitable for receiving our unending trash; they can react against us. No party in Earth's system can dominate without challenge; domination is not the name of the game in the long run, only respectful coaction is. Human beings are not the "owners" of the planet in the sense that we have a right to use it any way we choose for our short-term benefit. We are members of the planet system, and if we hope to survive, we need to start from this premise.[14]

Social Classes and Work

Inequality has had a long and almost ubiquitous history in human culture, preceded, of course, by social stratification and "pecking orders" among other animals. There are, therefore, strong arguments that such organization is only "natural," and it may be that people tend to sort themselves out according to their natural abilities and to gravitate to the work/role in the community that they do best and are most comfortable doing. But it is also true that classism is a social expression of the fact of exploitation of the less powerful by the more powerful. Where some people have the means of control over other people, there is a significant probability that they will exercise it to their advantage. It may be by brute strength or mental cleverness, by skill or by ownership of the means of wealth. However the edge over the others starts, it becomes magnified: to those who have, more shall be given.

Then our educational, economic, legal, and political institutions (think of segregated schools and restaurants, marriage laws, hiring practices, voting and office-holding restrictions) will follow these patterns of social discrimination. And our philosophies (and sometimes sciences) and our religions are arranged to indicate that our social classes and the laws about them are not only natural but God-commanded. Unfortunately, a lot of lies have been told and believed about human superiority and inferiority.

Classes can form based on all sorts of distinctions: sex, race, age, property ownership, occupation, language. Once classes are formed and ranked, we find that expectations are different for different classes, suspicions rest differently, and legal sanctions are visited on the classes quite differently. People are made to feel their position: they are not listened to; their ideas are not taken seriously until put forward by a superior-class person; they become shy in the presence of superiors; there is acute embarrassment or anger if their class is mistaken. It has even been found that when a person talks with a person of higher status, the inferior's blood pressure goes up.[15]

Usually each ruling class sees itself as the norm for humanity, the remainder being "lesser breeds." Those forced to the margins by their deviation from this norm are not heard. Their opportunities for self-fulfillment are restricted, often explicitly and de jure, but almost always de facto. Only the upper classes have the money, education, contacts, and experience to develop themselves as they choose. In this milieu we seek whatever badges of respectability we can lay claim to. Respectability, says Daniel Yankelovich, "draws its strength from the emotional power of the need to belong . . . to be part of an entity larger than oneself—a family, . . . neighborhood, a religion, an ethnic group, a social class, a profession," even a crime gang or a drug ring. According to one's belonging, one will dress and speak a certain way, follow a lifestyle of consumption and ostentation appropriate to one's position. One's appearance in these terms announces one's respectability in one's class.

Labels support this stereotyping of one's class and status. Names and titles, terms of respect or opprobrium, slang, how persons of different class levels may address one another, and who gets to say what the qualities of a given class are. Members of the lower classes, those who are dominated, lack full knowledge of themselves and their class, because their achievements and their history have been buried by their superiors, who control the instruments of social attention and memory. What knowledge the underlings have conflicts with what their dominators say about them, and such is the prestige of the power classes that the dominated frequently believe in the incapacity and unworthiness of their own peers.

Some subordinates react to this state of affairs by imitating their dominators and abusing and despising any class they can perceive as inferior to themselves. Some strive to acquire the qualities that the upper classes enjoy so that they can be respected on those levels, but attainment of these skills may just as well win them fierce rejection for trying to move out of their "proper" class, a behavior viewed by the dominant class—and sometimes by the subordinate class—as "unnatural." Only what the dominant group does is highly valued, and what is valued is restricted to the dominant group; others are not permitted to perform the same activities, even if they can. In this way the dominant group can continue to demonstrate that people of the underclass never achieve anything of quality.

Another curious wrinkle of the class system is that, if some aspect of the human experience comes to be associated with members of an underclass, it becomes impossible for the upper class to admit to it or engage in it. For instance, since women are very good at picking up other people's feelings and empathizing with them and showing their own emotions, men must never do these things, just as they must not be good at household tasks that are "women's work," or perform tasks at the office that are usually performed by women. If an ethnic group is especially skilled at some form of art, then the classes that look down on that group must take pride in *not* being able to do that. Of course this is a substantial loss for the upper classes, but their respectability in their own eyes and in the eyes of the underlings they have educated requires it.[16]

There are clear classes and ranks in the world of work. This shows in the dress of the various workers and in the accommodations provided for them in their workplaces. The upper classes actually have their offices on higher floors. The inequality shows also in ordinary social contacts: how persons are addressed (dominants receive titles; subordinates may be called by their first names), standing up when the superior enters a room; never contradicting the superior or interrupting—although the superior may do this and use insulting, coarse, and belittling language as well.

Most jobs are expected to be filled only by persons of certain social classes. An individual who takes a job out of the proper class may experience discomfort and social errors: the male nurse mistaken for a physician, the female board member called upon as a secretary, the cross-racial friend ignored as a servant.[17]

Ethnic, Gender, and Family Domination

Membership in an ethnic group is always a handy way of establishing domination ranks. This is done all over the world and has been going on for a long time. The dominated are easily recognized, and their subordinate status can be attributed to obvious differences. If it is desired that a certain group should be exploited economically, or if a scapegoat is needed to account for some disaster and to allow the populace to vent its anger on a body other than the rulers, then an ethnic group is the preferred target. If it is convenient to remove a population that is occupying desired territory or positions of power, then an ethnic separation is very useful; it allows the dominator group and the subordinates it commands to dismiss the target population as outside the "we," not human as we are human, not deserving of consideration in any context but their being an obstacle to our rightful move into their place. In our own case, the destruction and exile of Native Americans and the enslavement and repression of Africans are outstanding instances, with the isolation of Irish, Italians, or Puerto Ricans also being recognized. Jews are the classic example of subjects of religious-ethnic oppression, while the caste system of India and the tribal hostilities of Africa are not quite so well known to us.[18]

Domination/submission patterns based on gender are universal and, some claim, ineradicable. Peter Farb says that as soon as warfare came on the human scene, females were no longer equal members of the community, as they had been in hunter-gatherer society. Their primary function became bearing sons to be soldiers. Marvin Harris says it is the other way around: war was invented as an excuse for preferring sons and justifying female infanticide, thus keeping the population under control in regions of limited resources. In any case, patriarchy, warfare, efforts to control life and the environment, and the subjugation of women all appeared together. In fact, we might say that this is the origin of culturally institutionalized and religiously commanded *domination* itself. Women were depicted as the source of evil, as unclean and the cause of weakness and sin to men. Consciousness shifted from magic (trust in and cooperation with nature) to technology (alienation from and exploitation of nature). Ideas were developed as ways to learn to control—to harness—natural power. Suppressing the female principle was connected to the ambition to gain rational control over the cosmic forces. Jean Baker Miller says that the characteristics most highly developed in women and most essential to human beings are the very characteristics that are especially dysfunctional for success in the world as it is, the world in which the Domination Paradigm prevails. Women who are now moving against this world order are speaking on behalf of all people, for the full development of their total humanity, creativity, and personhood.

Meanwhile, however, the suppression and the exploitation and abuse of women goes on. Women do 66 percent of the world's work, say Alfonso Montuori and Isabella Conti, and get 10 percent of its rewards. Women's scientific and creative work is passed over and their pictures and music hidden and lost (some of which are now being recovered). Marilyn French has detailed an unbelievably extensive War Against Women, including not only economic and political suppression and female infanticide but systematic discrimination against women, nation by nation and religion by religion: genital mutilation, medical abuse and neglect, prostitution, starvation (see especially India), and murder (especially in the military). The statistics for what we may call "private" rapes are bad enough, but the numbers for officially permitted rapes in wartime are horrendous: in 1937 the Japanese sexually tortured and killed twenty thousand women of Nanking; in 1943 Moroccan mercenaries hired by the French were given explicit license to rape tens of thousands of Italian women; in 1945 Allied troops in "liberated" Berlin raped hundreds of thousands of German women. These acts were not considered war crimes. In 1971 more than two hundred thousand Bengali women were raped in Bangladesh as part of a conscious military strategy by Pakistan; in 1992 the Serbs began practicing systematic rape in camps set up for that explicit purpose, using unusual cruelty and photographing their actions, and in 1993 the Croats responded in kind. Nothing is done about this.[19]

Family abuse is an enormous problem, affecting wives, husbands, children, and old people. Part of it can be neglect and injustice, but a great deal is positive cruelty. The causes of abuse are multiple and complicated, and the abused to some extent are contributors by not reporting and not leaving soon enough. Historically husbands have had not only permission to beat their wives but encouragement to do so, especially from religious authorities. Beating children has also been recommended in a religious context. Overall, the public attitude has been to look the other way, although there are agencies concerned with the problem.[20]

Religion is a powerful influence in the whole issue of domination. Religions may practice domination in their own social structures; they may counsel domination in social relations among their adherents and support it in matters of state. Many wars have been religious wars. Religion itself may be a matter of domination, frightening people into compliance, and it may represent its Deity as a Supreme Dominator, usually called, therefore, "the Lord."[21] Religion is a primary source of overall culture, so if the religion is based on a Domination Paradigm and countenances attitudes and behaviors of domination in its own domain, the culture will almost certainly be governed by concepts of domination. The Domination Paradigm is learned in the home, in the religious setting, in the school, on the playing field, in marriage relations, and in government. Domination will show in a culture's arts— think of pictures, songs, theater—and will further sustain the legitimacy of relations of domination.

2

Our Basic Insecurity

The Psychology of Domination

People whose business it is to study human beings sometimes warn the rest of us that human behavior is an enormously complex subject and that unless we are specially trained in the matter, we should not offer opinions about it. We are advised not to go around saying, "the trouble with people today is . . ." and then proceed to reduce all our current ills to me-first-ism, the breakdown of family life, loss of religious faith, permissiveness, television, rock music, social deprivation, mixing of social classes, taxation, the welfare state, malnutrition, pollution, or whatever our pet scapegoat happens to be. We should recognize instead that all sorts of things go together to make up what we call "human nature" and to influence our behavior on any given occasion.

There is the whole question of our genetic endowment, and this varies from one generation to the next, certain characteristics being preserved in a population and others being lost because the individuals carrying them did not reproduce. Then there are all the learning experiences that have accumulated in our lives up to the moment of any particular action. We have habits of thinking-feeling-behaving that are common to our culture, as well as the personal ones peculiar to each of us because of our individual histories. And we have a certain scope of flexibility on every occasion wherein a great variety of motives may make claims on us.

In what follows I will try to take account of these various categories of concern, but I will also try to trace out their implications. I will ask what is the meaning-shape of an action-attitude-relation— what makes it possible? I think we can find a very general root for the behaviors laid out in chapter 1 as instances of "domination." I think

23

we can see all these as forms of the desire for mastery, which assumes insecurity, insufficient being, and therefore is rooted in fear.

Mastery by Destructive Power

If we go back to where we began in our list of ills—to war, violence, and general destructiveness—we can notice that glorification of fighting, as Mary Midgley says, is widespread and ancient. Many cultural features are superficial and ephemeral, she points out, but not fighting, not destroying. It's very deep. It must be saying something profound about human perception of the human situation. Herbert Butterfield says that for a long time and over a wide area, war was considered sacred, an affair of the gods; the gods commissioned and commanded wars, which were conducted against alien gods. Something at the root of Being was involved, something more than human.

Something in the core of human nature itself? Polling among American high school and college students and adults reveals that some 60 to 70 percent believe that wars are inevitable, given human nature. Although this assessment will be challenged by scientists (see chapter 8), it has to be admitted that, to date, neither the national leaders nor the masses of the people have shown the will to delegitimate war. On the other hand, military trainers take considerable pains to dehumanize the enemy in the perceptions and emotions of their soldiers so that the armies will be able to overcome their human feelings and destroy the opponents. Ashley Montagu says that it's not that we don't have inhibitions against killing our own kind but that our societies discourage such inhibitions.

In some ways it's easier now; we can kill at a distance, with technological precision. We don't have to get emotionally involved; we just have to know how to operate the machinery. Moral responsibility doesn't enter into it; people are hired to operate the machines, and they follow their instructions without entering into the decisions. They're only "doing their job," and when they do it skillfully, honestly, and loyally, their moral standing is high, not low. (Interestingly, such workers are participating in the Domination Paradigm not on the domination side but on the submissive and passive side.)

Was it different when one had to face the enemy, engage in hand-to-hand combat? What was the emotion that made war "glorious"? Was it the excitement, the concentration that drove all other thoughts out of the mind, so that even wounds were unnoticed? The "rush," the exhilaration? An "altered state" that could hardly be obtained any other way? Was it the courage that was required to set aside one's attachment to one's own life and run awful risks in order to accomplish one's mission? A transcendence of the usual world—thus "sacred"? Was it the bonding with one's comrades, the sharing of powerful experiences, the willingness to die for the others? Was it the thrill, the acute sense of *living*, of meeting Life on its own turf, in the pure form, Life as such and distinguished only from Death? Lifted above the mundane into the domain of the ultimate realities? A religious experience? Now that war is all mechanized and computerized and carried out against unseen persons who are mostly simple civilians who are in no way enemies of oneself but only people obeying their governments as we are obeying ours, not "worthy opponents" with courage and transcendence of their own, has the magic gone out of it?[1]

There are some old hatreds left that still move the people concerned—insults, offenses, and injustices whose blood still cries out from the contested ground and demands revenge. These can be personally involving, and their "small wars" are carried on by guerrillas and terrorists and in some ways even by civilians who can identify with the issues at stake. For the strategic wars engineered by the big powers for political and economic reasons, emotional support among their people has to be activated by carefully planned propaganda, advertising, images, and news selections—it's all too far away, too abstract. It has to be boiled down to elemental we/them feelings—we must conquer them, master them. We must be the winners.

Our fundamental value as a society seems to be to have power over others. Most nations spend a lot on their military preparedness, whereas caring for, nurturing, and developing *people* is at the bottom of their budgets. Governments, institutions, and churches order things to benefit the social class that controls them. Morality and love of neighbor are preached to individuals, but rarely is anything said about large social bodies (corporations, religions as such, or our own nation) abandoning or mitigating their intentions to dominate their opposite numbers. Inequality is not only assumed but promoted. The world tends to sort itself out into the relative oppressors and the oppressed, and the cultural institutions display and encourage the emotions to sustain this arrangement, making clear where the class lines fall, shaping the sense of virtue and proper behavior and feeling to fix people in the classes to which they should belong in the power structure. Deferential behaviors of language and gesture, as well as actual obedience itself, become matters not only of politeness but of morality and normality as well. "Insubordination" is a serious offense, in the military, in government, in business, in church, between races, and between genders and age groups. We are dealing here with a fundamental value in our consciousness. This is why the Holy Thursday Revolution, when it comes, is so radical, so profound, so great a shift, touching everything in our lives.[2]

Deference Ranks

The implicit hostility that underlies deference ranks shows at both ends of the spectrum of scale, from one-on-one interpersonal interactions to the relations between the human race and its environment. The power-over issue is central. Jean-Paul Sartre remarked on "the stare" (or "the look") with which we confront one another. So often we are sizing one another up to see who's going to be able to dominate in a relationship, or to see how we can use the other or relate to the other to enhance our being and self-image. This assessment of the other person as a means of enabling me to feel good about myself even passes for "love." Indeed, much apparently sexual behavior is actually about status, domination, and relations to persons other than the sexual partner. All these aspects are woven together in our concern for the relationship, but the bottom line is usually a question of who gets to define the nature of the relationship, the roles played by each party in the relationship, and the goal of the relationship. It is (so far) a rare relationship that has no touch of the domination/submission theme (including who is primary or leader and who is secondary or follower).

Our culture is so designed that playing one's part in the game may be accounted pleasurable, even if one is the dominated party. Self-esteem and the security of being "normal" may be strongly connected to having (or pretending to have) the approved emotions in the relationship. It is "wrong" (legally, morally, psychologically) for those cast in the submissive role to be or try to be dominant, and equally wrong for those cast as dominant to be submissive. Those out of character may be despised, regarded with contempt, or actually subjected to "treatment" to adjust them to their proper places.

These attitudes prevail in the case of race relations; there is strong hostility if the submissive ones show signs of reaching for equality. Third World countries are not quite on the same social level or accorded the same respect as First World nations, and they are exploited today in the same way they were when the colonial empires were functioning. Workers are in similar positions relative to management. Human beings are believed by many to be commissioned by God to dominate the rest of the planet, whose natural features and living beings are the property of the human race, created for the latter's service. If we don't care for the theological terminology, we can choose to see the universe as basically hostile to human life and the human vocation as being to conquer nature and make it serve us.[3]

When we look at the world in this way, competition characterizes everything. We believe that it is natural, inevitable, and highly desirable. To lose it would be to lose the spice of life, the driving force of progress and further development. It is natural law that there should be winners and losers, rich and poor, those who control/manage/command and those who obey, the powerful and the powerless. We need to realize how deep this view is in our psyches, individually and corporately. The psychology of domination encourages us to see helping others as possibly harming ourselves, to see harming others as a way to help ourselves. What else is war or any other effort to restrict the other's life lest it impose on ours? Life is a zero-sum game, one in which the plus signs (our side) cancel out the minus signs (the other side). We can't all be pluses; the only way we can support the "have" people/nations is by enforcing this natural law that there be "have not" people/nations.

We teach our children to vie for prizes and awards; education becomes a matter of learning not for its own sake but for the sake of obtaining the coveted grades and positions of rank. Sport is competitive; what is of most interest is who wins, who finally gets to the top. If sport turns professional, "playing" becomes "work," and work translates into money and celebrity, not into relaxation and joy. We do not react well to the suggestion that we could enjoy playing together without striving to win while the other loses. We don't invent many exercises or games that are not zero-sum; our imaginations and our emotions have difficulty with that. Our economy is not only run as competition between producers for "market share," but it is run by means of inciting competition among the consumers—buy this in order to be superior to your neighbor. Maybe the object itself is not of great quality, but if it has the right brand name on it, it advertises that you can afford to purchase it. That alone is worth the price. You are buying comparative self-esteem.

Comparison is the critical word. This is how we recognize our values. This arises quite naturally from the way our perception works: we see and hear by contrasting (comparing) an item of interest with its background, a figure against the ground, a signal standing out from silence or noise. We measure distances and sizes and weights by comparison, so it is only natural that we would begin to measure value by comparison, to view it as more or less. Thus, persons became stronger/weaker, quicker/slower, and more or less skillful or insight-ful—even more or less loyal, reliable, or helpful, thus more or less powerful and honored. It is a way of seeing that depends on separa-tion and difference. It looks not for the way things or persons are alike but for the ways in which they are different and measurably so. Moreover, judgment is attached to this, for one side of the difference is always preferred to the other. As the sorting progresses, the pre-ferred rise gradually to the top, and the disvalued sink to the bottom. This is how power, wealth, status, and fame accumulate at one pole, and oppression, poverty, and the underclasses at the other pole.[4]

The feelings that go with this process are pride and satisfaction as one rises and shame and dejection as one falls. Success breeds success, partly because the successful feel more energetic and hopeful. Those who fail, on the other hand, tend to lose energy and hope, especially if failing happens repeatedly. Those rejected from one level of success will try to succeed at a lower level, comparing themselves with those to whom they may yet feel superior. As long as there is someone below them, they are not totally deprived of self-respect. In this way the rank ordering falls into place, carrying with it the corresponding recogni-tion of and experience of honor and shame.

Even in a democracy, says Arthur Deikman, "we are always look-ing up at those who must be obeyed or down at those who must obey us. This is so because authoritarianism draws its strength from the same source that supports cult behavior: dependency on groups and leaders."[5] This probably derives from the parent–child relationship and from the evolution of social group behavior. Rank position may vary from group to group; an individual may be a leader in one group but a dependent in another. But position in the relevant group greatly influences behavior. As human beings (as primates?), we seem to have a "predilection for inequality." It underlies our sense of "rightness." "An unthinking submission to the communal will remains among the most emotionally potent virtues among 'good' people in the main-stream of society," says Edward O. Wilson.[6]

It can be argued that rank ordering in society was necessary for the evolution of intelligence, that it improved cohesiveness and coop-erative behavior in which planning and taking different but related roles improved the life of the whole troop or band. Human society in this sense is clearly descended from general primate social organization. It can also be pointed out that very aggressive species have more rigid social domination systems, while peaceful species have more equality and opportunity to change roles.[7]

The thesis of *The Holy Thursday Revolution* is that, while rank ordering and domination have been the rule in the course of evolution and have been selected for because of advantages to socially developing animals, human beings, with consciousness capable of empathy and ethical responsibility, can live by another set of operating principles. This was not a totally new idea on Holy Thursday, having already been voiced by the Hebrew prophets, but it is still shocking and confusing when put forward as explicitly as it was then laid out. It has emerged, more or less, at various times and places in the last few thousand years.

Specifically, for our discussion, it emerged clearly in the Revelation at Sinai, sometimes called the second creation. The giving of the Torah represents the appearance in human consciousness of this new set of operating principles, by which human beings become the presence of God in the world, as distinct from merely fancy animals. Animals have advanced by killing, stealing, deceiving, raping, cheating, and so on. But once human beings understand their reality as the image of God, and understand God as the One who liberates from the "narrow place" (Egypt) of animal social organization and enslavement to biological evolutionary laws, then fundamental changes can take place.

If we do not put other values and other rules "before" the God who liberates, then it is no longer necessary to murder, steal, deceive, rape, cheat, or even covet. The human being is illumined as—essentially defined as—the being that can live in the material world, having evolved from the biological-chemical-physical universe, in terms of divine values: love and self-gift and oneness. Anyone who can live in these new terms is truly a "new creation."[8] The paradigmatic events of Holy Thursday repeat, underline, renew, and boost this transformative passage. But every time such renewal takes place it is shocking all over again, for the revolution is long and drawn-out, and the old paradigm struggles against the new. The two sets of principles for successful living are both still present, perhaps related to each other rather as the cerebral cortex of the brain, with its capacity for thought, simply lies on top of the limbic brain, with its emotional feelings. We need to analyze these things, understand why the Domination Paradigm has such a strong hold on us, what it is rooted in, and then see the corresponding root, stem, and flower of the new Communion Paradigm.

Domination and Submission

It will be useful at this point to repeat the definition of domination put forward in chapter 1: *Domination is an asymmetrical, or nonreciprocal, relation of determination of being: of the fact that a being is, or of what it is, or of how it can act, or of how it is to be valued.* This is clearly a matter of the "expansion of being" of the dominator and is derived, curiously enough, from the truly great value of creativity—although not in this form. The forms of domination and its correlative, submission, are ways in which a limited being tries to expand its being. Those who choose the dominator strategy seek expansion by controlling the lives of others and thus using those others as extensions of themselves. Those who find the strategy of submission easier (or the only way possible) nevertheless gain expansion of their being by joining in the larger being of the dominator and the whole system that the dominator controls. The dominator feels glorified by being master of whatever realm is subject, while the submissive feels glorified by belonging to the dominator and sharing in the dominator's honor. It is not ideationally or emotionally clear to either party that there are alternatives to this way of life, that the desire for fuller being and belonging to a larger whole could be handled through quite different principles. What we will explore at this point is why this is not clear, what the alternatives are, and how a passage from where we are at present to where we might be could be approached.

It is important to point out that the domination/submission game has to be played from both sides. Submissives cannot always claim total impotence. Usually it takes two sides to play, so it behooves submissives to study the situation and understand how it works, understand it deeply enough so that if they choose to try to change it, they will not simply exchange roles. The trouble is that the oppressed are most often motivated by the desire to become oppressors in their turn. They do not think of changing the system as such but only their role in it. The Holy Thursday Revolution is about changing the system as such, and that means going very deep, for if the change is not made at a sufficiently deep level, there will be dominators and submissives again, played by other parties, perhaps in other ways. To the extent that the evils in our lives can be traced to the Domination Paradigm, both dominators and submissives bear responsibility and both are called to repentance.

Submissives generally know more about their dominators than their dominators know about them. Dominators know that the best ways to control their holdings is by keeping up the appearances of power and by preventing union and organization among the dominated. But submissives, while they must avoid open conflict (until they can actually mount a rebellion) in order to survive, can find a great many ways to harass their masters and to manipulate them to the submissives' advantage. This can be done either with respect to an individual or with respect to a whole institution or system. On the other hand, submissives usually have no knowledge of their own class history and no psychologically encouraging traditions; the dominators destroy and bury these and prevent new ones from arising by systematically ignoring the cultural achievements of the dominated. This has the effect of making submissives believe in their own subject position. They come to feel that they could not have lives of their own, for themselves; they conceive of their success only in terms of service to their masters. The two roles are tied together. We cannot have a nation of "servants." Servanthood and lordship, domination and submission, exist together and must perish—if they perish—together.[9]

But this practice and psychology of inequality is universal. It must have been fulfilling some vital need. It gives people identification, specifying who and what they are and what it is appropriate for them to do in their "place." It defines the deferential behaviors of the community, which organize the social cohesiveness. It clarifies the chain of command in case of emergency or even for noncritical decisions. Insofar as there is competition for positions of dominance, it encourages people to exert themselves in effort and imagination and to run risks, and these activities may benefit the society. For winners there are further rewards, and hope and ambition can drive many members of the society. There can also be a beneficent aspect to such organization, along the lines of noblesse oblige, by which the superior takes responsibility for the inferior and is supportive (in ways that do not result in upsetting the superior/inferior status) and providential, while the inferior in turn is grateful and loyal—and dependent. To most of humanity, for most of our history, this has seemed a proper and natural arrangement.

It is the rare individual who looks at this universal phenomenon and reacts, as Gandhi did, being amazed that people should feel honored by the humiliation of other people. But that is precisely what does make them feel honored, and any other way of feeling honored is not apparent—there has to be that sharp contrast. Where does this come from? Families practice dominance/submission behaviors based on gender, age, birth order, and who has the money. These psychological attitudes are then extended to age and gender outside the family, to social classes according to their rank, to teachers, clergy, government officials, and so on. All this the child learns, usually without question; it is part of belonging to one's social world.

For those who occupy the top places in this tree, life is not thereby made secure. They may become obsessed with maintaining their status and be constantly looking for ways to reassure themselves. This applies to nations as well as to individuals. One way of reassurance is characterizing other individuals, classes, nations, races, and so on as possessing certain faults or despicable qualities; it is especially useful to project onto others one's own suspected failings so that the failings can be powerfully denied by means of this contrast. By such devices people learn, in the Domination Paradigm, a limited range of feelings that are permitted toward themselves, their peers, their superiors, and their inferiors. Temptations to feel other emotions are shut out, repressed, denied.[10]

Some people have suggested that the central paradigm of domination/submission is the male–female relation. It has been reported by observers of animal behavior that the same gestures (presenting/mounting) that initiate copulation are used as social greetings and reaffirmations of social rank: inferiors use female gestures toward their superiors and the superiors recognize this by returning the male gesture. In our own societies, psychologists say, certain attitudes and behaviors have been restricted to women, and for men to engage in these is to act "like a woman," which is contemptible. Among the forbidden behaviors and feelings are being attuned to the needs and feelings of others for their own sakes, being sympathetic and moved by others' feelings, serving their needs, sharing with others, relaxing one's authority in the direction of equality, and so on. Accepting direction from another is bad enough; asking for directions is unthinkable! Men must not admit to feeling fear or weakness, whereas women must feel these things; for women not to feel weak and in need of a strong arm to direct them is to be unfeminine. Similarly, people in lower ranks for whatever reason are regarded as presumptuous, arrogant, impudent, and "uppity" if they behave with more self-respect and confidence than is appropriate to their status. We have only to consider how we use such behaviors as eye contact, posture, tone of voice, use of names, touching, interrupting, freedom to disagree, and ultimately obedience to clarify the dominant/submissive positions.

Our societies rank people a good deal by occupation. Jobs done by men are generally valued more highly than those done by women. When women move into those positions (historically, secretaries, teachers), the value of the job itself falls; a man is embarrassed to do it. We have seen the reluctance to allow women to do such things as stay over the winter in Antarctica or go on space missions, because if women can do these difficult and dangerous things, then men can no longer feel heroic about doing them. Gender-identity self-esteem is threatened. Women, on the other hand, often want to do men's work just because it is more highly valued. But if women can invade every niche that had been reserved for males, then the entire rank-ordering principle is at risk.[11] Institutions such as the government, the military, and the church, which are carefully structured in terms of rank orders and chain of command, would be undermined by a shift in the feelings with regard to inequality, and so they tend to hold the line. The Jesus Movement, encapsulated in the events of Holy Thursday, practiced social equality of every kind, which is, no doubt, the reason why it aroused such enmity in powerful quarters.

Domination is mostly a male characteristic, although females also will vie with one another and find ways to appear superior and to put others down. But the central concern to locate one's position in the rank order is a male issue. Males are much more concerned about their relationships with other males than about their relationships with females (they even dream more of males than of females), says Peter Farb in his anthropology text *Humankind*. But it is also true that having a desirable female as "his" gives a man standing in male society, and that having breeding access to females is what the competition was originally and is ultimately all about. Our societies are male-constructed societies, emphasizing separation, comparison, and ranking rather than context and cooperation, giving us class structure, empire building, slavery, and warfare. The socially cohesive activities are mostly relegated to women. The highly visible dimensions of our cultures, the action-determining axes, are privilege, property, and power. The danger to life today arises from conflicts inherent in large, highly stratified, and intensely competitive social structures.

Anthropologists have studied the cultivation of aggressive males and warfare, and the pleasure that men take in fighting, as well as in fishing, hunting, and rough contact sports. Favorite male deities have been (at least initially) war gods, some of whom have been metamorphosed into judge figures, preserving the motif of domination. Activity on the economic and financial markets is thought of and spoken of in terms of warfare, where success is described as "making a killing." Observers of children claim that even small boys are already instinctively aggressive, and of course culturally we encourage this by giving little girls dolls and little boys guns. (An American G.I. generously gave gifts to Vietnamese children to show them the true mean-

ing of Christmas. The gifts? Toy machine guns.) Little girls are prepared for their task in life, which is giving life, and little boys for
theirs, which is killing.

Killing is more respectable than giving birth (though this is con-
tradicted by seeing the latter as sacred). It is hard to find a hero celebrated in song and story who has not done a good bit of killing. The
stories are, after all, composed by men about men for men to use as
models. Killing is the ultimate form of controlling, of taking possession of, of being superior to. Power is the ultimate category. Do we
not worship God Almighty? Men need power, and power is located in
the will. Men are properly related to their superiors (see the Rules of
religious orders) when they make the superior's will their own, and to
God when their own will is surrendered to God's will. But jostling for
power is the game of life, and appearances play a big role. Fashion
offers us "the power look"; self-help teaches us to be assertive;
"image" is what counts, with "damage control" being brought in to
cover over appearances of weakness. Power is a fantasy game, an
inner experience, a sense of self.[12]

In animals the androgens (especially testosterone) are related to
status. Man is always in heat, producing high levels of these hormones, and this makes him intimidating. This is his "manliness." To
be safe, he must always be testing it against his peers, striving for
more power and honor. To keep it a keen and meaningful test, honor
must be always in short supply. And to diminish or lose one's manhood is the greatest disaster, therefore the greatest fear.

But what is all this ultimately in service of? Why play this game?
Why have such deep and strong emotions invested in such concerns?
Steven Goldberg has undertaken to explain why men rule, always will
rule, and there is nothing anything cultural can do about it. It's neuro-
endocrinological, he says, wired in by the genes. I think we can say
two more things. The first is that men rule because it is to men that
"ruling" is an issue. The whole idea of such a thing as "ruling" over
others is an invention of male status-seeking behavior.

But underlying that is probably a deeper genetic explanation.
What males are vying for is the right to breed—that's where the gene
comes from originally. The life stream passes through the females. The
genes in males are reproduced only when added to the genes in
females. (The reciprocal is not always true; females can reproduce
without males.) Among a great many species, all females may be confident of breeding, but not all males. In many species, only a few
males will breed, those that win in the dominance contests and those
selected by the females. Thus, a male-linked gene for aggression, drive

to power, rulership, fighting, possessing, and controlling will tend to enable its possessor to leave more progeny than those lacking it or having a weaker form of it. Since females who select males having this gene will have more grandchildren because of it, the gene spreads in the gene pool, and we have the attitudes and behaviors of the present.[13]

Scarcity and Fear

Most of us probably believe that people are naturally and primarily selfish. Generosity, when it occurs, is some kind of fluke. Eknath Easwaran, a spiritual teacher who started his students off with the Prayer of St. Francis, says that the reason we need this particular prayer is because "most of us suffer from the mistaken belief that it is in grabbing that we receive, it is in venting anger that we improve our relationships, and it is in having our own way that we find fulfillment."[14] We are mistaken, because when we want things, or especially when we envy other people and wish they didn't have what they have, our vitality is ebbing out, our natural power is declining, we are becoming depressed. When our horizon of consciousness is filled with demands that we be satisfied regardless of the rights, needs, comfort, or convenience of others, then our energy is at a minimum, our selfhood is tightly constricted. On a national level, such demands and blindness to the perspectives of others are the marks not of a great nation or a noble people but of an international bully, driven by anxiety and insecurity.

Because of our fascination with valuing by means of contrast, we are almost forced to wish others ill, that is, to desire that they should want what we have and not have it. If we can get it by depriving them, our satisfaction is greater. Hurting others is the best way to helping ourselves and helping others the surest way to hurting ourselves.

Why do we feel this way? Partly because we consider that the resources that supply our needs are limited. There is no reason to believe that they are going to be shared out equally or with concern for our needs; therefore, if we are going to get what we need, it behooves us to look out for ourselves. But we feel the desire to get ahead of others even when we already have plenty of what we need. Aristotle Onassis told us something to the effect that after a certain point, money is meaningless. It ceases to be the goal. The game is what counts. In other words, we can even invent ways to feel lacking and so be stimulated to put others down.

I said invent ways to feel lacking, but that isn't quite right. We do feel lacking; what we have to invent is a focus for the feeling, something to fasten it on, to give it some recognizable form. The real lack, deep down, is too frightening to face, so we transfer it to something common like more money or fame or honor. We hide from the realization that no amount of contrast with our fellows on this little planet, even if we were vastly superior to all of them, would fill this lack. In trying to trace back this real lack, it looks at a certain point as if what we lack is control, and that is why we keep trying to show that we have control over other people and over various aspects of our lives, our resources, our comfort, even our own psychology. But that is not the bottom; control by power, skill, knowledge, and will is not the answer. It doesn't give us enough value, enough meaning; it doesn't give us sufficient being. We are still finite, contingent, ultimately helpless creatures. All our efforts to maintain our biological life finally fail, and all our endeavors to prevail over our fellow helpless finite beings reveal themselves as ridiculous.

Our desire is to be real, to have value in a world that is not itself a tiny, vulnerable, contingent, lost-in-the-cosmic-clutter world but is itself a truly *real* world. This is the real lack, which we try to cover over with our strivings for position, power, temporary pleasures, and all the rest. A strategy of distraction. We pretend that if only we could have this or that, then we would be fulfilled, in spite of the fact that we are daily shown that So-and-So, who actually has this and that, is far from happy and fulfilled. Whom are we kidding?

There are those who tell us that real meaning and satisfaction in life come from caring for others, putting others first, loving our neighbors as ourselves. This is true, but it is putting the cart before the horse. We are not able to do this sort of thing to any great degree because we haven't got the horse to pull that cart. It isn't that loving others will make us feel fulfilled. It's the other way around: when we feel fulfilled, we will spontaneously love our neighbors—love them unconditionally and without motivation, not in order to gain anything but as a result of our own fullness of being.

Meanwhile the craving for secure and complete being drives us to bolster our petty, finite beings and little local honors in all these miserable and destructive ways. The sharp word at home, the snub at work, the one-on-one mugging down the dark street, the exploitation of the workers, the hostile takeover of the other company, the operation of healthcare facilities as a cost-controlled business for the benefit of stockholders, the deceits "necessary" in politics and government, the hate-inspired moves against ethnic groups, the small and large massacres, the weapons of mass destruction—all the horrors: so much foolishness, so much waste. None of it produces secure, invulnerable, top-value Being.[15]

There is a great deal of talk by spiritual teachers that the trouble with us lies in our ego and that we sin because of our pride. My own persuasion is that behind the ego and the appearance of pride is dreadful fear. It is fear rather than pride that drives us to do the unconscionable things we do. The ego is the level at which our sense of self is focused: the level of finite, limited, vulnerable, lack-laden selfhood, which holds itself tenuously in being by constantly comparing itself to its fellows. It takes all the energy we can muster to puff this ego up with enough pride to keep its head above water.[16]

We constantly need affirmation, usually by achievement and comparison, as well as direct word and gesture from our companions. We want to hear that we are better than others—at least that we are, like all the children in Lake Wobegon, "above average." We want accepting, respectful, even admiring attention turned in our direction. We are like green plants turning toward the sun. Our ego energy comes from such attention. Even hostile attention can be nourishing for the ego, because it means we are noticed, we are important, we make a difference in other people's lives. We will see, when we come to the story of Jesus and the new metaphysics it manifests (chapter 4), how shocking it is when we do get all of someone's positive attention, spontaneously and generously, without our having done anything to attract or merit it.

My argument is that if we got such attention, and if we could believe in its unconditionality, the central stress in us would relax. We would not need to put the other down in order to hold ourselves up. It takes a lot of energy to be hostile to other people, to think of clever ways to belittle them, tricky ways to control them and bend them to our bidding, heavy investments to conquer and govern them. If we felt safe in being, we would have no drive to expend energy this way. Consequently, we would have a surplus of energy. Energy is by nature radiant, so this person energy would overflow from us in the direction of our neighbors, becoming positive attention of valuing them. This would form a chain reaction, reversing the cycle of hurt leading to further hurt.

If that is where domination is coming from, if the terror from behind and underneath is what's driving it, can anything be done? The Holy Thursday Revolution preaches that it is highly possible but also very difficult. We have to learn to refocus our sense of selfhood at another level. There is positive attention available; we have to open ourselves to receive it. Why are we presently focused the way we are? I will answer that it is not bad will, not pure evil, not some control or even temptation from a supernatural source, not disobedience, not falling away from a previously held condition of purity.

Fear comes from a perception of ourselves as potentially *not being* and even now being *deficient in being*, always vulnerable to loss, to demotion, to depreciation. Where does that perception come from? If the politics of domination rests on a psychology of fear, on what does the fear rest? In the next chapter I will urge that it rests on a metaphysics of alienation (otherness) and a logic of identity by mutual negation. These are not willful evils; they are inevitable, natural arrangements. Nevertheless, the time has come to transcend them. We are, have been the last few thousand years, and will continue to be in a "phase transition," shifting from one set of basic operating principles to another, like ice melting from the solid phase into the liquid phase and evaporating into the gaseous phase. This sort of thing is natural for the cosmos, which has passed through, and continues regularly to pass through, various phases of transition. But now our personal consciousness and our freedom have a much greater role than they had previously, so that the new phase to which we are invited may be called "supernatural" relative to the previous phase. Therefore, the first thing we need to do is to understand the nature of the transition, and that is why it is important to see clearly where the problem is lodged in our perceptions of how Being itself is arranged and how our selfhood is identified and maintained.

3

How We Identify Ourselves

The Metaphysics and Logic

Success has been our aim—various kinds of success: in business, in our personal lives, with our talents. What is success? It is measured against some goal. Goal setting is a method for living that is much touted in our time. We may have the impression that if we don't do it, our living is slovenly.

Success and Failure

If there can be success, there can also be failure—only a few ways to succeed, only one success in the end, but many ways to fail and many failures. But even success is a failure. Why? Because the goal set was arbitrary and finite, in some sense artificial. If you can measure and judge whether you are achieving it, it is finite. Sometimes we translate "sin" as "missing the mark." If you can miss a mark, it is because someone has set the mark and you can measure whether it has been missed and by how much. The whole operation is finite.

Even hitting the mark, or gaining the success, only leads to setting another mark, another goal whose attainment will be a success, but whose nonattainment will count as failure. So we are constantly in a state of nonattainment and potential failure, a state of frustration and unhappiness. But this is what is driving us, we protest. Well, that's just the point: it's a form of "domination." It is the assumption that underlies the psychology of domination: meaning comes from winning, from succeeding, in a context that not only allows for, but threatens—and needs—failure. The value *comes* from the presence of the failures, maybe my own past failures, but now that I'm winning,

39

from other people's failures. If they didn't fail, my success would be meaningless. Unless I can have/do what they want very much but can't have/do, there's no value to it, nothing to feel elated about. If everybody has it, no response is called for. Someone has to be disappointed, deprived, unhappy—in that order—for me to feel uplifted by my success.

The *me* that craves this success, that feels indeed that it is necessary for existence, is what we usually call the *ego*. This is how it measures itself, values itself. The context is the assumption of *scarcity*—there is not enough meaningful success to go around—and the feeling is *fear*. I can never get enough to reassure my ego of its place in being. Everything in my environment is a potential enemy against which I have to struggle, which I have to dominate in order to stay in the valued being. So I fear everything, for everything has the potential of destroying my value. A kind of endemic paranoia. P. G. Wodehouse says of a character in one of his funny books, "He was suffering from that form of paranoia which makes men multi-millionaires. Nobody would be foolish enough to become a multi-millionaire, if it were not for the desire to prove himself irresistible."[1] This is the fragile ego.

The ego level is the level of our usual social interactions under the Domination Paradigm. On the one hand, we are asserting our egos to the detriment of others, and, on the other hand, we are politely avoiding offending other people's egos. Both of these concerns are active in most of our conversations and in our reflections on the conversations afterwards. Was the other person trying to dominate me? Succeeding? What lies behind what the other said? I feel suspicious, distrustful. Was my ego-selfhood under subtle attack? Did the other come off superior? Or, if I am anxious to succeed in a different sense, I will ask, Did I say the wrong thing? Could that be misunderstood? Will that injure someone's ego?

All this concern, which looks to us like a good thing, is necessary because we are all so insecure, so insular, so mutually hostile. But the very cure proposed works on the same level as the illness: it continues to focus attention on the ego-self. We study communication skills to learn how to avoid intruding on other people's egos and how to keep them from intruding on ours. The unspoken, unquestioned assumption is that this ego-self level is a real and worthy level of being. There is no recognition in this whole affair that the assumptions of this level are themselves the root of the problem. The more we focus attention on this supposed "reality," even on trying to "do it right," the more we strengthen its presuppositions.

Alienation: Why We Can't Love "Others"

What are the assumptions of this level? They are that the others are truly "other," *alien* to us, that this shows in their having descriptions different from ours, and that this descriptive self is the *only* kind of selfhood we have, one that maintains a shaky perch in being by contrasting itself with every other being.

I think this fundamental method of trying to achieve being and value by contrast comes out of our way of perceiving. Our sight is based on the contrast of one thing against a background; if the contrast is insufficient, vision is murky, uncertain, and unhelpful. It is similar with hearing: distinguishing signal from noise, judging tone, volume, location. Even tastes and smells depend on contrasts with one another in memory. The whole construction of the perceptual world is a matter of setting up useful (meaningful) comparisons. Measurement and judgment of these related percepts are crucially important for life. Values arise directly from these critical judgments: what preserves life is good, what harms it, evil. Even being afraid *correctly* is an important skill, derived from judgment about the environment, about perceptions of largeness, strength, speed, weapons, and so on. The items in our lives that support our lives and the items of which we are correctly afraid are both *important* items and stand out for special attention and careful treatment.

It is not strange, therefore, that conceptual thinking will follow the same pattern and we will seek "clear and distinct ideas" that can be definitively contrasted with one another. That is, they can be *defined,* their "endings," or limitations, made clear. It is in terms of these differences that the ideas will be subsequently related to one another. The sharper the contrast, the narrower the definitions, the more useful they are. This may be the case even for broad generalizations in which quite particular characterizations may be attributed to large populations by stereotyping, reducing the call on energy to make individual judgments. We can proceed to wholesale social actions without having to engage in case-by-case examinations.

The sharper the contrast, the clearer the choice of behavior. In this way our familiar we/they polarities arise. They function on various scales: when we are abroad, we are all Americans as distinguished from the "foreigners" we are visiting. When we are at home, we belong to our respective states, or ethnic groups, or whatever other classes we sort into. Locally, the distinctions are finer still—where you live, work, go to church, and so on. Finally we get down to the one-on-one, where the same method is applied: what characterizes the other that does not characterize me? And, most important, which description is to be preferred? Notice that even when dealing with an individual (in this way), we are not really engaging the individual person in full particularity but classifying the person into various appropriate (we assume) categories whose intersection then gives us the composite that we deal with. Actually reaching the true *uniqueness* of the person before us is a quite different process.

When we meet another, what is usually happening is that one set of descriptions is measuring itself against another set of descriptions in the context of a socially established preferred description. This is what sets up the feeling of *alienation*, that the other is *other* than I am, a "foreigner" on this small scale. We stand opposite one another, outside one another, over against one another. We are separated; there is space between us, no man's land. We have no intention of loving this foreigner as our self. This isn't our self; this is part of our environment and has to be dealt with to our advantage.

Winston King, in his foreword to the English translation of Keiji Nishitani's *Religion and Nothingness*, discusses "the basic building blocks of the Western thought structure." He finds *lordship* very much to the fore: God is Lord over his creation and "man . . . more Godlike than any other creature, [is] the little lord of creation under its Great Lord." This arrangement applies to the act of knowledge itself, even in "post-Christian philosophy": "man as subject . . . lordly in his relation to objects. Mind, soul, or consciousness alone 'within' the citadel of individual selfhood looks 'out' at everything else, whether human or nonhuman, as 'other.'" King goes on to say, which I will develop in a moment, that "out of this climate has arisen the Western dichotomous type of logical assertion that A is *not, cannot* be B." We stand here, and everything else is over there. "I" versus the "not-I."[2] Nishitani himself says, later in the book, that this view has caused the "not-I" to be perceived as a mechanism and the "I" to be experienced as an endless pursuit of desires. And since, we can remind ourselves, this pursuit takes place in terms of the essential *scarcity of being* that is the finite world, it ends up as "a sense of the meaninglessness of the whole business."[3]

Edward O. Wilson says that brains programmed to divide people into friends and aliens are predisposed for war. Zev-Hayyim Feyer, a returnee from the Holocaust, urges that we are all in danger of using Nazi ideology whenever "we make separations between and among peoples." In particular he asserts that "when we view the Holocaust as solely a Jewish tragedy, we allow Nazism to win, for we thereby declare that the killings of the . . . others are not worthy of our remembrance. . . .We . . . separate humanity into two classes: those whose tragedies we remember and those whose tragedies we forget." Furthermore, when we blame the Goyim in general, or even the Germans in particular, and punish the descendants of that generation by refusing to buy German products, "we act in accordance with Nazi ideology" by putting people into categories and dealing with them as monolithic entities. "We must learn," he says, "that all human beings—whoever they may be and whatever they may do—are God's children, created in the image and after the Likeness of our Divine Parent, and therefore, are our brothers and sisters!"[4]

But this is exceedingly difficult when we have been hurt so badly. Eknath Easwaran reminds us that the consciousness from which hurting others issues is itself first a hurt consciousness. A person whom others have rejected and abandoned, he says, who is looking at you through the selfishness with which he tries to protect himself, does not believe that you can care for him but expects you to sneer at him, reprove him, and desert him. These feelings can easily lead, by a series of steps, from this experience of oppression and social poverty to aggressive action against those one perceives as causing the pain. Michael Lerner agrees that oppression causes us to feel "distanced" from one another, and this causes blindness to the other's pain, thus facilitating the growth of pseudo-meaning structures such as fascism that further oppress and cause more pain. Thus the wheel of suffering turns, driven by positive feedback: more pain causes more alienation, which causes more pain.[5]

We Learn to See the World of Hurting

So this is our basic worldview: myself and the others, who may help me—indeed, whom I need—but who may hurt me. If we can form a relatively reliable helpful group, then we can regard other groups as the potentially hurtful ones. We also live with the idea that other individuals and other groups probably regard *us* as those who may hurt *them*. The potentiality of hurting holds us apart, and the distance between us increases our wariness of being hurt. Our feelings follow this perception, and our actions follow our feelings. Much of the suffering in the world is due not to real lacks of real things but to unwillingness to share because of these feelings and perceptions. Our basic perspective channels our political will.

This basic perspective may be supported by biological drives inherited from a long line of evolutionary selections, but in the human being it is also socially *learned* within a symbolic framework. It is in the symbolic frameworks of human society that our freedom is to be found, the possibility for creative action. We have an inner map of beliefs about the world, and while that map is supported by our experience of the world, it also is projected upon the world and we place our acts in the world in terms of the lines and the labels of the map. Thus, our epistemology (our way of knowing the world) and our politics (our way of acting in the world) are mutually reinforcing. We act in terms of what we believe and what we expect based on those beliefs, and then, sure enough, we experience more or less what we expect! At least we can usually highlight and interpret our experiences to confirm our expectations and our beliefs. In this way we constantly create the symbolic environments in which we live; the environment of perceptions and feelings limits the way we live, and the way we live creates the environment.

The trouble is that we believe that our view of the world is the way the world really is. We mistake the symbolic perception/feeling map for the real territory. But to the extent that the map, the symbolic environment, has been created and learned by us, it can be altered; we can learn a new way. Pope Paul VI said, in the context of achieving social justice, that we must learn to think in a new way. That is exactly right. It is the meaning of repentance, or *metanoia*. Change your *noia, nous,* mind, way of thinking. Think in a new way. We can. The symbolic world is the world of human creation; it is plastic, modifiable. Indeed, it is alive, always moving, somewhat changing, also being reinforced, just like other living systems. It changes superficially with the winds of fashion. It changes more deeply when we meet new experiences, such as the discovery of the roundness of the planet and the centrality of the sun, and with the invention of new technologies for labor, transportation, communication, and problem solving. If we want to change it profoundly, we must try to find the deepest layers of the symbolic framework and question these. We must try to find what we believe so securely that it does not occur to us that we are "believing" anything. We do not recognize that an alternative view is possible.

When we work on the deep level, we are open to feeling very disoriented. Shifting from believing that the earth is the center and that the sun and all the planets go around the earth to believing that the earth and the other planets go round the sun is disorienting. Many other ideas, values, and feelings were built on that basic view, and the shift dislodges all the superstructures. The discoverers/creators of quantum mechanics said that if one does not feel profoundedly disoriented by this theory, one has not understood it properly. These are deep shifts. Where do we stand while the "shifting" is going on? This sense of disorientation will come up when we go through the story of Holy Thursday; it is what Peter describes in his attempt to prevent Jesus from making the shift. But Jesus insists on making his move, on shifting the foundation of the symbolic environment, the basic way of seeing the world.[6]

It is in order to appreciate the nature of the shift that Jesus dramatizes in his Holy Thursday "showings" that we are tracing back the metaphysical assumptions of the Domination Paradigm, the archetype of "lordship," which he symbolically destroys in favor of the Communion Paradigm. Thus far we have seen that hurting is based on seeing all that is not myself (or ourselves in the case of group identification) as "other," as alien. Now I want to draw attention to the notion of *separate*.

Separated Selves

We see all the beings of the world as separate from one another—not just people but also human consciousness as separate from the cosmos and both cosmos and human consciousness as separate from Ultimate Being. Since we have (mythically, archetypally) eaten the fruit of the Tree of Knowledge according to Good and Evil, we see division everywhere, contrast and separation. David Bohm, who has advocated a theory of wholeness in physics, believes that the separateness we put between people has its origin in a way of thinking that sees things as divided; that is, things are outside one another, they *exclude* one another. Easwaran says that we are trying to resist evolution by maintaining our own separateness as though that were the best way to be. Here is where we need to confront a fundamental assumption and ask, Is separate the best way to be? This is a complex question, involving many considerations and different contexts, and different answers can probably be given according to the context. Nevertheless, it is a question that is important and should be given some thought.

According to Carol Ochs, a midrashic tradition holds that the original Human Being was Adam/Eve, one being. The fall from grace was their separation into two incomplete beings; we will regain Eden when we become whole again. Another tradition holds that when the First Temple was destroyed, the two cherubim atop the Ark turned their backs on each other. After eating the forbidden fruit, Adam and Eve hid from God. Interpreters say that we still hide from God and hide from ourselves the fact that we are hiding from God. Jean Baker Miller says that insofar as we accept and participate in the Domination Paradigm, we are hiding from the truth of the whole situation and not seeing how it injures both parties. (Indeed, Socrates said that to *commit* injustice hurt one much more than to *suffer* injustice.) We are hiding from the fact that we are unnaturally separating ourselves from our true wholeness. We do it in terms of economics, in terms of power and authority, and in terms of our consciousness of ourselves. Separateness and the fear it engenders keep us apart from our own deep essence. Out of touch with the universal matrix of basic energy, we try to increase personal energy by stealing it from one another.

In other words, we don't recognize God in each other. This blocks the "flow of divine plenty," says Rabbi Adin Steinsaltz.[7] Gerald May says that it is not possible to belong to the universe, to participate in its vital flow, if one is either being controlled by it or trying to control it. There is no hope of realizing unity in an atmosphere of either submission or mastery. The slave may smile at the master, but it is a false smile. The master may feel affection for the slave, but it is an affection eternally tainted with contempt. Michael Lerner repeats that cruelty is made possible by our not recognizing—acknowledging—the image of God in one another, and he asks, Why does that recognition break down?

My own idea is that it doesn't "break down"; it isn't there to start with. This is not to imply that it ought to have been there, but it is a biological/historical fact that it is not. I don't mean that the image itself wasn't there; of course it was. It's the conscious realization of it that has to grow. The mutual recognition that Lerner rightly asks for is gradually forming as a paradigm shift. It is a new thing on the face of the earth. Yet it has probably begun to surface about as soon as it could. This has to be seen not in a moral context alone but in a cosmic context. In fact, the coming of a "moral context" itself is a cosmic development. Nevertheless, as a paradigm shift, or a "phase transition," it constitutes a "revolution," a profound change of basic principles of operation in a space structured by different dimensions. O. W. Markley outlines the stages of dealing with a system transformation as first holding to the tradition, then tinkering with the system hoping to "fix" it without abandoning it, and finally experiencing some breakthrough in the approach to the problem that leads to a reexamination of the fundamental assumptions of the troubled system. Even simply examining fundamental assumptions causes a transformation in the perception of reality, for we are now looking *at* what we formerly looked out *from*, so we are already standing somewhere else. When the new perception has stabilized, a new world is seen, new dynamics in relations and feelings appear, and behavior is altered.

This is what is going on in the Holy Thursday Revolution. The long-term phase transition is being given a big boost by Jesus' ministry. Jesus, according to John Dominic Crossan, was "building [for the poor and the rejected a] community on radically different principles from those of honor and shame, patronage and clientage." In order to do this, I say, he has to perform the shift at the foundations, deeper than principles of social or economic organization, where metaphysical principles, perceptions of how being itself is put together and valued, and the root sense of existence and identity are found.[8]

The Logic of Mutual Negation

The metaphysics, I have argued, is one of alienation, otherness, and separation. What makes that possible, I will now urge, is a logic of mutual negation, a logic in which the principle of identity, A is A, is accompanied by a principle of exclusion: A is not-B, B is not-A. The separate things are outside one another; they exclude and negate one another. To see how this works, let us consider how we usually identify ourselves. If someone asks us to tell about ourselves, we begin to list our descriptive labels. One might say, I am a white, middle-class American, a Catholic, a Republican, a businessman, generally conservative; I'm married and have three grown children and five grandchildren. I'm interested in sports, especially football, and I like to go boating. They tell me I've got a "type A" personality: I want to get things done and done right; I can't stand incompetence; I'm ambitious and mean to get to the top. But I try to be honest in everything I do, and I give to charity and do a little volunteering when I have time. And so on. We give a physical and social description of ourselves, of our work, of our personality, of our character. There might be some more secret and subtle points, but they too would be particular descriptions. Where all these labels coincide, my self is supposed to be found. The descriptions tell about it—that's it, that's me.

We align similar descriptors for everyone we know or interact with. Sometimes the other party is identified very simply by a single dimension: ethnicity, occupation, nationality, political affiliation, sexual orientation, disability, criminal history, whatever. Sometimes that is all we need to know to decide how we feel about the person and how we're going to conduct ourselves in the relationship. We can appreciate here the power of naming. Whoever can put names on others and make them stick has great social power, a power that enters the minds of people and causes them to perceive their world according to the values of the names. Moreover, it is because we believe that we are our descriptions that we experience being hurt by others. What is going on? One set of descriptions is injuring another set of descriptions. And thus also it is because *we believe that we are our descriptions* that we find it necessary to hurt others.

The descriptions maintain their being precisely by their contrasts with one another; they maintain their value by dominating others. The very logic of the metaphysical situation requires it. The description, the concept, is what it is by virtue of being *not the other*, and it derives its value from being *more than the other* or *having what the other lacks*. Mutual negation is at the heart of language and therefore at the heart of humanness—under the Domination Paradigm. The human world is the word-created world; this is the world that we actually live in, not a raw natural world but a world experienced through the mediation of the Word, of language.

We don't have many words for qualities that are absolutely universal, perhaps a half-dozen or so: being, unity, truth, goodness, beauty—that sort of thing, the transcendentals. But the words we mostly pay attention to are the ones that apply to only some beings, not all. We say that X is a useless word unless there are some things that are not-X. Contemporary philosophers say that every linguistic element exists only because of "what it is not," that binary oppositions are the primary dynamics of language, that all propositions say that things stand to each other in one way rather than another, that "since thought works only with correlativities, a word or a concept which has no contrast has no meaning," that all structures characterized by relationships are "ultimately reducible to binary opposition." This being the case, there is a powerful urge, says Edward Wilson, to classify other human beings into two artificial categories; we are comfortable only when the rest are labeled as "with us" or "against us." Mary Midgley allows that such mutual negation may be built into our way of living so deeply that we cannot altogether get rid of it.

These are the ways we try to shore up the finite being which, after all, exists only as a set of relations to other finite beings. We want to find a principle of identity, something that exists always and remains constant throughout all changes. This, says Emile Meyerson in his *Identity and Reality*, "is the true essence of logic, the real mould into which man pours his thought." But David Bohm counters that the notion of *separately existing* entities is not basic to perception but is an abstraction from perception. What is truly primitive to perception is change itself, movement, process, from which something invariant is arbitrarily abstracted to serve as an "object."

I myself think that there is something terribly important about shifting from thinking that reality consists of *things* that have definite relations between them to thinking that *relations and processes* are the basic reality and that "things" are the patterns and the inter-sections of these processes. We have moved from geometry as funda-mental mathematics to calculus, which studies motion as such. Now, with quantum theory, we face a study in which, when we try to cap-ture the process in terms of measurement (which is a "thing" thing, comparing a supposedly well-defined being with a conventionally constructed definition, the unit of measure) we find that it cannot be done to an arbitrarily fine degree of accuracy. The "process" does not submit to such perfect definition and measurement in terms of its being a "thing." It is all relations and motion, and the measuring rod and we who would measure are also involved in the same holistic process, the members of which are not "separable."

It is a living world, being created by a Living God, and you will not find the Living One among the dead, the abstractions of mutually negating logical concepts. When we try to think of ourselves and other persons in these terms, we do not reach our or their reality; we reach a deadness, a shell, a mask perhaps, but not the quick, not the living one. None of us is captured by our appearances or by our his-tories. We exist only in the living moment, in the movement itself into the future. Judgments based on appearances and on the past (without openness to the future and hope) are fallacious, untrue, unreliable, and unhelpful. This is the meaning of *forgiveness*, to look *for*ward and empower the future for the living and not confuse the living with the dead.[9]

Revolution

Now we may begin to appreciate the sense in which a "revolu-tion" is called for and why merely moving the furniture from one side of the room to the other is not sufficient. There has to be a turn-around in the sense of self. The question to the human being who appears on the brink of expulsion from paradise is, "Where are you?" Where's your selfhood? Where do you fit into the picture? Is your self-hood defined by its comparisons with other apparent selfhoods as finite as your own? Is fitting into the picture a matter of your location in the various pecking orders of community life? Is God a Lord whose servant you are? Or are you a conscious subject-presence surrounded by an environment of the objects of your perception-analysis-desire? Are you alone in existence? Until we have entered into existential anguish, say the Christians, the Jews, and the Buddhists, we have not got down to where the problem is so that we can turn the whole perception around.

The problem is that we believe that we are nothing more than our set of descriptions, that this finite being is all that we are, just dust, fancy dust. Even if we claim that we believe in resurrection or immortality, it is still under the aspect of finitude, deficiency of being—deficiency of being, contingency of being, dependency of being, relativity of being, and at the same time isolation in being, cut off by the definitions, by the contrasts that give us the only being we have.

The revolution comes when we break through the ordinary mode of seeing and overturn our structures of consciousness from the ground up. This is *metanoia,* which—if we do it *thoroughly*—opens to us the "kingdom of heaven." This "kingdom of God" is always "at hand"; it wants only this fundamental shift in the sense of self to bring it into full reality. When the sense of my existential self-being shifts, everything else shifts too: world, God, destiny, meaning, value, duty, desire. If in some way the sense of being a deficient self could be altered, the entire world would have to reorganize itself.

"The thrust of repentance," says Rabbi Steinsaltz, "is to break through the ordinary limits of the self. . . . it is an ever-renewed extrication from causality and limitation."[10] What is wanted is an experience of the self as not limited by the descriptions and the comparisons, a self that is not defined at all. Transcending definition, the self cannot be isolated in being, cannot be deficient in being. Therefore it need not be anxious or defensive or greedy or envious, much less destructive or dominating or submissive. The self will not be an island, but the person-community-process will be a whole that the persons will compose as a living being by their activities: a new emergent that is transcendent with respect to its antecedents, revolutionary in its new principles of organization and operation.

This is a phase transition. It takes time to happen. Historically, it may have begun millennia ago, and it can easily be expected to take a long while yet. We contribute to it now by undergoing the transition of *metanoia.* A pot of water "boils" when its molecules, one by one, attain the energy of vaporization, make the phase transition. This, as I see it, is the context in which Jesus and his Holy Thursday Revolution are situated.

Story I

The Jesus Ministry and Holy Thursday

There has been a lot of interest lately in "the historical Jesus": Can you find him, and if you can, what have you got? Of course, the stricter you make your conditions, the less you've got. For my part, I think I can get by on a mere handful of stories that pertain to three main topics: the baptismal vision, the social expression, and the Suppers. The Suppers are part of the social expression, and the expression follows from the vision.

Let's start with the social expression. If we had only the following stories about Jesus, we would know what was going on: his interactions with women, lepers, and tax collectors. If you consider yourself a ritually pure Jewish male, yet you are willing to interact socially with these three classes as if they were your peers, you show yourself as someone in whom a profound transformation has take place. One spoke with women as little as possible. Tax collectors were traitors; lepers couldn't live in town; and all sorts of diseased and disabled people were considered to be cursed by God. They were rejected by the pure and righteous and experienced themselves as social orphans, "fatherless." Hanging over the whole society was the fact that God had allowed the nation to be subjugated by the Romans, so perhaps the whole people was being rejected and punished.

The Baptismal Vision

What was Jesus' transformation? Now we move to the baptismal vision. John the Baptist was preaching that God would soon come to rescue his people and that the people must prepare. John was offering a baptism of repentance, of *teshuva,* "return," turning back to God

51

and full compliance with the Teaching (Torah). Jesus, identifying with all the distress of the people—the diseased, the socially deprived, and the nationally defeated—asks for baptism from John. Emerging from the water, he finds that heaven has opened to him, and he hears the Voice of God: "You are my beloved child, in whom I am delighted!"

This was not really "new." Jews had considered themselves "children of God" for centuries (Deut. 14:1). But this story shows how this mighty truth has to come home to each individual as though heard for the first time with all its stunning power. In the story, Jesus *is* stunned by it. He runs away from the river out into the wilderness and stays there a long time, forgetting to eat, just living in the resonance of this Word, receiving, assimilating, *taking in* the full meaning of what was said. At some point he began to think about it, to draw conclusions from it. "If you are the child of *God* . . ."

The first conclusion—and you have to hear deeply to realize that this conclusion is *necessary*—is that this Word is spoken not to him individually, to Jesus of Nazareth, but to him as "Adam," as all humanity, as one who is able to *hear* the message, really hear it in all its immensity and not reduce it to something personal, provincial, and exclusive. All people are *really* children of God. Take it seriously; take it literally. Think what that means.

The second conclusion is that being children of God means that in this respect, on this level of our reality—and this is the deepest, truest level—we are all equal. No exceptions. No modifications. In a class-structured society, think about that! The third conclusion is that we are obliged to honor one another as equal children of God. We must recognize and acknowledge and respect one another. This is not a "counsel of perfection," or an ideal held so far out in front that we will never reach it but it's nice to know it's there. This is a present obligation. It is the *mitzvah* that underlies all neighbor-directed *mitzvot* and is obviously akin to honoring God. "Whoever dishonors the child, dishonors the parent."

What might this mean on a practical level? The fourth conclusion is that we must share our lives with one another. Noting again the social expression—all the stories of healing and helping, of lifting up the outcasts and welcoming all, showing equal respect to all (amazing those who observed him [John 4:27])—we come to the Suppers. This is how Jesus tried to get his insight across and get other people to see it and practice it with him. There are a lot of stories about suppers, dinners, and banquets, and they all show this central point: no social class distinction is allowed—everyone is equal, all are welcome. What John Dominic Crossan calls "open commensality," everyone eating at the same table was unheard of—scandalous! Do it, says Jesus, this is right, and this is our salvation.

This is the general background for the Holy Thursday Revolution, which is itself a capsule version of the whole Jesus Movement. I want to develop first the baptism and its conclusions, then turn to the social expression in what we may call "the Jesus program." Finally, we will examine the Suppers and Holy Thursday itself, with its significance as a revolution.

The most important thing about the baptismal vision is that, if we are to follow the Jesus program and contribute to bringing the revolution to pass, we need to experience the vision as deeply as possible. All the rest of this—social program, Suppers, everything—depends on really receiving that vision, really hearing that Voice speaking to *me*, and hearing it in such a way that I *know* that it's for everyone else just as much as for me. We have to be careful not to flit lightly over "everyone else" in some abstract way, and we have to take care not to lose "me" in "everyone" too soon, because there is usually a temptation to let that turn into "everybody except me."

You may remember from the Sermon on the Mount (Matt. 5:48), how Jesus stressed being *thorough* (*teleios*: seeing something through to the *end*, accomplishing the job, usually translated as "perfect"); here is an instance where that applies. The meditation on the baptismal Word needs to be repeated until it's in our bones and eyeballs and we can't feel or see any other way. Unless we do this first thing well, the rest of the program will limp, fail, fall apart; and even when our efforts go forward to some extent, we have to sweat and strain and push. And the old ways will come back. The Domination Paradigm rests on a way of *seeing;* that is what we have to change, and here is where we change it. So don't try to do it by will power (St. Paul tried that and found frustration).

Meditation and Reflection for Paradigm Shift

We perform this meditation by letting our own "heavens open" and welcoming the Spirit of God in ourselves, which is an exercise not in striving or struggling but in relaxation. We saw already that our troubles are caused by identifying with our descriptions and trying to acquire value for these by reducing the values in others. So take away the identification with the descriptions, with the labels. Give up limiting yourself to being what the label says. That's an abstract and artificial classification anyway. Let go restricting yourself that way. Just be *you*, being you without being what the label says. Remember that our God is One who brings out of the constricted places, out of bondage. Don't consent to being tied to your descriptions. Unbind them, one by one, until you can genuinely feel yourself being you without being the label. Practice. This is the way your consciousness, your "heaven," opens. It is also a way of understanding yourself as a child of God, for God has no labels, no name. Rabbi Lawrence Kushner reminds us that when Moses pressed God to tell him His name, God "said what He always says, 'I'm sorry but I can't help you; I'll be whatever I'll be. Alive and real. And therefore unpredictable.'"

Then listen to the Voice. Don't think about it, just listen to it. Feel good, listening to it. "Beloved," it says. "Delighted with you," it says. Hear that, stay with that, sigh and relax with that. Don't let yourself introduce reasons why it shouldn't be so. The Voice doesn't make conditions or exceptions. It's an absolute assertion of loving you and being pleased with you and claiming you as intimate family. Repeat this meditation every chance you get. Remember it in between times. Live with it. Live from it. In your interactions with other people, let your heart lead and do the generous thing to help others feel accepted and affirmed. This will tend to free them from being preoccupied with their own needs and will open them to their heaven and to other people.[1]

Now let us reflect on the conclusion that we are all equally children of God. Several points follow from this that we will be taking up in greater detail in Part II. I want to mention them briefly at this time so that we will have a sense of the context in which the events of Holy Thursday take place.

If we review the teaching of Jesus and his actions, we see that he evidently concluded that being children of God meant that we were to be as impartial (perfect) as God, who sends sun and rain on just and unjust alike, both the good and the evil (Matt. 5:45, 48). It means that we are to love our enemies as well as our friends. We are to deepen our purity beyond ritual observance and not let insistence on any purity practice divide us or set us at odds with our fellows. It means that we have grounds for rejoicing even in the midst of temporal troubles. It means that in God's eyes all are equally worthy, equally unworthy, for worthiness is not the issue. This is an example of the way Jesus throws out whole categories for thinking/feeling about our relations with God and one another.

To be a child of God means that your real life is maintained by God and is not valued in terms of your manipulation of the environment. It means that you forgive and heal your sisters and brothers endlessly, as God endlessly forgives and heals you, continuing to pour life into you from moment to moment. It means that you live your true life in each other person, as each of them lives in you. It means that you give your life to be the nourishment of all and hold nothing back for yourself alone. It means that the more you give yourself to others, the more you are living true to your reality and the more your being is affirmed.

To be a child of God means to be incomparable, as God is incomparable. As we will discuss further in Part II, a sense for our own absolute, or nonrelative, being is the key to the freedom that will enable us to see ourselves in a new way. As God is transcendent, we also in our personhood, are transcendent. To be a child of God is to be essentially an act of loving, even as God is. We should be ready to realize our true nature by coinciding with the act of existing that we are, with that fountain of living energy that springs up in the midst of us and actually is eternal life. Sheer existence, beyond form. Active self-giving that means indwelling the other and receiving the other into our own life. Being outside one another is another principle that Jesus discards, substituting being inside one another. More of this later, too. But this is what leads to the interactive community that forms the Living Body of the Messiah, in the image of the Living God. From that it follows that to be children of God is to be incarnate as creative process, to participate in the divine creative life and activity.[2]

Jesus' Social Program of Boundary-Breaking

This brings us to Jesus' social program as he saw it embodying these theological principles. (We always have to remember that Jews never linger long in the purely abstract and theoretical but move promptly to the field of action, putting into practice on this plane of the creation what they understand to be the intention of God.) The first thing that is obvious is that a lot of boundaries have to be shattered, especially the boundaries between those accounted "righteous" and those considered (by them) "unrighteous," contact with whom would render one "unclean."

To illustrate this, Jesus tells the story of the Good Samaritan (Luke 10:30-35). The man who was beaten and robbed is said to have been left "half dead" by the side of the road. When the priest and the Levite come by, they observe that there is some question about whether the man is alive or dead, and on the chance that he may be dead they are careful to pass by on the far side of the road, because coming within a certain distance of a corpse would render them unclean and they would have to go through a purification ritual when they got to the end of their journey before they could conduct their business. The Samaritan, on the other hand, goes to see, for even if the man is dead one has a duty to see that his family is informed and his body properly treated. But it turns out that he is alive and the Samaritan cares for him.

The story hits several issues: my convenience coming before a life-or-death issue for another, the purity regulations coming before a matter of real concern, and the despised Samaritan turning out to be the hero. (It may be that this story is the creation of a Christian community many years later, when Christians were moving away from the Jewish priesthood and the stricter points of the Mosaic Law and when Samaritans were joining the church in large numbers—in which case the storytelling itself illustrates the principle of domination by putting down the people it sees as adversaries, possibly unfairly.) But any way we take it, we see how the basic theological principle that Jesus brings strongly forward—the universal divine filiation—translates into particular social action in several ways.

It is interesting that in our own day Michael Lerner, in *Jewish Renewal,* is complaining about people pretending to be highly *hala-kic,* "superobservant or supernationalistic," who are effectively "assimilated," for "when they go into the economic marketplace or into politics, they think and act in accord with the logic of a system that encourages unlimited accumulation of power and money without regard to human consequences." "Woe to you Pharisees who tithe mint and rue and herbs of all kinds, but neglect justice and the love of God!" (Luke 11:42). Same complaint. But then, Jesus was a Jewish Renewalist in *his* society!

Another boundary that is expanded by Jesus is that of the family. On one occasion, when he was teaching in a crowded house, a message was brought to him that his mother and brothers were outside and wanted to see him. He took advantage of the moment to say that he considered all those with him in the house to be members of his family as well: "Whoever does the will of my Father is my mother and my sister and my brother." When a woman blessed his mother for bearing and nursing him, he appreciated the blessing but added that she was more to be praised for having heard the word of God and having kept it, with the implication that blessing is appropriate on everyone who does that. It isn't flesh and blood that count, it isn't family lineage, it isn't ethnic descent, it isn't biological achievement—it's hearing the word of God, that we are all God's children, and then following through on that word. That's what counts. John the Baptist had already scolded the people for thinking they were privileged as children of Abraham: "God can raise up from these stones children to Abraham!" How *do* you live right with God, then? "Whoever has two coats must share with anyone who has none; and whoever has food must do likewise" (Luke 3:8, 11)—the practical social application of fundamental theology.

Another boundary that has to go is that between the social authorities and the common people. Jesus treats everyone the same: respect people as persons, showing no deference to power and no condescension to the poor. Richard J. Cassidy points out that "universalism is a striking feature of Jesus' social stance. Luke describes him as including persons from a wide range of backgrounds among his disciples, and shows him accepting dinner invitations and hospitality from men who were wealthy. On occasion Jesus' cures and healings also benefited the rich and the powerful."

The boundary between the rich and the poor was to be overcome by more than evenhanded social manners. The rich were expected to share—indeed, everyone was to share—and surplus material possessions were to be distributed. This is a very difficult thing to get any society to accept, but it may have been preached by Jesus as a way to social salvation under the circumstances of Roman occupation, heavy taxation, and property loss.

The boundary between the diseased and the healthy had to be stretched. Jesus himself touched the "untouchables," the lepers, and even dead bodies. He refused to countenance the idea that people who had some physical disability must have been cursed by God. He approached those from whom others ran away. Nor did social disabilities count with Jesus. Tax (toll) collectors were called to join him, and he ate in their houses.

His most scandalous behavior, probably, was the respect with which he treated women. They traveled with him as did his male disciples; he conversed with women he met on his travels, even having very important discussions with them about theology and about his own mission; and he sent women to be witnesses for him, something legally impossible. He undertook to protect women charged with adultery or divorced by their husbands, recognizing the deep injustice of the laws on these matters. The *Gospel of Thomas* suggests that Jesus deliberately intended to treat men and women exactly alike.

The very hardest of all Jesus' boundary-breaking stances was that between friends and enemies, but it is based on what he saw in his vision and realized about God. God sends sun and rain on the good and evil alike, and God's children are expected to be perfect, like their Parent. Anyone can love friends, people who are nice to one and do favors for one; but if we are to live up to our true natures we must love even our enemies, those who treat us badly, cause us loss and injury. Moreover, we must always be ready to forgive. After all, God could consider us "enemies" often enough, and we want God to forgive us, so we must do the same thing. This will win through to peace and even to freedom sooner than fighting. Violence only begets violence. Get to the root: don't desire power over others.[3]

It all sounds very idealistic—or maybe not even that, maybe not desirable but rather threatening to the existing social order—but could it actually be done? Jesus breaks boundaries in his own life and causes a lot of shock, and he tells other people that anything he can do they can do also. Follow me, be the light of the world, all of you. You can do it. The kingdom is at hand: you don't have to wait, you can do it now. The power of God is vested in you—hidden in you, perhaps, but it's there. Believe in it, let it shine!

The Two Showings of Holy Thursday

That is the background, the context of the teaching that Jesus practiced by word and deed. Now we come to the two great showings of Holy Thursday. The first is the footwashing. Remember the definition of domination, that it is nonreciprocal. Footwashing is a good way to show a relationship that is nonreciprocal. Servants wash the feet of their lords—in all sorts of ways, literally and, even more so, figuratively, as we have seen. Very often both parties are invested in preserving the arrangement. In certain ways we like to have lords over us. It relieves us from taking the ultimate responsibility; we have someone to turn to, someone else to make the decisions. We enjoy looking up to great people, gaining our little glow from being associated with them without having to face the risks they face, and so on. Remember the argument the Grand Inquisitor gave Jesus when he turned up again in Spain in the sixteenth century, started preaching freedom and equality again, and was promptly picked up by the police and thrown into prison. "We've taken the responsibility *for* them, we carry the burden and relieve them. People don't *want* your dreadful freedom!"

The story of the footwashing is told as though Jesus' disciples are in this mood. They are followers and believers and worshipers, and they like it that way. Jesus doesn't. He shows them an image. He leaves his place at table, takes off his coat, rolls up his sleeves, gets a long towel that he ties around his waist, takes a jug of water and a basin, and begins to wash the feet of his disciples. This is unbelievably shocking. The master is acting like a servant. Peter pulls his feet away and admonishes Jesus: "Lord!" (calling him back to his proper role: you're supposed to be the lord) "You shall never wash my feet!" Notice the paradox: the servant is telling the master what he can't do! But Jesus, undeterred, tells Peter firmly, "If you can't consent to this, then you can't participate in what I'm about." That's how important it is. Somehow this gesture carries the weight of the whole program. If your position, your perceptions, your feelings, your way of life, are such that this behavior is incompatible with them, then you haven't got the insight into the kingdom. Come on, Peter, don't tell me you don't understand it at all, that you don't see that it has to come to this.

What was Peter so afraid of? Was it that he *did* see all the implications? Did he see that the whole world was being turned upside down? Did he know that if he consented to this, nothing could ever be anything like the way it had been? (That is, if he held true to it.) Did he suddenly get the picture of the Temple crumbling to pieces all around him? If the Lord washes my feet, how shall we be governed? Whom shall we honor and how? How can we run the world unless some have power and others obey? How will this affect families? Businesses? It's too disorienting. I would have to readjust all my relationships, all my values, all my attitudes. . . .

Nevertheless, Peter reluctantly consents, and Jesus goes on around the circle and resumes his place at table. "Now, then," he says, "do you understand what I have done? You've been calling me lord and master, and in the old system that was correct. We've been living in a world organized in terms of lords and servants. What I have just shown you is what I think of lordship. When the 'lord' acts as a 'servant,' then being a 'lord' or a 'servant' doesn't mean anything anymore. 'Lords and servants' is not a good way for us to think of our relationships. What I have done is destroy that whole concept. It's been a kind of 'Temple' for us, in which we have worshiped, done business, understood all our activities and relations. That's why you're so upset. It's very fundamental. I've just destroyed that 'Temple.' But I'm going to build a new one. Or better, *grow* a new one.

"I will no longer call you servants but friends. There is to be no distance between us. You are entirely in my confidence. Everything I have heard from my Father I have told you. I have not kept anything back, and I have not claimed any privilege. We are friends, all equal. Everything I have done you can do as well. You can do more, and I hope you will. Sharing my life with you has been my love for you. No one can have greater love than this, to be willing to give your whole life to your friends. Do you see how it is? That a friend's life lives inside you? and you live in your friend? It's that kind of love. That's the kind of love we have with the Father. The Father is in me and I am in the Father, I am in you and you are in me; the Father is in you and you are in the Father; you are in each other.

"Let me show you another sign to make this clear. Here is bread, the fundamental food, our body. If I break it, so, and give it to you, saying 'This is my body, my life, eat it, receive it into yourself and live by it,' can you perceive how this is really true? What seemed to be outside you and someone else has now come inside you. You have eaten it and it will become you. What was *my* body will be *your* body. Do you see? My life is given to nourish your life, to make you live more fully.

"Let us do it with the wine, too. This is the cup of joy, of blessing, of salvation. Let me give it to you, saying, 'This is my very life, my soul, poured out for you. Drink it and live!' It is a single cup; share it among you. It is a common life among us all. Now, you must do the same thing. I have given you the example. You also share your lives with one another, feed each other with your very bodies and souls, lay down your lives for each other, dwell in one another.

"And do you see what has happened? We have come together in our sharing, in our indwelling, in such a way that we form a new living being composed of us as its limbs and organs. *This is the kingdom of God*, this is the salvation of Israel, and not of Israel only, but of the whole world. If people everywhere could live like this, give themselves into each other this way, it would take away the sins of the whole world."[4]

The Suppers Inaugurate the Kingdom

Michael Grant, in his book *Jesus*, says that the Supper was already identified in Jesus' mind with the first manifestations of the kingdom. Bruce Chilton concurs. He says that "Jesus had a well-established custom of eating with people socially," but that he had "a special understanding of what the meal meant and of who should participate." All Israelites, provided they were willing to forgive and be forgiven, were welcome, and the meal itself was a "sign of the kingdom of God." Participants were expected to bring something of their own to contribute, and of course they had to be willing to sit at table with everybody else. Their own material and social generosity imaged the generosity of God for which the meal was a thanksgiving. The idea is that Jesus and his companions traveled around organizing these Suppers, held often in someone's home, but occasionally outdoors, when large crowds took part (see the feeding of the five thousand and of the four thousand). Chilton says that these meals were an "anticipation" of the coming kingdom, but I (remembering how Jesus began with "the kingdom is at hand" and later corrected Martha, who expected the resurrection of her brother at the end of the world by saying that resurrection is here and now) would prefer to say that the Suppers are the actual inauguration and real presence of the kingdom.[5]

John Dominic Crossan says that Jesus was using his practice of open commensality as a strategy for building peasant (unpropertied people in villages and small towns) community on radically different principles from those of honor and shame. The basic idea was an egalitarian sharing of spiritual and material resources at the grass roots. Jewish practice today publicly announces the commitment to radical egalitarianism by the presence of the blue thread in every tallis (prayer shawl). Alfonso Montuori and Isabella Conti praise "radical human egalitarianism" in terms of seeing "all of reality [as] a single, complex, interrelated life system" in which "both people and things are to be cared for and nurtured, not exploited or shaped to one's private will," and they hope for an increase in our experience of "human interconnectedness."

Crossan also points out all the symbolism involved in the meal and accents the appropriateness of *eating* as an image of human interconnectedness. He quotes Peter Farb and George Armelagos: "eating is the primary way of initiating and maintaining human relationships. . . . Once the anthropologist finds out where, when, and with whom the food is eaten, just about everything else can be inferred about the relations among the society's members." After noting that "reclining" at table implied the presence of servants and that rank was expressed in terms of position at table, and even sometimes in the quality of the food served at positions farther from the host, Crossan points out that Jesus refuses to use any of those practices and deliberately does things to show the equality of those at the meals. Words that we still use in our liturgies, the verbs *took, blessed, broke, gave*, have "profound symbolic connotations. . . . They indicate . . . a process of *equal sharing* whereby whatever food is there is distributed alike to all. But they also indicate something even more important. The first two . . . *took and blessed*, and especially the second, are the actions of the master; the last two, *broke and gave*, and especially the second, are the actions of the servant." By doing all of these himself, Jesus shows again that masters and servants are no longer distinguished, but all are equal.

I myself think that using the physical act of eating to express spiritual intimacy is brilliant. If a new idea is offered, we first have to be "open to" it. Then we have to take it in, "receive" it. We taste it, "savor" it. We may have to "chew on" it for a while. Some things we find "hard to swallow," some we just can't "stomach." But if we have swallowed the idea, we have to give ourselves time to "digest" it. Perhaps finally we actually "assimilate" it, make it part of ourselves, and begin really to live from it. In the Jesus story, we are invited to apply this imagery to someone who is offering more than an idea—a vision of reality and a way of life, a vision and a way completely embodied in the person offering. The "way" is himself, what and who and how he is. This is how we feel about it, and he himself feels totally identified with and by his vision. If we "participate" in the vision, if we eat it and digest it and assimilate it, then it becomes *our* body, *our* selfhood. And if we all do it, then *together* we compose *one body.*

There is another interesting thing about the fact and the symbolism of eating. Christian de Duve, in his history of life entitled *Vital Dust*, remarks that what some living creatures don't have by their own synthesis, they must obtain by eating other creatures that do make those chemicals. This is what is going on in the food chain. Moreover, eating a compound ready-made saves the time and energy required to synthesize it oneself. All this shows "eating" as the ultimate "domination." One takes over another's life and literally builds it into one's own structure. Now, in Jesus' Supper, we see this intention reversed: he offers to be food for his friends. This is the opposite of domination; he is the un-dominator, the un-lord.

Furthermore, this negates the assumption that we necessarily live in a context of scarcity, which we discussed earlier. In a context of scarcity, anyone who consumes something appropriates it not only against its original owner but against everyone else who might have had it. (Remember our discussion of value.) But to use the symbolism of giving oneself to be life in others is to destroy this whole pattern of perception and value. Jesus is not destroyed in being "eaten." He continues to live in himself, and his life is actually *expanded* when he also lives in the others. And their lives are expanded when they are augmented by receiving his life, and they are expanded further when they also give their lives into their companions and receive their companions into themselves.[6]

The Multilevel Revolutionary Supper

It seems possible that Jesus was organizing Suppers to meet the practical needs of the people as well as to introduce his concepts of equality, reciprocity, mutual indwelling, and abundance. When people *share* what they have, they often find that there *is* enough to go around, even more than enough (baskets of leftovers can be taken up). I like to think of Jesus setting up these Suppers somewhat on the order of the "base communities" of "liberation theology."

Borrowing a model from the Hindu tradition, I interpret the Suppers as taking place on five levels of human reality. Individual human beings and the human community are composed of a series of "sheaths," one inside another. The outermost sheath is made of food. Sharing on this level means literally sharing food and anything else made of matter: housing, clothing, tools, and so on. Inside this sheath is one made of energy. On this level we can work for one another, help with tasks, and also share emotional energies, supporting one another in joy and sorrow. The next sheath is that of the mind and memory; we share our stories, our news, our daily lives, and experience ourselves as a community. When this feeling and level of sharing deepens enough, we may become willing to share our secret insights, our dreams, our visions, our sacred revelations. When a community reaches that level of intimacy and trust, shared joy breaks out in its midst; we are in the sheath of bliss.

I sometimes end this recital of the sheaths by saying that Jesus' Suppers, when they reached this pitch, ended as all good Jewish parties do, with singing and dancing. In that vein, I would like to share a bit from Rabbi Lawrence Kushner's *Honey from the Rock*, a description of a communal Sabbath meal enjoyed by seven families (with three times that many children!) crowded into a suburban recreation room. Activity begins with lighting of candles, sanctification of the wine and the day, parents blessing children, husbands praising wives, blessings over bread, and food—lots of food.

> And the laughing. The sharing. And the singing. One melody is scarcely spent when another comes forward. We don't even notice the racket of the children. There is a great holiness in this room. It grows from the sharing. [I take a large ceramic Kiddush cup, fill it with wine, offer it to my wife and then to the man next to me, who] hands it to his wife with the solemn instruction, "Here, keep it going." And we do. From hand to hand. Drunk from and refilled. Time and time again.[7]

This is a vision of a *revolution*. It begins with a mystical experience, which is developed through thinking and feeling into a social
program with economic and political dimensions. It begins with the
realization of divine filiation and works out as a multilevel human liberation. Liberation theologian Gustavo Gutiérrez says that for people
suffering under domination mere "reform" and "development" from
the existing status are

> timid measures . . . ineffective . . . to achieving a real trans-
> formation. . . . [We] must attack the root causes of the prob-
> lems . . . the domination of some social classes over others.
> Attempts to bring about changes with the existing order have
> proven futile. . . . Only a radical break from the status quo . . .
> a profound transformation . . . a social revolution . . . would
> allow for the change to a new society. . . . What is at stake . . .
> is the possibility of enjoying a truly human existence, a free
> life, a dynamic liberty . . . a society . . . free of all alienation
> and servitude.

What makes it a *revolution* and not merely a "reform from
within" is the depth at which the shift takes place. Jesus does not
move the furniture from one side of the room to the other; he tears
the house down. The level at which his revolution in human life takes
place is the level at which being is conceived/perceived in its most fundamental way: instead of being myself by virtue of being not-you,
over against you, I am myself by virtue of giving myself to you, loving and affirming you. Thus, instead of being outside you and separate from you, I am within you and symbiotic with you. But this is not
merely a shift in sentiment and attitudes at an individual person level.
It includes the community level—all of "us" together, being "in" one
another and therefore incapable of "dominating" one another.

This has to become apparent in the way our institutions are organized and operate. Our economic life, political life, religious life, family life, education, recreation, and art all have to manifest this new
reality, or it is all a matter of hypocrisy. "By their fruits you will know
them." It is not enough to say "We believe such and so." Salvation—
good health—implies mutual indwelling, expanded "selfhood"—the
big "WE." Exactly what forms these manifestations might take we do
not completely know; our imaginations are not yet sufficiently into
the new paradigm to allow us to formulate much detail. But some
things are already happening and we do have some ideas. In any case,
our life is a growth; it is never a shift from one static arrangement to
another.

Historian Hannah Arendt has important things to say about revolutions. A true revolution always starts a "new story" with its own inner coherence and development. A social shift is revolutionary only if all of the old beliefs, values, meanings, traditions, and structures are disturbed and profoundly modified. A genuine revolution always advances the cause of human freedom. She distinguishes between "freedom" and "liberation." "Liberation" concerns the restoration of rights and is a necessary precondition for freedom. "Freedom" is the creative action that liberated people can take. Arendt calls it a "treasure." It is found when people can join with others in shaping their lives and their meanings. It flourishes only when the focus is not wholly on private satisfactions but extends to the larger community and revolves around the conviction that people sharing their lives can overcome obstacles to full human living.

Revolution and Torah

Michael Lerner affirms that revolution is the central Jewish idea: "the world can be radically transformed from what it is to what it ought to be [because] the fundamental spiritual reality of the universe makes this transformation possible." God is revealed to Moses in terms of the intention to make available "good health" (salvation) on every level of human existence, but we have to do the transforming. Lerner says:

> Our task is to hear the voice, to recognize God's availability to us, to make space for it in our lives. This mystical experience is tied to an ethical and political awareness in a way not typical of most mystical systems. . . . What Moses understands is the true nature of the universe: that spiritual enlightenment and moral obligation to struggle against oppression are not two separate things; they are inextricably united. . . . The God of the universe has made it so that transcendence and transformation of the world are both possible and necessary. . . . Human beings become more fully themselves through a process of mutual recognition, and part of *what* is recognized is the God within each of us (namely, the way that we are created in the image of God and hence equally worthy of respect and love). . . . The process of recognition is itself a manifestation of God's presence as a force of healing and transformation in the world. . . . [This] revolutionary conception of God . . . [is] rooted in Torah. . . .

"Torah," says Rabbi Adin Steinsaltz, "is the original pattern, or inner plan, of the world. . . . Torah expresses the inner will, the direction and mode of operation of the relations between the world and God, it is the spiritual map of the universe. It is not, however, a static chart of things as they are but a dynamic plan of the ever-changing world. . . . One who is immersed in Torah becomes a partner of God . . . participating in the planning, the spinning out of the idea, the common dream of the existence of the world."

This is the Torah that Jesus avows he is committed to "implementing" (*plērōsai*, Matt. 5:17). The transformation of the world, its transition into the next phase of its life, is a cosmic event. It is not the recovery of a previous state of unity and purity, nor is it merely a moral conversion and political rectification. It is a true "phase transition" to a new set of interrelational principles and modes of process and operation, creating a new level of being. Being "in Christ," says the apostle Paul, is being "a new creation." The "Body of Christ," the living community that is the Messiah, that is the kingdom of God, that *is* the era of peace and justice and fullness of life, is a new creature constituted of the interactions, the life sharings, of the persons who compose it. It is like making a new kind of molecule. The composing atoms share their electrons in such a way that the electrons no longer belong to their original atom but to the molecule as a whole. Something like this happens when human beings share their love energies and feed one another with their individual lives. We can say of this transition what can be said of many another cosmic transition: "Life had moved another step, beyond the networking of free [energy] transfer to the synergy of symbiosis. Separate organisms blended together, creating new wholes that were greater than the sum of their parts." This was said by Lynn Margulis and Dorion Sagan about bacteria, but it's the universal pattern (Torah?) of the creative cosmos. Fritjof Capra generalizes it: "symbiosis [is] a major evolutionary force [with] profound philosophical implications. . . . Life is much less a competitive struggle for survival than a triumph of cooperation and creativity."[8]

This is the core of the Holy Thursday Revolution, where the "turn" takes place. We will take up next the logical and metaphysical foundation of the new Communion Paradigm and show how it is expressed in a psychology of love and a politics of *friendship*.

PART II

Person as the Basis for the New Paradigm

4

Person and *Perichōrēsis*

A New Metaphysics

Under the Domination Paradigm, people are encouraged to think of themselves as identified by their descriptions and to see themselves as real insofar as they are distinct from others. This distinction is achieved by mutual negation: each party says, effectively, "I am I by virtue of being not-you." So defined, people feel the insufficiency of their being, which is always vulnerable, always at risk. Consequently, people are insecure and anxious. Strongly pressed to preserve and enhance what being they have, people are easily tempted to believe that helping others may hurt themselves and that hurting others may be the best way to help themselves. After all, the others *are* "others," and our first priority is ourselves. "My" well-being has to take precedence over "yours."

Jesus Offers Unconditional Positive Regard

In the Jesus Movement, several things happen that undercut these views and feelings. First, Jesus offers people unconditional positive regard. He gives full attention, sympathetic support, respect, and something else. The something else is that he does not interact on the basis of one's social description. In by-passing the description, he is going to something deeper and more real in the person. When he turns his unconditional positive regard on this deeper self beyond the descriptions, that self has the opportunity to wake up, to experience itself. When it does, it discovers itself as full of being; it no longer feels deficient. It was the identification with the descriptions that produced the sense of deficiency.

A self that cannot be captured by descriptions is a self that is not exactly "finite." And it is discovered (or "awakened," or "liberated") in an interaction with another person who is not acting from a position of description and who is not establishing selfhood by *negation*. On the contrary, this "positive regard" is entirely *affirmation* of the awakening self. The awakening self, finding itself beyond description or definition, has no motive (drive) to negate anyone else; it is not necessary in order to establish one's being. The basic being-energy of the self, therefore, is free to radiate, to move outward in positive regard, in its turn. It reflects the affirmation. We have two trans-descriptive selves established in free and full being by *mutual affirmation*.

Second, Jesus explains to people that each person is a child of God. God is undefined, indescribable, intimately personal, and unconditionally loving. God does not interfere with the cosmic order, does not alter circumstances to benefit this or that person, nation, or any other kind of group. God does not play favorites. God loves all equally. Children of God are supremely safe in this love (but not protected in the world), and children of God are themselves capable of this kind of loving. That is what it means to be a child of God: it means to be one who loves all equally and unconditionally.

Third, Jesus gathers people into communities in which the mutual recognition as children of God is the foundation for social interaction, and the social feeling is mutual affirmation. In the community, each person does the same thing that Jesus originally did: loving another person on the level beyond any description, beaming full attention (with all one's heart, soul, mind, strength) of positive regard. This can awaken the sense of selfhood in one who has not yet known it, and in this way the community expands.

This largely undefined, almost indescribable *doing* is what characterizes the community. Social descriptions make no difference in the community; the community does not recognize descriptions as the level of reality on which it operates. All people are absolutely equal and each is absolutely unique. The sharing within the community is thus richly textured and very creative. Being unified, loving, and creative, the community is the "outreach" of God, the very Presence of God as world.

We now have what we may call a Communion Paradigm: a *symmetrical, reciprocal relation of enhancement of being: that beings may be, may become all that they can be, may act in maximum freedom and be valued for their incomparable preciousness.* Here I am I by virtue of being in-you/with-you/for-you, not outside and not against— not even separate. Consequently, helping one another is always helping oneself, for the "selfhood" itself has expanded in a complex, systemic way. And the drive to create comes forward as more funda-mental (naturally for a child of God) and yields a deeper satisfaction than the desire for gain or protection. There is more free energy avail-able than under domination, less inhibition by self-defensive fears, so there is a great deal more cultural development.

A New Selfhood: The *Person*

This is a capsule version of the Communion Paradigm. Now we can start to look at it in more detail. The first and most basic thing to understand is the *person* beyond the descriptions. I am going to use the word *person* now in a special sense to mean our deep reality, our true *self,* beyond the descriptive self. I will call the latter the *person-ality.* It is important to learn to distinguish our person from our per-sonality. Most of us tend to confuse them, to speak of the person but mean the personality. Usually we are very interested to learn more about our personality, what type we have, how it typically behaves and feels, what kinds of work it is good at, what sorts of people it gets along with, and so on. Sometimes when we hear about finding our "true self," we might think that it is what our personality really is, as distinct from what we've been pretending to be. That is worth know-ing, too, but that is not what I mean.

Think of answering the question, Who are you? Make a list of answers: I am gender, race, nationality, religion, work, marital/parental status, and all the rest of the description. Now try to sit firmly in the I AM part of the sentence, to feel yourself *be-ing* in those ways. Next, alter the description; if you are tall, imagine yourself short; if contem-plative, active; if irritable, patient; and so on. Then, take away the descriptive items, one by one, while remaining clearly and vividly aware of *be-ing.* Try to work down to just a few very general descrip-tions; then begin to erase them, acting from the central position of I AM. . . . You may be able to let them all loose, remaining in the I AM without any following predicate, without any modification.

If you can do this, you will discover something amazing: just as in a solar eclipse, the solar disc disappears little by little and everything gets darker and darker, until at the moment of totality the solar corona breaks forth in all its glory—just in that way, when you work your way down to the bare undescribed I AM, when you reach total-ity, your radiance will suddenly erupt, and you will find that the I AM is also MAY YOU BE! This central, undefined *be-ing* is you, the *person.*

Do not think that you can approach it or move toward it. You can only draw back into it. Nor can you look *at* it. It *is* you, the one who does look-ing. It is not something you have or an aspect of you. It is you. This is the true self. The descriptions are never the true self. They are all memberships in classes, in categories, in sorting schemes. As such, they are all masks, costumes, character roles in the cosmic play. They are not the living You.

This is the child of God. Daniel Walsh, who taught philosophy to the Trappist monks at Gethsemani after his retirement from Manhattanville College and Columbia University, had a powerful experience in his youth of being pure being. He gradually worked out an explanation for it. He distinguished *person* from *nature*. The nature is what I've called the descriptions. It includes human nature. This is created, he said, by the free will of God. But the *person* is not created; it arises from the being of God, not created but from the being of God. As the Nicene Creed says of the Second Person of the Trinity, it is *genitum,* not *factum,* generated or born, not made. The First Epistle of John speaks several times of our having been "born of God" and being "from God."

This is the heart of the revelation, this is the ever-living word that Jesus heard from his Father and passed on to us. It is important not to limit it or water it down by importing some notion of contingency or mediation into it. It is supposed to stand forth in all its awesome unconditionality. Only if this is so and only if we understand and believe it to be so will we be able to live the divine life and practice divine love.

There must be no hint of insecurity at this point; the foundation must be of rock, not of possibly shifting sand. There is no deficiency of being for the person. The person is born of God and is filled with divine being. This, of course, is the grounding for the equality that Jesus is preaching and practicing. Realizing ourselves on this level is what is going to enable us to love our neighbors as our selves. Unconditional love is the characteristic divine act. We receive it, believe it, deeply know it, realize that we are it, and act as it. That's the heart of the revolution, what makes it possible.[1]

The Nicodemus Story

Remember the mystical conversation that Nicodemus had with Jesus, deep in the nondescriptive "night." In order to "see the kingdom of God," Jesus tells Nicodemus, you have to be "born *anōthen.*"

The teaching turns on the double meaning of the Greek word *anōthen*. It can mean "again," and so Nicodemus asks, "How can human beings be born again? Are we to enter again into our mother's womb to be born?" This is a little like trying to find the personality that is the "real you." Another human birth isn't going to get you any closer to the kingdom. It is also a little like asking, Can we change human nature? Can *anthrōpos* be born again? asks Nicodemus. But Jesus says, "Unless you are born of the Spirit, you cannot enter the kingdom of God. That which is born of the flesh is flesh, and that which is born of the Spirit is spirit. Do not marvel that I said to you, You must be born from above." *From above*—that is the other meaning of *anōthen*.

That which is born of nature is nature, and that which is born of God is the person. Unless you are born of God, there is no way that you can belong to the kingdom of God. Unless you were born of the Spirit, you wouldn't be here asking me about the kingdom, so don't be so amazed. You must know this. The Spirit is like the wind, blowing wherever it wills, but having no origin and no destination. "So it is with everyone who is born of the Spirit." This is your true self. At the very core of you, you know this, you have to know this.[2]

In this story, Jesus is not telling you that you have to *do* something or *acquire* something in order to be eligible to enter the kingdom of God. He is drawing your attention to something already true, *always* already true, your deep self, very likely hidden under culturally received notions, habits, distractions, and descriptions. He is opening you by his affirmation of you, so that the real you can feel itself being, the you that is born of the Spirit and therefore *is* spirit, and therefore *belongs* to the kingdom of God.

The effect of this "opening" by affirmation, if one "believes" it—that is, really accepts it, sees it, experiences it at the greatest depth and no longer has to depend on someone else affirming that it is so but knows it on one's own authority—is to confirm absolute security in being and thus undercut at the very root any need to manipulate another, either as dominant or as submissive, or to contrast oneself in any way with another in order to obtain a feeling of greater security. This is where the revolution at the root takes place.

An efficacious way of bringing this about is by way of the loving look, the unconditional affirmation by another person. It happens on the person-to-person level. That's what makes the awakening one experience being a person. We should note that the awakening does not necessarily have to come through another human being's love. Jesus himself heard a Voice from heaven. The Buddha simply sat with himself until it broke through. Those who are thus freed can help others by affirming them, but it is also always the case that anyone may break through to realization without human aid.

Eros and *Agapē:* The New Logic

The breakthrough can spread through this unconditional positive regard, and will spread that way. So let us look at this act of love more closely. It is the quintessentially divine act, called in the New Testament *agapē*. God is said to be *agapē* (1 John 4:16). Those who can act with *agapē* manifest by so doing that they are children of God. What is *agapē*? From Lutheran bishop Anders Nygren I learned to distinguish *agapē* from *eros*. Both of these Greek words can be translated into English as "love."[3] *Eros*, says Nygren, is self-seeking love or desire. I love someone or something insofar as it is good for *me*. It is pleasant or advantageous. I may love my studies because they make me knowledgeable, maybe even wise. I may love my teacher for the same reason. I may love God because God sustains my being and gives me good things. (This love often comes into question if the good things cease coming and disadvantageous or painful things come instead.) *Eros* is the love that seeks the good of the lover.

Agapē, on the other hand, is the love that seeks the good of the beloved. It asks or expects nothing in return. Return is not a question that arises, one way or the other. The benefit to the beloved is all that matters. The lover wills and acts for the good of the beloved. In terms of the loving itself, the lover projects positive person-energy—if we may call it so (for we don't have a proper word for it)—toward the beloved with the intention that this should enter into the beloved and increase the beloved's being and life and well-being.

This *agapē* is unconditional. It does not love the other because the other is lovable, has pleasing aspects, does the lover good, is morally meritorious, deserves to be loved, or for any such reason. Neither does the lover love the other because the other is in moral need of being loved or because to love someone who doesn't deserve it would be meritorious on the lover's part, or for any such reason. *Agapē* is not a *reactive* love. It comes from the lover as an original *first* action, not as a response to something about the beloved. There is not even a choice about whether to love or not to love. Thus, the freedom with which this love is posited may be called *creative*. It arises from the very being of the *person*. It can also be said that the person arises from love inasmuch as the person arises from God and God is love. We'll come back to that presently.

Agapē reaches out to the beloved, it "flares" out, like a solar flare; it enters into the beloved to nurture the beloved, to give life, to give being, to bestow value. This is the significance of Jesus' expression of love under the guise of giving oneself as food for the other's life. It intends to put oneself *inside* the other and to receive the other inside oneself. "I am in you, and you are in me." This is the alternative to being "outside" one another. This is what the I AM does. The MAY YOU BE is simply its flip side, or even just another way of saying the same thing. The central, indescribable, transfinite You is this. This is what/who is born of the Spirit. This is your true identity.

Now we can see how this is a new and different logic. It establishes identity not by mutual negation but by mutual affirmation. What makes you to be you is not how you have a different description from others but how you love the others with unconditional *agapē*. The more you give yourself away in *agapē*, the more you are you, the more being you have because you are doing your true-being thing. Under identity by mutual negation, the more you try to save your life by acquiring advantages for yourself, the more you lose your life, because you are doing the opposite of the truly living thing.

We still have differentiation, but by another method. Descriptions are *what* persons *have*, and they are *different* from one another by negation. The indescribable I AM/MAY YOU BE self is *who* the person *is*, and the persons are *distinct* from one another by their acts of loving each other. Notice that in a world that organizes in terms of differences among descriptions, one principle is needed for determining the differentiation, and another principle must be called in to establish any union among these different beings. It takes one thing to make them different, another thing to bring them together. But among persons living by *agapē*, a single principle—the *agapē* itself—both differentiates and unites. One must go out from oneself toward the other to be *agapē*, but *agapē* intends union with the other, so both the differentiation and the union are established by the one principle. This is important because to be creative we must maintain both differentiation and unity. This is why the Trinity is such a good way of speaking of the absolute ground of being. In this logic, others do not exclude one another but include and confirm one another.

The logic of the Domination Paradigm had said, "I am the one that is not-you, outside you, separate from you, over against you, preferring my welfare to yours." That was supposed to be the real self;

that view is still considered "realistic." The logic of the Communion Paradigm says, The real I is the one that lives in you, the real you the one that lives in me; your welfare is my welfare; you and I are a "we." Power-over relations and the possibility of cruelty belong to the Domination Paradigm and its mutual-negation logic; love and creativity belong to the Communion Paradigm with its mutual-affirmation logic. In my view, it is the latter that Jesus is preaching, teaching, exemplifying, and celebrating. He proclaimed then (and still does) what Michael Lerner calls "the most central aspect of Jewish destiny: to be people who testify to the possibility of a different logic in the world than the logic of cruelty and power."[4]

You Have to Do It Yourself

I want to stress the importance of living from this realization of being in an authentic way. By that I mean that one must come to see this for oneself, beyond taking the word of someone else about it. We can recall the story of the Samaritans saying to the woman who had had the interesting theological conversation with Jesus, "We are no longer dependent on your report, for we have seen for ourselves." And the story of Jesus declaring to his friends, "I will no longer pray to the Father *for* you, for the Father himself loves you." In other words, you don't need me as intermediary. This conversion to living from the person-self works only if one does it oneself; it is not sufficient to say one "believes in" it when hearing another talk about it. Such a positive disposition is initially helpful, but it is not the turning, or the awakening, itself.

In a tradition that has long emphasized the virtue of believing certain propositions as salvific in itself, it is necessary to point out that the revolution we are discussing is not actually achieved that way. The realization of being a child of God has to be one's own indisputable conviction based on one's own experience in order to be proof against all the ideas, images, and feelings generated by the domination culture. That's why Jesus himself says that it's no use just listening to him and applauding; you will be blessed only if you *do* what he says. If we understand that this is the case, then we won't think we have done what is required if we simply assent to a nice idea and occasionally make an effort to behave in terms of it. That's trying to force one's nature by sheer will power, and it is well known that that produces frustration, weariness, distress, and despair. People wind up teaching each other that we'll never do it "in this life."

What Jesus is insisting on is that we *must* do it in this life—it's in this life that it's significant, and we *can* do it. He's not teaching how to be welcomed into the next world but how to manifest God in this one—that is the original purpose of the creation and the special vocation of human beings.

What we are to do is to open ourselves to hearing the Voice, seeing the truth, knowing how it is with us, that we are born of the Spirit and therefore find ourselves "in" one another and feeding one another in mutual positive regard. This is the truth that makes us free. If we know about it and expect it, at least we won't ignorantly or deliberately shut ourselves off from the possibility of realizing it. We need to know that we are so much more than we usually think we are, so much deeper and so much freer, so much more able to manifest God-as-world. This conviction and confidence need to become our ground consciousness, the place from which we think and feel and act.

Another image may help. Most spiritual traditions say that the ego is *the problem;* get rid of the ego and you'll be open to reality. What is the ego? The suggestion is that this troublesome ego is like a focal point: it's where the action lines of the heart, soul, mind, and will converge. Where they all cross is where we feel that we are situated, where our self is. (Maybe that's the meaning of "Where the body is, there the eagles will gather," only the other way round: where the eagles gather, that's where we feel the body is.)

What we can do toward "opening" ourselves to realization is be aware that this focal point can shift. It's not a *thing*, not an entity, therefore not something to put down or go against or "die to." You just focus somewhere else and that previous focal point disappears. Practice focusing on your neighbor's welfare, on carrying God into the world; the ego focus will weaken and dissolve. No violence is needed, just a shift in interest and attention. Also, use your own images, ask your own questions, and listen for your own answers. Doubt whatever doubts you like. For now, doubts can be helpful, they move the contents of consciousness around and thus aid opening.

The whole idea of being a child of God brings up the question of how we should think/feel of God. What do we mean when we say "God"? I am going to say that it is the Love-Ground of the *person* community. But before we get into that, I'd like to share some God-language from Rabbi Zalman Schachter-Shalomi, a contemporary guru of Jewish renewal. This language may sound strange but that is what's needed to help us shift our focus and our feelings. The main idea is that God is not a thing, a being, an entity, and therefore should not be designated linguistically by a *noun*. Verbs are better. Some time back, about thirty years ago, Mary Daly said that God is a verb. And Reb Zalman is composing poems and prayers and songs and whole liturgies in this context. Here's the sort of thing he says—this is from a book to help parents answer children's questions: the unpronounce-able Name of God has meaning letter by letter

> and then together, they make for the simultaneity that is the most goddest God godding endlessly. . . . Infinitely inging. . . . And that infinite/inging was the most pervade/ing, sustain/ing, create/ing, love/ing, care/ing, feel/ing, understand/ing, image/ining, integrate/ing, conceptualize/ing, BE/ing, blowing our minds with identity beyond belief, shattering our concepts as inapplicable to that reality, rebirthing us as loved children of the universe who have every right to be here and now and for all the devastation of that living through, it also gave us renewed life, vigor, energy, zest. . . . The holy AND became the strongest paradigm of our theologies . . . the And between good and evil, Jew and Gentile, *Shabbos* and the week, holy and secular; this And, the infinitely *And*/ing ONE. To serve this ONE means to let oneself become aware of one's identity with the ONE . . . to function in the flow of the ONE. And we make it up as we go along.[5]

This may be a good preparation for a discussion of *perichōrēsis*, the theology of the Trinity, because it indicates clearly that we are talking about something dynamic. Zalman says that the One is constant beyond all our changes and changing beyond all our endurances. Our notions of change and motion and flow and process are poor for the dynamism that is God. *Perichōrēsis* means "proceeding around," or possibly "dancing around." (When you're doing mystical spirituality, it's customary to play a little loosely with etymologies!)

Perichōrēsis: The Metaphysics of the Trinity

Perichōrēsis is the metaphysics of the Communion Paradigm. It's the way *persons* indwell one another in God, dancing into each other's hearts. With respect to the Trinity, classical theology said that each divine Person is "in" each other. The intensity, depth, and thoroughness of this "in"dwelling makes God ONE. It is the ONEness of *agapē*. God is *agapē*, says the Johannine epistle. *Agapē* is God, says

Dan Walsh, putting us in mind of Gandhiji, who said that earlier on he had thought that God was truth, but later realized that Truth was God.

Agapē-Love is the foundation of all, the metaphysical ground, what is implied by everything that is real, what must be the case in order that everything else may be as it is. But love is always only love-*ing*, only action, doing, not a thing. Dynamic, not fixed. Not even a something or someone who then does the loving—and might or might not do it. No, the Loving Itself is first. The Persons of the Holy Trinity are the first effusion of Loving, says Walsh. The persons who are gifted with created natures, such as angels and human beings, are the second effusion. The persons arise out of Loving and loving arises out of persons. If we want to speak of "grace," this is where we do it, because the notion of "deserving" has absolutely nothing to do with any of this. The persons, whether of the Trinity or of angels and humans, give grace to one another in these acts of loving. Grace *is* divine life, divine living, doing the divine thing.[6]

Now, to get a deep sense of how loving unifies, or how Loving and ONEness are the same meaning, I want to offer some more images for the Divine Dancing. This is going to be what I call the "I–I" relation. I think it's important, because we have to transcend all sense of subject–object consciousness. Subject–object consciousness is a deep level of the Domination Paradigm: subjects know and thereby possess objects. Objects are "acted upon" by subjects. Think of how we talk about someone who is not present in the third grammatical person: we say "he" did thus and so; this happened to "her"; let me tell about "them." Those talked about are not subjectively participating in the conversation. The speakers are very external to the objects of the talk, very separated. This is an "I–them" relation.

Now, imagine that one of those spoken about comes into the conversation. We suddenly have to shift gears; we have to address the one who is now present, whose own subjectivity has been added to our community. We say "you." We face the one we call "you." We do not talk *about* that one but *to* that one. The feeling is very different from the "third-person" talk. The energy of the subjective presence of the "you" is very strong. It demands attention and care. Our own subjective presence goes out to the other's subjective presence. There is a feeling of meeting, of giving and receiving, of not being in total control, of not knowing what the other may do or say; there is creative tension, something new each moment, a new dynamic. Nevertheless, we do speak to the "you" and we do listen, for the interior of the other is hidden from us. We share in the other's reality only to the extent that the other reveals it and we are able to translate the media of the revelation into terms of our own subjective reality. It is an incomplete fusion, although an enormous leap beyond the "I–them" relation. This is the second grammatical person, the "I–you" relation.

Can there be anything beyond this? Can one person enter more deeply into another person? What is meant by "the Father is in the Son, and the Son is in the Father"? Are they as "outside" one another as our "I–you" conversations suggest? We have to say no, for God is strictly ONE. The whole point of saying that the Persons are "in" one another is to show that no intimacy or union is left unfulfilled. Each Person is totally open to the other and totally sharing with, revealing to, the other. Nothing is reserved. In the "I–them" relation, the "them" was clearly object and nothing but object, while the "I" was subject. In the "I–you" relation, "I" is subject and "you" is partly object, but not totally object, for "you" is also active as subject to which the "I" is partly object. One feels in the relation that one is engaged with another who is, in that one's own right, a subject just as I am a subject. I address another subject. But I do not know that subject as the subject knows itself, as I know myself, from the inside. I acknowledge the inside of the other and I get peeks as the other reveals it, but I do not entirely enter into the other's interior.

Now, the Persons of the Trinity cannot be objects at all, not objects of anyone's action, anyone's knowing or speaking to. They are all pure subjects, totally active. Therefore, their relations to one another are subject–subject relations. I call this the "I–I" relation. It means that each Person knows the other Person as that Person knows itself. There is complete coincidence, or (remembering this is all dynamic) confluence. There is only insideness, no outsideness. The Person is totally "in" the other Person, and this is reciprocal, "to know even as one is known." This is the archetype of "communion." The sacrament of Jesus' Supper, the imagery of eating, is representative of this original communion. The Supper is supposed to be a manifestation of, a realization of, the fact that each of us is "in" each other and therefore we are "one" as the Persons of the Trinity are ONE (John 17:21, 23). The community so formed is the image of the Trinity.

I think we can see that this subject–subject coinherence can be true only for *persons*. Personality natures, defined by their differing descriptions, would be held too far apart, for it is their nature to exclude one another logically. That is proper to them, but it is just as proper to *persons* to indwell one another. The revelation is that on the deepest level of our being *we are already engaged in such a commu-*

nion. As persons we are eternal children of God and therefore are ONE as God is ONE, by being a perichoretic community. But as human beings we are endowed with natures that belong to the cosmic reality, the creative effort that is still going forward.

Creation Metaphysics

Our mission in this world is to let the *person* communion shine through the cosmic order. To do this is to be *theotokos,* the God-bearer, giving birth to God in the forms of organized matter. Creation is getting more and more intense. The physical-chemical-biological "underpainting" is in place, now the real artwork can begin. There is no way of knowing what it will do, for "we make it up as we go along," it being truly a matter of creation, and there may be no end to it.[7]

I am proposing what we may call a "creation metaphysics." It applies to all that exists, to the entire cosmos, what classical Christology says of the union of two natures in one Person. The uncreated person-community becomes incarnate as the physical cosmos. We are trying to hold together the extremes of the spiritual uncreated and the material created. It is a Great Work. I said earlier that to be creative we must also hold together differentiation and unity, and that this is why the Trinity is such a helpful way of talking about the Ultimate Reality. Now that we have explained how *persons* are united and how *agapē* sustains both differentiation and union, we can say more about how the person-community manifests in the world and how the world is made in the image of the Trinity.

The great problem of metaphysics has always been how to give an account of the joint reality of the One and the many. The world is obviously multitudinous and diverse. Reasoning and spiritual insight convince us that the ultimate Source and Ground of the world must be One. How does this One become (or produce) many? Here we see the beauty of the Trinity. The Ultimate Reality itself, the very Ground of Being, is both One and Many. There is no need to cross over from one to the other. Further, since the Ultimate is *agapē*, the oneness of this principle implies the manyness of the persons, and the manyness of *agapē* must be resolved in oneness. If the Ultimate were either One or Many alone, it could not be *agapē*. Many other metaphysical doctrines have allowed for multiple deities or for one absolute deity, but I think only the Trinity insists on holding both together without reducing either to the other. Moreover, I think we can say that only

Christianity has seen God as a Community—has seen Community as a way to talk about God.

This seems to me a very important point and the brilliance of this tradition, for it connects the structure of the universe and the structure of human society directly with the Creator and shows precisely in what the "image of God" consists. It is not individuals who bear the image but the whole creation and communities within it. Everything in the physical cosmos operates in terms of an appropriate community, some kind of system in which every part has a role to play, makes an important contribution; and the character of the system emerges as a result of these interactions.

The interactions are always energy-sharing processes, and the higher-level organizations that appear as emergents from these sharings have new properties and new processes, new actions that they perform as wholes, as new units on their new level of organization. Thus quarks unite as nucleons, nucleons unite to make nuclei of atoms, atoms share energy to become molecules, molecules interact chemically to form living cells, cells collaborate as organs and systems and emerge as a unified body. Animals share their lives in communities of various sorts, and eventually human societies take shape. We are still in the transition to whatever the next emergent will be. Pierre Teilhard de Chardin called it the *hyperpersonal*; early Christians called it the Messiah, understanding themselves in their unity to form the body of the Messiah—in Latin, *Corpus Christi*.

The divine creative action, or process, can be seen in terms of a life cycle in which the uncreated manifests itself as evolving cosmos and the cosmos evolves to the point where it becomes conscious enough to "remember" or "realize" that it *is* the uncreated person-community expressing itself in this incarnate process. The realization brings the consciousness back to its true selfhood, closing the cycle. John 1:18 tells us that the Ultimate is necessarily invisible, transcending all form, but it generates a *monogenēs theos* that resides in the "hollow" of its Parent, and simultaneously "exegetes." The exegesis is the world. The world lays out in an unfolded way and makes explicit what is enfolded, implicit, in the Invisible One. But through consciousness the explicit is gathered together again in the realization of the Supreme Unity. Oneness manifests itself as manyness, and manyness realizes itself as oneness.[8]

Our task in this is to realize and again to manifest. When we become enlightened, know that we are the uncreated children of God clothed in the skins of the created world (see Gen. 3:21), we do not linger in the mystical union, but, joined to the divine action, we participate in the creation of the world. This is the same life cycle, seen from the creaturely side.

In terms of our own personal spiritual practice, what we need to do (says this view) is shift our focal point. Whereas the energies of our heart, soul, mind, and will had been focusing at the ego, so that we sought in everything the welfare, comfort, pleasure, and interest of the ego, we now focus on the creation and development of the world, God's action, God's process—God's dance, if you like. Instead of concentrating on what we can get, we concentrate on what we can give, how we can contribute, how we can help. We conceive of ourselves as partners with God, even participants *in* God, since "God" is a verb, a "God-ing," a living process.

Notice that we are so far beyond the Domination Paradigm now that not even God can be correctly styled a "dominator," a Lord. Our relationship is too intimate for the old-style lord/servant description. Jesus is showing this in his metaphor of the Supper: we are "in" one another as food is in the eater. An epistle attributed to Peter says that we are "participants in the divine nature," and Paul quotes one Greek poet, Epimenides, as saying that it is in God that "we live and move and have our being," and another, Aratus, who affirmed that "we too are [God's] offspring." Later Paul invents the image of our being the Mystical Body, which reinforces the dynamic feel for what is being taught, the strong sense of being God-present-and-active-as-ourselves in the world. We are all members of this divine body and individually also members of one another.[9]

It is thus clear how entwined we all—all humans and God—are. This is why many of the categories and images we have used for God and for the God–human relation are really not suitable categories or images. The relationship is not essentially one of obedience, for instance, not a testing of wills; therefore, Judge is not a good image for God, and reward and punishment are not good motives for human participation in the great creative work. There is not enough separation between us and God—in fact, there is no separation, says the revelation—not a separation that would make such relations as obedience, judgment, reward, and punishment even make sense. The relation is too intimate, far too intimate for that.

That is something worth getting your eyes open to, for many, many people have suffered fear, anxiety, guilt, distress for their friends and relatives, alienation from God, spiritual loneliness, and despair because of such images, ideas, and preachings. Even the image of God as parent may not be adequate, depending on what kind of parents one thinks of. Parents can be very dominating, oppressive, fear-inspiring, and guilt-inducing. Only a God of *agapē* can set our souls completely free from affliction and open us up, liberate and energize us for creativity.

When this liberation really takes place for us, then the excitement begins, then "spiritual life" really takes off. Then all of life is seen as "singing and dancing," that is, as direct expression of the interior reality. The song is the singing, which is the singer in action; and the dance is the dancing, which is the dancer in action. So all our life in the world is ourselves acting and acting *artfully*, that is, creatively and expressively. We are the "God-ing," which is God in action.

That is the meaning of our lives, and it feels perfectly integral and natural. We do not experience ourselves as a ghost operating a machine. Nor do we experience ourselves as puppets at the end of a string, or robots inhabited by a divine program. We experience ourselves as thoroughly ourselves, but it's a big OURselves through the intimacy and intensity of the *agapē* interactions, the cross-feeding of the Supper that is living together. It feels very authentic, thoroughly real, vividly awake, and aware. Spirit is incarnate in matter, expressed as life; godliness is permeating worldliness, and world is shaping up as image of God.

There is a clear and strong sense of wholeness. It is not the same as a "herd" feeling or peer pressure. The uniqueness of the person (that it cannot be compared at all) acts happily through its incarnation in a particular individual nature that brings its special gifts into the Supper sharing, into the cross-feeding that constitutes the whole, the messianic body. The diversity of the composition is what makes it beautiful, what keeps it moving as a melody, advancing, as Gregory of Nyssa said, "from grace to grace," as *agapē* energy, beaming across the community in every direction, "making it up as we go along."

5

Living inside God

The Psychology of Love

Sometimes in the past, when I was telling about this revolution—and even just now in the Story—I have made use of the report that Jesus spoke of destroying the Temple and then rebuilding it. In my version I have had him claim that his act of footwashing was the "destruction of the Temple," meaning the all-governing institution (paradigm) in which we had been worshipping, doing business, adjusting our family structure, identifying ourselves. The analogy was all right, but the image suggested that tearing down the Temple was a good thing to do, rather than a violently destructive and unspeakably tragic event for a whole people. What is needed is an image of a societal and ideational structure that centralizes and covers all the thinking, feeling, and behaving of the people. But the real point of the analogy lay in the kind of difference that was to be displayed between the old structure and the new one. It wasn't just a question of rearranging the old stones into a new pattern and putting up new decorations, while still going by the same sort of architecture and engineering, physics and geometry, as the old one.

Rather, a whole new set of principles was involved: Suppose the new Temple is made of glass rather than of stone and wood. Suppose the glass is blown, not molded or bricked. Suppose that there are bubbles inside bubbles (you can do this with glass, just as you can with soapy water). Glass is not a solid; even in our window panes the glass is in the liquid state—the panes are slightly thicker at the bottom than at the top. The glass bubbles hold together, therefore, not by being stacked one on top of another, but by the cohesion between the molecules, their attraction to one another, sharing their own energies with each other, rather than being coerced by the external force of gravity. The spherical bubbles are symmetrical in all directions, and the liquid-state molecules can slip over and around one another in a smooth, easy, always moving, and rearranging way. The bubbles are all transparent to one another, rather than opaque with hidden interiors. Moving bubbles can subdivide or can join together.

This is what the analogy is intended to convey: the new "temple" is a very different kind of thing. The revolution is not a matter of throwing out one bunch of rascals and installing another. It is not a matter of letting the last now be first and obliging the former first now to be last, as though that would satisfy all justice and make things right. That wouldn't change the structure or the principles that make the structure possible. A new collection of "first" people will be just as dominating as the former incumbents. So we must examine our desires carefully to see whether we really want to give up domination as the game, or whether we merely want to change places, letting the losers win for a while.

We should also say that while the analogy to a glass bubble gives us a chance to show how the physical principles are different, if we switch to the image of a living body, the difference from the stone building is far greater. The indescribable complexity of this integrated system of systems of systems is by far the best analogue for the human (plus nonhuman) community.

One Great Living Body

Now we are going to talk about how it feels to live as members of a great living body. How do we sense the *wholeness* of the body and our place in it? How do we relate to the other "cells," other systems of cells? We need a new outlook in which the One manifests as many and the many realize they are One. Then how do we comprehend the constant *movement* that actually is the life of the body and our life as components thereof? How does it feel to be "inside" God instead of having God somewhere outside yourself? Or, even closer, how does it feel to sense yourself as being a "participant in" God-ing? What are we going to do about our ideas, concepts, images, names, sense of orientation, and communication?

Clearly this will be a mind-set very different from the one under the Domination Paradigm, for the sense of isolation will have disappeared, to be replaced with a sense of participation, of being a unique and valued movement in a warm, affirmative, personally intimate, and supportive process. One has a feeling of moving comfortably and creatively (a kind of dancing) in a space that leaves plenty of room to be oneself and yet feels close in friendship, confidence, trust, pleasure. It's going to involve our images of ourselves, society, culture, nature, body, action. All of these will be characterized by "insideness" rather than "outsideness," and we will transcend ourselves. From being creatures of the world, we will be creators of the world.[1]

The shift in perspective does this, focusing the energies of our consciousness beyond the ego, so that the "self" feels itself as an active member of the God-community that is expressing itself as the world rather than as merely a passive product of that activity. We ourselves, as individuals, are perceived as member-artworks of the world-dance, a constantly changing, growing reality. Likewise, our societies, cultures, and deliberate actions are all molecular movements within the living texture of the great body of which we are members. Nothing appears to be everlasting or absolute or the last word, though some last long enough to give us comfortable familiarity and reliability. We firmly opt for the best value available (conceivable) at any given time, but the ideal keeps being refined and heightened, so that our aspiration and our standard become more demanding of us.

In this context we are living out of our own shared intelligence and good will (conscience) rather than in obedience to an outside authority. "The days are surely coming, says [God], when I will make a new covenant with the house of Israel: . . . I will put my law within them, and I will write it on their hearts; . . . no longer shall they teach one another, . . . 'Know the [reality of God],' for they shall all know me, from the least of them to the greatest" (Jer. 31:31ff.). Our motivation shifts with this, so that the prayer "Your will be done" is an act not of subservience or surrender but of eager desire that the Great Will, in which our own will is a confluent participant, should move forward, expand, develop, and fulfill itself.[2]

All the components of our consciousness will be integrated; qualities formerly polarized and reserved for one type of person or another (male or female, master or servant, etc.) will be present in all, balanced and harmonious. Desire will not struggle with understanding; imagination will not run away from judgment; reason will not hold itself aloof from joy; will and intuition will be two sides of one coin. We will not feel under tension because of internal conflict but will feel natural and at ease in our own integrality and comfortable and happy in our movement in the network of the community.[3]

Our attention will go out freely to others, to be aware of their situations and feelings, uninhibited by prior concern for our own interests first. This will happen of itself, not by effort but quite spontaneously. Living in/with the other's life will be the normal way to live; others will live in/with us and we will not feel crowded by them or intruded upon; we will not need to hide or be private, concealing our affairs and our feelings, being anxious about our reception by our fellows. Even now, during the transition, we can gradually experience how helping others actually helps ourselves, though there are many temptations until the consciousness definitively shifts and relocates its focus.

There is a realization that being for each other is the natural and normal way to be, that the frightened everyone-for-one's-self approach to life was an aberration and an illness. We easily recognize one another as ends rather than means, as embodiments of holiness, as all equally characterized by dignity and freedom, all infinitely precious. It will follow from this that there is no urgency to tag items in our lives as "mine," to put up signs saying "Keep off," "Private." Indeed, while each creative agent needs to be in close touch with the means of producing whatever that agent creates—needs to have ownership or "creative control" in order to be properly creative—the agent is being creative precisely to be able to share the creative work with all others who can benefit from it. And as all share their works, all will be happily aware of how they and their activities and their products constitute a whole, and everything is flowing into everything else. By reason of this intuition also, we will find comparison not relevant, not even possible or making sense, and this will leave us happily unencumbered to enjoy each other to the full.[4]

Enjoyment in this outlook will be the usual tone of life rather than the special and rare experience. Our work will be interesting to us and a pleasure to do because of its rightness and its contribution to the well-being and happiness of others. We will be expanded to the point where we spontaneously experience our work on the level of "building a cathedral" rather than the level of "dressing stones" or "earning money." In general, we will experience our lives as contributions to large-scale processes of the world, aimed at improving life. These large processes will be felt as "our" processes, for which we naturally take our share of the responsibility. No sense of "burden," no need to withdraw.

We will value and rejoice in the common and widespread and available things of the world, as Thomas Traherne discovered:

GOD being, as generally believed, infinite in Goodness, it is most Consonant and Agreeable with His nature that the Best Things be most frequent; and only Things Worthless, Scarce. Then I began to Enquire what Things were most Common:

Air, Light, Heaven and Earth, Water, the Sun, Trees, Men and Women, Cities, Temples, etc. These I found Common and Obvious to all. Rubies, Pearls, Diamonds, Gold and Silver, these I found scarce, and to the most Denied. Then began I to consider and compare the value of them, which I measured by their Serviceableness, and by the Excellencies which would be found in them, should they be taken away. And in Conclusion I saw clearly, that there was a Real Valuableness in all the Common things; in the Scarce, a feigned.

Energized by such insight, we will all give ourselves to concern for the well-being of our food, our homes, our health, our education, and similar common issues that had not been considered of primary importance and were left to be attended to by the underclasses. Similarly, universal love, in the sense of concern for the well-being of others, will seem obvious and natural and be present without strain. In this consciousness it will be unthinkable that anyone should hold, as a local citizen did in a letter to the editor, that the "best reason" for not passing laws requiring employers to pay employees a "living wage" (the lowest at which one could live decently, $7.50 an hour at the time the man wrote)—is that "No one has a right to confiscate the property of an individual (in this case, his money) and, without compensation, force him to use it in a manner that will do him harm (e.g., reduce his profit)." We will no longer believe that helping others is harming oneself.[5]

Altruism in Our Genes

Those are some examples of what it may "feel like" to live in a Communion Paradigm. We may wonder, since genetic endowment was suspected to have a lot to do with the Domination Paradigm, whether we can get any help from our genes, or whether it is going to be uphill all the way. Happily, we can report that there is a genetic heritage of altruism—helping the other, even at cost to oneself—going back a long way. Richard Dawkins, who first drew attention to the "selfish gene," also pointed out how various animals practice behaviors in which certain individuals subordinate their own welfare to that of their near relatives. His calculations showed that the degree of sacrifice was directly proportional to the closeness of the kin, to the percentage of genes shared, but nevertheless such behaviors are a start in the direction of true concern for others.

Ethologist Frans de Waal stresses that calling a gene "selfish" is only an attention-getting metaphor and says "nothing, either directly or indirectly, about motivation, emotion, or intention." Gene-directed behaviors will always be self-serving in the sense of favoring their own replication, but they may well include food-sharing, mutual grooming, protection, common defense, and other cooperative activities that are forerunners of genuinely moral acts, which are based on conscious intention. It is natural selection, after all, points out de Waal, that "has led to symbiosis and mutualism . . . to sensitivity . . . to the needs of another, and to joint action toward a common goal. . . . Genetic self-advancement . . . has given rise to remarkable capacities for caring and sympathy."

Because practices of cooperation can themselves evolve when set in a context of dealing repeatedly with the same partners, reciprocal altruism can develop. This benefits all participants, so those parties with genes that promote reciprocal altruism will see their genes spread, and they will spread better when the individuals begin to have subjective feelings by which they can react to those who can be trusted to reciprocate and to those who cheat. In this way the sense of "justice" may have arisen, together with feelings that the "good" should be rewarded (cooperated with) and the "bad" punished (deprived)—because, probably, the evolution of the system of cooperation itself favors a program called Tit-for-Tat.

Psychoanalytic theorist Paul Gilbert concludes:

> over the course of social evolution, change has occurred which has shifted motivational systems away from isolated and aggressive social styles to positive interactional styles. Those who are able to live in this domain, by creating safety in themselves and others, tend to be happier and more satisfied with life. Those who remain egotistic and hostile or who are on the defensive are less happy and more prone to disorder. . . . Evolution, therefore, points out clearly the road we humans should try to tread.

Empathy—the ability to coincide imaginatively with what another is experiencing—clearly gives many advantages in life, enabling the one who can do such a thing to predict more accurately what the other is apt to do next or do in response to action on my part. When this is joined to the motive of caring for the other, we begin to have a movement toward real morality. Such feelings develop through self-consciousness, introspection, awareness of one's own feelings in a given context, and notice of similarities with the other. Studies of human infants' disposition to begin crying when they hear another infant cry led some researchers to suggest that we have "a rudimentary empathic distress reaction at birth." Alfie Kohn, pointing out the brighter side of human nature, says that "our species may be primed . . . to be discomfited by someone else's discomfort." The seed present in the newborn develops through stages, showing unhappiness in the presence of another's distress, later trying to comfort the other, until by preschool age, helping and sharing are regular occurrences. The interesting thing is that the sense of concern and the desire to help seem to be there long before there is a more mature cognitive reaction to the situation.[6]

True morality appears when a person has enough imagination and empathy to recognize that there are subjective feelings in the other very like one's own, that the desires to live, to be well, to have needs met, and to be happy are in the other even as they are in oneself. Furthermore, just as one feels that it is not right that someone else should prevent these desires from being fulfilled in one's own case, so it is not right to interfere with their fulfillment in the other's case. A sense that the other has a "right" to certain desires and their fulfillment develops, and with it comes the sense of "obligation" on one's part to respect the other's "right." When this is clear both as idea of correctness and as feeling of "ought," then we can speak of true morality. It comes out of the sense of "we," those whom one recognizes as having feelings like oneself. This doesn't include everyone else at first but expands only very gradually. Those outside the "we" are not perceived as having these rights, and the obligation to respect them does not apply. Sometimes they are not perceived as having the feelings, desires, disappointments, and pains that we recognize in others like ourselves. Foreigners, enemies, and the underclass in one's own society do not have the rights that the power classes have. Human cultural evolution can be tracked in terms of the expansion of the sense of "we" and the recognition of those people whose rights exist and must be respected.

In the Communion Paradigm, the basic recognition is that everyone, absolutely everyone, is a child of God and as such is absolutely equal in dignity to everyone else. The "we" sense is thus unlimited. The sense of "right" and "obligation," however, is not expressed as "ought," as demand to which we force ourselves against our natural feelings. Our "natural feelings" are spontaneously identified with the welfare and good feeling of all the others; there is no need to say to ourselves that we "ought" to do such and such; we quite naturally *want* to do so and do not even think about the fact that we want to do so as though it were a strange thing. We care for the other as naturally and unthinkingly as we care for ourselves. The feeling therefore is of a greatly expanded self, of living a much larger life, of experiencing on a far wider scale than could be possible through one life alone.

Life in the Messianic Body

There is a rather telling story that illustrates this idea. The Hindu saint of the nineteenth century Ramakrishna was ill with cancer of the throat that had reached the point where he could not swallow food. His disciples begged him to pray for healing, but he was reluctant. He had not been used to praying for anything but devotion, but he finally consented. He prayed to God as Mother, saying, "Please make it possible for me to eat a little food." He reported to his friends that She pointed out all of them to him, and said, "You are eating through all these mouths, and you want to eat through this one as well?" This is the same man who was sitting quietly talking with his disciples when he suddenly fell down and began crying out in pain. Welts and bruises appeared on his body. Someone went out on the street and found a man beating another man. The pain was experienced by Ramakrishna as his own. Life in the messianic body is supposed to be like that. In the New Testament the apostle Paul writes to the Romans:

> Love one another with mutual affection; outdo one another in showing honor. . . . Contribute to the needs of the saints; extend hospitality to strangers. Bless those who persecute you; bless and do not curse them. Rejoice with those who rejoice, weep with those who weep. (12:10-15)

This is an attitude of our minds and feelings that is a step beyond what we are used to calling "morality." This is divine love. Henry Ward Beecher, Presbyterian minister, said, "Love is more just than justice." It is an interesting remark. Justice consists of giving everyone what is "due." But the ministry of Jesus shows us a love that is not a response to "worthiness." It is not a "response" at all, and worthiness or unworthiness has nothing to do with it. The love that transcends justice is an original act, not a reaction. It is not measured according to the qualities or the behavior of the one loved. It is a creative act.

Brad Young, in *Jesus the Jewish Theologian*, comments that the parable of the Good Samaritan teaches that even one's enemy is one's neighbor and is to be loved as such:

> The meaning of unconditional love for every human being created in God's image cannot be diminished. The esteem one demonstrates to [the] neighbor is not based upon what a neighbor has done to earn or merit love. Godlike love is for everyone, friend and enemy alike. Divine love is more powerful than human hate. Esteem for others mends the world [*tikkun olam*]. . . . Now is the time to decide about unconditional love. Love demonstrates its force in action. To love one's enemy is to fulfill God's will [*agapē*].

This is Jesus' interpretation of Leviticus 19:17-18: "You shall not hate in your heart anyone of your kin. . . . You shall not . . . bear a grudge against any of your people, but you shall love your neighbor as yourself: I am the Lord." "The Lord" is a substitution for the Tetragrammaton, YHWH, which stands for the unspeakable Reality that is the Ground of Being. *That* is what underlies this expression of mutual love toward all. Neighbor love is the "exegesis" of the Divine Ground.

I have a clipping from a newspaper, old enough to be quite discolored, a short letter to Dear Abby from Arthur H. Prince, who writes:

> in your reply to *Angry in San Mateo*, you wrote that "love generates love." The late Martin Luther King Jr. showed us that hate generates love, too. In his *Stride Toward Freedom* (Harper, 1958), he wrote: "I can only close the gap in broken community by meeting hate with love. If I meet hate with hate, I become depersonalized, because creation is so designed that my personality can be fulfilled only in the context of community. . . . When I love, I restore community."

The same truth is expressed in the *Dhammapada*, a collection of the sayings of the Buddha: "In this world hate never yet dispelled hate. Only love dispels hate. This is the law, ancient and inexhaustible." In our day, the Dalai Lama, responding to a question about how he feels toward the Chinese Communists, who have destroyed his country, culture, and people, said,

> Buddhism gives us a different attitude toward one's own enemy. . . . We believe a negative experience is due mainly to

our own previous life. . . . Due to that, unfortunate results happen. So therefore the so-called enemy, or the external factor, is something secondary. The main force is one's own. . . . That is really helpful in . . . that it induces us never to feel negatively toward the external factor.[7]

These are contemporary testimonies to the possibility of responding to even severe provocation with peaceful and positive attitudes. We are more familiar with ourselves "believing in" the Sermon on the Mount, with its recommendations for a life free from hatred and domination, but we find them difficult to put into practice because we are not able properly to energize our "beliefs." That is why I argue that we must attend to matters below the level of our psychology in order to release and correctly orient the energy needed. If we fail to do this, if we try to change our behavior artificially without changing the underlying structure of our life orientation, then the path of least resistance will lead back to the original compensatory behaviors. That is very likely, but it is not true to say that displacing hatred by love is impossible. If it were impossible, no one would be able to do it, yet we have many examples of people who have done it. What we need is a reorientation of basic ideas that will allow the shift in attitude that will enable many more people to do it.

When we do have that shift in attitude, we feel very good. A sense of satisfaction, a kind of completion or fullness is our ground-floor feeling, on which we build further feelings of interest, caring, eagerness to help and share, and drives toward creativity and expression in beauty. Even without a full-depth reorientation, we find that we behave more lovingly and more helpfully when we are feeling good, and helping generally makes us feel good in return. The kind of "feeling good" that promotes these good actions can include feeling concern and sympathetic distress for another's suffering, with consequent urgency to set the matter right. The reason that this is also a "good feeling" is that it arises out of our own secure belief that we have sufficient "being" that we can share, energy and time and emotional grace that we can donate to another without loss. *Agapē* is an overflow phenomenon, as distinguished from *eros,* which is a need phenomenon.

Feeling needy is the background to seeking power and being stingy about love. Feeling satisfied obviates the interest in power and turns attention and awareness of pleasure to other-benefitting love. There may even be some secondary effects on bodily health: being fixated on the need for power and trying to gain more being tend to reduce the effectiveness of the immune system, and we have more ill-ness, whereas a sense of security and satisfaction leads to relaxation and joy, right functioning, good health. This is not to say that ill health is a sign of spiritual failure; there are plenty of instances of great saints suffering a lot of sickness. So don't read this relation backwards.

Nevertheless, we can recognize that thoughts produce feelings, attitudes, and behaviors, and that the way to good feelings and good behaviors is to fill the mind and heart with contents of meditation that help us to realize our security and fullness in God, so that we become transparent to the divine light shining through us. When we have done this, we will know what Easwaran means when he says that it is "so pleasant to work hard for the welfare of those around us."[8]

The Communion of Friendship

A favorite biblical verse says, "How good and how pleasant it is, when all our family live together in unity!" (Ps. 133:1). This is the feeling of the Communion Paradigm, of the messianic body, the messianic full family, the communion of friendship. Jesus says plainly, "I will no longer call you servants but friends" (John 15:15). This has to be taken literally and taken seriously, its implications being faced and (we hope) acknowledged and embraced. Friendship, as Aristotle pointed out, either discovers or creates equality. Equality is the keynote of friendship as it was the keynote of all of Jesus' ministry, and it has numerous implications. The one we see first is that we are all to perceive one another as social equals and treat one another with the honor and dignity that comports with that perception. There are spinoffs from that, such as that we *should* make sure that everyone receives a "living wage" even if it *does* cut into our precious "prof-its," and we shouldn't have to pass a law to see that this happens. If all are equally children of God, if all are members of one family, if all are friends, then it shouldn't even be necessary to mention such a thing. It should be our *pleasure* to make sure that all are comfortable and well cared for. The joy of friendship is joy in seeing our friends living to the full.

We may also note, listening to Jesus' announcement, that *he* intends to be a friend rather than a lord or master. That was the con-text. But letting Jesus be our friend may be hard for many people. I recommend that we try to look at it from his point of view. I contend that he doesn't like being isolated on a pedestal. He wants to be one of the crowd. He feels that that is the holier way to be. He prays that everyone else may be "with him where he is" (John 17:24). People accustomed to thinking in terms of grades and different levels of respect are afraid of putting Jesus "on the same level with" even the greatest saints and spiritual masters. They want him to dominate everybody else, be first, be the greatest, be something beyond anything that anyone else could possibly be. At the same time, we repeat his saying, "I have given you an example." We should all be like *that*?

The Domination Paradigm is hard to give up; we fear we will lose a proper sense of value. But what the revelation is trying to tell us is that *domination as such* is the wrong way to appreciate divine value. Divine value shows itself in pouring itself out, "taking the form of a slave" (Phil. 2:7), suffering in the service of others if need be, but especially being *together with* others. You can't be "together" if you're not friends, and you can't be friends if you're not equal, not "on the same level with." So you are called "Friend," and invited to "come up higher" in your acceptance of your own reality, come up to your divine level as a child of God, be together with Jesus, all on the same level!

This friendship, therefore, is something that strongly characterizes the psychology of the Communion Paradigm. The sense of all together, all in one family, everybody intermingling, no sorting out into ranks—a felt sense of closeness and trust, happiness in being together, being close, being confident. A friend is someone you can touch, someone you can laugh with, someone whose thoughts you can share, someone you can work with, play with, sing and dance with, someone with whom you share devotion to common values and tasks and creative projects. Jesus and his friends are continuing the creation of the world. *Tikkun olam*—healing the world, repairing the world, continuously creating the world, making it more interesting, more beautiful, more diverse, more interfaced, more united.

Friendship is the human image of the *perichōrēsis* of the Trinity, the mutual indwelling, the dynamic grace-giving sharing, the strong bonding to be ONE. It is a relationship that we ought to pay much more attention to, that we ought to study and think about, feel about, cultivate. It ought to be explicitly held in high honor in our thoughts and our social talk. We need to recognize and to practice it as sacred, as sacramental, as the Presence of God on Earth. There used to be rituals for cementing friendships, sharing wine with linked arms, sometimes sharing blood between cut fingers. Maybe we should allow these memories to reawaken us to the deep ground being pointed to by these rituals, and we should reflect on friendship, on what it implies, what foundation it must rest on, what values it represents, what its special pleasures are.

Friendship, we may say, is the goal of religion. Religion, which seems to be a natural expression of human beings, a symbolic representation of our experiences in a context of meaning, will be a happy art form in a Communion Paradigm. Currently practiced as highly divisive and productive of hostility without and often fear and guilt within, religion would be transformed by insight, security, empathetic love, and friendship equality and appreciation into a way of bonding throughout the human race. On an ever-shrinking planet, this is a much-needed development.

In a Communion Paradigm, religion would not seek to set up special groups of people cut off from their neighbors by supernatural privileges, but would encourage all to reach out and bond with all neighbors, looking for what we all have in common, cultivating lines of unity in the perichoretic way, that is, by interweaving the diversities, making beauty, enriching insight, keeping celebration ever fresh. It would not seek to frighten and thereby control its adherents but to proclaim the acceptability of all, to reassure and strengthen, to develop by faith and encouragement the values with which all are blessed (only needing someone to believe in them in order to come out).

Religion would create peace and joy, open up new lines of interest in the world, support invention, development, composition. It would busy itself with the further creation of the world, which means (among other things) enhancement of interactive and mutually supportive diversities, perichoretic diversities, which deepen and enrich unity. Varieties of symbolic expressions would be welcomed, many ways of saying what we deeply experience, many artistic gifts being nurtured as celebrations of the Presence of God in the world. The world itself would be honored and drawn into the realm of the sacred. Dichotomies of sacred and profane would be overcome as all human activities were experienced as infused with Divine Life. Nothing is to be lost; all are to be brought in, all to find a home, be part of what the family does.

Saints and Mystics

This means that a further dimension of our existence, beyond the ordinary material experiences of our usual life now, would be commonly recognized and lived with. The orientations of perception of the enlightened ones, the saints and mystics, would be much more widespread than they are now—though we should note that transforming experiences and altered lifestyles are even now more present among us than we may think. Andrew Greeley made a survey some years ago which showed that 35 percent of Americans had had experiences akin to those set forth in classical literature on mysticism— that is, direct intuitions of the Presence of God, a sense of the universal Oneness, a sense of being beyond one's superficial descriptions and being a member of or assimilated into the Wholeness.

Like the people who have had what we now call the near death experience, many of these "amateur mystics" have been afraid to say anything about their experiences because others might think them peculiar, even crazy. Professionals in psychopathology in particular tend to regard these experiences as artifacts of abnormal brain activity or diseases of psychological relationships. Andrew Bard Schmookler, in *Out of Weakness: Healing the Wounds That Drive Us to War*, says of this that "by intimidating people, the reductive explanation inhibits people from telling others about their mystical experiences, thus excluding the force of mystic revelation from the realm of respectable public discourse." In a Communion Paradigm this would not happen. People would feel quite free and comfortable with sharing their deep experiences, as we projected in the description of Jesus' Suppers, the fourth level of intimacy in the multilevel Eucharist, the thanksgiving for all the ways we live together.[9]

This would be extremely valuable, for out of this level of experience and this degree of sharing will come the most beautiful creations that we will add to the developing world. What we need to realize is that insight into the Divine Presence in the world is not the end of the story, not the "and they lived happily ever after, but there isn't any story about that." On the contrary, attainment of the realization of the Divine Presence as world is just the beginning of spiritual life. This is where the real story begins; what came before was the foreword, the preface, the introduction.

I emphasize this because many people, knowing nothing but the Domination Paradigm, suppose that without it, life would be too dull to talk about, with nothing exciting ever happening, no stimulation to further growth or achievement, no sharp contrasts to give a proper value. An important part of the revolution is coming to know that there is another way to be and to live and to develop and create and enjoy.

We need religiously sensitive people, contemplatives, to help us through the phase transition, people who will devote the time and effort necessary to break down the barriers and inhibitions that prevent Light and Presence from coming through, people who can reach out to their companions in other spiritual traditions to exchange ideas, practices, and experiences. In our tradition we need contemplatives to help us see that the saving transition is not going to come as long as the concept and name and image of God is *Dominus*. It is the contemplative, the deeply devout and holy person, who sees realistically beyond this name and enters into the revelation of Jesus that God is better named *Amicus*, Friend, and *Amator*, Lover. It is this breakthrough that signals the end of the age, "the end of the world." This is the sense in which it is a new world with new concepts and images (the new heaven) and new actions (the new earth).

This is how life acquires meaning. Having "meaning" means being situated in a larger context. We need mystics because they help us to see everything in the largest possible context, the context of Absolute Being and its self-expression in our world (possibly among others). Rodger Kamenetz reports that the Jews who went to visit the Dalai Lama in Dharamsala and the Buddhists they met there said to each other that each tradition had a "spectrum of perfection," and different traditions focused more on certain ranges within that spectrum, relegating the remainder to "minor themes." Actually, "if you look even more carefully," they cover the whole spectrum. For instance, says Kamenetz,

> both Judaism and Mahayana Buddhism are religions of transformation. Our transformation is dominantly of the world, but to transform the world means to transform ourselves too. Whereas their transformation is primarily of themselves, and by so doing they transform the world. And . . . when the world is transformed it paves the way for the kind of spiritual perfection they are talking about, anyway. So it's really not separable, and if you really are reaching out for that kind of spiritual transformation, it would be of this world as well.

Rabbi Lawrence Kushner says something similar:

> Notions of inside and outside may just be cultural convention. A once helpful, but now insidious trick persuading us to regard the locus of our consciousness within what we ordinarily call our bodies. Perhaps awareness is also outside us; independent of organic matter. What if what we call "God" is intimately related to a mode of consciousness and our collec-

tive beings that we are not allowed or accustomed to call part of ourselves? For, in addition to being within us, it is also without us. Is this not the One who unites us all? The One who is beyond us, but whom we are forbidden to name as part of us? The One who is certainly our infinite potential, The Holy One of Being?

This is an example of how to look for new meanings, new concepts, and new images in the context of a Communion Paradigm, new ways of perceiving our living so that new excitement in existence is aroused and eagerness to take part in the Divine Life is heightened.

Here is another way of saying what the mystics find. The kabbalists tell us that "in the beginning, all of existence was the Endless Light of the Endless One." When finite beings were created, they were receivers of the light, which was the giver. But the light was too strong and the receivers broke into fragments. The world we are living in now is made of these broken vessels, and our job is to mend the world and strengthen it so that it can bear the Light.

In the story of Abraham, God blesses the one who was willing to leave a previous way of life for one new and unknown, saying, "I will bless you . . . and you will be a blessing." The meaning is that the power of blessing is being conveyed to us. The power of blessing is the power to draw more of the Light into the world, and this power is now in our hands.

God wants to give us Endless Light—it is the nature of God to give and to share—but this kind of gift, which is the Divine Life and Reality itself, can be received only if we want it. The ability to hold it without breaking is related to the depth of desiring it. But we can help ourselves to realize how much we want it (rather than the superficial goods of wealth, fame, material pleasures, etc.) by prayer and other spiritual practices. That realization is joined to the realization of our selfhood being widened to the whole, so that "we want to receive the Endless Light not just for ourselves but for the whole world."

Rabbi David Aaron, who is telling this story, says that sooner or later "the soul calls the ego's bluff and cries, 'This is bogus. This is not what I really want!' From deep within, the soul recalls the memory of the real thing, the Endless Light—the light of true oneness, genuine love, endless personal growth, Great Self consciousness, immortality, freedom, peace." Prayer and spiritual practices "help us bond," restoring our broken union with one another and with God. "We can receive the Endless Light only when we are willing to share it. We can do it only one way—together." That is the vision of the Communion Paradigm.[10]

Togetherness in Creation

Togetherness: "Outside the Church there is no salvation." The Torah cannot be liturgically read until a *minyan* has assembled. "Human nature only really exists in an achieved community of minds." The image of the Trinity is the community, community of minds, of souls, of spirits, of *persons*. The sharing among the members of the community heightens the awareness of each participant, and the increased sensitivity and insight of each raise the consciousness of the whole. The result is creativity. We see that already. When people collaborate, really acting together and not vying with one another in some way, marvelous things can be done, and the joy and satisfaction from this joint success are not only far greater than for any solo achievement, but they are of a different quality, too. We know that the cooperation, the very fact of the selfless collaboration, is an achievement—never mind what it was that we made together. The togetherness in creation was the joy, is the joy.

We feel that we have touched something new and deeper, happier in ourselves. We have learned to experience ourselves as simultaneously our single selves and our collective self. Our single specialness was enhanced by this, reached a new height of expertise through the creative energy coming from the other people, and was enabled to blend in with them so that harmony happened, a new sound, different from single tones emitted one by one, separate from each other, or in conflict with each other. This is the image of the Trinity and the participation in the dynamic of creation of the world.

We also experience a new sense of freedom, a spaciousness of the scope of our action, of our living. We are able to do more, to bring forth more, and therefore to be more by giving being more. That's (a little taste of) what it feels like to create. The consequence of the transition from the Domination Paradigm to the Communion Paradigm is therefore increased life and awareness, interest, inventiveness, expansion, activity. No chance of being bored.[11]

6

"In the Days of the Messiah"

Friendship, Communion, Politics

Toward the end of Yom Kippur, when everyone is miserable and exhausted from the long fast, the Book of Jonah is read. Jonah was sent by God to Nineveh, to "cry out" against them for their "wickedness." Now, Nineveh was a serious and dangerous enemy of Israel. Jonah therefore didn't want to do this and he ran "away from the service of God." But God arranged that he be delivered, nevertheless, to Nineveh. And there Jonah proclaimed that in forty days Nineveh would be destroyed by God. But Nineveh repented, in sackcloth and ashes, with fasting and prayer. And God forgave them and withdrew the "planned punishment." Jonah was thoroughly disgusted and said to God, "I knew this would happen, that's why I didn't want to come; I'd just as soon be dead as see this happen. I knew you were a God of compassion and mercy and forgiveness and kindness."

Why is this story set at the end of the Day of Atonement? Here is my interpretation. We have fasted and confessed and prayed and been forgiven and blessed for another year. Now we must be ready to carry the message of repentance and forgiveness and mercy and blessing to our worst enemies and be prepared to rejoice (if and) when God forgives and blesses them, and not resist their prosperity and honor in God's sight. We all have our Ninevehs, as individuals, as nations, as races, as religions, or as whatever category would be relevant. Under the Domination Paradigm, in terms of its psychology, we resist the very idea that our enemies should find favor in God's sight. We don't want to admit that they also are made in the image of God.

So we struggle with God about it. Maybe that's part of why we're called "Israel." It's a hard struggle and we continue to be a little "out of joint" as a result of it. Historically we haven't given up the struggle—the wars and the exploitations and the private quarrels are still going on—but God hasn't given up either. Special persons, and sometimes whole traditions—we should call particular attention to Buddhism—keep arising with the same message: change your way of thinking-feeling-seeing, and that will change your way of living. It takes some effort to do it, but we can help each other; it can be done. The Buddhists say that we can find refuge in the examples of those who have done it, in the teaching and explanation and the very structure of Being itself and in the community of those who are trying to make the transition.

The Messiah Phase Transition

This is the context in which the story of Jesus and the Holy Thursday Revolution are set. Another attempt is being made to open our eyes to what is really going on in the creation effort and to the transition—the "phase transition"—that we are now being called to make. As I said before, on an evolutionary scale phase transitions may take thousands of years, and we will continue under pressure until the new phase has fully emerged.

This transition is called, in our tradition, the *Messiah* and was initially visualized as a single individual. Further meditation has revealed it as a community, an era, and a new way of living and being. At this time it has already been in the making for three or four thousand years and still has a long way to go. It is important that we understand that this is not a magical event, not something done by someone else; it is important that we not take a "cargo cult" attitude toward it. It has to be done by ourselves; it consists of changes in ourselves. If we don't transform, Messiah doesn't come. Everybody knows that the Messianic Age means peace, justice, and universal forgiveness, amnesty, even generosity, unity, and joy. These are things that characterize the way we ourselves think and feel and behave toward one another. So we have to take responsibility for bringing them about.

A phase transition means that a new state of being is entered into, a new set of operational principles begins to function, and often a new level of organization is achieved. It is because the change is this fundamental that I have called it a revolution. A revolution is a *total* social process and has to include worldview and social, political, economic, and cultural dimensions. "Cultural" dimensions include education, religion, recreation, sport, art, science, humanities, and anything else you can think of. When the basic outlook and principles change, all dimensions change. Unless their change is intended and provided for, you haven't got a real revolution.

It is usually thought that a revolution means conflict, but that is not true of this revolution. Since it is a shift from domination to compassion and community, it takes place in terms of compassion and community. It moves by inclusion rather than rejection. It is true that the revolution intends to replace the Domination Paradigm as the basic social image, but it doesn't do this in hostility, because hostility would mean acting still within the Domination Paradigm. Replacement must come by free choice because of the obvious advantages of the new paradigm.

On the other hand, changes in all these dimensions of our lives will not come about merely through loving attitudes. We have to have knowledge and creative talent and make efforts to design new ways of living together. Expertise will get a good workout; innovators will have a field day. This is where the spiritual lore that says that God intentionally made the world such that it had to make itself, and especially so that human beings had to exercise intelligence and free goodwill to create the stages they were active in, seems a prophecy fulfilled.[1]

Gustavo Gutiérrez, in his efforts to mount such a revolution in Latin America, said that liberation means "in a deeper sense, to see the becoming of [humankind] as a process of the emancipation of [people] in history. It is to see [the human race] in search of a qualitatively different society in which [we] will be free from all servitude, in which [we] will be the artisan of [our] own destiny." Sir John Eccles warns that this begins to happen only when people realize that what they had believed before was really superstition. A certain amount of spiritual maturity is called for, and more will be required as we go along. Hannah Arendt says that a revolution starts a new "story," with its own inner coherence, plot, and meaning. All of the old beliefs and structures are disturbed in the cause of freedom—real *freedom* comes after "liberation"—and the new outlooks and ways of living come in that involve commitment to larger communities.[2]

Morality and Technology: The Enhancement of Being

Revolutions that work usually include two main dimensions: moral and technological. There have to be practical new ways of living, and there has to be an accompanying insight into how the new way is more meaningful than the old. For instance, it was hardly a matter of morality that slavery was wrong until it became economically feasible, even advantageous, not to own slaves because machinery was cheaper and quicker. Then we allowed ourselves to see that it was scandalous that human beings should be considered the "property" of other people. (The analogous positions of wives and children, economically dependent on and legally subject to the "head of the household" was not seen at that time—isn't altogether seen yet—as morally unacceptable, because there was no concrete alternative that was seriously plausible.) It seems that insight into value and the physical possibility of doing things another way go together.

True *morality* implies insight into the absolute value of each person and therefore the essential equality of all. The Domination Paradigm doesn't, on this definition, have a proper "morality," but only rules of conduct in a system of honor and shame. The system itself is based on the perception and the protection of *inequality*. Because it *is* a system of "domination," it is quite strict in enforcing its rules of attitude and conduct, whereas the Communion Paradigm, which believes in freedom, acceptance, and inclusion of those who are different, may seem to be "looser." Nevertheless, it is the latter that has the better claim to being "moral," by virtue of its acknowledgment of the unique value of each person and the consequent obligation to respect each equally, not allowing any to claim that their advantage, convenience, pleasure may rightfully take precedence over another's. The Communion Paradigm tends not to impose a set of rules but to rely on the insight and mutual recognition of value to guide each person and each organization to appropriate behavior in each situation.

Our definition of the Communion Paradigm says that communion is a symmetrical, reciprocal relation of *enhancement* of being: that beings may be, may become all that they can be, may act in maximum freedom and be valued for their incomparable preciousness. The reciprocity means that helping others implies helping oneself, since all are members of a single system. The will to freedom and full development means that the desire to create is more fundamental and yields a deeper satisfaction than the desire for gain or for protection.

The moral guideline to promote creativity is thus tied to the other main dimension of the revolution—the technological, or concretely practical. However fine our ideals, they become significant only when we can actually put them into practice, and this requires development of technical possibilities, although the latter by no means guarantee that the moral ideals will then be realized. We have the capability now of feeding the world, stopping destruction of the environment, and realizing various other desirable goals, but we do not yet do these things because our moral sense and political will have not endorsed them. But certainly without the power to perform the ideal, it would never be performed.

The most hopeful and exciting technical development tending to the actual practice of some of these ideals is that of the information sciences and technologies. Marshall McLuhan said that our consciousness would be shaped by the very nature of the media of our communication. Perhaps we are beginning to see this, as our rapid interactions by way of our electronic media give us an enlarged sense of the "society" in which we move. Computer-aided manufacturing has made a difference in industrialization, extending hope to Third World countries that they may soon bring their standard of living up to the levels enjoyed by more fortunate nations by learning and participating in the new processes. We are also witnessing prosperous and well-educated nations teaching those nations who want to learn and helping them to get started in industrial and informational operations. More producers mean also more markets and more intelligent interaction, more development, more interest for everyone. There is beginning to be appreciation of the idea that where another prospers, all prosper. The world feels very interconnected. The sense of a single organism is growing upon us.[3]

The technology feeds back to the morality by providing an environment in which equality of action is almost demanded. Superiors have very different roles in the information world from those they had in the industrial era, to say nothing of earlier times. Close and free direct communication has the effect of leveling, putting people in immediate contact with one another without need of rituals of deference (to an increasing degree). Knowledge can't be held within physical boundaries, and knowledge begets knowledge. The knowledge-world is global by nature, making nations increasingly irrelevant. Territory, in the sense of land, is becoming less and less necessary for development, success, and wealth. These lie in the information itself, an immaterial reality. Thus, one of the grounds for ancient quarrels is disappearing. Not that it is completely gone; the Middle East and oil-bearing lands in general are a prime example at this time, but the trend is to transcend physical territory.

In addition, the production of our goods is a world-interactive enterprise, components being manufactured in perhaps a dozen countries and assembled and sold in dozens of countries. We are all becoming more intimately related to and dependent on one another. We are thereby in the process of being motivated to feel commonality of interest and to cooperate with one another. Exploitation of cheap labor is still going on, and transnational corporate power has largely overwhelmed national power, but the more the technology develops, the more such exploitation should decline, education should go up, income should go up, self-esteem and expectations of equal respect should go up and be met.

Continued economic growth in the information world uses comparatively little in the way of natural resources or energy, but is a voracious consumer of intelligence. Intelligence expands only in an environment of freedom and comfortable stimulation, of opportunity for curiosity and creativity to express themselves and opportunity for conversation and sharing among the researchers. Thus, it behooves everyone in this world to nurture these intelligences, researchers to help one another, because, despite continuing competition among their products, the knowledge itself does not come except by massive cross-processing among the competent intelligences. This approaches the morality envisioned in the Communion Paradigm. Free communicating is becoming the model, the paradigm, in terms of which we view our relevant and significant world.

Political scientist Robert C. North says that "justice . . . requires that . . . each person should enjoy a right to resources and a share in the total human enterprise equal to that of every other living person on the planet—with equal responsibility for care of the resources so held in trust." Otherwise, justice "is flawed at its base." He therefore proposes a political worldview and lifestyle of "equal access."

Within an equal-access framework, the interests of the individual and the group are closely aligned: any improvement in the general welfare will mean an improvement in the situation of the individual, but no individual will gain at the expense of another, and any decline in the general welfare of a society will be felt more or less simultaneously *and equally* by all.

Margaret Mead stresses that we must operate with a sense of responsibility for each other, and therefore we need a vision of the world and our life that will evoke the strongest and most reliable commitment from us. It would, in a Communion Paradigm, be clear enough and strong enough that threats and sanctions would hardly be required to persuade people to behave mindfully toward one another. Each of us would quite spontaneously and sincerely want to do what is right and best for the whole. We would not even be tempted to cheat on our income tax or exceed a speed limit, because we would perceive that such behavior would break the bond of faith with the community.[4]

The World as the "Great Work"

Commentators on the Bible often say that it is characterized by justice and kindness. Justice says, "What is yours is yours." Kindness says, "What is mine is yours." Between them they define the attitude with which we are to meet one another and live together. Humanity is a work in progress; we are not determined but are constantly in quest of new possibilities. We can start with a utopian vision, and we need that to orient ourselves. We can gradually work toward it, making concrete progress despite obstacles and setbacks. We are trying to heal the world, but all of us are ourselves wounded. Nevertheless, we advance, as Rodger Kamenetz says, "with imperfect and partial steps, pragmatic and unrelenting . . . all the steps [themselves having] equal dignity with the greater vision."[5]

For the world is not an illusion, not a mistake, not the work of an alien deity, not something to be left or abandoned or avoided. It is the Great Work: to express godliness in the forms of finitude, forms of matter, energy, time, and space. All the dimensions of human culture, which includes our relations to all the other creatures of the world and their relations to one another—all these are features of the creative work. When we understand that we are united with and in the Creator and are thereby freed of our fear-motivated efforts to secure worldly goods for ourselves, then with joy we participate in modeling the world, inventing cultural modes to express justice, kindness, and beauty.

The biblical tradition suggests that there may be a "plan" for the creation, but it is a very general plan, something like "Let's make a world that can make itself, that will become conscious and that will consciously make the world further, creating more realities and exploring them." When we start to think in these terms, along these lines, we can see how narrow is the life view under the Domination Paradigm. It seems to have rather little imagination. But God is made known to us as the One who "liberates us from the narrow place [Egypt]." These familiar words begin to take on new meaning. The Paschal message is that the Source of Being is an energy in the world that makes possible transformation, that is primarily given to creative possibilities and transformations and liberation from narrow places, one always calling us to leave whatever we've settled down in, the old country, and go out to a new land. That is the pattern, so now when we look forward to the future, we expect that this is the sort of thing that will happen again.

But it is never a daydream; it is always a concrete, historical reality. The hope of the future, what we call the coming of the Messiah, carries both the ideal and the practical dimensions, the Presence of God in the world with specific strategies for ushering in the next age of the creative work. Don't look for a *last* age—that's another "narrow place." Look for the *next* age and expect many after that, growing, as Gregory of Nyssa said, "from glory to glory." There is always another "world to come."

The vocation, the call to leave one world and enter into the next, always includes convincing us that it is possible. And since the world we are in is a "narrow place" relative to "the world to come," it may be hard to believe that we can make the transition. There are several stories of Jesus about this—healing stories. We usually take them as bodily healings for individuals that miraculously set aside the laws of nature. I want to interpret them as types of social healing and to apply them to large groups of people.

The first story is that of the man with the withered hand (Matt. 12:10ff.). Jesus finds him in the synagogue and calls him to stand forth. In the context of the story, this is a brave thing to do, because "healing"—practicing medicine—can be construed as "work" and therefore should not be done on the Sabbath but postponed until the new week begins. However, Jesus does not see benefitting life as contrary to the Sabbath, and he orders the man, "Stretch forth your hand!" The man does so, and the usefulness of the hand is restored. The social interpretation says that the man with the withered hand stands for men who feel that their power of action is inhibited, restrained, even dried up, that they are not able to act effectively. This could apply to certain classes and groups in a domination society, or even to a whole society under foreign domination, as Israel then was.

The social situation is often such that people lose heart; they think that nothing can be done, that it is not possible for them to get anywhere. If someone suggests trying, other voices may be against it: don't do it now, wait a while. Jesus doesn't usually *wait* (if he does, the waiting itself is in service of the action at hand; it is not mere procrastination or postponement). Jesus is generally a do-it-now type and urges against holding back or being shy or doubtful. "My Father works until now, and I work" is one of his mottoes. His attitude is confident and vigorous.

What he says to this man is, "Stretch forth your hand." "The hand that is withered?" "Yes, go ahead and stretch it out." Take some action, try. The story is telling us that if you do so, you will find that the hand does have power of action in it.

The story also warns the formerly powerless that the bystanders may not be altogether pleased that you have now become active, that your right hand is back in business. The phase transition from domination to communion can be expected to have difficulties. When the formerly powerless stretch forth their hands in normal strength, the power classes may be alarmed. Be prepared for that, but do it anyway. Don't hesitate. It is your right to have full life and you don't have to wait for it.

There is a parallel story about a woman (Luke 13:10ff.), which also takes place in a synagogue on the Sabbath. The woman is described as bent over (*sygkyptousa*), unable to stand up straight. The Greek word for her state (*astheneias*) means powerless, oppressed.

When Jesus saw how it was with her, he called her to him and declared, "Woman, you are *set free* from your infirmity." And "he put his hands on her and she at once stood up straight and praised God." Again there was complaint against his having done this, but Jesus, in response, said that the woman was "a daughter of Abraham" (equal to the sons of Abraham) and that the condition of her not being able to hold her head up was a bondage laid on her by Satan. Jesus' way of celebrating the Sabbath included rescuing and restoring life, setting those who were bound free.

A general story is the one about the paralytic who was let down through the roof (Mark 2:3ff.). The context is that the state of being paralyzed (unable to act) is equivalent to being cursed for one's sins. In this instance, Jesus denies that the paralytic is burdened with sin, and says, "Since you are not cursed and made inactive by God, stop being paralyzed. Get up and go about your business." The message is to all the oppressed classes who imagine that it is God's will that they should be dominated by the power classes: Don't you believe it! This is not true. Stop believing that you can't take your place in the human world and make your valuable contribution. Get busy!

Everyone Unbound, Active, and Sharing

Jesus is asking that everyone be unbound, set free to be active in the human community, for everyone has something precious to offer. Robert Haywood, a vice president at Pacific Gas & Electric, sees this in a concrete form in running a business and planning its future:

In situations where you need to anticipate incredible change in every area, the old models [of communication and decision-making] have become quite anachronistic. . . . They don't work. . . . What works instead is . . . getting everybody involved, building consensus . . . no hierarchy, we are all searchers for truth. As each person brings to the table his or her piece, a lot of communication goes on.

This is one practical form of the Jesus Supper. Everybody has something to "bring to the table." Sharing it is "communication," communion. The aim is to find what is "true," what is good, what to do next, and that emerges in the sharing, in the communication, the cross-feeding. If we used such a method (and others growing out of such an attitude of mutual respect), we could build what Jesus has in mind: a Just, Empathetic, Social Unity System. *Just* means "what is yours is yours," as said above. *Empathetic* means what we said about kindness, "what is mine is yours," and also what is your joy or pain I accept as mine and will act accordingly. *Social* means all of us together, interacting. *Unity* means that we make a One, an integral being. *System* means that our diversities are protected and enhanced, and that each of us contributes, each of us is an initiator; we are all on equal terms; we all affect one another in forming this one community. That's how you spell "God Saves." That's how Messiah comes. That's the Name in which we should pray.

Fundamental equality of dignity and respect for each one's unique contribution, then interaction: that's the key. The traditional figure of Jesus–the-Example can be seen as a "Democriton," one who interacts with all other particles. This is what gives rise to all the specific forms of the Communion Paradigm. Rabbi Zalman Schachter-Shalomi, inventing language showing God as a verb, urges various forms of interacting. For instance, we need to learn *interpeacing*. Because that's the only way we're going to get to it. Sharing, interacting, is the key. Peace, shalom, is what emerges for the whole community when the communiting interpeaces. ("Communiting" is a neologism. It turned up accidentally as a typo, but perhaps we should keep it. Comm-uniting inter-peacing—reminding us that it's all *activity*, it's all *living*.) Everyone has to contribute; we can't sit back and wait for someone else to do it for us. All of us, acting together, interpeacing, are Messiah.

Reb Zalman also speaks of *share-flow*. He says, "The scarcity mentality is counterproductive in achieving its aims. More productive is the grateful mentality that produces a greater *share-flow* of goods, services, and communication." He applies the concept to religious, personal, and esthetic activities.

Barbara Marx Hubbard does a similar thing. Long active as a futurist, she has developed many ideas, structures, activities, and words to guide and encourage us. Her *Conscious Evolution* identifies eight sectors or pathways to social transformation toward a peaceful, cocreative world. These are governance, education, economics, personal growth, science, spirituality, ecology, and culture. Each of them is "a vital system of the whole, offering a visible matrix of the emerging social body in which we place our creative acts."

The clues to the direction of the emerging social body can be found in the previous developments of the cosmos, increasing complexity and consciousness, new wholes forming from the interactions of simpler wholes, increasing freedom and scope of action, increasing community and synergy—working together for the good of the whole. We are looking now, Hubbard says, at the ways in which innovations can be introduced, developed, related to one another, "synergized." Contemporary efforts already constitute a "Global Collegium," a network of people knowledgeable about innovations, who identify breakthroughs and systemic changes, share information and nurture innovations that work. The dynamism for this "new social process" comes from "the community of co-creators—social innovators and builders of the new world—you and me."

This "co-creative society" has been envisioned by many writers these last few decades. Buckminster Fuller, who undertook to pioneer the future by intentionally working fifty years ahead of where the rest of us are, said that we must cultivate "synergetic comprehensions . . . omni-inter-relevancy of all phenomena" in a "metaphysical revolution" of "spontaneous universal cooperation" for "total human success." Lewis Thomas, in his popular *Lives of a Cell*, said that thinking together, we may become a new community, self-thinking, by a symbiosis of consciousnesses, exchanging information-energy. This will be the beginning of the community consciousness that will become reflexively conscious and finally mystically conscious. Jesuit Joseph Bracken, in *Society and Spirit*, sees wholes made of wholes, acting in "collective agency," to form a new emergent.[6]

Getting More from Less

All this inter-ing, inter-facing, makes the whole smarter than the parts—and not as simple as a "sum of" the parts. Interactions create something new; this is the general phenomenon of "emergence." This is what "creation" does: it gets more out of less, greater things from combinations of lesser things. As computer scientist Daniel Hillis says, "The most interesting thing in the world is how a lot of simple, dumb things organize themselves into something much more complicated that has behavior on a higher level." We are now organizing at the level of societies into supersocieties.

These emergents are not tyrannies and cannot be, because the very interactions that constitute them imply that all components are equal. Any attempt to reduce a cocreative *system* to an order of domination would simply destroy the system, with all its higher-level characteristics and operations. Systems do not work by "top-down" monarchical commands. They don't work from the "bottom up," either, because there isn't any "bottom" or "top." They work by "cross-feeding," the eucharistic way. This is the beauty, the innovative power, and the futuristic genius of the Jesus Supper, why it can be the model for the new politics. Any Just Empathetic Social Unity System can be such an emergent, a limb of the living body of the Messiah, and can serve as a "demo" for other social bodies formed of interacting consciousnesses.

The Jesus Movement seeks to create a multilevel, integrated, simultaneous, sharing, and connection system rather than a linear sequence of control in one direction. Its communications are not filtered through central processing (Crossan's "broker" or "the Lord" in the Holy Thursday idiom)—not passed through a central authority and back to the community again. Rather, the members communicate directly with one another; it's all grass-roots stuff and stays grass roots: there is no privileged position in the system, no hierarchy, no monarch. This, says Fred Hapgood in *Up the Infinite Corridor* (a book about MIT), is how nature works, and how we should work socially. "Problems [are] transformed [directly] into solutions . . . answers . . . generated directly by locally interacting neighbors communicating." Gregory Stock, in *Metaman* (the interconnecting community of consciousnesses, assisted by our invented peripherals), says that this emergent entity is already operating in response to global perceptions, for example, the problems of global warming and ozone depletion. Concerned humans from all over the world are exchanging information and suggestions, working on solutions, without any central control: "no single group is coordinating this."[7]

Hazel Henderson described the "network model" of social change in 1981 in *The Politics of the Solar Age:*

They have no headquarters, no leaders, no chains of command, but are free-form and self-organizing, composed of hundreds of autonomous, self-actualizing individuals who share similar world views and values. . . . They ebb and flow around issues, ideas, and knowledge. Many hundreds of thousands of these networks exist today in and between media-rich, industrial societies; . . . their chief product is information processing, pattern recognition, and societal learning.

It is interesting for us, studying the Jesus Movement, to observe that many of these networks are created by people marginalized by the power classes, and they cut across the institutions established by these classes to form new share-flow "communions." It is also interesting that what makes the *connections* in the network possible is the new communications media. Technology enables the implementation of the moral vision. Jesus, the *tekton* (mason, carpenter, etc., Mark 6:3), the *technician*, the practical man, has set himself to "fulfill" (*plērōsai*, implement) the Torah and the Prophets (Matt. 5:17).

Henderson sees these developments (as I also do) within the context of cosmic evolution. The budding of new units of organization is a kind of feedback that recalibrates the evolutionary process "while encouraging diversity, experimentation, and continual learning and adaptation of the whole system to change. . . . Networks, counter-cultures, and dissident views are always vital for societal and institutional renewal."

Institutions go through seasons of growth, culminating in "winter" when they are on the verge of collapse: disorder increases and the (domination style) government has little popular support and suffers from scandal and crisis. Four possible responses are then likely: muddling through, descent into chaos, increasing authoritarianism, and transformational change. Henderson's own model of the last includes increasing demands for member participation at all levels of decision making, rapid "grapevine" communication among the dissidents, growth of networks with their "heterarchical" (as opposed to hierarchical) structures, and renewal of individual responsibility.[8]

What we need to add from the Holy Thursday model is the basic mystical vision of the divine filiation, which implies universal equality of persons, and the consequent share-flowing in a context of sufficiency, even abundance. This discussion gives us a helpful sense of how such transitions can take place, and it underscores our view that such transitions are natural rather than supernatural and belong to the usual pattern of evolutionary advance.

A Major Shift from Domination

If we now review quickly some of the departments of human social life that we looked at under the Domination Paradigm in chapter 1, we can say that, of course, the great wars and persecutions and tyrannies of the Domination Paradigm would be unknown in a Communion Paradigm. This would be a major institutional shift, war having been a prominent dimension of human society for all of historical times. But it does seem—despite current violence in many parts of the world—that on some level, in some sense, it is already true that "the age of nations is past," as Teilhard de Chardin said years ago. Somewhat later, though still a long time ago, Senator William Fulbright told us that our survival depends on our being holistic politically. The network unities that are happily functioning in benign neglect of national boundaries seem to be where the growing layer of our organic being is located now. The cumbersome bureaucracies of the old institutions are perhaps already dead but don't know it.

These developments are moves in the right direction, in the view of a Holy Thursday Revolution, but the revolution urges that if we are to be able to hold the equality and the sharing and the flowing and the uniting, we need to base them on an insight and a realization of our transcendent personhood sufficiently deep and strong that we will not fall back into psychologies of domination.

Michael Lerner insists that if we are going to do real politics in the context of healing the world, we have to work the micro (individual) level together with the macro (institutional—or replacement with communication network) level. The highest moral principles must govern both. Global issues of hunger, ecological devastation, and human rights have to be addressed everywhere. "The economies and consciousness of the entire world are ever more . . . interlinked," and everyone's survival "depends on the health of the totality." We need to apply ourselves to "the strategic thinking necessary" to plan how to build communities in a unified world that "can embody and manifest . . . the God of love, kindness, and healing." If God is ONE, and if people and even the whole world are made in the image of that ONE, then functional oneness must characterize our relations.[9]

On the economic level, we will be looking for positive-sum games rather than zero-sum, win-win rather than win-lose. This will be possible because we will admit that we are operating in a theater of sufficiency/abundance, not one of scarcity. Economic systems evolve together and progress if *all* progress, not if some are depressed for the temporary advantage of others. Economic justice—indeed, economic health—requires a sharing process whose central element is the reciprocal recognition of participants who operate in freedom and in mutual respect and even care for one another. Our economic life will be an ecological life, characterized by cooperation, nurturance, and partnership. Such an interdependent economy creates security that is much greater than any military establishment can promise. Military establishments anticipate hostility; economic sharing is invested in peace and friendship.

Kenichi Ohmae, a managing director of the McKinsey consulting firm and advisor to large companies in many industries around the world, tells us that the corporation, if it is to succeed and fill its place in the world, must learn to see itself as a social institution beyond the well-being of its stockholders; it is called to provide security and a good life to its employees, its customers, its vendors, and its subcontractors. If it does not keep these values in mind, it will surely fail, for all these are intertwined in the life of the world. We are entering the era of the global corporation, Ohmae says, which is "fundamentally different from the colonial-style multinationals of the 1960s and 1970s." Notice in his description the notes of the Communion Paradigm, indicated in boldface.

> It serves its customers in all key markets with **equal dedication.** It does not shade things with one group to benefit another. It does not enter individual markets for the sole purpose of exploiting their profit potential. Its value system is **universal, not dominated** by home-country dogma. . . . [Local managers] need to escape the center's rigidities. . . . The old, pyramidal organization . . . used brute force . . . today [this is] . . . neither necessary nor effective. A **new form of organization, organic and amoebalike** . . . [characterizes] a genuinely global mode of operation. . . . [This] new ground [requires that companies . . . denationalize . . . and create a system of values shared . . . around the globe [that are] country neutral. . . . Everyone is hired locally [and] can communicate fully and confidently with colleagues elsewhere . . . through a **network** of . . . individuals, connected to each other by **crisscrossing** lines of **communication rather than** lines of **authority.** . . . **These linkages mean that creative work can** happen . . . **anywhere in the network. There is no conflict because no one**

instance of first-rate performance detracts from . . . any other. What holds this network together is our shared sense of identity, supported . . . by our shared set of values.

In the old multinationals, the separate pieces were linked to each other through the authority of the center. In the true global, "the pieces are linked, individual to individual, not through the center but through a shared set of values . . . [and especially through] commitment to a single, unified global mission."[10]

Part of the radical change of our consciousness that can be expected to come with a Communion Paradigm is the rise of an ethics of ecology. Ecosystems may be seen as having *rights*: that is, their protection and nurturance are validated not by their service to humans but simply by their own existence. They are not means to others but ends in themselves. So far, we are still urging correction of "the environment" for our own sakes. We do not very often see the natural world rather portrayed as God's creation that should be protected for its own sake and helped for God's sake, so that the creative act may go forward. Indeed, Christianity has mostly represented human-kind—"man"—as having dominion over, and having a right to exploit, all the other creatures.

Those who hold this view quote Genesis 1:28, saying that we are to "fill the earth and subdue it; and have dominion . . . over every living thing that moves upon the earth." However, it is clear from the following verses that the humans are not to eat or otherwise exploit the animals. What is given humans and animals for food are seeds and the fruits that enclose them. Eating these does not harm the living plants but even helps them to spread their respective kinds. An attitude more in line with this directive might be more characteristic of a communion ecological responsibility.[11]

Both strengthening and expansion of the family might be expected in a Communion Paradigm of social life. The feelings of bonding and commitment, joy in being together, sharing, helping, and supporting would be central in a natural family, but this would be more extensive than our present parents and children, reaching further generations and lateral connections. In addition, "family feelings" would take in close friends and in appropriate analogies coworkers and more distant acquaintances. The conscious recognition of universal kinship would be a constant background. Ethnic discrimination would be a thing of the past, even forgotten. Very probably there would be so much intermarriage that visible ethnic lines would be well blurred.

All ages would be valued and treated with respect. Violent punishment visited on children, as is common in our culture, would be unknown. Children would be reared with love and would grow up without having the model of power, hostility, hurt, and fear as a central force in their lives. This one point alone would remake a great deal of our social life.

Equality of respect between men and women would be a fundamental position of a communion society, without artificial expectations of either competencies or incompetencies. Differences can be enjoyed and honored as well as samenesses. People would not be either pushed into occupations or excluded from them on the basis of sex. Work would be so arranged as to allow parents ample time with young children. Family values—gender equality, child care, elder care, time together—would be more to the center than work-related concerns, as things are now. Work would support the family, not supersede it.

Child care means birth without frightening the baby; support for mother–child bonding; sensitive, informed nurturance of bodily and emotional health; gentle, enjoyable education in social behavior and cultural skills. Education takes place in every interpersonal or cultural contact, not just in schools. As Socrates said long ago, we are all of us always teaching the young by everything we say and do. The very structures of our families, our schools, our religious institutions, and our governments proclaim to the maturing mind what is considered the right order of the world and what is acceptable behavior.

Communion Paradigm schools would, by their own organization, goals, and feedback practices (grades, diplomas—or the absence thereof), support the form of the world and the value of human society that they are explicitly teaching. Curricula themselves would undoubtedly be integrative, entwining disciplines that today are distinct; they would recognize diverse learning styles and would encourage exploration, invention, and creativity; they would respect dissent, divergent opinions, and skepticism within a framework of eagerness to learn and respect for one another. Education, learning, and exploring would be highly respected and would go on all one's life. These activities would take place in real contact with the subject under consideration rather than from books.

Sport would be enjoyed for the experience itself, not just for winning (much less winning *bets* on the winning), and would include new games in which the goal would involve cooperation on the part of all participants instead of setting them at odds with one another. Art would also be more of a participant experience than it is today, when most of us merely observe the artistic products of others. It would not be primarily a professional occupation, any more than sport would be, but a dimension of experience for everyone. Neither sport nor art would be reducible to money earned, or a medium of investment, as both often are now. Religious liturgies as art forms would display graphically how the participants see their world as ordered and valued and would be creatively revised as needed.[12]

In his book on the new science of complexity, Michael Waldrop says that once the whole intellectual fabric was seamless—and maybe it could be that way again. This is what we are even now reaching for, seeing the interconnections everywhere. Fritjof Capra says that living systems build up worlds by their interactions with their surroundings and are themselves members of one another's worlds, so that an "ecology of worlds" emerges, "brought forth by mutually coherent acts of cognition."

That is to say that we live in an ecology of minds and souls. Minds and souls are free creative beings like their divine Progenitor, who says, "I will be whatever I will be—alive and real—and unpredictable." We are engaged, as Barbara Hubbard says (furthering Teilhard), in conscious evolution. That's the name of our game. It's unpredictable, yet it's intentional.

The phase transition from domination to communion won't take place unless we intend and will it, yet the whole history of the cosmos supports it. We ourselves are the "elements" of the next creative union; thus, it will not unite except as *we* unite. And we cannot thoroughly unite beyond all need to seek private advantage over our fellows unless we are in touch with the deep self, the *person*, the transcendent one beyond the labels. *Persons* are naturally in living communion with one another and naturally engaged in creation. When we know ourselves at that depth, we begin our conscious evolution.

Far from anticipating the "end of the world," the spirituality of this outlook knows itself to be on the brink of a limitless future. The variety of life we have known up to now is a tiny edge of what we may expect to find and to create. We are not coming toward the denouement; we are only about truly to get started. When we will have passed through the phase transition of the Holy Thursday Revolution, from domination to communion, then "the morning star will arise in our hearts" and a new day will have begun.[13]

PART III

Human Nature

7

"You Can't Change Human Nature!"

But isn't this whole thesis just another utopian dream that ignores reality? Competition, domination, and rank ordering are perfectly natural and unalterable. They are the very fabric, perhaps the backbone, of nature itself. As the comic song "The Reluctant Cannibal," by Michael Flanders and Donald Swann, has the cannibal's father admonish him, "What do you mean, don't eat people? People have always eaten people. What else is there to eat? If the Jou-Jou had meant us not to eat people, He wouldn't have made us of meat!"

Prophets and preachers, mystics and avatars have, for millennia, urged human beings to love one another and seek each other's welfare on a par with their own. Nothing ever happens. Admirers nod, disciples worship, but human social forms and practices don't change. The institutions built on the following of the prophets become new occasions for domination and warfare. In our current computerese we can sagely tell ourselves that domination is "hard-wired" into us. It's not a superficial piece of software that we can pull out of its slot and replace with a "communion disk." In all fairness, the avatars and other advocates of human-heartedness have never claimed that the transition would be easy or uncontested or quick. They have only pointed out that the time has come. We must begin. Domination has had its day; it has become obsolete, and, like many obsolete forms, it is now a hindrance.

Domination Is Natural

So the levelers say. But is that true? Can we ever outgrow competition and domination? Look how universal it is! Take warfare, for instance, arguably the most explicit and destructive form of domina-

123

tion. It is still the outstanding concern of our social life, one of the half dozen or so dimensions of human culture studied by anthropologists, an "institution." Doesn't that argue that it is natural and inevitable? Can't we even show that war drives the advance of civilization, that it weeds out the weak, the backward, and the unworthy, and unleashes fresh waves of creativity in the victors and all those who convert to their lifestyle? Don't the more intelligent and better integrated have a responsibility to govern those not so well put together and keep them from preying on and slaughtering one another in their centuries-old tribal hatreds? Doesn't a little bit of war—"limited conflicts"—act as a safety valve, letting everyone's violent passions experience release and thus avoid hugely destructive global combat? Doesn't warfare stimulate the economy and encourage invention? Doesn't it unite the nation and give people a sense of something to work for and die for, a transcendent meaning to their otherwise banal and insignificant lives? Even the *threat* of war focuses and energizes national activity. Invention, manufacture, and sale of weapons, efforts to be first in space with a trip to the moon or a long-term space station or a convenient shuttle or satellites or energy collectors . . . all these are stimulating and unifying, life promoting! Death threats are life promoting. Oxymoron? Or the curious way nature always works?

Competition and efforts to dominate obviously characterize our economic life, and we can well ask, Could it possibly be any different? In the first place, life is about access to the means of life: habitat, food, mates. These are not evenly distributed on the planet, and the humanly developed means—material, financial, and intellectual capital—are not either. They have to be sought out, developed, and defended, fought for. In the second place, this unevenness is again the driver, the context in which meaning is found and success identified and enjoyed. Can we imagine what it would be like to live in a world in which these forces were not in play? If life's motto is "Be fruitful and multiply" in an environment of limited resources, how can it be any other way? All of us living creatures are built to live in such a situation. We're not designed, not engineered to exist in a steady state, with all our needs fully met. That's why we have to keep the frontier open, the frontier of the world of limitation and desire. As fast as we satisfy present wants, we must invent new ones, keep up the dynamic. Don't let the music stop. Unless the momentum circulates, we will all die.

Life momentum is also generated by our cultural structures and activities. Aren't most of our social organizations and structured recreations informed by these very same principles? Sport is most often "playful" warfare, mutually aggressive "sides," strategies for winning—winning for one entails losing for the other—thus domination, possession of the trophy, the rank position, the fame, and usually the money. Not only players experience this, but spectators. They enter vicariously into the loyalty, the hostility, the effort, the hope, the triumph or desolation, and sometimes they act out their participatory feelings. Owners, advertisers, and those who place wagers may not experience the same kind of identification with a chosen team or athlete, but they are playing a metagame off the field that has its own risks, urgencies, and rewards or losses. Is "Excitement" only the nickname of this game, or is it its real, legal, tax-paying name? Is it essential to life?

And rank ordering in society, which the egalitarians inveigh against, is found almost everywhere in the world—and always has been since we became more than simple bands of food gatherers. A social *structure* is bound to involve recognizing some as superior to others. Even an amorphous group, left together for a reasonable time in particular circumstances, will spontaneously evolve a structure appropriate to the circumstances. Leadership will emerge, theoreticians will be identified, activists will be evident, those who prefer to follow directions will be clear, and those who try to avoid taking either action or responsibility will be known. This is natural. It doesn't have to be imposed from the outside. In fact, if we want to have egalitarianism, it will have to be imposed against the resistance of this natural ordering tendency. Why should we struggle against the manifest will of nature simply to fulfill some ideology?

Human Nature Is an Animal Nature

To carry this nay-saying argument further, consider the nature of the human being as an animal. In particular, consider our biochemical arrangements. It can be argued that we are competitive and aggressive by instinct, that is, by genetic predisposition. We are supplied with hormones that release certain behaviors when properly triggered. For instance, male dominance, ranking, and violence are connected with the hormone testosterone, about which Dr. Ben Bova says, "The most potent and dangerous drug in the world is testosterone. It is a major driving force behind today's terrorism and crime."[1] Of course, it is also behind highly useful protective and constructive behaviors, as well as exploratory tendencies, risk taking, courage, and perhaps perseverance.

The point is that testosterone and the other hormones, and the behaviors that they support, are *natural*. People are made this way. The human being is basically an animal and thus shares in common animal traits—behaviors, biochemistry, genes. Humans share the need for loyalty and cooperation skills with other hunting carnivores; we share with birds the importance of eyesight and the energy investment of rearing our young; in length of life and accumulation of wisdom and long-term relationships, we are like the elephants. But in the matter of dominance and social ranking we are like almost all animals that live in communities.

"Pecking orders" are observed among birds, lined up according to who may peck whom, an order that governs feeding rights. Horses in the wild travel in a fixed order: stallion in the rear, top-ranking mare in the lead, with her foals (the youngest being closest), then the rest of the mares (with their foals in age order) according to descending rank. Each animal "knows its place," so the herd can keep together and no one will be lost. It is interesting that horses and other herding animals that have this ranking practice will, for that very reason, accept human (or in the case of sheep, dog) leadership and can be readily domesticated.[2] Is human "domestication" indebted to such an inherited tendency to rank ordering?

Dominance shows in decorum. The appropriate behavior for the top-ranking animal (especially if male, as it usually is) is proud posture, gait, eye contact, gesture. The head wolf, for instance, walks stiff-legged, with majestic pace—head, ears, and tail up, staring freely at others. Subordinates dare not look; they lower their heads and tuck their tails, keep their teeth covered, grovel and slink, while yielding food and space to the top animal, who takes what he pleases. Rhesus monkeys behave similarly. The alpha male walks regally, head and tail held high, and climbs handy objects to obtain a position above the others. He outstares challengers and slaps the ground ("snaps his fingers") to insist on deference and compliance. Male and female subordinates walk furtively, head and tail down; they keep their mouths shut (when the boss is around?) and back off in the presence of authority.[3]

Carl Sagan points out that gestures of sexual display are used to establish dominance ranks. Japanese macaque males of lower rank take up the sexual posture of a female in oestrus ("presenting") and are briefly and ceremonially mounted by higher caste males. The behavior is derived from copulation practices but has been transferred to a quite different context: symbolically renewing the social order.

"Mounting" translates as "I am the master," say the scientists who study this phenomenon. Sagan remarks that sex, dominance behaviors, and aggression are all tied together by neuroanatomical connections. Mating rituals of many animals initially look like fighting, and among some insects and spiders mating concludes with the female actually eating the male. In the case of human beings, socially offensive language derived from sexual behavior is characteristically used to express insult and hostility. This may happen linguistically because the words chosen for sexual acts come from roots meaning hostile and violent actions.[4]

Edward O. Wilson takes advantage of such descriptions to point out the resemblance he sees between "animal submissive behavior . . . and human obeisance to religious and civil authority." He believes that this is due to *Homo sapiens* having "only recently diverged in evolution from a nonhuman primate stock. . . . True to their primate heritage, people are easily seduced by confident, charismatic leaders, especially males. . . . Their power grows if they can persuasively claim special access to the supremely dominant, typically male figure of God. . . . Unruly subordinates, known as 'blasphemers,' are squashed."[5]

Being of low rank can have more than social disadvantages. Within female primate societies, there is ranking of the matrilineal families. From far back in evolutionary time, the mother–daughter bond has been the stabilizing factor of the community, but these families could be high-ranking or lower, with daughters inheriting their mothers' status. Low-ranking mothers, whose own "self-esteem" is low, often become child abusers, being poor mothers to their own infants and sometimes injuring the infants of other mothers. The offspring of these animals become antisocial in their turn and again poor parents. On the other hand, high-ranking females, with secure social placement and self-confidence, tend to be attentive and nurturing mothers. Robert Jay Russell says, "It is a pattern we can trace for more than twenty million years, from the extinct jungles of the human past to our homes within contemporary society."[6]

Russell also argues that prostitution is "a cold, hard, amoral fact of ape and human life." The practice of "bartering sexual access for resources (like food) or intangibles (like proximity to power)" may go back to the dryopithecine ancestors of both humans and modern apes. What the female gains is food and protection for herself and her children, and the bargain is based on the fundamentally different sexual strategies of the partners: females produce relatively few gametes in which they make a large energy investment, while males produce a huge number of gametes (carrying genetic information but no food or embryo protection) in which they make a minimal investment.

The male therefore seeks to have as many mates as possible to whom he owes nothing further, while the female seeks to retain the provisioning services of a mate for at least the term of rearing their offspring. But this negotiation takes place in the context of social ranks. Both parties seek to be mated with partners of high rank, thereby improving their own positions. This leads to sexual matters becoming means to social position ends. It elevates a woman's social status to wed an established, successful, and wealthy (usually therefore necessarily older) man, and it glorifies a man's social position to be able to display a beautiful and charming young wife.

"Our difficult game of courtship," Russell concludes, "is layered each day with the complexities of power struggles, preferential treatment, leadership, and survival. . . . Love, expressed as some form of egalitarian ideal that works for both men and women, must work hard to conquer all the evolutionary legacies of our past."[7]

Egalitarianism is not desired even by the subordinate parties in chimpanzee society. An alpha male is obliged by his rank to reassure those under him by strutting about and acting pompous, strong, and authoritative: as someone who can lead, handle emergencies, protect, settle disputes, and generally be a hero worth worshiping. At the same time, he is always in danger of being deposed (perhaps by a conspiracy) and replaced. But it is not the destruction of tyranny as such that is sought, only the displacement of that particular tyrant.

Alliances are formed opportunistically and can fall apart overnight as all the adult males scramble for position on the dominance ladder. Not only physical qualities are needed to succeed but "people skills" and "political savvy." Those who are able to manipulate the hopes and fears of other members of the community have an important advantage. Carl Sagan and Ann Druyan, in *Shadows of Forgotten Ancestors*, sum up:

> In chimp society, the combination of dominant males, submissive females, deferential but scheming subordinates, a driving hunger for "respect" up and down the hierarchy, the exchange of current favors for future loyalty, barely submerged violence, protection rackets, the systematic sexual exploitation of all adult females—all this has some marked points of similarity with the lifestyles and ambience of tyrants

of all political persuasions [and in all sorts of leadership/power positions] and with the actual lives of many of the figures in history adjudged "great." We find humans behaving like chimps at their worst in the chronicles of the most ancient civilizations, in the sacred books of many religions, in the tragedies of Euripides and Shakespeare, and in endless succession of modern popular fiction.[8]

Even animal societies already begin to exhibit the complexity, flexibility, and ambiguities that characterize human communities. Straight domination is not the whole story. There are also cooperation and occasional bonding among those who are otherwise rivals. Animals that hunt and that make war especially display the ability to suspend the dominance game in favor of relations more on a level and including concern for one another's welfare. William F. Allman, in *Stone Age Present*, points out that on the one hand, aggression plays a key role in keeping the peace within a social group, and on the other hand, well-developed powers of cooperation make warfare possible. Closing the circle, warfare, says Russell, like hunting, evolved and persists to redirect male aggression and socially bond overly competitive males.[9]

Power Differentials Are Cosmic Forces

It is not only in biology that inequality appears as a central organizing principle. Contests, exclusions, preferences, and gradients are common principles at every level of cosmic organization. The currently popular view of the universe at time zero (if there *is* a time zero; if not, then at the earliest time) is that it is found in a state of perfect symmetry. All the forces are of equal strength and range, and their corresponding particles are all interchangeable. As long as this condition prevails, nothing happens. There is no development.

But, thanks to random quantum fluctuations, the symmetry breaks. In a series of steps, the four fundamental forces separate into their respective ranges and strengths, and an array of elementary particles appears. The particles seem to be symmetrical, matter and antimatter, but it turns out that what we call matter prevails, for there is slightly more of it, some being left over after the matched particles have been mutually annihilated. Masses have been "chosen" for the various particles from a field of possibilities in which there had been no preference. Now some are more massive than others, and it makes a difference. In addition, they have different sorts and different senses of "charge," some being positive and others negative.

Inequality would seem to be the foundation of cosmic development. Louis Pasteur thought that dissymmetry was the very characteristic of life. Whether by chance or by choice, one alternative from a field of possibles becomes active in a new situation, and the chain of consequences deriving from that selection amplifies the "preference" and sets the universe on a course different from what it would have been if another possible direction had prevailed. Ilya Prigogine has enlarged this idea in his far-from-equilibrium thermodynamics, showing how such a system is very sensitive to changes in its environment, making the system free to "adapt" much more readily than an equilibrium system could.[10]

Sometimes the imagery of conflict is used in discussing the mysteries of inequality in nature. George Wald was puzzled about the preference for one of a pair of mirror-image molecules. This is true, for instance, of sugars and amino acids and is common in nature. A right-handed arrangement should be just as good as a left-handed one, but once one way gets started, other components built into the system have to be the same or the structure will lose stability and the characteristic shape that makes it work. Wald says he talked with Einstein about this strange preference in nature, and Einstein confided that he had wondered why the electron was negative, because negative and positive should be symmetrical. And he finally told himself, "It must have won out in the fight!" And Wald agreed: "That is just what I think of the [left-handed] amino acids. They won in the fight!"[11] Other examples might be dominant and recessive genes and the dominant and subdominant hemispheres of the brain.

Then we have examples of exclusion, beginning with Wolfgang Pauli's famous Exclusion Principle governing the collection of electrons around an atomic nucleus: A unique set of quantum numbers defines each position that an electron can occupy; if that position is already filled, an approaching electron cannot take it. On the biological level we have the phenomena connected with the immune system. "Inflammation" means the effort to exclude strange cells and molecules from the home system in order to establish a definite identity for that system. This is useful and adaptive, because otherwise there would be a more general "flow" of life without specific forms, a merging and sharing without organization.

Gradients are also important everywhere in nature; some aspect of a system is increasing/decreasing and other aspects can relate to this scale in terms of whether that increase or decrease is favorable to them. There are gradients in physical realities such as gravity, light, electricity, heat, and in proportions of chemicals such as salt or acid. The growth of an embryo follows certain gradients to form limbs, for instance, knowing in this way how long to continue making a tissue and when to stop. And simple one-celled creatures can follow a gradient in light, heat, and salinity to find their way to a more favorable habitat. If all these quantities were equal, the organization of the cosmos and of life would not be possible. It is precisely nonequilibrium, asymmetry, and not everything having the same probability of happening that brings order out of the original chaos of symmetry and no preference.

But the most important of these gradients and the strongest argument against equality come from thermodynamics. Action that gets anywhere moves from a state of lower entropy to one of higher; it uses energy to change the situation, after which there is more organization but less available energy. The local feature of organization has to take in more resources than it eliminates in order to build itself up. This is obviously the case with living things. That is why there are contests to obtain these resources and all creatures try to acquire what they need to live and reproduce as cheaply as possible. For instance, if one creature eats another, it saves itself the energy of synthesizing the molecules it has just ingested ready-made. Or, if you can join your genes to those of another creature who is also going to provide protection and food and nurturing to maturity for that embryo, then you have successfully reproduced at minimal cost. Or, if you can trick another set of parents into feeding your offspring (cuckoos) instead of their own, you have gained. Killing, stealing, raping, and deceiving can be advantageous, and it is the order of nature itself that makes them so.[12]

The Sociobiological Argument

The sociobiological thesis is that social behavior (in people and other social animals) is guided by genes, just as cellular or organ behavior is. Genes tend to structure all these behaviors in ways that favor the replication of the genes. Since there is (it seems) no feedback from the front lines to the genes, the implication is that it is very difficult to alter social behavior and probably impossible to alter its central principles, such as those governing social organization. Only behaviors that actually prevent gene replication will be extinguished. Surviving genes for social behaviors will favor the "inclusive fitness" of the kin groups that carry those genes. "Inclusive fitness" accounts for cases in which single individuals may not be favored by the behaviors that they are guided to perform, but since the genes that urge them so are also in their relatives who are favored by the behavior, the genes will flourish. This makes possible an argument that what looks like unselfish or even self-sacrificing behavior is, on a larger scale, really self-serving—for the genes.

Edward O. Wilson, who is regarded as the chief spokesperson for this view, says that "variation in virtually every aspect of human behavior is heritable to some degree, and thus in some manner influenced by differences in genes among people." He adds that "this should come as no surprise. It is equally true of behavior in all animal species. . . ." In particular, the dominance hierarchy "is a general trait of organized mammalian societies. Like humans, animals use elaborate signals to advertise and maintain their rank."[13]

Some critics feel that these are exaggerated claims and so broad that they cannot be falsified in proper scientific fashion. Social scientists are especially resistant and wish to stress the role of cultural transmission of social behaviors and other alternative explanations. Still others urge that sociobiological claims must be understood correctly and that there have been some misapprehensions. Sociobiology does not claim that the animal is motivated by the intention to further the interest of itself or of its kin. It says nothing about motivation, only about the effects of the behavior and how that behavior has genetic roots.

There are some lively disputes, however, about whether the way things are by the apparent order of Nature is the way things *ought* to be from a human moral point of view. Wilson argues that if sociobiology is correct, it "challenges the traditional belief that we cannot deduce values from facts or moral prescriptions from scientific information." But this should not be too quickly read as a blanket endorsement of behaviors among other animals that we reject for human beings. Science in general takes the view that if we want to change something in the world—including ourselves—we must first find out how it works, what its own rules are; then we can determine to what extent we can change it, and we will know something of how to go about doing so. Wilson himself, who is a liberal who nevertheless thinks that some form of intelligent planning is inevitable for human society to survive in peace, hopes that the scientific discoveries of sociobiology will relieve the "constant turmoil" that afflicts the "human spirit." The conflict comes from the various levels of good that the human brain recognizes—for the gene, the individual, kin, larger groups. Wilson believes that if we can find "a single strong thread" that runs through all life that lives in community, we will be in a better position—together with help from other fields of human effort—to frame the principles that will lead to better social living."[14]

Our question, of course, is, Can we change human nature? This is initially a vague and open-ended question, inviting further questions. What is human nature? Do we need to change it in order to reach a desired state? (What state do we desire?) Is it possible to change it? Or some aspects of it? Or possible to modify its expression? Or compensate for it? And so forth. To the question whether there is an inborn human nature, Wilson answers, "The evidence accumulated to date leaves little room for doubt. Human nature exists, and it is both deep and highly structured." It is dependent on more than just genes. It has what Wilson calls "epigenetic rules," concerning how the living being develops under the joint influence of heredity and environment. Finally, it is shaped by the "universals of culture," of which there are dozens. It may be important to say explicitly that this "nature" includes the means for (and limitations on) its own variation.

Niles Eldredge says that it is "time to drop the either-or dichotomy of nature-nurture and to confront just what this fusion of consciousness, cognition, culture, and biology that we call 'human' is really all about." He argues that we must use our intelligence to relate ourselves correctly to the rest of the natural world. This includes both recognizing how humanity is embedded in nature as a whole and changing many of the ways we have been expressing our own nature alone (especially increasing our populations beyond what the planet can support). *We can use our nature to change our nature.*

Richard Brodie, who is into "memes," argues that just doing "what comes naturally" no longer works. The genes' urgency to replicate can get us into serious trouble. Furthermore, merely following the behest of our genes is not a sufficiently human life. The peculiarly human part of us not only allows but drives us to act beyond the biological imperatives. Alfie Kohn, looking at the "brighter side of human nature," presents evidence that human behavior does not fit the norms of "inclusive fitness." We can, and often do, act against it, and we normally do kindnesses, even risky ones, for people who are not kin to us and who will not even have an opportunity to reciprocate our altruism. He quotes anthropologist Marshall Sahlins: "no system of human kinship relations is organized in accord with the genetic coefficients of relationship as known to sociobiologists."

Perhaps the safest thing to say is that no one knows the total potentiality of the human. All our notions of "human nature" may be quite selective, shaped by whatever experiences and interests we have.[15] However, let us continue to listen to those who hold that any hope we might have of deeply turning humans from domination to communion is ill-founded.

Social Status Values Can't Be Uprooted

Whether mandated by the genes or not, the habits of forming social ranks and finding occasions for conflict are so well entrenched in human culture that many people believe it would be impossible to eradicate them. We have developed these traits over millennia (at least), built our social institutions on them, grown into our psychological sentiments and responses in accordance with them. Domination and competition may not be all that some moralists would like, but they are strong roots of our human *cultural* nature, and we are stuck with them.

It is possible that the forms to which we especially object came into our lives comparatively recently. Eli Sagan argues that tyranny cannot be explained by attributing it to "human nature," because it had a time of beginning in human culture. And Wilson offers us a diagram (based on K.V. Flannery) that shows that social ranking began to be practiced only after people began to live in villages and larger towns. It is a characteristic of civilization and emerges as people clump together first in bands, then by tribes, later under powerful leaders, and finally in formally organized states. Egalitarian social relations appear here as the practice of the primitive societies and gradually give way to task and power structures.

Cultures have their own way of evolving, rather parallel to the biological way, using "memes" rather than genes. Memes are units of culture: words, modes of dress, manners, gestures, songs, dances, rites, beliefs, social organizations, and many others. They survive by being copied—more people begin using them. They adapt by being modified until they are being copied well. Really successful memes have built into them characteristics that cause them to be copied (much as DNA codes for the enzymes that help it copy itself). For instance, a meme that includes the injunction "Teach this to your children," or the belief that anyone who fails to copy it will be in serious danger, will copy well. This sort of advantage (there are others: making sense, being what the elite or the authorities do, being fun or pleasurable) accounts for the rapid spread of memes through a cultural population. Items such as "If you forsake this meme, you will be in serious trouble" help the meme to persevere. When memes have been well established for some generations, they acquire the included item that they are either "natural" or "divine," in either case unchangeable. Religions, of course, are obvious examples, but patterns of domination are also—forms of government, family structure, morally acceptable/unacceptable behavior, and so on. Not questioning the status quo becomes a powerful supermeme protecting all the memes under its umbrella.

The hierarchies of dominance that currently characterize business, government, the military, and the church have evolved culturally, claims Richard Brodie, to embody the feelings that men have about knowing their place on the power ladder. The meme cluster included "wanting power," and men who didn't push for power or who didn't enjoy exercising power lost out. In our society not to want power or not to act as though you have power makes you a "wimp," a bad thing to be. You lose respect, you lose jobs, and you lose out in the mating game, because potential mates believe in the power meme too.

Verifying your devotion to the power meme is most easily done by showing readiness for conflict, eagerness to displace another. Philosopher J.M. Fritzman tells us that "it is the nature of humanity to seek disagreement with others." He argues that if the purpose of communication were to achieve agreement and if the regulative ideal of all communication were to reach consensus, then all conversation would cease once that consensus had been reached. Consensus is not the ideal for human communication. Part of the power meme is giving ourselves permission to feel more competent when we disagree, find fault, criticize. Indeed, it wins us more respect from others, as Teresa Amabile showed with some cleverly devised psychological experiments.[16]

Stephan Chorover, discussing the meaning of human nature and the power of behavior control, points out that "dominant groups will propagate whichever myths about human nature will justify those structures [that maintain the dominant group in control]." The endorsed myths will represent the status quo as natural and inevitable for secular hearers and as God's will for believers. For instance, in a modern society there are differences in status, wealth, and power. The promulgated myth says that these differences are right and unavoidable because they are due to intrinsic differences in ability. A further development can say that the natural differences can be measured; and, being natural and intrinsic, the differences must be ultimately genetic, thus unchangeable; and, being genetic, they will be shared by interbreeding groups, thus producing the observed differences between classes and races. Meme institutions, says Brodie, devote themselves primarily to their own survival and replication, even in preference to the purpose for which the institution was originally founded.

However, Brodie continues, it does little good to blame anyone. The memes will evolve, just as genes do, with or without intent on anyone's part. Cultural evolution moves in the direction of more powerful memes. In order for memes to replicate, to be copied in our minds and behaviors, they first have to catch our attention. The three best attention catchers, says Brodie, are danger, food, and sex. These appear to be "hard-wired." If you want to sell something—product or idea or action—tie it somehow to one or more of these three.

Aaron Lynch explains why gender equality is going to be hard to come by because of the way memes work. The dominant/subordinant roles—which translate as "responsibility"/"helplessness"—outpropagate their alternatives because they are tied to many other aspects of culture, including jobs and products, and because they tend to lead to earlier marriage and more children sooner. By acting helpless and childlike, explains Lynch, a woman can test a man's willingness to take responsibility to protect, care for, and provide for the children their marriage might produce. Marriages actually made between partners playing these respective roles will tend to produce a next generation seeing these roles as "natural" and "right."[17]

Division of tasks is based on this view to a large extent, and it in turn strongly influences product design and advertising, which reinforce the role identities. Art and entertainment, toys and stories, sports and contests, courtship and marriage advice, some laws and religious teachings all reinforce these roles. It's a powerful meme combination. Attempts to change it threaten other aspects of the institutions involved.

If this item of religious teaching is challenged, it casts doubt on the divine inspiration of the whole body of teaching. If some laws are changed, precedents may be set that will logically engage other laws (e.g., military service). If roles and tasks become less polarized, many industries are affected, not only in the products and services they offer but in the way they are internally organized and the way people pass from one job to another. If women are admitted to male jobs, will they adopt the male memes of competition and status and power seeking? Moreover, if women can run big corporations, head nations, machine-gun down the nation's enemies, pilot high-speed aircraft, stay over a winter season at the South Pole, and go to the moon, what is left to do that is heroic? Without being heroic, without the power meme, without domination, what will happen to personal identity and self-esteem? To the meaning of life?

Don't Change It—We Like It!

Even if we could change the Domination Paradigm to the Communion Paradigm, a last argument urges, we wouldn't want to do it. The first part of this argument adduces instances of attempts to switch from domination to communion and shows that they don't work. The obvious example is the worldwide failure of communism. Attempts at economic leveling and making "everybody" own everything really produce terrible tyrannies with even more powerful elites and oppressed masses. People lack ambition and inventiveness and don't exert themselves. Consequently, they feel depressed, become lazy, and take to drink. They don't experience their connection to the "means of production" in a personally meaningful way. Allowing bureaucrats to decide who will work where at what is a program for human disaster. People have talents and interests and important connections to other people. This makes a complex system that can't be successfully "programmed" from on high but must be permitted to work itself out by spontaneous arrangement. People need to choose their own goals and be able to work their way toward them. Otherwise they don't enjoy their lives.

Most people can't expand their existential sense of "we" (or even of "I") to some borderless extent. They need a defined "space" in which to identify themselves. This surfaces as movements to drive "others" away from the relevant "space" (not necessarily physical). Mary Midgley argues that this is "something essential for most advanced creatures and deeply connected with the higher development of feelings—with social responsiveness and also with affection, loyalty, persistence and enthusiasm." Social animals learn to relate to others with either hostility or friendship or with a mixture or even an alternation of the two. The very ambivalence is important, according to Konrad Lorenz, who counts it as a "central element, a structural factor," involved in a variety of valuable traits. Therefore, attempting to get rid of it would be foolish and harmful, as well as probably impossible.[18]

Therefore, this line of argument can proceed: We shouldn't try to love all our neighbors as we love ourselves. There needs to be some discrimination and a gradient, even perhaps refusal. Selfishness shouldn't be regarded as a "bad" thing; it's necessary and highly useful, as well as satisfying. Pleasure in life comes from selfish needs and desires being satisfied. So, if you're going to love your neighbor, you'd better do so on condition that your neighbor show some love for you in return. That's the only way to order a viable community.

Unconditional altruism would be the ruin of an organically interacting world. You have to be careful about how you help the weak or your enemies. You may simply ruin yourself and not obtain an ideal world, either. In a way, if we were to rid the world of war, crime, and hunger, we would undermine the whole economic—not to mention political—structure. Think of all the institutions, all the businesses, all the jobs, that are directly or indirectly dependent on these "evils" in our lives. In trying to rescue one set of victims, we might create another, even larger and more fundamentally injured, set.[19]

Here's another way of looking at it: If you help people too much, you deprive them of the pleasure and satisfaction of gaining what they need and want for themselves. They may then transfer that normal way of obtaining self-esteem and contentment to a meta-level of political action, where the needy contend that they have a "right" to help of various sorts and once again have a meaningful opportunity to *struggle* for it. People *enjoy* emotional stimulation. A certain amount of trouble and threat and fear is energizing. A social structure of gains and losses, rewards and punishments, concretizes the values and orients the emotions. No society so far has organized itself without calling on these forces.

That's why *unequal* rewards are important. They are experienced as vindications of one's worth—primarily of one's effort, but also of one's talent, sometimes of one's luck or merely of one's accident of birth. A comic strip of some years ago puts it all in a few lines: Three teenage boys are walking and talking. Boy 1 says, "Wouldn't it be neat to be rich, guys?" Boy 2 says, "Yeah! Wouldn't it be neat if everyone was rich—if nobody in the whole world was poor?" Boy 3 says, "There's gotta be poor people. There's always gotta be poor people." "Why?" asks Boy 2. "'Cause without them, the rich people would have no fun being rich!" explains Boy 3.[20]

Fun. Is that a serious dimension of our discussion? Is it true that what we consider "valuable" is simply what turns on the pleasure centers in our brains? Was Freeman Dyson on the right track when he declared that if we think we want to avoid the destructiveness of war, we must first "understand what it is in human nature that makes war so damnably attractive"? In the Media Lab at MIT they tried to explain about war to an especially sagacious computer they had invented. "Interesting game," the computer concluded; "the only way to win is not to play." But if we don't play, will we all wind up in "paradise" and fall under the spell of the "leisure-disease" of the South Pacific islands? Where there is nothing to arouse us, nothing to challenge us, even temporarily to frustrate us, will there be nothing to activate the reward centers in the brain, so no sense of pleasure?[21]

So, say our nay-sayers, let us remain in our Domination Paradigm, where there is always something interesting going on, where there is constant jostling to secure a higher position, something to try your mettle on, something to be rewarded for and something to be rewarded by. You can't change human nature. Besides, we like it this way. To paraphrase Ben Bova, in his efforts to persuade a doubtful audience, "No, they do not really believe human life without domination is impossible. They believe it is undesirable."[22]

8

It's the Nature of Nature to Change

It is worthwhile to go through the arguments against trying to shift from a paradigm of domination to a paradigm of communion and friendship because it shows us in a graphic and compelling way how fundamental the problem is and what kinds of questions have to be dealt with in our discussion of it. This is why, in Part I, I pursued the psychology that drives the politics of domination to the underlying metaphysical and even logical levels. Even if some of us do want to convert from domination to friendship, it can't be done on the political or even the psychological levels. It is necessary to go much deeper. Nevertheless, I will now argue, such a transformation is natural, has natural precedents, and is presently stirring among us.

The Need for Change

Many voices are now raised to urge that we undertake a fundamental shift in our worldview, our attitudes, and our behaviors. The main reasons for this are the unprecedented degree of destructive power that we now possess, the global interconnections that have developed in our economic exchanges and personal communications, and the insight that many scientists have into how nature itself moves from one stage to the next. Our present position, however, is new in that the shift now before us will not happen without our highly conscious intention to bring it about, because it is essentially a transformation in our conscious intentions themselves.

Let us listen to a few of these voices: Jonas Salk says that a "point of inflection" is at hand and a great change is needed. Barbara Hubbard tells us that a lot of things are not working now; there is a breakdown in the system and we are being pushed toward change.

Jeff Gates reminds us that our senior scientists have been warning us that we are seriously endangering our habitat by persevering in our social and economic patterns. Magoroh Maruyama finds that, beginning a generation ago, independent social groups were already moving from a linear, competitive, hierarchical logic to an interactionist, mutualistic, symbiotic one, and that this convergence was "an indication that the total structure, not component structures, of our society had become obsolete."

Michio Kaku, sharing his visions of how the computer, biomolecular, and quantum revolutions are changing our lives, says that "the sheer power of the three scientific revolutions will force the nations of the earth to cooperate on a scale never seen before in history . . . tearing down petty, parochial interests while creating a global culture." Michael Lerner agrees that we cannot stick to narrow and selfish goals while expecting to see transformative social movements: "Realistically, to change society means to think more globally, not less so, and to strive for the largest changes, not the smallest." Hazel Henderson perceptively remarks that current interests in extraterrestial life and extraordinary powers of mind (even if fantasy) "help us project ourselves out of modes of thinking and being that are now evolutionarily blocked"; issues now have to be joined at the planetary level.

Robert North knows that the change is going to go deep and that we will have to "replace many assumptions and rules of the past with new understandings and policies." O. W. Markley concludes a study of consciousness in transformation by prophesying that we must "undergo an institutional transformation as profound in its consequences as was the Industrial Revolution, and simultaneously a conceptual revolution as shaking as that created by objective science." Niles Eldredge realizes that "our ecological and evolutionary history has taken us to a state very different from any condition . . . any . . . living species . . . has ever experienced"; our influence on the global system is unprecedented, unpredictable, and unrepeatable: there is no respite from our pressure on the natural world in which natural evolution could be triggered and the ecological system adapt.

Robert Ornstein and Paul Ehrlich think that biological evolution is too slow; "the only permanent means of resolving the paradox that our minds are both our curse and our potential salvation is through conscious change." David Bohm and David Peat declare that we can no longer rely on the natural cycle of civilizations' growth and decay to promote an "overall generative process." We are global, and the challenges that face us have never occurred before; what is required is "a new kind of consciousness." Peter Russell repeats Vaclav Havel's insight that consciousness precedes being and not the other way around, as Marx had claimed, and affirms that "without a global revolution in human consciousness, nothing will change for the better."[1]

Changes Are Already Appearing

Fortunately, not only is it possible for "human nature," consciousness, and behavior to change, but some of the needed changes are already starting to appear. Some of these are in quite early stages, and the former conditions are still very much with us. No amount of optimism can overlook the fact that in 1994 some eight hundred thousand people were brutally slaughtered in a genocidal war in Rwanda. In Europe, by contrast, after two catastrophic world wars, the nations who fought one another for centuries, with the loss of millions of lives, have finally taken steps to set up the political and economic institutions that should enable them to enjoy the fruits of peace and a shared prosperity for many generations to come.

What remains worldwide is terrorism, a new kind of global war against the power of the West and its secular values. It seems that the terrorists and those who support them see this kind of struggle, with its suicide bombers and its attacks on civilians and even on children, as heroic and glorious. But the large public consciousness, exemplified, for instance, by the very existence of the United Nations, has definitely shifted from seeing war as the glory of manhood (as it was seen for many centuries) to seeing it as what most needs to be rejected. It should be said, before leaving this topic, that people who feel so oppressed, threatened, deprived, and powerless that they must resort to terrorism deserve to have their needs and their point of view seriously considered and negotiations undertaken to deal with the reasons for their complaint. Meeting destruction with worse destruction certainly isn't the way.

Thus, we have made some recognizable moves in the direction of eliminating our worst ill. Among other important concerns, there are some for which progress can be reported. Acknowledgement of the equality of all people, while far from being in place everywhere, is nevertheless much spoken of as an obvious and valuable truth. That we are one world is now undeniable; feelings of national loyalty, while still present, are clearly in the process of being modified in the direction of a sense of all-of-us and global "belonging." We continue to exploit and pollute the planet, but publicly we admit that this must cease.

Some deep changes have already been launched. In an interesting

way, global commerce—despite its exploiting Third World peoples—
is undermining racial/ethnic prejudice. No one can say anymore that
this or that people is incapable of technological thought and operation, for they are in fact doing state-of-the-art work for high-tech corporations. Ethnic types cannot be ranked as superior or inferior; that
image, with its accompanying feelings, is being forced out of consciousness. We are obliged to undertake a politics of pluralism,
accepting other nations and cultures on equal terms. This is a big
change from colonialism and "the white man's burden" and indicates
that fundamental adjustments in human social outlook are indeed
possible.

It can even be argued that we are becoming (in some ways and at
some levels) less competitive and more cooperative. Interdependence
is clearly the way of all life, and, interestingly enough, greater acceptance and practice of interdependence lead to more autonomy, as the
old dichotomy of individual versus society weakens toward collapse.
Symbiosis on the economic and social levels is as powerful a way to
rise to a new world of emergence as it is on the biological level. In *No
Contest: The Case Against Competition* (why we lose in our race to
win), Alfie Kohn speaks of "an impressive pile of studies substantiat-
ing" the advantages of cooperative experiences: increased productivity, success, satisfaction in the activity; improved sensitivity to
other(s), enlarged perspective and orientation, receiving other points
of view for creative incorporation; advances in communication, trust,
and liking for others.

We have, in the past, developed these themes within the view that
"intragroup cooperation," can be tolerated and encouraged as a
means to improve "intergroup competition"—bonding with allies
against a common enemy. The received wisdom was that we have no
operative sense of "we" except as opposed to some "they." But studies in this area have confirmed that this is not so. Far from supporting intragroup solidarity, external enmities actually do harm to
developing feelings of trust, confidence, acceptance within the group.
Rivalry, distrust, and hostility at any level tend to find reflection at
other levels. Furthermore, the popular idea that aggressive and com-
bative sports provide a releasing alternative to war has been proved
to be exactly wrong: aggressive sports and aggressive politics go
together; homicide rates also go up during or after a war and aggressive playground activity follows the viewing of violent films. Aggression breeds aggression.[2]

Scholarly studies by theoreticians are not the only evidence of
deep level shifts in consciousness, values, and practice. Grass-roots

citizen organizations are sprouting all over the world and achieving notable results from their efforts to cope with poverty, educate populations, save natural resources, empower women, protest injustices, and deal with various other causes and social human needs that are being ignored by governments. Their proposed remedies often involve fundamentally changed values and attention to issues such as peace, human rights, disarmament, educational exchanges between cultures, humanitarian relief, and resource-preserving development. Many of these movements have such popular support that governments and agencies, even at the international and global levels, have been obliged to recognize and take account of their concerns. These are vectors pointing to the win-win world that Hazel Henderson advocates.

Kenichi Ohmae gives further examples of reassessed values and practices in his *Borderless World*, citing commercial partners interested in each other's welfare without threatening each other's autonomy. We are experimenting with cooperation. Robert Axelrod, who has studied cooperation closely, says that

> cooperation can begin with small clusters. It can thrive with rules that are nice, provocable, and somewhat forgiving. And once such rules are established in a population, . . . the overall level of cooperation tends to go up and not down.

His thesis is that *continuing relationship* is what allows cooperation to develop without the domination of a central authority. When cooperation and mutually rewarding relations become so commonplace that they can be implicitly trusted, the we/they antipathy has disappeared and "the separate identities of the participants can become blurred." We are bringing forward on larger and more public scales the empathy to which we have been predisposed from birth, in our natural capacity to share in and respond to the affect of others. We are gradually approaching a state of conscience that requires us to use our empathy for victims as a prime criterion for the righteousness of any activity. Gil Bailie says that "no event can be fully assessed until its victims have been heard from." This is the turnover in values perception in which we are presently engaged—not yet arrived, but on the way.[3]

Changing Views of Human Nature

Our basic question of what constitutes "human nature" and whether it can be changed is itself receiving new answers. Psychologist Robert Baron, in his book *Human Aggression*, cited more than three hundred studies supporting the conclusion that "aggression is *not* essentially innate. Rather, it seems to be a learned form of social behavior . . . influenced by . . . social, situational, and environmental factors." In 1986 a special meeting of psychologists, neurophysiologists, ethologists, and others in the natural and social sciences from all over the world was convened in Spain to study the roots of war. It issued "The Seville Statement on Violence," which declared: "It is scientifically incorrect to say that we have inherited a tendency to make war from our animal ancestors, [or] to say that . . . violent behavior is genetically programmed into our human nature, [or that aggressive behavior has been selected for, or is automatic in the brain, or] caused by instinct or any single motivation."

The aspect of human ranking behavior that appears in the distinction between owners/managers, on the one hand, and workers, on the other, undergoes blurring when workers become owners. Labor unions can practice "investment bargaining." If workers become owners of the corporations for which they work, they are better placed to see that they are accorded fair wages and safe working conditions; as owners who are workers, they can be more flexible in their demands, and the whole assumption that humanity is engaged in a "class struggle" can give way to a common concern for excellence of product, financial responsibility, and creativity and innovation in company development.

The pecking order represented by the industrial "pyramid" is disappearing in some areas. Operations can no longer wait for instructions to come down through channels to the level of action. Critical information doesn't flow from the top down but disperses in all directions, feeds back, and shares. There is participation in a network, respect and decision-making responsibility in all positions. Old-style domination doesn't work anymore. "Supervisors" don't supervise, because operational people don't need it; instead, they act as resources, consultants—they give guidance and advice rather than orders. Everybody is active, none passive; deference and obedience are no longer prime virtues. Everyone acts intelligently out of a shared vision and set of values.

In spite of the exploitative character of the practice of outsourcing—the way it takes advantage of poor people in Third World countries and leaves job-lost people behind in home countries, and the way the great transnational corporations and their alliances inflict their rules on national domestic policies—I hope that in some quarters we are moving closer to a Communion Paradigm. Where we used to believe that people would perform well only if they could see something in it for themselves, now we recognize that there is another powerful motivator: the opportunity for people to give something of themselves to one another. What they give is opportunity for the other to fulfill potentials to the very best. The workplace can become a community of high-quality relationships. Mutual enrichment, rather than control, can be what is going on. The company doesn't just make money; it makes meaning.

The Domination Paradigm is weakening on the home front, too, in many families. Male–female relations need not include an element of domination/submission. Western educated people at least are mostly of the opinion that relationships and marriages should express equality and mutuality. That's where the satisfaction and sense of significance come from. Failure to find and express respect and equality is seen as insensitivity and verges on being unhealthy. So what at one time was considered obviously natural has shifted to being regarded as undeveloped, or even distorted. We can now look at living systems in general and recognize the basic "friendship" dimension in many of their relationships; we are more open to seeing how much of "living" consists of some form of symbiosis.

Has "human nature" changed? Or just our view of human nature? Or is that somehow the same thing? Is the "human" aspect of human nature the part that can and does change as our view of it changes? Democracy, based on the belief that all people have equal rights to fulfill their own lives and to contribute to the common life, is spreading into many cultures (though strongly resisted in nations and organizations committed to domination systems). Encouraged to recognize their own incomparable value as persons, people wake up to their dignity, realize respect for themselves and expect to receive respect from others. They no longer believe in the old paradigms of rank ordering, inequality of worth and honor, and the naturalness of domination.[4]

Human Nature Is Made for Changing

One of the great advantages of human nature is precisely that it is capable of change, that it can learn. The human being doesn't arrive completely preprogramed, with all its behaviors and motivations, attitudes and feelings set up and ready to run. We all have to be socialized, schooled, led, and taught how to feel and act in our particular culture. The great variety of ways in which this can be done is one of the things that enables us to adjust to the different requirements of our environments. Evolution gives high marks for flexibility, and humanity goes to the head of the class.

For instance, the Netsilik Eskimos studied by anthropologist Richard de Boer have lived "for over five thousand years [in] an unusually viable and stable culture without resorting to any kind of dominance hierarchy. . . . There are no leaders, chiefs or bosses . . . but . . . Eskimos . . . work together." De Boer offers this as evidence that "dominance hierarchies are not innate in species sapiens, dominance behavior is learned." Another anthropologist, Edward T. Hall, thinks that we tend to confuse culture with human nature and that it is of "crucial importance" to study "how one arrives at a definition of the relationship of [human] nature to . . . culturally conditioned control systems." Michael Lerner remarks that "many people have come to think that it is the mark of sophistication to imagine that . . . self-destructive selfishness is actually 'human nature.'" And comic strip artist Bob Thaves, author of *Frank and Ernest,* drew an explosive Earth surrounded by missiles and rockets, being inspected by a large, puzzled and unhappy God-figure, accompanied by two small but vocal angels, one of whom says to him, "Maybe you shouldn't have used human nature as an operating system."[5]

But, argues Alfie Kohn, when we examine socially acquired values and behaviors in a particular culture, find there an image of the human being as self-interested, competitive, and violent, and then attribute these features to "a postulated underlying nature," we are calling on "the comforts offered by any version of determinism: an escape from responsibility." If we don't want to change our social arrangements, we declare that they are meeting the obvious needs of "human nature." It is the inevitability of nature itself. And, adds Kohn, we easily find that the most efficient way to "head off social change" is "to dismiss the very idea of change as naive."[6]

Yet these very endeavors to control our cultural expressions demonstrate the power of the human being to mold the fundamental perceptions from which the cultural expressions arise—in other words, to modify "human nature." We might say that it is the nature of the human being to value, but what is valued changes. Even the way of valuing changes: whether we value for the sake of the individual or for the sake of the community, whether we value for ourselves (either as isolated or identified with a larger entity) or for others, whether we value by means of contrast or transcendentally, in itself.

The human being is capable of such activity and capable of such shifts. It is the nature of the human being to be so. When we talk casually about the "human nature" we claim can't be changed, we are usually thinking of the culturally conditioned behaviors and values we are accustomed to in our particular world. They obviously do change—we change them. So it is actually a mark of human nature to change the values by which we live. Deeper than that, it is a mark of human nature to change the way of valuing. And deeper than that, it is a mark of human nature to critique the way we choose among ways of changing our values. Capacity for self-change is at the very root of our being. It is probably what most characterizes us. *The human being is the self-changing being.* It is the nature of human nature to change human nature.

Joseph Needham says, in *The Grand Titration,* that in the West the basic idea has been that the divine lawgiver determines the natures of things, while in China the natures of more complex wholes grow harmoniously by the organic cooperation of less complex wholes. What I am suggesting in connection with the revolution in valuing that Holy Thursday represents is that the divine lawgiver makes the natures of things such that they can make their own natures, partly by harmonious cooperation to achieve more complex wholes and partly by insight and choice. So when we find our "true nature," we find our participation in Original Creativity: what is "fixed" in our nature is that we must be of unfixed nature. We know that we are "children of God" and *therefore* "what we shall be has not yet appeared." We are still in the process of creating it and do not expect ever to "finish." "God is still working" equals "we are still working."[7]

Fritjof Capra declares that "human nature is most changeable" and that we have created "human nature" as we have evolved. J. Z. Young concludes that "human nature has changed in the past and is likely to change ever more rapidly in the future." How it will change is strictly unpredictable, partly because the human being, and even more the human community, is a "complex adaptive system" for which knowledge of a future state cannot be derived from knowledge of the present state. There are too many different kinds of interactions with the environment and too many ways of responding to any one interaction. The complexity is "unsimulatable"—it cannot be modeled by any system less complex than itself, and thus its dynamic evolution cannot be predicted.

Add to this the fact that the human activities in which we are interested are "intentional," or semantic, dynamic systems, systems of *meanings*, requiring consciousness and understanding for their interactions. Finally, the changes in the structures of these systems are subject to the "insight and choice" actions of the human systems themselves. Even the continuation of a given structure requires at least tacitly renewed choice in each generation. The human being cannot escape responsibility for its own nature's development.[8]

On the spiritual level, Eknath Easwaran asserts that "what makes me a human being is the limitless potential for growing to my full stature through the practice of spiritual disciplines, standing firmly on this earth while rising beyond . . . the galaxies, in my capacity to give to others and to serve life." Human nature, far from being forever stuck in selfishness, greed, hostility, and ambition, is precisely that nature most open to creative impulses, capable of growing, of renewing and ever transcending itself, evolving in an open-ended context of continuing development. Easwaran quotes Leon R. Kass, who denies that all of life can be explained in terms of molecular biology and urges that "we . . . must do better . . . in articulating . . . with real power, a superior vision of the nature and meaning of our humanity."[9]

To claim that it is the nature of human nature to change is no more than to assert that human nature is embedded in nature in general. It is the nature of all nature to change. That's what evolution, what cosmogenesis, is all about. Natural forms are always subject to change, even to shifting the very principles of their life strategies or their physical interactions.

Protons, for instance, ordinarily repel one another by the electromagnetic interaction, because like charges repel. But if the protons are very close together, as they are in the nucleus of an atom, then they bind to one another by the strong nuclear interaction. Not only their behavior changes, but the very principle governing their behavior changes. Shall we say that "proton nature" has changed? Or that it is the nature of protons to shift from one pattern of interaction to another?

Reproductive strategies among living things show not only variety but changeability. Certain fish have the ability to change sex from female to male if a shortage of males in the mating population should develop. Did "fish nature" change? Or is it the nature of that fish to change a fundamental principle of its life in that way? Indeed, the very invention of mating types at all was a deeply fundamental change in the nature of the living things affected by the invention.

Let us go back further, to the origin of the eukaryotic cell, the next great step in evolution beyond the bacteria. It seems that after the cyanobacteria (bluegreen algae) synthesized chlorophyll and began the photosynthetic production of sugar with the waste product of that reaction, free oxygen, most of the bacteria perished, destroyed by the oxygen. But some of them were able to survive, and these formed symbiotic unions: those whose membranes did not succumb to oxidation taking in those that could actually use oxygen to make phosphates and store energy. The engulfing bacteria changed their nutritional policy from digesting the engulfed to protecting and nourishing them, and "in return" received the immense advantage of access to a reliable source of stored energy for all their biochemical needs. That is a very big change in "bacteria nature," so great that it became the ancestor of all the subsequent new forms of life.[10]

If we generalize the meaning of "symbiosis," reading it as any kind of "living together" and applying this even to nonliving things as a way of indicating closeness and mutually supportive interactions, we can say that symbiosis is a general principle of advance in compounded complexity that is repeatedly verified in cosmogenesis. "Symbiotic unions" of quarks make nucleons, which make nuclei; nuclei plus electrons are atoms, whose symbiotic unions make molecules, simple compounds joining to make more complicated molecules, such as nucleic acids and proteins, whose extraordinary symbiosis is the foundation of life, as each promotes the formation of the other. Membrane-enclosed hypercycles of mutually catalytic molecules constitute cells, and communities of differentiated cells are living organisms, which in turn can form societies. All of them are instances of generalized "symbiosis," cooperative unions of formerly separated entities, even formerly hostile entities. It can be done. It is perfectly "natural" to do so. Changing "human nature," if that is the question before us, is not impossible. It is the nature of nature to change.[11]

The Natural Goodness of Human Nature and the Evolution of Cooperation

When we say to those who are being unacceptably idealistic, "You can't change human nature," what we really mean is that you can't change people from seeking power, being greedy, comparing themselves to others, separating and excluding others, insisting on always being right, and in general trying to have the upper hand in a world that lives by upper hands. I have argued that such qualities are not necessarily "human nature" but are the consequence of being socialized into certain worldviews. Change the basic worldview, with its characteristic logic of self-identity and its derived psychology, and you can change the social relations. Now I propose to point to the evidence for human beings already having the qualities that we consider idealistic, and then outline how cooperation and helpfulness develop in the course of human relationships.

Alfie Kohn opens his book *The Brighter Side of Human Nature* with an epigram from Charles Horten Cooley, who in 1909 declared that those who emphasize the "selfish aspect" of human nature and write off as sentimental any altruistic view of it "make their chief error in failing to see that our self itself is altruistic." To improve our social relations, we need to develop and apply these altruistic traits. In my view, Cooley has put his finger on the essential point: we need to revise our ideas about our deep selfhood, that is, shift from the belief that the self is essentially, necessarily, and ultimately selfish to the belief that it is foundationally interactive, sharing, caring, community-bonded, and indefinitely capable of transcending itself.

Kohn believes that we find that goodness makes us uncomfortable. Indications that what is naturally normative for humans might be goodness rather than our putative inherited and therefore unavoidably selfish nature, challenge us so painfully that we prefer to believe that we have built-in "evil" inclinations that we need not expect to overcome. We feel tense and threatened by stories of "heroic" generosity and caring, but relieved by accounts of someone giving in to temptation. For this reason, Kohn says, "helping, caring, rescuing, and sharing were not systematically studied until the mid- to late 1960s."

When the studies were finally done, he reports, "the overriding truth that emerges" from them is that "people of all ages usually do go out of their way to help, particularly when they believe that no one else [will]. . . . Ordinary people often lend a hand sometimes . . . heroically." For instance, "83 percent of blood donors [have] indicated a willingness to undergo anesthesia and stay overnight in a hospital in order to donate bone marrow to a complete stranger." Most Americans (almost 90 percent) give to charitable causes, and about half the population does volunteer work. Kohn finds this "remarkable in light of the fact that we are socialized in an ethic of competitive individualism." If it is also the case that we feel uncomfortable about "being good," perhaps we are not lifting up these characteristics of our own behavior sufficiently and labeling them as significant evidence of "human nature."[12]

Apparently the capacity for both competitive behaviors and cooperative and empathetic behaviors is innate, but it is not particularized. It is a ground from which to learn various cultural ways of expressing these possible attitudes. It is especially interesting to see expressions of these basic feelings even in newborns, a view of the "ground," before there is any cultural development. As remarked earlier, babies in hospital nurseries are more likely to cry and cry longer when they hear another baby cry than when they hear comparable sounds, and this can be interpreted as sympathy, or "a rudimentary empathic distress reaction at birth." At ten to fourteen months, the child will show signs of being upset by another's discomfort, and at eighteen to twenty-four months will begin to try to relieve the other. By preschool age, helping, sharing, and comforting are regular and frequent behaviors. There is also selfish and antisocial behavior, but it is not more fundamental, earlier, or more "natural" than the prosocial attitude and activity.[13]

David C. Korten, in *When Corporations Rule the World*, says that we humans have demonstrated our capacity for "hatred, violence, competition, and greed." But we also have a "demonstrated capacity for love, tenderness, cooperation, and compassion." The argument is about which of these has the better claim to being "human nature" and about which set of attitudes and behaviors fulfills human nature and leads to healthy societies. Korten supports the view that encouraging greed and competition produces dysfunctional societies with characteristic hatred and violence, whereas nurturing cooperation and compassion creates a healthy society of caring communities, sustainable livelihoods, and good living.[14]

But what constitutes "good living"? Is it being at the top of the pile? Able to dominate everyone and everything in one's life? Is it ever-expanding growth and consumption? How shall we measure "success" in life? More basically, what do we really want? Surely most people want a stable life, job security, a loving family, and opportunity to develop their creative interests. Why should we not consider a social-economic pattern that actually produces such a way of life to be the most "successful"? Since we seem to seek the society of our peers, why should we favor a dynamic that increases inequality? If we did not have to exhibit "ambition" in order to be acceptable, would we not be more relaxed and happier and healthier? Would we not be able to increase "good living" among our neighbors and enjoy doing so?

Most of us have had enough experience to know that cooperation in creative enterprises is a great source of pleasure and fulfillment. We want to enjoy experiences together, not alone. We want to express our insights and feelings in a supportive community setting. We feel best when balancing giving and receiving. We like to work, to create or produce something good, and we like to offer our creation or product to others for their use or enjoyment. Well-being and happiness arise from such activities.

Cooperation and mutual care are absolutely required for human life. They are not optional, let alone idealistic. Competition takes place on the foundation of, and in the context of, the fundamental cooperation of the human group. Even the famous "selfish genes" are selected by evolution for their ability to cooperate with their most immediate environment, other genes. This gene pool is that of the entire breeding population, so we are into holistic considerations. That population survives insofar as it adapts to, fits in with, "cooperates" with all the other gene pools in its external environment. This says nothing about "intention"; it is simply a fact of mutual survivability.[15]

But as "intention" becomes possible, it enters into the behavior responses. In human society, mutual support makes survival possible, and even selfishly intended actions evolve, in repeated interactions and long-term associations, in the direction of cooperation and mutual friendliness. Reciprocity, as in Holy Communion rather than footwashing, is the key to the common prosperity of cooperating parties. When independently operating agents interact with one another repeatedly over a long (enough) term, cooperation tends to emerge, because it enables both or all parties to prosper. This is discovered by experience, coming about in a spontaneous way, not mandated by a central authority. This will happen even if we assume that all parties to the interaction behave in their own self-interest, without concern for the well-being of their partners. When the dynamic principles that lie behind the increased prosperity coming from cooperation have been understood, *intentional* cooperation can vastly enhance the well-being of all and thereby of each.

What is discovered is that if each party acts always only out of self-interest, there is a poor outcome for everybody. If one agent tries always being nice, regardless of how others behave, that agent will be exploited and will lose. But if each agent responds consistently by giving back in kind, partners to the interaction will gradually learn that the best way to gain a favorable outcome for themselves, over the long term, is to grant favors to those from whom they desire favors. This is reciprocity, and it can start from such a selfish basis and evolve toward an objectively mutually protective and supportive community. The name of this strategy is Tit-for-Tat, and it wins repeatedly in computer simulation contests. The basic condition for the strategy is that the parties will interact again and again, so that they have a stake in future interactions and so that they have sufficient opportunity to learn how others can be expected to behave.

Given that proviso, the four rules of the strategy are: (1) Avoid unnecessary conflict; cooperate as long as your partners do. (2) If another hurts you, respond in appropriate kind. (3) But then forgive, cooperate again. (4) Be consistent, so that the pattern of your behavior is clear and your future actions can be predicted. Robert Axelrod, who has been teaching this since 1984, claims that the computer simulations of repeated interactions show that cooperation can get started, even in a very selfish world, if there are small communities of interacting agents using reciprocity, even if they do not restrict their interactions to one another. Such reciprocity can thrive in an environment in which various other strategies are being used. And reciprocity cooperation, once established in a community, can robustly protect itself against invasion by less cooperative strategies.[16]

Charles Darwin said, "each man would soon learn from experience that if he aided his fellow-men, he would commonly receive aid in return. From this . . . he might acquire the habit of aiding his fellows; . . . [this] habit strengthens the feeling of sympathy, which gives the . . . impulse to [further] benevolent actions." In 1966, George Williams repeated this: "an individual who maximizes his friendships and minimizes his antagonisms will have an evolutionary advantage." In 1971, Robert Trivers developed this idea in "The Evolution of Reciprocal Altruism." Studied now by computer, with the aid of game theory, the evidence for this assertion is still growing.

Games are holistic systems in which various parties interact. An ecosystem or a trading community is such a system. All the players interact with one another and adjust their moves in the "game" according to what other players do. The question arises whether exploiting and cheating are not better strategies for "success" than cooperation and mutual care. Game theory shows that the answer depends on whether the parties will continue in their interaction over a long enough term for them to learn what to expect from one another. Human life is necessarily interactive and necessarily long-term. We will continue living together, interacting, and learning how our companions behave. For us, mutual care and cooperation are definitely better options.[17]

For us, as for all parties to long-term evolutionary systems, evolution is co-evolution. Our very biological background teaches us that all species that have ever evolved have co-evolved. Those that can't cooperate don't survive. Biologist Lynn Margulis points out that "greedy and bully" strategies that try to take advantage of their inter-acting partners are the worst performers. Ruthlessness doesn't pay; over time, cooperation grows and wins out. Bullies become extinct. Life isn't a "zero-sum" game, in which what one party wins another loses, the gain and the loss balancing to zero. In a non–zero-sum game, all parties either win together or lose together. This is the gist of the argument for ecological protection and social parity. A strategy that encourages positive feedback—rich get richer while the poor get poorer—is a strategy headed for disaster for everybody.[18]

Learning to Change: Redefining Success and Well-being

Fortunately, human nature is that nature that is especially capable of changing, of learning, of redesigning itself. We can so transform ourselves that we perceive whole new worlds in which our values rad-ically rearrange themselves. This is what the Holy Thursday Revolu-tion suggests we do. There is a world outlook that shows us a separated and insecure self, alienated ("othered") from the rest of the world and other people, frightening us and urging us to protect and advance ourselves by preferring ourselves to everyone and everything else. We have learned a Domination Paradigm.

In the Holy Thursday story we see this paradigm graphically dis-played (as footwashing) and radically rejected as the *dominus* (lord) washes the feet of the servants, inverting and thus abolishing the rela-tion. It is then replaced by a new paradigm, Friendship in Community, built on an alternative experience of selfhood as secure, affirming oth-ers, uniting with them in expressing neighbor-love, and thus forming friendship communities of caring and sharing. The shift in outlook is summed up in our attitude of saying to everything else in our experi-ence, "I no longer call you servants but friends" (John 15:15). It is equally graphically expressed in the action of feeding everyone, nur-turing everything, from our own lives.

Relations that we take for granted, assuming that they have no workable alternatives because they represent the "natural" order of things, are really relations and attitudes that we have *learned*. Our cultural institutions (nations, religions, schools, sports) and commu-nications media (news, advertising, entertainment) picture "natural" reality to us in their several ways, and we believe in it. We are por-trayed as divided, threatened, competitive, and seeking "success" by purchasing the means to exceed others.

Holy Thursday undertakes to show an alternative: We can experience ourselves as united, safe, cooperative, and finding a successful life by enhancing the well-being of others together with ourselves. The "revolution" consists in making a transition from the one view to the other. We can learn to do it if we want to do so, and the new paradigm will position us to deal effectively with the various ills in our lives by introducing different strategies and different structural dynamics into the systems by which we interact with one another and with the natural environment.

The first reaction, whenever any living arrangement is not working, is questioning the received paradigm. We try to locate the assumptions, the axioms from which the principles in play have been derived but which have now passed from direct consciousness. In the case of our question, the basic assumption is that human beings are always driven by self-interest, even when we seem to be doing something helpful for another. We can question this assumption; we can try denying it and see what the consequences are.

Herman Daly and John Cobb give us a start by saying, in their book *For the Common Good,*

> However much driven by self-interest, the market still depends absolutely on a community that shares such values as honesty, freedom, initiative, thrift, and other virtues whose authority will not long withstand the reduction to the level of personal tastes that is explicit in the positivistic, individualistic philosophy of value on which modern economic theory is based. If all value derives only from satisfaction of individual wants, then there is nothing left over on the basis of which self-interested, individualistic want satisfaction can be restrained. Depletion of moral capital may be more costly than depletion of physical capital. . . . The market does not accumulate moral capital; it depletes it. Consequently, the market depends on the community to regenerate moral capital.

Building on this, we read Timothy Gorringe, in *Fair Shares*: "the immense expense, effort and talent put into advertising suggests . . . that we are not really driven by self-interest and an insatiable desire for commodities after all, and that the growth economy succeeds only by a massive effort to reconstruct what it means to be human. . . . Advertising does not just sell us products, but . . . [its version of the desirable] human image." He quotes John O'Neil: "the economy teaches us to disvalue [our human image] in its natural state and to revalue it once it has been sold [the advertisers' version of desirability]." "Massive exploitation," O'Neil calls it, and Gorringe follows with: "The economy no longer exists to serve human needs, but human needs have to be distorted to serve the expanding market."

The point being made here is that all these values, attitudes, outlooks, and worldviews have been *taught* by our culture; we have *learned* them. They are not "natural," unavoidable, inescapable, divinely established. They can be questioned, and alternatives to them can be examined and tested. Part of our learning to do this concerns understanding how the dominative structures are composed and how they work. Daly and Cobb help again when they explain the differences between academic economics and ordinary housekeeping. The former, which studies and advises the large corporations that so dominate our economic life together now, seeks ways of manipulating property and wealth "so as to maximize short-term monetary exchange value to the owner." The latter, which characterizes management of a household, acts "to increase its use value to all members of the household over the long run."

There are three important differences: (1) Household economics looks to the long run rather than the short run. (2) It takes into account the costs and benefits to the whole community of any endeavor, not merely the benefit to the buyer/seller immediately involved. For instance, a new manufacturing firm comes to town, bringing new people and therefore increased business for all sorts of shops in the town as well as being a source of local employment; on the other hand, the cost is that the new plant discharges noxious wastes into the atmosphere and the local river. (3) Household economics focuses on "concrete use value" and "limited accumulation," rather than "abstract exchange value" with its "unlimited accumulation."

This last distinction is most interesting and helps us to understand something that can be quite deceptive. "Concrete use value" means that the value of the "product" is that you can actually use it. It's a refrigerator, or a service of nursing, or an education. When you have enough of it, you stop buying more. You don't accumulate refrigerators without end. "Abstract exchange value" means what you can sell it for, and the "it" in question may be a kind of entitlement to something that doesn't even exist yet. The party that buys "it" from you isn't interested in acquiring the goods in question, but only in selling "it" again at a higher price. Since the "price" thus becomes the "value," and although it is only the expectation of a future resale, that price is counted as your "wealth."

We are measuring wealth in terms of prices for possible resale, rather than in terms of the use-worth of a real product. The traffic based on prices in themselves and their changes becomes a "virtual" economy, distinguished from the "real" economy, which is exchange of actual concrete goods and services. There is no limit to the accumulation of this "virtual" wealth as long as the participating players believe in the value of what they are purchasing. This is a large part of the reason for the great gap between the rich and the poor, so we need to learn what it means and how it works. Then, if we propose to change these arrangements in some way, we must find not only a new arrangement that people can live by—that meets the needs of people for basic necessities of life, plus social dignity, education, opportunity for creative expression, and other values—but we must find a safe way to move gently from one practice to the other.

It is often argued by professional economists that maximizing short-term monetary exchange leads to the people as a whole gaining from this manipulation. The argument is that "rational self-interest" brings this general welfare about in a spontaneous way, without any need to cultivate concern for people in terms of justice values or caring or loyalty. The market reduces "the need for compassion, patriotism, brotherly love, and cultural solidarity as motivating forces behind social improvement." If our own experience and observation, plus the news from abroad, make us doubt that this is the best way to bring about the well-being of humans, then we need to learn how to find a better way. We have learned the market way, how to do it, how to believe in it. We can learn how to adjust it, modify it, change it, if we believe such efforts would be better for human beings. The Holy Thursday argument is that all economic activity is for the sake of people—all the people—*people* are the bottom line.[19]

Michael Lerner calls on us to acknowledge that our fundamental human needs are for personal connection, for recognition of our humanity in common, for meaning in life, and for celebration of ethical and spiritual values in community, so that we empower one another to build societies that manifest people's highest ideals. We need to *unlearn* the cynicism that has lulled us into spiritual unconsciousness and the belief that self-interest is the only true reality. The power for new learning is within us, renewal forces that testify to the possibility of transformation, rooted in intense realization of the spiritual Ground of all existence.

Jeff Gates, who has made some specific proposals for taking first steps toward such a transformation (see Part IV below), brings up another basic human need that "the market" overlooks: the opportunity—and the resources—to give to others. "People *want* to give to each other—to their spouses, their children, to others in their community." But our economic arrangements are such that we have to keep running faster and faster just to keep up. People "cannot afford to give either of their time or their money," and that "not only erodes marriages, families, and the bonds that comprise community; it also eats away at one's sense of self-worth, reinforcing feelings of inadequacy, isolation, alienation and impotence." People "can no longer afford to create . . . cannot afford to spend more time on relationships." They are so insecure in the present that they cannot give proper attention to the long-term future. The household is being forced to be as short-sighted as the market.

Gates, like Lerner, also issues a prophetic call,

> a call to the financial leaders of this finance-dominant era to devise ways to finance the future in such a way that a steadily broadening base . . . can afford to participate in what has long been hailed as the uniquely "human work" . . . : caring for others, literature, music, the arts, politics, spiritual practices, raising children. . . . The very human need for such participation, for a sense of being in community, is a primary theme underlying this work.[20]

Voices such as these—and there are many more—indicate that we need to reassess our sense of *success:* How shall we define and describe, image and feel about "the good life"? What should we strive for, admire, feel content with? Shall we reduce everything to money? Or, perhaps deeper yet, to social status? To comparison and exceeding? Does our "feeling good" really depend on our assurance that others are not so well off as ourselves? If we come to recognize that *we have been taught* to have such ideas and judgments and feelings, does the resolve arise in us to investigate whether we have been taught correctly? Perhaps there are other views. Perhaps this is not the deepest truth. Perhaps something has been concealed or somehow remained hidden from our sight. Following on this wondering and doubt, does a desire arise to liberate ourselves from such conditioning and seek out our truth for ourselves, looking to find a deeper, more secure happiness in human life?

The Holy Thursday imagery—one-sided footwashing vs. mutual

feeding—intends to provoke such doubt and such insight: we really prefer and long for the communion way of life, giving and receiving in equality, rather than the alleged satisfaction of belonging to the class waited on by servants. I have urged here that we have not given "human nature" its full due; we have sold it short under the pretense of being "realistic," not taken in by sentimental values. Actually, human nature is far more powerful—full of potentiality—and open and drawn to creative growth than our present images of ourselves show. We are right to want something unlimited, but it's not a list of priced "securities" (not truly "secure" at all). It's something about ourselves, about being *persons,* about having a share of creativity, wisdom, and love.

In the next chapters I will try to awaken realization that we deeply want freedom from the Domination Paradigm and entrance into the Communion Paradigm. I will use the biblical story of the escape from Egypt, the revelation at Sinai, and the giving of the Torah as guidance to the Promised Land to dramatize this idea of the paradigm shift. It will also be described again as a "phase transition," for which the Jesus-led covenant-renewal movement to "implement" the Torah will offer some detailing. Then we will focus on the transformation in consciousness that lies at the root of all social regeneration in preparation for our final layout of life according to the Communion Paradigm.

9

Memes, Mysticism, and Phase Transitions

Having looked at the arguments against "changing human nature," and having looked at arguments in favor of making some such change, we can now study how to go about making changes. In this chapter we will consider the radicalness of the needed change: it touches our view of the goal of life, of what constitutes "success," and of who we are and the ground of our security. How such cultural concepts are formed and spread—our ideas about personal identity and success in life—will be studied under the heading of "memes," units of culture that are copied just as units of heredity, genes, are copied and thus spread. Then we will look at mysticism, which is where the radical changes have to take place. There we have to make clear what we do and do not mean by mysticism and then delve into how one avails oneself of its insights and realizations. Finally, I want to say something more about "phase transitions," a term coming to us from the physical sciences but susceptible of a wider application, I believe, just as "symbiosis" is. Generalizing the range of applicability of these terms can help us see how our human development is embedded in the broader cosmogenesis.

Changing the Whole System

Bernie Glassman Roshi, in *Bearing Witness*, talks about the perception/commitment attitudes of people who are open to witnessing grave social ills. He tells of visiting a city park in Zurich called the Letten, in which the government had set aside space, under guard, where drug addicts and their suppliers could meet in peace and safety. The idea was that this was one way of dealing with the problem. The government also supplied clean needles—sixteen thousand a day. The area was jammed with people, mostly already under the influence of the chemicals, drug dealers, and huge sums of money. This was very near the center of the city. Glassman says:

> The Letten was full of greed, anger, and ignorance. It was also a living metaphor of a society in denial, blaming those who were suffering, aiding and abetting the perpetrators, thriving financially on the proceeds from that suffering, taking no responsibility, simply looking away.

The experiment didn't last very long; too many foreigners came into the city, and the authorities closed the area. But the experience gave Glassman a concrete situation for showing different perceptions and responses that people can make to such a scene. One person may see only the suffering of the drug users and will set up a drug rehab program. Another may see the suffering of the dealers as well—which perhaps they don't themselves perceive clearly—and try to arrange for them to enter other lines of work. But what Glassman is after is someone who can bear witness "to the entire system, from the users to the dealers to the banks to the businesses to the citizens to the government that carefully supervises such a system." Such a witness "will see how money from drugs permeates the economic and social life of the city and the world." What will this witness do in response? Someone who perceives the whole connection "will try to change the entire system." That's the point. That is what we are looking at: you can't change just one piece of it, because it's all interconnected. We have to consider changing the entire system.[1]

The thesis of the Holy Thursday Revolution says that Jesus was/is such a witness, that the Jesus/kingdom/covenant community program is such a program for change, and that we still confront such issues as he confronted and can still try to apply the (general) remedies that Jesus and his program proposed. Whether you read him as historical or mythic doesn't matter for this purpose; his story means the same values, the same social attitudes, the same radically mystical way of shifting perception and commitment to the point where we can make some concrete changes to relieve human ill. Both ill done and ill suffered.

It is part of the perception of the interconnections of the system that the ill-doers are trapped as well as the ill-sufferers. The remedy sought must intend to liberate and heal both. The underlying paradigm of perceptions, beliefs, values, and directed energies entangles all parties in its circulating dynamic. In its most general form, this is the Domination Paradigm. Alfonso Montuori and Isabella Conti, in *From*

Power to Partnership, quote psychologist Stanley Krippner saying, "Societies, like people, can change their myths, but it requires considerable effort, because social myths are the result of so many different influences over the years. It usually takes a catastrophe."[2] The Holy Thursday Revolution is an attempt to shift the paradigm without a catastrophe. Catastrophe is to be replaced by mystical insight and moral conversion, but it is no less radical a transformation. Myth changing is a very big and very fundamental change, but understanding can help a great deal. This is why we need to study memes, which are, in a way, atoms and molecular bonds of myths.

Edward O. Wilson, in *Consilience,* quotes George Scialabba, who asks: "For those who believe that neither God nor natural law nor transcendent Reason exists, and who recognize the varied and subtle ways in which material interest—power—has corrupted, even constituted, every previous morality, how is one to live, to what values can one hold fast?"[3] Behind the Holy Thursday event in the Jesus story lies the baptism, the mystical realization—seeing into one's own nature, as the Buddhists put it—that makes the rest of the program possible and feasible.

This insight is what gives us the values to which we can hold fast and by which we can live. It is a matter not of "believing" but of direct vision and experience, like the intellectual perception of first principles or "seeing" that a conclusion logically follows from premises. As for being corrupted by "power," part of the insight is that the concept of "power" —social power or "power over"—has to go. It doesn't just transfer to another party or take another form; it disappears. The "entire system" shifts at the level of its deepest principles.

Our problems and their solutions are rooted in something deeper than government and science, says Michael Lerner. It's in the whole way society approaches reality. There's a hunger for meaning that's not being met.

> [There's a] contradiction between our form of life and the glimmers of a fuller way of being, rooted in a deeper understanding of our role as expressions of the ultimate moral and spiritual realities of the universe . . . a yearning to be more fully an expression of God . . . of [that Ultimate Reality] that is compassionate and caring and loving . . . [and] that makes for the possibility of the transformation of that which is to that which ought to be [and which reveals] to us and through us dimensions of its Being.[4]

Looking at our present mentality in terms of memes, we have internalized the memes of the market: all people are self-interested, committed to maximizing their own benefit, gaining their own advantage, and seeing others in terms of what they can get from them. But if we're really *not* like that, if that's where the contradiction is, where the meaning isn't coming through, then human life can't be reduced to a market and the way is open to admitting other motives and measures. The memes are strong, and there is, as Robert Kuttner asserts, a "fundamentalism in the market conception of society and human nature." It behaves like other fundamentalisms, punishing dissenters who don't believe properly in the model. "The purists insist that politics, family life, law, and even . . . charity can be understood as variants on markets." And "a dissenter who calls into question one fundamental aspect of the model threatens the entire edifice." The memes are an interconnecting system. It's the whole system that's at stake.[5]

If we're looking at the possibility of finding meaning by changing the whole system, what is it that has to change? This idea of self-interest. Although people often act in terms of it, we also feel that we don't want self-interest to be the prime value in our lives. We want a believable and workable way to build our lives around something deeper, bigger, more than just ourselves in our selfishness. We want to be free to care about others, give to others, relax our efforts to "get ahead," "maximize," have more and more; we want to be able to enjoy and trust in the community, protecting and enhancing others as they protect and enhance us.

If we really want that, why can't we have that? We can have that, but we will have to pull together to get it. It's a community value and meaning, and we will have to act in concert as a community to gain it. But it can be done. We need first to understand how the memes work, how they can trap us, and then practice our way into the mystical realization of true selfhood. Insofar as we stand in a freer place because of our practice, we will begin to create new memes and copy them in our communities, and the new paradigm—the "kingdom of God," if you like, or the Messianic Era—will gradually come into being. The gradualness will be a "phase transition," which we will also understand and be able to develop.

The Methods of Memes

To begin to see how the memes function in human culture, let us consider two related notions of importance to our whole topic: success and the goal of life. Do we want to be successful? If so, what do we mean by "success"? How did we come by that meaning? Did we learn it in our family, at school, from public media, from companions? In American culture, can we have a concept of success that does not equate to, or at least significantly involve, money? If not, why not? What happens to us if we do not define success as money? Will our companions think us peculiar, ridicule us, be suspicious of us? Will employers be unwilling to engage us? professional training schools reluctant to invest in us? Will we be imaged as unsound, "flakey"?

However you answered these questions, you begin to see how the memes work. You pick memes up from your social environment; they are constantly reinforced by social institutions; and it is socially dangerous to go against them. Some memes are more important then others. Not everyone has to be keen on golf or baseball. Liking classical music may be either advantageous or disadvantageous, depending on the social milieu. Hairstyle can be critical, however, determining your social status at first glance, before anything else is known about you. These are the powers of memes.

Memes are units of culture that are *copied* in a social world and can be used to classify, grade, and value the members of that world. Basic value memes are vitally important; in some social settings they can be literally matters of life or death.

If we're to speak of life and death, shouldn't we declare life itself, its preservation in health and happiness, the fundamental meme? You would think so, and in many situations that is true. For instance, the memetics analysts have found that *danger* is a prime dimension for memes. If you attach a new meme that you are trying to get copied to a threat of danger, you will catch the public's attention. The enemy will have more missiles than you, the foreigners will take away your jobs, you will be socially rejected unless you use our cosmetics, you will go to hell unless you believe our religion, you will be suspected of subversion if your political views are too far off center, etc., etc. This is one powerful way that the memes work.

On the other hand, if we suggest that life itself is the prime value, good health more important than riches, happiness in the home more important than high rank at work, satisfaction in developing your particular skills more important than winning prizes, then things become rather ambiguous. Popular memes urge us to do many things that are injurious to our (and others') health, happiness, satisfaction, and peace. We are often not brave enough to adhere to the prime value but follow popularity to injury. Perhaps *popularity* itself is more important yet—doing what "everyone else" does, not being different, not standing out from the crowd. How do we sort and measure our memes? Are we even aware of how the meme environment is manipulating us?

There are *method* memes as well as substance memes. Popularity is an example of a method meme that says "be alike." But the values of the danger situations listed above depend on the *comparison* method. Its meme is "be more." In general, our success meme is guided by this method meme. This is why we do not usually define success in terms of meeting our desires and being satisfied with good health, happy homes, our gifts in practice. The overriding method meme requires the value to be compared with our neighbor's and to be "more." More than the other's and always more. *Growth* is a strong meme in this culture. Together, these two method memes say to us: Be like everyone else in wanting to have and be more than your neighbor and more than you had yesterday.

Insofar as this meme is in place, it can come into sharp conflict with the meme of valuing human life, health, and happiness. Constant growth of an economy, a company, a corporation, its "market share," the price of its stock may dictate that the values of others' lives, health, happiness can be appropriately neglected. We detailed this sort of thing in the first chapter. In America "success" is built around share price; in Japan it has been built around employee well-being. These are basic memes that determine the more particular ones derived from them.

Can we change our substance memes and even our method memes? Robert Axelrod and Michael Cohen, in *Harnessing Complexity*, suggest a way of shifting a substance meme by using an existing method meme. People want to excel, to surpass their peers. Let some wealthy and celebrated people come together and offer a prize to the corporation that shows the most concern for the well-being of its employees, one for protection of the environment, one for high-quality products, and so on. Like Oscars for movies. It should be done with a maximum of publicity and celebration. Perhaps this would get all corporations to start practicing these virtues. Perhaps we would have shifted the definition of "success" a little.[6]

The meme of success is one example of how the memes work in society. It can be quite instructive to trace out the various methods that characterize copying of memes. Aaron Lynch, in *Thought Contagion: How Belief Spreads Through Society*, outlines the methods clearly. I'll sketch them briefly. The first way to copy memes is by teaching them to your children—and having a lot of children. The meme system that wants to spread, therefore, should include as part of its program the injunction to have large and stable families. Don't divorce and don't use contraceptives. This is the mode called "quantity parental."

There is also "efficiency parental," which suggests that the family be very close-knit and that children marry within the belief system. Members of the system should be sharply defined and differentiated from members of other systems, and members of the given system should exclude members of other systems. This can apply to religions, nationalities, political organizations, economic systems, and other classes and castes, as well as ethnic groups and sometimes professions. The "children" do not have to be biological children only but can be converts or new members or apprentices or other carriers of a lineage.

The next mode is "proselytic," meaning that the system has built into it the injunction to bring in new members, to pass the meme on, to influence others to copy it. Try to spread democracy, capitalism, free trade, and the American way of life. There are various ways of making entrance into the system attractive. Rewards can be offered, and disadvantages of not taking up the offer can be pointed out. Once committed to the meme system, a member must not drop out. The "preservational" mode makes staying with the meme mandatory and presents dire threats to apostates. This happens in the political, business, and academic worlds, as well as religious ones.

If there are alternatives to the given meme system, then the system can tell its members that they are "right," the "best," the "favored" ones, the wave of the future, more enlightened, and so on. They can be compared with the opposition by using the "adversative" mode: show the others to their disadvantage, try to sabotage their programs, frighten their adherents with propaganda and outright hostility.

Switching from emotional to "cognitive" mode, the system can bring out arguments in favor of its positions, persuasive discourses, appeals to common sense and/or special intelligence. If, in fact, the system does have good arguments, this can be quite effective. Of course, what appears to potential copiers to be good cognitive arguments will depend on all the other cognitive items already in that society. Finally, the "motivational" mode will affect the meme system's copying success. If people find that they are "better off" in ways that matter to them (for which they already have memes), then they will tend to copy the system's memes. For instance, our old friend "popularity" can be a great motivator. The more people sign on to a given meme, the greater the likelihood that other people will too. Don't be different, do what everybody else does.[7]

The Holy Thursday Revolution, of course, intends to be a meme changer. In particular, it targets foundational memes and method memes, such as "self-interest," "comparison," and "maximization of profit." Its memes cluster around a new sense of self and the goal of life. It hears the force of the question, What do economists economize? and recognizes the answer: Caring for people. That's where the "economy" is, where we cut and minimize and neglect. Cheap labor and no regulation on healthful working conditions make for larger profit margins. Holy Thursday's images invert this attitude: people first, profit margin last. "The last shall be first."

When we put profit that far ahead of people, we have, as Frank Lloyd Wright said long ago, "lost sight of the true aim of human existence." We have accepted "not only substitute means but substitute aims and ends." When this happens to us, when we buy into that set of memes, we may live to regret it as "Morrie" did in *Tuesdays with Morrie*: "I traded lots of dreams for a bigger paycheck, and I never even realized I was doing it." As Michael Lerner says plainly, "The goal of the economy should be to help produce and sustain human beings" who are nurtured to realize their highest personal and creative potentials. This means they have to have their basic life needs met first. "If our goal is to provide . . . good living for people," says David Korten, then we need to rearrange all sorts of things. He makes a radical suggestion:

> An important part of the demand for economic growth comes from the carefully cultivated myth [meme system] that the only way we can keep people employed is to expand aggregate consumption to create jobs at a rate faster than corporations invest in labor-saving technology to eliminate them. We neglect an important alternative—*to redefine the problem* and concentrate on creating livelihoods rather than jobs. . . . A job is a source of money. A livelihood is a means of living. [Italics added.][8]

The goal of life, the meaning of life, the real thing, not a substitute, needs to come to the forefront of our individual and collective lives. The meme systems need to be seen for what they are. We need to identify and consider our memes, especially the most general, the method memes. The thesis of Holy Thursday includes the assertion that our meme of *comparison*, the belief that the only way to give value to something is by its being "more than" something else, is defective. There is an alternative, adumbrated in the above remarks. Until we can find the meaning of life in the Absolute, in what cannot be compared, which is not "better than," "more than," or even "deeper than," but simply *is* in its own right and glory, we will continue to be restless with an Augustinian restlessness and will continue to try to satisfy it with our puny "more thans."

We can live a meaningful human life by realizing its rootedness in incomparability, the value that is in Being itself, being a value in itself, not valued by comparison with others. Not a value that dominates but a value that communicates. The discovery of this incomparability, our rootedness in it, our own incomparability and that of everyone else, is what I mean by "mysticism." It is this discovery that enables us to make the turn from the logic of identity by mutual negation to the logic of identity by mutual affirmation. This turn constitutes the "Revolution," the transition from the Domination Paradigm to the Communion Paradigm.

Mysticism without Mist

People are always worried about my use of the word "mysticism." They're afraid it will be mistaken for New Age occultism, or supernatural or preternatural interests, or some sort of spookiness in general. I, for my part, hold that I have a right to use a word in its original and proper meaning and, strictly speaking, should not have to justify or account for it. However! Etymologically, "mysticism" is one of those things that the Greeks had a word for, and the word was *mystērion*, from *myein*, to be closed, as of eyes or lips, or to initiate into sacred rites and doctrines. In Greek philosophical religion, it came to mean a truth that was seen with closed eyes and told through closed lips. In other words, something that transcends finite objects and particular ideas. The seeing, therefore, and the expressing—the movement toward and the movement out from—imply *union* with that ultimate reality, and that is the critical note in the definition. The dictionary says, "the experience of direct communication with ultimate reality."

In metaphysics, this would be the Ground of Being, or Being Itself. This all-inclusive Reality, which has no environment, no opposite, no alternative, which is "One without a second," must be of the nature of *subject* rather than object. If it could be approached and apprehended as an object, there would be a "second" to it, the subject doing the approaching and apprehending. So it is known from the outset that it must be apprehended as a Subject, therefore "known" from the inside, in its subjectivity, that is, by subjective union. You cannot "look at" it, you can only realize your own "location in" it. This is where we need to make our turn, the moment of change in the revolution.

In tracing the origin of human ill, I argued that we tried to deal with the world in terms of domination because psychologically we were possessed by fear that we did not have a secure hold on being, on existence itself and on all those things that we felt held us in existence, food, mates, power over the environment, and power over other people. This sense of insecurity was further traced to our perception of our position in existence as isolated and alienated, "othered" from everything else, and therefore essentially at risk. The self that was at risk was experienced as defining itself by this "otherness," by being what the "other" was not, by not being what the other was. Mutual negation.

This perception of selfhood is just the opposite of the sense of selfhood indicated by what was said about "mysticism" above. "Otherness" is replaced there by *union*, being "outside" by being "inside." If we can come to a genuine realization—not just the abstract concept—of being in union with Ultimate Reality, we can turn this whole thing around. That is the thesis of the Holy Thursday Revolution. If we are grounded in ultimate security, we will escape the existential fear of not having a reliable hold on Being and therefore having to do all we can to grasp the means of being, against all the rest of the world, if need be.

How do we go about doing this? Basically by seeking the self that is not contingent on various conditions in its environment, where "environment" includes one's body, history, personality, social relationships, and beliefs. To say that these are the environment of the self is to say right away that they are not the self itself, although they are the media through which the self expresses itself in the world. This is, of course, the key to gaining the security that will enable us to free ourselves sufficiently from self-protection and advancement that we can engage in neighbor-protection and advancement. Our present bondage is a result of our confusing the self with this intimate environment and believing that we are contingent on favorable conditions in those areas.

This is the general method found in all spiritual traditions, whether theistic or not. Buddhism, which is not theistic, is perhaps the most successful of them all, for it addresses itself directly to this problem without involving any myths, dogmas, or theories. However, mystical insight is attained in all major traditions, often with the help of scriptural teachings, stories, theologies, and devotion to personal religious figures, though these are usually transcended in the end.

That the self is not identical with this intimate environment is shown by the fact that the human being is characterized by its urgent questioning about the self, by the sense of not knowing who one truly is and what one is ultimately "for." It is, says Hazel Henderson, "the oldest puzzle of our species: Who is the 'I' that is studying and judging all this? Every great religion and spiritual tradition has posed this question—through meditation . . . prayer . . . contemplation [directing attention to] this profoundly beautiful mystery of . . . [our] ever-expanding awareness [inhabiting briefly a] miraculous physical body."[9]

The investigation of the self beyond the intimate environment is not an easy task. It usually begins with moral virtues and psychological practices, carefulness about our actions and our attitudes, with the intention of freeing ourselves from the obsession with our own insecurity in being, broadening our concern to others. Gradually, our questioning of why we desire and fear as we do goes deeper: We desire this because it will give *that*. But why do we desire *that*? If we repeat the question until no further answer can be given, this will bring us to the existential confrontation with our faith in our finitude. We believe that we are finite, nothing but finite. And we do not want to be nothing but finite. We have some sort of sense of going beyond our finitude, and yet we identify with the sum of our finitudes. This is the root of insecurity and falsehood. We have to have some participation in the infinite, else we could not conceive of it, desire it, have an exigency for it, a tropism toward it. The drive to the infinite is already embedded in our finitude itself.

Where is this drive coming from? Who is it that experiences this desire? Who has this desire to be free from finite desires since they clearly do not deliver freedom from want, fear, and insecurity? At this stage of the investigation we already know, as Eknath Easwaran spells out, that "as long as we are subject to . . . the expectation of getting money, prizes, prestige, or power . . . we . . . have no access to the deeper capacities in our consciousness." Up to the point of realization of our noncontingent self, we are not really alive. We are more like puppets pulled by forces outside our true self, or like corks on the sea. We are obliged to run after pleasure, prestige, and power and to attack whatever threatens these or our self-will. We have enough insight at this point to know that only when we are free from these forces can we begin to live an *authentic* life, one that is our *own* life. Our eyes are open enough to see that material possessions, social status, even supreme power, are not It, not ultimate at all. We have only scratched the surface of our capacity for consciousness and creativity.

Now we come closer to realizing our self as subjectivity, that is, as the witness and the agent, the one who experiences, and the one who originates action. We "sit with" the desire for the beyond; we become one with the drive for the root of Being. This has to be a real experience, not something read about or thought about. The doubt about whether we have a secure root, where it is, what is our reality, what is our meaning, has to become Doubt with a capital D, a consuming quest. This cannot be done by spending an hour a week evidencing our loyalty to our particular religion.

This has to become our overriding concern, what we are in search of in everything that we do. It is not another thing that we do besides our regular activities. It is the whole of what we do, however we do it. There is sitting-practice, when we do nothing but search within, and there is work-practice, when we try to act from the deepest and truest place in ourselves that we have yet found. The two practices help each other. Both of them show us that *we* are not the ego, not the constructed social self, the self that feels the insecurities and tries to protect/advance itself. We can now see ourselves doing that still, but we are alert to the fact that we can *see* it, which proves that the seer is not the seen. We are coming closer to the real subject.

Alongside these practices, we work on disengaging from our socially constructed self-image. Looking at the image helps us see that *we* are not that image. A useful exercise is to make a list of all the predicates that we believe describe ourselves: I am a man/woman, of such a race, nationality, religion; with such a bodily appearance, with these abilities/disabilities, age, other particularities; with such a personality type, family, history, relationships; I do such a work with such success; I have such tastes, interests, opinions, principles; I have such desires, yearnings, aspirations, beliefs, convictions.

The aim of the exercise is to see if you can still experience yourself *being*, experience your *self* being, as these descriptions are gradually removed. Some of them are easier to disconnect from than others. Start with the easy ones. Do the exercise existentially, not theoretically. Not as something outside you but as something you experience yourself as *being*. Feel, coincide with, yourself as being one of these descriptions. Then try altering the description: I'm short, I imagine myself tall. Did the deep inside sense of self change? Am I still I whether short or tall? *Be* the inner self that is independent of shortness or tallness.

It's this awareness of the *independence* that we're after. Notice the independence, not being trapped, limited by the description. Notice the *awareness* of the independence. Notice the *capacity* for being aware of independence. *Be* the one who is aware of being free of identification with/by the description. As Witness, know it; as Agent, *be* it. You, the Subject, are that Witness, that Agent.

Years will pass in the earnest quest for freedom through these practices. Along the way we will begin to marvel that we let ourselves build our lives around the belief that we, the real self, were identified with these various descriptions, which descriptions required so much protection, justification, grief, anger, fear, pride, and so on. So much vital *energy.* We exhaust ourselves in the support of our descriptions. And with that breakthrough about our own lives will come compassion for others. They're going through the same thing! All this effort, all this suffering! They're feeling inside the same things I feel. But it's all unnecessary! That's not who we really are. Let us meet one another in the peace and freedom of this insight.

The more we disengage from the belief that we are our descriptions and are obliged to protect, sustain, and enhance them, the closer we come to the experienced sense (as distinguished from a theoretical "sense") of the noncontingent and incomparable. Antoine de Saint-Exupéry said in *Wind, Sand, and Stars,* "In anything at all, perfection is finally attained not when there is no longer anything to add, but when there is no longer anything to take away, when a body has been stripped down to its nakedness." The "naked self" that the mystics so often speak of is what is liberated when we have escaped identification with all the descriptions. The naked self is not specified by its relation to an environment or to an opposite, not any more than the Ground of Being is. Neither has any particular predicates. Only I AM can be said.[10]

The Noncontingent, Secure Self

Now we are at the heart of the issue of security, which, according to our thesis, is at the heart of all our troubles. There are two kinds of security: essence-security and existence-security. When we identify with our descriptions, we try to find our security in them, in *what* we are, our "essence." We may try to change our description to that of something more valued in our society, or we may try to make our description more appreciated. We may take refuge in the community of those who share our description—this is the usual way. But the descriptive self, the list of "whats" that we are, is fragile by nature, vulnerable, contingent. This is why we feel so insecure when we identify with it. If this is all that we are, then we really do have a very poor hold on Being.

On the other hand, there is the naked I AM self that we have just discovered. No descriptions at all. No essence. Just existence. Unlimited Existence. Not contingent. This is our participation in the Ground of Being, in Absolute Existence, in the Infinite and the Eternal. This is where security is truly lodged. The Gospel of Matthew (5:19-21) expresses it this way:

> Do not store up for yourselves treasures on earth, where moth and rust consume and where thieves break in and steal; but store up for yourselves treasures in heaven, where neither moth nor rust consumes and where thieves do not break in and steal. For where your treasure is, there your heart will be also.

The "heart" is our sense of centeredness, self-ness, and our energy of valuing. If we center ourselves in and value what is vulnerable by nature, we will always be insecure, anxious, and struggling to protect and advance ourselves. If we center ourselves in and find our value in what is by nature invulnerable, we cannot be insecure. The difference shows in this snippet from Rachel Remen's beautiful book, *My Grandfather's Blessings*:

> My family of . . . professionals were always struggling to learn more and to be more. It seemed there was always more. . . . It was never enough. If I brought home a 98 on a test from school, my father would ask, "And what happened to the other two points?" I pursued those two points relentlessly throughout my childhood. But my grandfather did not care about such things. For him, I was already enough. And somehow when I was with him, I knew with absolute certainty that this was so.

"Already enough" and "absolute certainty" are the experiences I want to highlight here. They speak of the naked selfhood of the mystic and the mystic's existential security. Remen acknowledges that "we may have to [travel] a long hard road to get to the place where we can remember once again who we are . . . this place beyond competition and struggle, this place where we belong to one another."

In the Jewish tradition, the Source of Being beyond all names is sometimes referred to as The Place, and we are encouraged to mark our memories of the occasions when we knew ourselves to be in The Place. In the Book of Exodus, God says, "Build altars in the places where I have reminded you who I am" (Exod. 20:24), and "The altar shall be most holy; whatever touches the altar shall become holy" (Exod. 29:37b). Whatever connects us to the remembrance of the Eternal and of our own embeddedness in the Eternal is holy. Remen reports a prayer recited by one of the participants in a physicians' seminar:

> Days pass and the years vanish and we walk sightless among miracles. Lord, fill our eyes with seeing and our minds with knowing. Let there be moments when your Presence, like lightning, illumines the darkness in which we walk. Help us to see, wherever we gaze, that the bush burns, unconsumed. And we, clay touched by God, will reach out for holiness and exclaim in wonder, "How filled with awe is this place and we did not know it."

The awesome place, the mystics tell us, is the depth of our own reality. It is not elsewhere, it is right here. All of us, as Easwaran says, are "full of dazzling beauty waiting to reveal itself," if only we can wake up to its presence and power. Taking refuge in the Buddha, says Tibetan Buddhist Gelek Rinpoche, does not mean going outside of oneself to find the Buddha, but rather going within, to "that place" in everyone which is a "buddha seed," the capacity to realize ourselves as enlightened. Christian teacher Meister Eckhart also calls it "God-seed": "The seed of God is in us." If we tend it with intelligence and diligence, it will "grow up to God, whose seed it is; and accordingly its fruits will be God-nature. Pear seeds grow into pear trees, nut seeds into nut trees, and God-seed into God."

We are seeing some maturation of the God-seed, the buddha seed, the inward beauty, the awesome place, when we are no longer concentrating on trying to get rid of our insecurity. This can happen by believing that you have been given adequate security, or that you have gained the security, or that you have discovered that you always had it. Christians speak of "being saved." How do you know when you're "saved"? Perhaps we may give one meaning: You're saved when you are sufficiently convinced of your own security to be able to reach out to others with compassion and nurturance. "We know that we have passed from death to life because we love each other" (1 John 3:14).[11]

Instructions on how to practice meditation are readily available in all traditions. An easy Christian practice being made popular by Trappist monks Basil Pennington and Thomas Keating is called "Centering Prayer." One chooses a sacred word to use to recall the wandering mind, then one sits attentively and "centers" oneself in the presence of God, comfortably, effortlessly, safely, as being at home. There is no striving, only full attention, awareness of the reality of God and of one's own act of living in God. There is a sense of peace, of being at the foundation of Being, of happiness, of enjoyment, of being one's true self, of satisfaction. If the mind wanders, then one repeats the prepared sacred word to recall it and again focus intentionally.

The method taught by John Main and by his successor, Laurence Freeman, in Christian Contemplation is similar: a mantram word is given and is repeated by the meditator throughout the practice period. St. Francis of Assisi used a practice like this, repeating *"Deus meus et omnia,"* "My God and everything." Sometimes the mantram is fitted to the breath, part on the inbreath and the rest on the outbreath. Hindu meditation practices usually include a mantram repetition at an early stage of spiritual training. Zen training with koans sometimes sharpens to the repetition of a single significant word.

These are all devices to focus the attention and the intention, to come to a consciousness-shifting, self-awareness-shifting realization. It is important in any practice not to sacralize the means to the point of forgetting the end. I am focusing on meditation's role in bringing us to such a sense of selfhood that we can be freed from the Domination Paradigm sufficiently to enter into the Communion Paradigm. I am looking for the kind of effect Bernie Glassman speaks of when he says:

> When we meditate, we begin to see the self-sufficiency of our own mind. We don't need to add all sorts of things. We don't need to build ourselves up. We don't even need to "improve" ourselves because we have everything we need right now.[12]

The object is to bring us to a vivid sense of ourselves as transcendent of all our descriptions and as satisfactorily secure in ourselves and keenly aware of our profound and multitudinous interconnections with all other beings. The individual self, although fully valuable in itself, uniquely and irreplaceably precious, is not *separated* from others but rather intimately entwined with all these other uniquely precious beings. This is the point about our selfhood being established not by mutual negation but by mutual affirmation and even indwelling. Meditation-practice, complemented by work-practice, is intended to bring us to such an experience of *being* this way that we always perceive and act from such a position as the real, natural, and normal position.

The Fiat and the Phases

Meditation practice brings us to self-discovery. It is important to repeat that this is not a matter of believing in a theory. It has to be an actual experience strong enough to reposition the general outlook of the person. When this is the case, a further discovery is made. The "name" of the discovered self, we may say, is I AM, one of the divine names because it is unqualified, unconditioned. And, I argued, because it is unconditioned, it needs no protection and no aggrandizement. If this is so, then all the energy—physical, emotional, intellectual, moral, spiritual—that was going into those efforts at protection and aggrandizement suddenly becomes available. It reminds me of $E = mc^2$. The apparently small mass becomes an enormous energy.

The further discovery is that this energy goes naturally into care for others. As soon as one discovers and says I AM, one says MAY YOU BE. It is the second divine name. I am calling it the "Fiat" here because of the Latin version of the creation story in which God says *"Fiat lux!"* "Let there be light!" These two divine names, divine utterances, are our central words with respect to Being. They are almost the same word, so close are they to one another.

Earlier I had explained the difference between *eros* and *agapē*, two Greek words for love. *Eros* seeks the good of the lover, and *agapē* seeks the good of the beloved. This MAY YOU BE is the expression of *agapē*. Like its companion, I AM, it is unconditional. Carl Rogers spoke of the healing power of "unconditional positive regard." This is in that line. It is unconditioned will to good being, which is more than just witnessing the other. It is a proactive enhancement of the other's being, the intention that the other should be, should exist, and should be an expression of transcendental unity, truth, goodness, and beauty. There is no limitation on the goodness that is willed.

When we stand in the Place of I AM and speak the Fiat, MAY YOU BE, we are using the logic of affirmation rather than of negation. Our being, our selfhood, is identified not by what it is not but by what it does. And this comes from the unconditionality. Just as we are not identified in our central selfhood by any description, any condition, so our act of Fiat is not conditional on the other displaying any particular description. Fiat is not a re-action to the other; it is a first action. It is "in the beginning." This is the attitudinal position on which the Holy Thursday Revolution is based.

So, the self is secure, the self is enlarged. Deep penetration into the self makes possible empathy with others, and this arouses compassion: the other is understood from the other's own viewpoint, and we care about the other as we care about ourselves. We are able to say, "I am in you, you are in me." If we say that human beings are created in the image of God, then we can say that it is through union with the other that that image appears. Speaking of God as Hashem (the Name), David Aaron says, "This is a very important concept. A lone individual does not reflect the image of Hashem. An individual in unity with an other does." Indeed, as Joseph Jaworski said, paraphrasing Mach's Principle and adjoining a possible implication of Bell's Theorem, "Everything in the universe affects everything else [Mach] because they are all part of the same unbroken whole [Bell]." And Michael Lerner points the moral: "It is our estrangement from the oneness of all being . . . that is the source of" all our ills.

Here we begin to move from speaking of the individual to speaking of the collective consciousness, the cultural consensus, the tacit agreements on the structure of reality and the values we ought to pursue. For the self-interest that we fingered as the culprit in our analysis of human ill characterizes the concept of our collective selfhood. Timothy Gorringe, in *Fair Shares,* gives many examples of how corporate and governmental practices have sought profit and price with "no regard . . . paid to the real needs of the countries concerned, but only to commercial self-interest." Looking at the aspiration to achieve social equality, Mickey Kaus says that something like a collective conversion is needed, the discovery/creation of "a basis in common, cross-class *values.*"

Jeff Gates turns to Alexis de Tocqueville, who suggested that "the remedy required" might be "the slow and quiet action of society upon itself." This means, says Gates, the whole array of public institutions in which people interact with one another and express their views and values, what gives "moral texture" to our "multilayered relationships. . . . Good citizenship and moral behavior emerge not by force but by a complex blend of persuasion and practice" that become our "habits of the heart." This gradual emergence into operating by a new set of principles is what I am calling a "phase transition."[13]

A phase transition effects a radical transformation but it does so gradually. The mystical realization takes time to develop fully. The memes have to spread. The application of the new insights to the multitude of practical affairs we want to transform has to be figured out, tested, adjusted. This is a *revolution* because it is deep, it affects basic principles and perspectives, but it is like *evolution* because it grows from within, adapting to real needs. Much of our present difficulty is that we are dealing not with real human and planetary needs but with artificial ones, such as fluctuating prices, social status, and misguided self-images. Understanding and transforming will take time and be a phase transition.

A phase transition begins in a system that is already in a certain "phase," that is, governed by certain principles, rules, laws that prescribe the behavior of its elements. Then it starts to change. What makes it change can be either something new coming from outside or something new emerging as a result of interactions taking place inside the system. An example of the former would be ice melting as energy comes into the system, and the water's phase change from solid to liquid; and an example of the latter would be the formation of a living cell from the interactions of different sorts of molecules. Usually there is a long gradual buildup in which the energy is accumulating or the molecules are developing their mutual catalytic relations. Then, at some point, things begin to move fairly fast. What is happening is that the elements of the system begin to operate according to a different set of principles or rules of behavior.

When ice melts, energy has been accumulating in it for a while, eighty calories of energy for every gram of frozen water. During this time the structure of the ice crystal doesn't yet change. Each water molecule holds its position in the lattice with the prescribed angles to its companions. But at some point, a molecule has gathered so much energy that it slips from its fixed position and begins to slide smoothly past the others. The others are also gathering energy, and one by one they begin to slide away. Soon the crystal structure is gone, and instead we have flowing liquid water. You can watch it dripping off the toe of a glacier or see the puddle widening around an ice cube on your kitchen counter. The rules have changed. Rigid fixed positions are gone and sliding while staying in touch is the order of the new phase.

The transition from simply chemical rules to biological rules is much more complicated, but the result is similar. What we recognize as "life" emerges from a sufficiently unified set of cyclical chemical behaviors in which the molecules abet one another's assembly. The nucleic acids and the proteins act as catalysts for each other, and the lipids of the enclosing membrane aid them by keeping them together with each other and with the raw materials for their mutual assembly. When the membrane closes, and there is a clear distinction between "inside" and "outside," the new phase has been entered, for a new level of entity has been formed that will henceforth relate to its peers as a whole body, a new unity formed of the interactions of its constituents, governed by new rules that had never existed before.

I have already pointed out that phase transitions are part of cosmic nature: changing the rules of operation happens. Therefore, such change is neither impossible nor unnatural. On the other hand, the great transitions, such as from physics to chemistry and from chemistry to life, and from life to consciousness, bring such newness and such increase of possibility and range of action and relation, that we might correctly call each succeeding phase "super-natural" with respect to its predecessor. It has transcended the limitations of the earlier phase.

So, making use of these analogies to make the desired points, I say that the Holy Thursday Revolution can come about as a phase transition in the natural way, as one more step in the cosmic sequence of transitions to greater complexity and consciousness, increasing unity and outreach, and can be "supernatural" with respect to the phase from which it emerges and which it replaces. This transition consists of two aspects: the individual, in which each consciousness awakens to a new awareness of its own nature, and the collective, in which these persons interact with one another in a symbiotic way to form an interpersonal community that advantages all participants. But this will not "just happen." We have to *do* it. The new community, the new phase, *consists of our actions*, our freely placed, understood, and intended actions arising from our awakened consciousness.

The slow buildup period is our practice of bringing ourselves to awakening to our deeper selfhood, our personhood beyond the vulnerable descriptions. It is accompanied already by efforts at expression in the collective order. Many failures are to be expected. We must not give up but must continue to learn, as all complex adaptive systems must. Look for the gradients, the trends, over long stretches of time, more like tens of thousands of years than like lifetimes or centuries, though some progress can show even on that scale. We must resist discouragement when there is a major setback just when we believed we were getting somewhere. Up and down, but gradually rising. And the more we can understand how the system works and how changes can come about, the faster the transition will go. Not that understanding alone will bring it about. There have to be deep transformations of perceptions, worldviews, attitudes, and motivations. It is a major effort, our greatest effort, to remake ourselves, to lift ourselves by our own insight and concerted action, to the next level of cosmic organization.

Michael Lerner relentlessly preaches the God who is the possibility and power of transformation, in whose image lies our own reality: the possibility of being radically transformed. This is what is meant by a *"living* God," who says such things as "Watch! We're going to make something new!" (Isa. 43:19). In this tradition, we are partners in all this making, all this newness. Divine transformative energy moves us to come out of our constricted views of ourselves and our world, "to transcend our alienated separateness and [join] in transforming reality."[14] This is the message of the story of Sinai, with its proclamation of liberation from the old paradigm and invitation to live by a new set of principles.

Story II

The Revelation at Sinai

A Phase Transition

The giving of the Torah at Mt. Sinai is the greatest moment in Jewish religious history. The Torah is the heart of Judaism. "God, the Torah, and the Jewish People are one" is a common saying. But what the Torah is, what the full significance of its "giving" is, and who "the Jewish People" are can be unpacked endlessly, because all comes from God, who is infinite.

The word *torah* means literally "instruction," or "teaching." (It is often referred to in English as the "law," but the word for the law is *halakah*.) In its expanded sense, Torah includes all Jewish teaching right up to the present moment. There is also a heavenly Torah, which God used in the beginning to create the world. Torah is always a general view, or pattern, or a kind of blueprint and set of principles for operating. Approaching our Torah, in particular the Five Books of Moses, writes Avigdor Bonchek, it is important to ask questions, to recognize difficulties, and to struggle with them; don't repress them and pretend you are making an act of faith. Neither should you think that there is only one correct way of reading:

> The Talmudic Sages taught that every passage of the Torah has seventy facets, perhaps a metaphorical number meant to reflect the seventy scholars of the *Sanhedrin*, whose job it was to interpret the Law. The number seventy would then mean that each mind interprets the Torah in its own way.[1]

The Many-Leveled Torah/Teaching

There is general agreement that interpretation of Torah rises through four main levels of understanding, called the "Garden of the

182

Torah." The word for "garden" is *Pardes* (from which we derive "paradise") and it is used as an acronym, PaRDeS, for *P'shat* (plain sense), *Remez* (literary allusions, allegories), *Drash* (homiletics), and *Sod* (mystical meaning).

It is important to say this clearly, because many people believe that there is only one right meaning to scripture, usually the literal level. If you reduce the Torah to that level, it would be easy to compile a better book, say the Jewish sages. But the Bible is much more mysterious than that. It is, so to speak, "disguised" in these stories, for "the world could not endure the Torah if she had not garbed herself in garments of this world. . . . Thus the tales related in the Torah are simply her outer garments, and woe to the man who regards that outer garb as the Torah itself. . . . People without understanding see only the narrations, the garment; those somewhat more penetrating see also the body. But the truly wise, those who serve the most high King and stood on Mount Sinai, pierce all the way through to the soul, to the true Torah which is the root principle of all. These same will in the future be vouchsafed to penetrate to the very soul of the soul of the Torah . . . the Ancient Holy One."

Thus, in the Torah, God is both concealed and revealed. God, after all, is not an object to be known from the outside. Just as we cannot know from any observation of someone's outside what the person is thinking or feeling, but must wait for the other to tell us, so the hidden reality of God has to be revealed to us by God alone, say the sages. The paths we are accustomed to using, they say, paths of emotion, reasoning, or acting, are all helpless before the Infinite. From these human operations only human conclusions follow. Knowledge of the supreme Spirit can come only from the Spirit, which transcends all things human. But because of God's self-revelation at Sinai, even ordinary earthly things become avenues of reaching the Divine and connecting with God according to God's own intention.[2]

But, the rabbis continue, we still have to open ourselves on successive levels to receive the revelation. "Lift up your heads, O you gates," says Psalm 24. The degree of Torah that one receives from God depends on how far one opens the gate—and how many gates one can open. Even the revealed aspect has a gate through which we must pass, and having passed, we will again encounter both revealed and concealed portions, gate after gate, more and more inward, until understanding is exhausted and only vision remains.[3]

There is always that in our souls that recognizes the Voice of God and awakens to it. Having been made by the Word of God spoken, we can never utterly forget it. Even in the worst of circumstances, we can remember when we hear it again. Indeed, "the Word of God is hidden inside each created thing and is the root of all existence," points out Moshe Braun. "When the Torah was given, [this] Word of God became revealed." The world is a mixture of good and evil, Rabbi Braun teaches, so that the good is often concealed behind the evil and the Word of God is hidden. But "at Mt. Sinai, . . . when God gave the Torah, . . . the inner reality became revealed. For an instant, the light of creation lit up the universe. Everything was clear." Just as there is Torah that comes into us from outside, so there is Torah that comes out of us from inside. There is hidden inside each of us "pure good . . . that is never defiled nor mixed with evil."[4]

What happened on Mt. Sinai was that God revealed not only the Torah of the outside but the Torah of the inside. The Voice of God spoke from the mountain and was heard and answered by the Voice of God with the people. In Deuteronomy, Moses reminds the people that "the Lord spoke with you face to face, out of the fire" (5:4). God is represented as coming down upon the mountain, and the people come as far up the mountain as they are allowed. In the tradition it is said that at Sinai the people had a mirror-face so that the Face of God was visible in it. It is also said that when God spoke out of the fire and the thunder and the dark cloud and the people recognized it, their souls rose up out of their bodies as they realized that their life is from heaven and not from earth at all. The Torah in the People responds to the Torah from the mountain.

When we follow the precepts of Torah, we transform them from potential to actual. We enable the Word of God to take flesh among us. We strengthen the Torah that God has implanted in our hearts and thus draw God on to continue to imbue our hearts with deeper and deeper levels of Torah.[5] But God is infinite and people are finite. How can they meet and commune? How can they dialogue and respond to one another? How can the people cross the sea on dry land? How can the bush burn and not be consumed? There is a story that accounts for this (retold by me, claiming midrash privilege to alter a bit):

From all eternity the radiance of God filled all space. But God grew lonely and wanted to create something. Where to put it? For the Divine Radiance was everywhere. So God constricted (*tzimtzum*) the Radiance; he drew some of it in and put it in clay jars, capped them, and put them on shelves in his pantry. Then there was a space in which something could be created. And God made the universe, all the stars in galaxies, many of them with planets, including the earth.

On the earth he made mountains and rivers, clouds and winds, butterflies and worms, hedgehogs, pansies, aardvarks, orchids—everything you can imagine (and many things you can't). And he had a wonderful time doing it! He was so pleased with it all. "How good it is!" he exclaimed.

But, meanwhile, back in the pantry, things were heating up. The Divine Radiance was not used to being shut up in jars with caps on. It was used to expanding, to spreading itself out everywhere, to shining and beaming. It strained and pressed against the clay jars, and at last they burst. The clay was broken into tiny fragments. These fell on the newly made earth and became the bodies of people. And the scintillae of the shattered Divine Radiance also fell onto the Earth and became the souls of people.

This is why God's people always recognize him, always love him spontaneously, can never be separated from him—because they have his own Radiance in themselves as a further soul. Besides the vegetative, the sensitive, and the rational souls, God's People have a part of God's own self within them.

This soul is called *neshamah*. According to the Hasidim (at least), "unlike the created beings in the various categories, the *neshamah* was not created," says Shmuel Boteach. "It is not a separately created entity that now apparently exists 'outside' the unity of God. Rather, it has always been part of God Himself." Like the flame of a candle taken from a torch, which lacks the intensity of the torch and is an "offspring" from it but nevertheless is itself also flame and fire, so the souls of God's people are not separate from God but are more like an extension of the Holy One. This is what fits them for the revelation that took place at Sinai.[6]

On that occasion the inner essence of everything was revealed. The whole earth fell silent and motionless and listened. There is nothing in all the worlds that is not God's manifest glory and essence, Gershom Scholem tells us.[7] Every created thing has God's Voice within, giving it vitality, expressing it in being. And the original Light of creation, Moshe Braun concludes, is still "found in the inner part of every created thing. Thus, although on the outside, things appear to be separated, in their inner spiritual nature, they are united. And when God reveals Himself, as He did on Mount Sinai, the physical differences disappear, and all that is left is the inner light, which is Divine and unified as one. It is the original light of creation that shines from one end of the universe to the other." God's kingdom is hidden in the natural world, "in every particle of nature, and if people would see it they could not possibly sin." For that breathless moment at Mt. Sinai, God's people did see it, God's glorious Presence in every part of creation, and "it was perfectly clear to everyone that sin was impossible."[8]

A Universal Revelation

The revelation was to all flesh. Usually we think of revelations as being to individuals. What is unique about the theophany at Sinai is that it had no limits. It was to all people and even to all creatures. The reality and glory of God were not withheld from any being. As the prophet (Second) Isaiah says near the beginning of the Book of the Consolation of Israel, "Then the glory of the Lord shall be revealed, and all people shall see it together, for the mouth of the Lord has spoken" (Isa. 40:5).

When the mouth of the Lord speaks, God's Will is revealed in action, and all the beings that have come into existence by that Will, that Voice, and that Word respond. They all—we all—respond according to our several natures. Our moment-to-moment existence, life, consciousness flow out through that speaking mouth (Deut. 8:3). They are gifts received. But they are also responses, our words in return. Our living, our being conscious, is also our own act. People, in particular, live and act by hearing the Word of God and performing it (Luke 11:28). In Exodus 24:7, God's people respond: "We will do and we will listen." We will do what we already understand, and we will listen to learn what we do not yet understand. It is a full—yet open-ended—response.

This is where the will of the people meets and unites with the Will of God. Sometimes this union of wills is thought of in terms of willing the same object. And the Torah can be read on the level where it means certain literal things to do. But the union of wills transcends and preexists any particular application of will to external objects. The Presence of God at Sinai, the revelation and the dialogue, are meant to raise the people to a union with the unobjectified Will of God, with God as Subject. People as subject unite with God as Subject, within the divine unity. God is not one being among others. God is the One Being, the Only One of Being, the very Oneness of all being. That is why the only adequate worship of and response to God is union.

The union of wills takes the form of intimate mutuality: "I will be your God and you shall be my People." (Try reading this not using designations of class—"god," "people"—but using personal names, for example, Abraham speaking to his bride, "I shall be your Abram, and you shall be my Sarai.") The pledge between them, what unites them, is Torah. The invisible Torah of the divine Will, the written Torah of the tradition, the living Torah of our every action, word, and thought. Torah is eternal, Torah is historical, and Torah is still being spoken. The people of God are those who live by the Torah (if not the particular Mosaic Torah, then the eternal and the ongoing Torah). The people have the divine-spark soul; they are the medium through which the Radiance of God shines, those whose vocation it is to bear witness to the Oneness of God by recognizing the oneness of all creation. God also bears witness to the people that we are a "treasured possession" (Exod. 19:5) and are entrusted with the task of extending, developing, and deepening the unity of the creation, so that the Presence of God in it becomes ever more evident.

Torah is related to the emergence of created reality from the unspeakable, the inconceivable, the qualityless, the undifferentiated. It is a concentrated form of that which develops in time, space, matter-energy, and complexity. It parallels in language the creation of the world, which act of creation is therefore seen as divine speech. Gershom Scholem says:

> Strictly speaking, the Torah does not so much mean anything specific, though it in fact means many different things on many different levels, as it articulates a universe of being. God reveals Himself in it as Himself, rather than as a medium of communication in the limited human sense. This limited, human meaning of the Torah is only its most external aspect. The true essence of the Torah . . . is . . . the complete mystical name of God, the Torah [as] a living organism, and the divine speech [as] infinitely significant [so that] no human speech can ever exhaust it.[9]

In Second Isaiah, the Prophet, speaking for God, says: "For as the rain and the snow come down from heaven, and do not return there until they have watered the earth, . . . so shall my Word be that goes out by my mouth; it shall not return to me empty, but it shall accomplish that which I purpose, and succeed in that for which I send it" (55:10-11). God speaks Torah. We also speak Torah. The Sinai experience is sometimes thought of as a kind of mutual reflection. The covenant oath itself is simply this full presence to each other. The experience can also be read as a kind of coming to consciousness of humanity: seeing ourselves for the first time, and even seeing ourselves as seeing ourselves. We are the self-consciousness of the universe. When we are conscious and knowing and caring, the universe is conscious and knowing and caring. If every blade of grass has an angel hovering over it, whispering "Grow!," surely the angel of God that was put into humanity to tell it to grow has encouraged it into the awareness of being God's "precious treasure," God's beloved children.

Stardust has knit itself up into a thinking, speaking being that inquires into its own existence. The Word from the divine mouth has indeed not returned empty but has brought "accomplishment" at least to this point. The universe has become a way of looking at itself and looking beyond itself. Was there ever a greater miracle? This realization, this meeting God face to face, "speaking" to each other, is one of the deep meanings of Sinai.

The Turning Point and the Supernatural Life

This is the great turning point, as all the teachers agree. The mission of God's people dates from the meeting at Sinai. The whispering angels within have brought the universe up to this point. They have had to use self-seeking and self-preserving and self-augmentation devices to do it. But now, at Sinai, self-conscious, God-conscious people deliberately undertake to live a supernatural life, a life in which the self-consciousness and the God-consciousness meet. An emergent has appeared out of the complexities of biological interactions that transcends and even reverses the actions of its components.

Stealing, deceiving, and killing have worked well up to now. All animals and even plants do these things. The roots of our "sins" go back to the very beginning.[10] But now the Big Brain that the genes have evolved has become capable of something else, capable of seeing from the other's point of view and empathizing with it. Capable of what Rabbi Hillel said in summarizing the whole message of Judaism for a Gentile while the latter stood on one foot: "What you do not want done to yourself do not do to others." "That's it," he said. "All the rest is interpretation."

One of those interpretations occurs in the Talmud (*Leviticus Rabbah* 28:1): "Under the sun there is nothing new, but over the sun there is something new."[11] This "super-sun" world is a "super-natural" life for those who can understand and follow it. The revelation at Sinai with the giving of the Torah is the opening of the path to this new kind of life. It is not easy. The "instructions" of the Torah have to be bound tightly to the hand and arm (representing the bodily faculties of action), though less tightly to the head (representing the mental faculties of understanding and willing). This is why the *tefillin* are worn the way they are.

God did not make a mistake in creating the world in such a way that it would have to be corrected later on. The natural self-seeking stage was a necessary one. Genesis 36:4 says: "I Myself will go down to Egypt, and I Myself will take you up." Egypt is "the house of bondage." This is why the revelation at Sinai follows the liberation from Egypt. Egypt means limitations and boundaries. The redemption means freedom from limitations and boundaries. Egypt is natural life; Sinai begins the super-natural life.

Clearly, in this usage "nature" means the set of operating principles whereby a finite being maintains and extends itself. I have urged that we see the Holy Thursday Revolution in the context of cosmogenesis, in which a series of phase transitions reorganizes the elements of the natural order into more complex patterns of interaction. The point there was that such change is perfectly "natural" and therefore possible and acceptable. Now, if we try the effect of speaking of something "super"-natural, we highlight another dimension of this change. We acknowledge that developed human consciousness really is something new, over-the-sun new. Two powers especially characterize it: the capacity for empathy with other beings, and the ability to conceive the Infinite. Both of these transcend the needs of the finite being's intention to maintain and extend itself. In this sense, human consciousness transcends the entire "natural" order. The revelation at Sinai is a proclamation of this reality.

The Proclamation of Liberation

For this reason I like to present the Decalogue as the Proclamation of Liberation. I am going to suggest that these ten statements are not "commandments" but announcements. They declare what the state of affairs is, what the meaning is, and what new set of operating principles is now overlaid on the set by which this state was reached.

The First Announcement sets the stage for all that follow: I am your God who brought you out of the land of Egypt (the "Narrow Place"), out of the house of bondage. God went down into Egypt and

God comes up out of Egypt (Gen. 36:4). This is the intended development of the world that is God's own self-expression, Word. "Egypt" is limitation and bondage or boundedness, and the present new state is liberation from, or transcendence of, that limitation, narrowness, and constriction. Finitude is now well established, and infinitude begins to shine through. But this is a phase transition, which means that both sets of operating principles are functioning, with a certain amount of struggle between them.

The Second Announcement we can read as both encouragement and promise: You are not bound to the needs and limitations of biological genetic evolution; you have access to human empathy and divine contemplation. So remember, take care not to let those former principles take precedence over these new ones. Don't set other desires and ambitions, even supposed necessities of existence, ahead of this principle and energy of liberation that is now your guiding light. Indeed, it will always be with you; you cannot fall back into the non-conscious state; your Liberator will always be with you. You can realize that you don't have to limit your sense of your reality and value by making icons of the drives of the flesh or the personality or the will (see John 1:13). You don't have to invest your mental and emotional energies in such things. Your true self belongs to the domain of the divine. Nothing can be compared with it, and nothing can ever adequately represent it.

The Third Announcement continues this theme by pointing out the sublimity of the True Name, I AM. Be aware of its transcendence; don't belittle it by attributing unworthy qualities to it. Realize the Holy One, whose Name you also bear, as inclusive of all and not to be invoked as a partisan to some limited view or biased care. God is the God of all. You participate in this Name and this Reality and are called to live up to It.

The Fourth Announcement invites to rejoicing in this Divine Life while in the incarnate state: The Infinite One—Present as the Sabbath Day, with its rest, peace, contemplation, and joy—is the meaning of all labors and finite efforts.

The Fifth Announcement puts into perspective the present state, just beginning, and the previous states of the world that have led up to it. What a wondrous path you have traveled. Therefore, honor your Divine Source, your parents on Earth, all your predecessors in the universe process, the way by which you have come to this point of entering the super-natural life. Do not despise that path. Nevertheless, you are now going to transcend it, and the way by which you have come is no longer the way by which you will go. For you are now ready to become God's people on Earth, a special presence of the Holy One, commissioned to bring all beings into the Original Light and Oneness.

The Sixth Announcement begins the detail of the Liberation. You no longer need to kill enemies to advance your cause. All have come from the same Source; all are to be cherished and honored for that reason, and it is now possible, in the light of the God-contemplating and human-empathizing consciousness, for all to live together well in peace and mutual care.

The Seventh Announcement liberates all from any sexual acts that do not arise from the God-and-human honoring consciousness and life. Biological evolution frequently rewarded both rape and promiscuity. The freed human no longer has to live that way. Even your biological activities partake of your place in the Divine Life. Not instrumental, not objectifying, not demeaning, they honor God and one another and become occasions of worship and joy.

The Eighth Announcement declares that when properly used, Earth provides plentifully for all. There is no need to steal goods, people, status, or any value from another. In your awakened consciousness, you rejoice in arranging for the distribution of all goods to the benefit of all. It is a way of your expressing your divine qualities of creativity, wisdom, generosity, and goodness.

The Ninth Announcement points out that deception is likewise unnecessary in the new life, although it too had been rewarded in the ancestral evolutionary path. Caring for one another, you have no motive to trick anyone, no motive to sequester your wisdom. You rejoice in sharing the great blessing of knowledge, and you expend your human energies in gaining more knowledge of how to live well together with the earth. You are trustworthy in all your dealings, even as God is faithful and true to you.

The Tenth Announcement summarizes the new state of participation in Divine Life by proclaiming that you have no need to covet anything, for God and the human community provide for you. You, indeed, individually and communally, rejoice in the opportunity to provide for one another, for this is a divine act, expressing the divine *hesed*, the loving-kindness and care that characterize God (Exod. 20:1-17).

The World Filled with Holiness

It is interesting to observe that after setting forth these implications of the Liberation, the God of the Exodus then requests, "Ask them to make me a home, so that I may dwell with them" (Exod. 25:8). Is this what it is really all about? Shmuel Boteach insists that the intention of the Sinaitic commandments is to "infuse the world with holiness." The purpose of the Torah, unlike an ordinary code of laws, is not to preserve orderliness, or even to establish justice, but to permeate every aspect of our daily life with the consciousness of God and to make everything we do sacred.

> The *mitzvos* at Sinai . . . were not given to serve as human moral and ethical standards, but so that the world would be a spiritual-physical domicile housing the Almighty. . . . God invested His intrinsic Self into the Torah, enabling [us], by virtue of our fulfilling the *mitzvos*, to bring Him into the material fiber of the earth.[12]

Boteach explains further. There is the Creator, and there are the created, he says. "God willed to unite the two. He wished His Presence to be manifest not only in the spiritual but in the physical realm." Now there are two distinct ways in which this can be done, the way of water and the way of fire. The way of water is God descending to Earth, as effortlessly as water flows downhill and enters any vessel available to it. So God's loving-kindness, *hesed*, comes to the world through the sheer generosity of God, and the recipients are passive, receiving. Although the world "plays no active role, it still becomes holy because godliness has enclothed itself within it."

Fire, on the other hand, does not descend but rises, symbolizing *gevurah*, which can be interpreted here as strenuous effort. Boteach argues that it is the latter that really changes the world, for in this case the world has not only been overshadowed by godliness but has also changed to become godly, to rise to a higher plane. "Divine transcendence" here "involves the physical elevation of the finite world. This creates a residence fit for spirituality, which draws the Divine Presence into it."[13]

Creating a residence fit for the Divine Presence is one way of saying what we are doing in the world, what our meaning is. Samuel Dresner, in his introduction to a collection of the sayings of Abraham Joshua Heschel, *I Asked for Wonder,* says this:

> To Heschel the question of religion is not "what man does with his solitude," but "what man does with the presence of God": how to think, feel, act; how to live in a way which is compatible with our being a likeness of God; how to *be* what

one *is*; how to so conduct ourselves that our lives can be an answer to God's question.

Heschel, he says, had "an awareness that man dwells on the tangent of the infinite, within the holy dimension; that the life of man is part of the life of God."[14]

God is clothed with the physical world. So how shall we live with God in the world? When we first began to leave Egypt, we knew that we had to do it *together:* Moses said, "We will go with our young and our old; we will go with our sons and our daughters, with our flocks and herds, for we must hold a feast to our God" (Exod. 10:9). That is the first point. The second is that we must do it by *universal* principles. The Torah is given in the wilderness, not in any particular place, but in an undefined space that could welcome all the peoples and did.[15] The third point is that now *we* have to build that dwelling for God in our midst. God has given the general principles; now we, the images, have to apply our own creativity to working out the details of the implementation, constructing the divine dwelling. These three points, together with the Decalogue, indicate a relationship between God and people that we call the covenant. It is a bonding relation between God and people and among the people ourselves. The covenants we make with each other follow the same principles as the covenant between people as a whole and God.

My thesis says that this is the context in which Jesus is moving and that his Holy Thursday Revolution is a reaffirmation of this covenant relation and the Proclamation of Liberation. He is applying Torah traditions to the problems of his day and in so doing is developing a general teaching that we can appropriate and apply/test/adapt to our situation. The last part of our study will be devoted to the implementation of the Torah and the renewal of the covenant community as a social transformation that is still needed today.

PART IV

The Covenant Community

10

Jesus and
the Covenant Community

I used the Holy Thursday story to dramatize my contention that humanly induced ills are so many different instances of what I call the Domination Paradigm. I argued that there is an alternative to it, which I call the Communion Paradigm, and I quoted the biblical text, "I will no longer call you servants but friends" (John 15:15). The reorientation of outlook characterizing the Communion Paradigm was so radical that it provoked strong arguments that it constituted changing human nature and that it couldn't be done. I considered rebuttals to this claim and examined the source of the change in mystical experience.

The second story that I presented, the Revelation at Sinai, makes the same point—that human beings can make the transition from slavery to freedom and friendship, and I offered some social detail to show the expression of the new set of relationships. No claim was made that either story was historical. But now we are going to look at how we can actually transform our relationships, from the one-on-one scale to the global, and in that context I want to look at the possible historicity of the Jesus story, not for specific incidents but for the conditions of the times, the resistance movements in Palestine, and the general principles of what we may vaguely call the Jesus program.

This means that the Sinai Proclamation of Liberation is the active background of the Communion Paradigm of the first century: living experience of the One God is the core, and ethical behavior of respect and compassion is the efflorescence. The continued theme is the covenant community of human beings, who have a covenant with God and a covenant among themselves.

The Historical Jesus

When we begin to talk about Jesus himself, as distinguished from what other people made of him afterwards, matters become very problematic. How are we to sift out a real, historical Jesus from materials constructed by writers who have their own views, agendas, received accounts, and so on? Historians use a respected method of determining the oldest stratum of text and asking for (in most cases) two independent witnesses to any particular item. They also examine the language and culture, make anthropological comparisons, and consult what is known from other sources about the history of the period and the people involved. For instance, what we think we know about Jesus depends in part on what we know about the Roman Empire. In this way, scholars hope to isolate historical reality from its elaborations, extensions, and exaggerations, from parallels to older stories and texts, from conventions of storytelling, and so on. All such study, of course, requires a great deal of careful, detailed work.[1]

I have a suggestion for a method of rough approximation that we might try in the meantime. It starts with storytelling just as storytelling. Suppose all our stories about Jesus are fictions. Organize the stories according to various categories: supernatural events; healings; preachings; relations with friends, strangers, enemies, power figures; and so on. Then ask whether there is any category or set of Jesus stories that are unlike storytelling in any culture up to that time—or even for a long time thereafter—any story in which the hero is represented as doing something that heroes are never represented in storytelling as doing. All the supernatural and miraculous stories, all the moral-teaching stories, all the claim-to-divine-status stories, and all the helping-humanity stories have parallels. But there is one general category of story and one particular subset within it that depicts the Jesus character as behaving in a unique way. This is not yet history; we are only comparing stories. These *stories about* Jesus are different from other *stories*.

The category of different stories consists of those that portray his relations with what we now call "marginalized people." These include the poor, the diseased or deformed, those outcast from the general social life for one reason or another, and children. Into this general category also falls the particular set of stories about Jesus' interactions with women. He is shown in the stories as treating women as peers and friends. The women are not portrayed as inferior to him or as supernaturally or magically superior. He is depicted as interacting with them as ordinary social equals, with whom it is appropriate to have serious conversations.

This is a special case of the general category of interacting with marginalized people, to all of whom he shows the same respect that he gives to close friends and to powerful figures. No more, no less. He is never depicted as showing deference or contempt or condescension to *anyone,* marginal or mainstream. Some interpreters argue that the stories about women represent a worst-case scenario. If the hero can be shown to deal with women as equals, then the hero's *character*—if it is to be consistent—must be such (in the storytelling) that he can be expected to behave this way with *any* marginalized type, or with any mainstream type, or powerful type.

If this can be admitted about the storytelling, then we can approach the question of history. Why do the storytellers tell such stories about Jesus? These stories do not improve his heroic status or strengthen the divinity claims. They do not even set an example for the storytellers' communities, which (perhaps after a brief period of experimenting with such social attitudes) did not themselves practice such equality. Even within the pages of the New Testament, it is explicitly forbidden to regard women as equal to men (1 Tim. 2:11-12). Certainly in its subsequent history (postapostolic age) the Christian church has never permitted such a position. So why show Jesus this way?

One possible answer to the question of why they tell such stories is that the man Jesus actually behaved this way in his lifetime. This behavior was so peculiar (John 4:27), so unconventional—indeed, so *uncopied*—that it was remembered and spoken of as one of Jesus' outstanding features. The "criterion of difference" allows such an argument to be made. I propose to take advantage of this possibility to urge that the mystical-psychological-social-economic revolution that characterized the original mission of Jesus is based on this type of no-exceptions social equality. Across the whole board, equality is the central principle of the social revolution that Jesus is preaching, explaining, and modeling.[2]

This supposition can help us grasp the logic of the whole program, help us see the deep context in which to situate particular local activities, and appreciate a vision not just of a distant ideal human community but of *commonsense,* realistic human relations. The equality is portrayed by the Jesus of the stories, by his way of *acting,* as obvious and natural. He does not seem to regard his attitude as extraordinary. This orientation begins to open up Jesus' whole context, in which it is our usual and accepted conventions that seem warped and unnatural.

He doesn't make a big issue of what he's doing and doesn't talk *about* it. He just quietly and naturally goes on *doing* it, as though it's the most ordinary thing in the world, while everyone around gasps in shock and horror as fundamental assumptions about the nature of things, principles on which whole societies have been erected, simply fall away, blithely ignored, negated, and replaced with alternative visions of reality.

We think that Jesus is radical and innovative. *He* apparently thinks that he is merely following out the original idea for human beings in the world: he's deeply *conservative*! Conventional practices, in his view, demonstrate the hardness of many human hearts. We tolerate this harsh usage, but, says Jesus, "It was not so from the beginning" (Matt. 19:8). Our conventions of inequality and domination are departures from the first order of nature ordained by God, and are therefore *un*natural. So the relation of what is real, right, and natural to what is a departure from the seemingly right way is turned on its head, one of the reversals spoken of in the gospels, such as "the first shall be last and the last, first." What is conventional now, seemingly right, will be realized to have been wrong, and we are called to return to a correct order of nature.[3]

The Social Situation
in the Late Second Temple Period

Let us suppose, for the purpose of developing our theme of domination being replaced by friendship and communion, that it was with such an insight and such an orientation that Jesus undertook to deal with the situation of his people in his lifetime. By working out this view, we can reconstruct a paradigm that we can adopt and adapt to our needs in our time and to our social and economic and even religious conditions.

The late Second Temple period, Douglas Oakman tells us in his *Jesus and the Economic Questions of His Day*, was a time of major social stress. Palestine was a conquered and occupied country, a province of the Roman Empire. The combination of insult and injury was severe, especially as experienced by the peasants. They were living in a strong centralized state, with absentee landlords, high rents, and taxes. More than 90 percent of the population were peasants, dominated by domestic and foreign overlords. The peasants' social unit was the village, the land traditionally divided among extended families, with work proceeding throughout the year. It was thus an agrarian, not an industrial, society; the unit of production was the family. Traditionally, production and consumption had been mostly local: the village families farmed, made tools, built houses, made clothes, helped one another. This lifestyle was threatened and considerably disrupted by the administrative and economic system imposed by the conquerors and their representatives in the Jewish homeland.[4]

The basic crops raised by the peasants were wheat and barley, plus grapes, olives, and figs. Beans and lentils were also popular, and peasant farmers also produced various fruits and vegetables, such as pomegranates, dates, apricots, peaches, citrons, leeks, onions, turnips, cucumbers, and several types of condiments. But with the coming of the empire and incorporation into its "globalization," there was pressure to concentrate production in large plantations given over to cash crops. A family that lost its land, therefore, or the right to control what was planted on its land, lost also its secure livelihood, its capacity for subsistence.[5] (We have seen this happen also in modern times to a number of countries whose economies were being "helped" to modernize and grow by shifting to export crops; when the export did not produce income for the family, the family no longer had a backyard garden from which to sustain themselves.)

The question, therefore, of who controlled the land was crucial. The traditional position of the peasants was that the land itself was the inalienable property of the clan. The people lived on their land and cultivated it themselves. People and land existed together and took care of one another. Jewish law protected this concept of land ownership and control, but powerful people found ways to circumvent it. Conquering kings took the position that all the land was theirs to bestow on their friends and vassals. Thus, gradually landholdings coalesced into large estates under the control of the foreigners and the native aristocracy subservient to the conquerors. This already divided the conquered people into a favored elite and the peasants, with the peasants becoming more and more a kind of "human cattle" who worked the landlords' holdings (compare the "commodification" of labor in our globalized economy).[6]

Many peasant families in this period had already lost their land when it was incorporated into one of the large estates. Many were working as tenants on their own ancestral acres, now the property of the invader or his client. Some were daily wage earners with no connection at all to any particular piece of land. Families fell into debt as a result of the taxes extorted by the conquerors and their native representatives. The farmers lost their land and were displaced.

There were several heavy taxes, most of which were sent out of the country: taxpayers did not receive services but rather supported the army, the administration, and the aristocracy. The first portion was the Roman tribute, the collection of which was often farmed out to a local client-king or other native connected to the empire, such as Herod Antipas. Antipas then took his own cut, which was considerable, and used it not only to support his lavish lifestyle but to build cities and monuments in other parts of the empire. The Temple tithe continued as always, but the Galileans may have had mixed feelings about it, since the high priest was now a puppet of the Romans and unable (uninterested?) to help the peasants in their plight. Then there were various tolls levied on travelers (Matthew was a toll collector) and various local obligations in one's own community. Altogether, between one-fourth and one-third of a peasant's earnings was taken in taxes. If one considers the peasant's lifestyle as a subsistence farmer and calculates the production of the land and the number of calories needed to sustain the family, it comes out that there was not enough left after taxes to take care of the family's needs.[7]

If, in addition, there was bad weather, crop failure, or some other disaster in the family, the peasant had to go into debt in order to meet those obligations and needs. The debt was to be repaid out of the next year's harvest. But if the next year was not a good year either, the family would incur further debt with no end in sight. The working peasant became more and more dependent on the creditor and gradually lost all right to and control over the ancestral land. Thus, release from debt and land redistribution were standard demands in resistance and protest movements of peasants against governments, landlords, and other power elites. Poverty and destitution were outstanding characteristics of the social situation in Jesus' day. When we read in the prayer attributed to Jesus by the evangelists that he recommended to people that they pray that they may have bread day by day and that their debts may be canceled, we should understand this in the literal sense of the pressing practical needs of the people.

Peasant values are typically reverence for the land, a feeling that agriculture is good but commerce (selling products one has not oneself produced) is bad, and that to be industrious is to be virtuous. But these values were systematically undermined by the Roman economic arrangements. For instance, people who had plenty of money wanted to invest (parable of Talents), so they encouraged farmers and urban poor people to borrow from them and repay them with interest (like banks and other large organizations advertising credit cards and urging people to accept them sent through the mail, which people do, using one card to pay off another until they are all "maxed out").

Further, the Roman administrative districts were set up in such a way as to make the districts compete with one another and so that they would not form a common loyalty with one another against the empire. The way business was conducted set town against country, with the townspeople finding ways to profit in the Roman system so that they were unsympathetic toward the country people. Landless and unskilled people were obliged to compete with one another for daily jobs (see the parable of the Workers in the Vineyard). A person's value was whatever the labor market was paying that day. The old covenant values of sharing and cooperation so characteristic of village life were disappearing, and the result was that hostility was growing where there had been trust and generosity.[8]

But it was far from clear what could be done about it. There had been a peasant uprising following the death of Herod the Great in 4 B.C.E., and there would be massive revolts in 66-70 C.E. and in 132-135. All of these attempts ended in disaster, further destruction and oppression of Jewish life and land at each successive confrontation.

Between these large-scale events were numerous smaller efforts. Social banditry and small-scale insurrection were common resistance moves. In the gospels there are a few references to "bandits" (Matt. 26:55; 27:38 and parallels) and at least one insurrection (Mark 15:7; Luke 23:19).[9] Homeless people, driven off the land, took refuge in caves in the hills and preyed on the wealthy classes, local aristocracy collaborating with Herod Antipas. They also broke into Roman armories to steal weapons with which to attack chosen targets. Places where records of indebtedness were stored were favorite targets.[10]

Many bandits also engaged in redistribution of goods, stealing from the rich and giving to the poor, on the principle that the invaders and their supporters had originally stolen from the peasants. Richard Horsley and John Hanson point out that there was a strong bond between social bandits and peasants. Bandits tried to right wrongs that the peasants suffered, and peasants protected bandits. Bandits were seen as symbols of hope and champions of the common people.[11]

John the Baptist Announces the Kingdom of God

It is in this general social context that Jesus—and before him John the Baptist—pursued a vocation to aid the injured people. John had stationed himself on the Jordan River, outside the city, on the edge of the desert. He was announcing the imminent coming of "the kingdom of God," or the reign of God, or God's domain. Or possibly, the kingship of God, that is, that God alone is King; all other claimants are imposters, usurpers, and thieves. The people are to be governed directly by God, with leaders chosen by lot, without domination, establishing a just socioeconomic order and protecting the people in peace and prosperity. In the manner of the ancient prophets, John urged the people to purify themselves and prepare for the coming. To this end, he encouraged them to "confess their sins," and he then immersed them in the river as in a *mikveh*, for ritual purification.

Roy Hoover, a fellow of the Jesus Seminar, raises an interesting question: Why the Jordan? Why this relatively inaccessible place, away from population centers and on the edge of the desert? The explanation he suggests is that "John is playing on the appeal of the wilderness and the Jordan as symbols of Israel's origins when from the banks of the Jordan they first took possession of the Promised Land. [Many insurrectionist bands also gathered in the desert and then crossed the Jordan to approach their chosen targets.] That he offered baptism as a cleansing from sin [officially, one had to go to the Temple] implies that . . . the . . . authority [of] the Temple . . . had collapsed. It had become religiously bankrupt, incapable of mediating the . . . moral renewal the nation needed. To gain access to that . . . new beginning, Israel would have to return to the ideals of its origins." Back to where we came in, across the Jordan, from the desert.[12]

My own midrashic fantasy about John the Baptist is that by being baptized by him people were making a commitment. They were saying in public that even if the invading Romans now controlled their Temple's high priesthood, they could still practice their religion by taking steps to procure justice. They could commit themselves to undertake actions that would move toward an alternative lifestyle independent of the establishment. They could go back to essentials and find vitality in them.

What were the essentials? Where did we "come in"? Was there an original covenantal community? There seems to have been at least the idea that no one individual or family was to dominate others, have power over them. By pledging themselves to one another, the various tribes committed themselves to a set of rules to protect justice in their social, economic, and political relationships. Their polity was first *theocratic*; they believed that it was ultimately and intentionally God who really ruled them, and only to God did they bow. Second, their society was *egalitarian* (for adult males) and democratic, any free man being the equal of any other and as eligible for a leadership role.

Horsley and Hanson remark that "the parables of Jesus, along with his other sayings, indicate that the Jewish peasantry entertained ideals of a (restored) egalitarian theocracy . . . inasmuch as it was members of the peasantry who not only heard such sayings, but also preserved and transmitted them."

In particular, there were covenantal provisions for avoiding peasants' loss of land through indebtedness. Debts and debt-slaves (people who were giving their labor in lieu of land or crops or money) were released every seventh year. Exodus 21–23 gives details of the regulations by which the people were to live, in which the effort to be just can be seen, even though people today might not approve of all of them. Particularly impressive is Exodus 22:20-26, forbidding wronging strangers, widows, orphans, debtors; 23:1:9 is sensitive to egalitarian values, compassion, and forgiveness, as well as truthfulness.[13]

These themes are further developed in the prophetic writings. Rabbi Milton Steinberg, in his little handbook for inquirers, *Basic Judaism*, calls the prophets "pioneers and discoverers . . . of the spirit" and points out as examples "Nathan and Elijah who rebuked kings for deeds of oppression"; Amos, "who proclaimed the universality of God and the primacy of justice in His service"; Hosea "who, out of the capacity for forgiveness he found in himself, leaped to the dazzling vision of a God inexhaustible in mercy"; and Isaiah, who looked forward to "God's Kingdom of universal peace and equity."[14]

The central idea that emerges from all these considerations is that the God of the Jews stands with the people—in particular, with the poor, and even more with the oppressed or the helpless. God is merciful and generous. It is the obligation of God's people, said to be made in God's image, to be likewise. So these are the essentials; this is the "original idea." This is the heart of the Teaching (Torah).

Jesus Implements the Torah

Matthew's Gospel has Jesus say, "Do not think that I propose to set the Torah aside. On the contrary, my whole intent is to *implement* the Torah, to put it thoroughly into practice" (Matt. 5:17).[15] Of course, the author of Matthew has his own reasons for including this speech, but this saying is consistent with other words and actions attributed to Jesus. In the very context in which the saying appears (the Sermon on the Mount), the "thoroughness" of the divine action is pointed out as the model for human behavior. We are to be "perfect" as God is perfect (*per* [thoroughly] *facere/fecit* [do]). And how is God perfect? By sending sunshine and rain impartially on the good and the evil, just and unjust alike (Matt. 5:45).

Looking at the whole of Jesus' ministry, it is easy to see how this plays out as unlimited inclusivity, egalitarianism, and refusal to judge, condemn, or even make comparisons and govern goodness by proportionality. Unlimited generosity is the characteristic portrayed, and it is described as *scandalous*, not what was generally admired or even considered strictly "moral." So when Jesus undertakes to implement the Torah thoroughly, he has to mean implement his insight into the central teaching of the whole tradition, including the prophets, who were also concerned with implementing the central teaching.

The rabbis of his day would ask one another, "What is the greatest *mitzvah* in the Torah?" much as Buddhists asked one another, "Why did Bodhidharma come from the West?" meaning "What is the essence of Buddhism?" "What is Enlightenment?" When Jesus was asked to declare his view of the essence of the Torah, he replied, "Love God thoroughly and your neighbor as yourself" (Matt. 22:36-40). If you do this, you will not miss anything that you ought to do or avoid. When this raises the question, "Who is my neighbor?" and it turns out that the neighbor is everybody and anybody, we understand better what "thoroughly" means. And when we further comprehend that the ability to do this springs from our prior thoroughness in loving God with all our faculties, then we begin to get a glimpse of the new world that these intentions make possible.

The orientation of love toward God with all one's heart, soul, and resources (Deut. 6:5), or with all one's heart, soul, and mind (Matt. 22:37), with one's total being, is the same as laying claim to, and realizing in one's concrete experience, the liberation from restriction that is the escape from Egypt. What it means, in a nutshell, is that our central selfhood is not defined by, contingent upon, or constricted by our circumstances, where "circumstances" include our body, personality, history, and social relations. This shows later in the Christian motto, "There is neither Jew nor Greek, male nor female, slave nor free." The true, central self transcends all these relations and finite characterizations. The "child of God," or "image of God," is not limited by such classifications but is "perfect" in its own reality.

The Kingdom of God

The central message of the ministry of Jesus concerns "the kingdom of God." John the Baptist had also preached that the kingdom was coming soon but was not here yet. Jesus seems to be saying, instead, that it is already here. Or does he mean that it is always possible and will be present to the extent that people make it to be so? Does it have to do with the issues we were wrestling with in Part III— whether we are going to believe that it is possible to transform our consciousness and our social relations?

Neil Douglas-Klotz, in a book on the Aramaic background of the Greek gospels, has an interesting speculation on the word *malkuta*, the Aramaic equivalent of the Greek *basileia*, "kingdom." He says that the root letters *mlk* are associated with well-formed and focused energy, creativity, and empowerment, "that which says 'I can!' to life." People who had the vision and the courage to say "We can" became leaders and their leadership role became *malkuta*.[16]

It seems to me that an important dimension of Jesus' ministry as it is recounted to us is that he and his companions encouraged the people they were trying to help by saying energetically, "We can!" They believed that things could be improved, that people can change their attitudes and behaviors, that the deep meaning of life is goodness, generosity, caring, sharing, and happiness. The "kingdom of God" is the world in which such values prevail, and it is brought into being just as fast as people actually assent to those values and express them in their daily lives. In this sense, the kingdom is both within the people and among them, in their relationships. Kingship is not vested in any one particular person; it consists of the net of relations among all the people. It is the faithful and creative "We can!" of all the people together.

The first thing that this renewal movement has to do, therefore, is to deny the prevalent belief that since sin produces suffering, any suffering must be owing to sin. This is the problem of Job: Job insisted that he had not committed any sin that should occasion the suffering he was experiencing. Job's lament and his anger can be seen as social protest. His so-called comforters were actually engaging in what we now call "blaming the victim." In Israel's history it was common for the prophets, the government, and the people to explain their ill fortune in terms of their not having been faithful to the covenant. They had not kept their side of the pact adequately, so God was letting other nations punish them. Individual misfortune was likewise divine punishment for sin.

Conversely, of course, it is argued that a successful life is proof of God's favor. So the link between favor and fortune, on the one hand, and between sin and suffering, on the other, becomes a principle for social organization, arguing that the powerful hold their positions by

God's approval and the unfortunate are receiving due punishment for their sins. According to this theory, it didn't even have to be one's own sins; it could be one's ancestors', three or four generations back (Exod. 20:5, etc.). That this was still believed in Jesus' day is shown by the story about the blind man. Jesus' friends asked him, "Who sinned, this man or his parents, that he was born blind?" (John 9:21).

Michael Samuel, in his book *The Lord Is My Shepherd*, devotes a chapter to the problem of Job in which he points out that Job's challenge to the prevailing explanation was a threat: his words "endangered the social system of the wealthy and the powerful. The wealthy were blessed by God, while the poor were cursed. The social realities reflected God's justice and maintenance of the social order. Job's fearless words could create a social upheaval among the poorer classes." Therefore, his companions tried to intimidate and silence him. But Job finally saw in his vision that the world is run by great laws that can't be adjusted to fit each individual's state of purity or sinfulness. Being in God's love doesn't mean that you will be preserved from misfortunes that may come in the course of nature and human history. Job finds his personal healing in praying for his "enemies" and showing compassion to other sufferers.[17]

This is the sort of thing we see again in Jesus' ministry, applied now to the nation. In the story of the paralyzed man who was let down through the roof, we find again the link between sin and suffering, and the action of Jesus can be interpreted as a definitive dissolution of that link. The assumption of the people observing this event was that the man must be a great sinner to be so handicapped, so Jesus' first response to the situation is to declare the man free from sin. Released from the belief that he is under God's curse, the man is no longer paralyzed but is able to do useful work. The message to the nation is: Stop believing that our present condition is our fate. God is not against us but for us. Don't think we are paralyzed. We can do something to help ourselves. We can!

Having exposed and negated the fundamental impediment to the realization of the kingdom of God in the notion that unfortunate people must be sinners and helpless, we can turn our attention to other misconceptions and false labels. In Jesus' society there were a number of such labels with their respective powers or paltriness plainly indicated. The New Testament shows people easily categorized: rulers, Pharisees, rich men, tax gatherers, prostitutes, lepers, Samaritans, Gentiles, and so on. The appropriate attitudes to take toward them were attached: suspicion, hatred, contempt, respect, deference, obedience, and so on. The kingdom of God cannot grow until these attitudes have been dissolved, and that entails rejecting the categories as well—in fact, it entails the rejection of the practice of categorizing people at all.

This task of changing attitudes is undertaken in the Sermon on the Mount, where it is explained that the old ways—hating your enemies, doing favors for your friends—are practices available to all cultures. If the kingdom of God is to be different, something new and better, it will have to exceed that kind of behavior. Don't give gifts with strings attached—expectations of getting something for your apparent generosity. Don't curse people who hurt you—pray for them and do them a good turn if opportunity offers. And—take a deep breath!—love your enemies! But if we do that, then they're not enemies anymore. Bingo. If you're a master, and you serve your servants, then who's the servant? Who's the master? Stop putting people into classes and valuing them and treating them accordingly. Each person is unique and uniquely wonderful, a child of God, just as you are yourself, and deserving therefore of your respect.[18]

These are unsettling ideas. If the poor start to have that kind of self-respect, and if they can't easily be divided and set at odds with one another, then the whole social system will shift. There are far more "common people" than there are "rulers." So, from the "people's" point of view, these may be fine ideas, even exciting and hopeful ones. But they will not be verified in our experience unless we DO what they outline.

In fact, although the kingdom of God grows to some extent whenever even a single individual turns to this way of life—and who knows how far its "ripple effect" extends?—we need large numbers of people to interact with one another in order for the full kingdom to be effectively present. We need whole communities reordered on these lines in order to bring about systemic change. It isn't a matter merely of individual and personal conversion and rectification. Individuals are members of communities, and it is the systemic values and actions on the community level—family, village, town, province, nation, world—that we are particularly concerned about changing.

The virtues at stake are virtues of *interaction*. The kingdom *is* the net of interactions themselves, not something separate from them, not something for which they are preparatory or something that will in itself make them possible. The kingdom of God is not something in the far future that is going suddenly to come down from heaven and settle on you and magically turn everything right. You yourselves are It. It's in and among you; you have to do It or It will never come.

This is the reason that Jesus sent out "apostles," people charged with announcing that the time had come to organize community life in this generous and responsible way in order to counteract the system being imposed by the Roman polity. To be successful, it requires a large number of people to participate, to make a large enough *interaction*. We need a "critical mass" to encourage still more people to join in, to commit to the caring and sharing that would make the plan work. It seems that the general idea was to broaden the attitudes and practices already in place within an extended family group to include whole communities—indeed, to be open to anyone willing to commit to this "new covenant." The same kind of caring for one another and sharing of resources that people had been willing to do with their blood kin they are now being invited to do with those who are their "brothers and sisters and mothers" by this free-will commitment (Mark 3:35). On the metaphor of "family," a new ethics and a new economics were to grow.[19]

The Jesus Program

This effort to implement the vision of the Torah and the Prophets had its own internal logic. I laid this out already in the first "story," but now we can develop it a little further and speculate on its practical consequences.

Jesus had a fundamental vision-faith that all people are "children of God." This is the *theological* perspective of his "program," on which everything else rests. I am supposing that he took this seriously, more or less literally, as the Kabbalah does in teaching that each person has an uncreated soul that is actually a continuation of the Divine Life itself. When he met a person, therefore, he really believed that God was somehow present in that person, so he looked for that presence through all the overlying contradictions to it, until he found it. Then he addressed himself to that point in the person. As the Hindus also say, the divine in him saluted the divine in the other. When anyone does that, it tends to awaken the divine in the other, who is thus invited to speak from that place in return. This is the sort of thing we will need to accustom ourselves to doing if we are to succeed in developing the further levels of the program. This is why I insist so strongly on the "mystical" aspect, the existential *experience* of what we objectively declare in our metaphysics. We need to learn to focus our social vision at this ontological depth, so that the ethical principles will form correctly and then the social and economic practices will follow.

Connected with this theological view of the ontological equality of all persons is Jesus' vision of the *unconditionality* of God's generosity. Metaphysically we would say that it is the nature of Being to give itself, share its reality with all without previous conditions (how could there be conditions prior to the existence of the finite beings?). But Jesus experienced this directly, seeing that God's sun and rain come to all indiscriminately, the birds are fed without their asking, and the flowers are clothed more grandly than Solomon. People, being God's own offspring, should naturally be like this, especially toward one another. And people can be, if only we will remove the artificial obstacles to our being so. This seems to have been Jesus' view, about which he told stories and which he himself enacted.

But unconditionality has its problems. It transcends justice. Douglas Oakman has an interesting discussion of the story of the Workers in the Vineyard, the ones who were all paid the same although they had worked different lengths of time. How are the workers waiting in the marketplace going to feel about the vineyard owner next day? Will they all want to linger and be hired late? What happens to the owner's reputation? Is he capricious? Unreliable? You don't know what he's apt to do. He says he has a right to do what he pleases.

I see justice as being a bit like determinism in physics. There are regular relations, so you know the outcome. Just as Einstein was uncomfortable with quantum mechanics, believing that it undermined the reliable regularity of the universe and amounted to God "playing dice," so Jesus' contemporaries may well have felt that his unconditionality undermined justice.[20]

It had been a great achievement to move from the capricious deities of earlier ages to the just God of late Israelite religion, and now here comes this dreamer declaring that "worthiness has nothing to do with it," God loves and cares for everyone anyway. And *therefore* we also should care for all, including "enemies." "Love your neighbor as yourself" had become so broad that it left no one out. This "unconditionality" looked very much like the old capriciousness. With strict justice at least you always knew where you stood; there were rules and laws and penalties. With Jesus, apparently, there were no penalties and no rewards: sharing the Divine Life was already the greatest "reward" anyone could have and you have it. You don't have to "earn" it, and actually, you can't avoid it either. It's just the truth about yourself. But you are strongly called to live up to it and stop the suffering that people unnecessarily inflict on one another because they don't recognize this truth.

It is from this theological position that the claim of human social equality follows. It also appears later in the Mishnah: All human beings have the same origin, so no one can claim a superior ancestry! But it is simultaneously true that each person is absolutely unique: "not one person identical to another. Therefore every single person is obligated to say: 'The world was created for my sake.'" This view, which I am attributing to Jesus, is seen today as standard Jewish teaching. David M. Elcott begins his *Sacred Journey: The Jewish Quest for a Perfect World* by enunciating this principle:

> Each human being, regardless of birth, status, or native abil-
> ity, has the right to be seen as created as an image of God,
> filled with infinite worth, equal to all other human beings, and
> so unique that he or she can say that the world exists only for
> them. On the other hand, since each and every person can
> make these claims, the only way all people can create a world
> that recognizes them is through relationship, that is, the part-
> nership between each person and God, as well as the connec-
> tions between all human beings. The traditions of Judaism,
> which build on this fundamental philosophy, provide mecha-
> nisms by which such a world can be achieved.[21]

The theology of human "connections" is developed in David Aaron's *Endless Light*, where he points out that it is in the wedding ceremony that God is blessed for having created the human being in the divine image, for it is in the *uniting* of people that the image of God is most closely reflected. He says, "This is a very important con-cept. A lone individual does not reflect the image. . . . An individual in unity with an other does. . . . Until an individual makes a space to include an other, and allows that other to do the same, we do not have the oneness that reflects the image" of God. But "creating that kind of oneness is not simple."[22] This is why it is so important to spell out in detail the *equality* from which our work has to begin, enumerating the marginalized groups who are included in "all people" who are "all equal."

The equality to which people aspire, and which many of us want for others than ourselves, is *social* equality, equality of *respect*. Most of us presently live in societies with high differentials of respect. This is what the Jesus program proposes to change. The mystical-theolog-ical insight that each person is a unique child of God obliges us to treat each person with the same respect, a respect that is an appropri-ate response to the theological insight. This means that we respect one another for what each one *is*, not for what one possesses or does or belongs to or is labeled as. If we can shift our criteria of valuing from, for instance, wealth, power, and celebrity status, from sex and race, religion and class, if we can focus on the personhood of the individual and the importance of that person's connections in the great social body, then we can begin to develop a society in which all people are truly respected.

Mickey Kaus, in *The End of Equality*, argues that we can meet the threat of losing equality (equality coming to an *end*) by a strongly proactive creation of the social goal (taking the right means to the *end*) of equality. Achieving financial equality is difficult, and efforts to do it often cause other social ills that are even worse. But if we simply cease caring that much about money and care about each other in our common humanity and personal lives, then the worst of the problem disappears. If money doesn't gain you more respect, Kaus says, what does it matter how much you have? He wants to see what he calls "civic liberalism," in which "the public sphere will . . . have the sort of primacy to which religions have aspired." He wants to see people from different economic classes, as well as different ethnic groups and whatever other categories we use to divide people, mixing socially on a daily basis, living in the same neighborhoods, so that "virtually every local institution—every gas station, drug store, tennis court, and supermarket—becomes a formidable social equalizer."[23] That assumes, of course, that there will still be local markets and drug stores rather than branches of enormous transnational conglomerates.

In the Jesus program, mutual social respect does result in a certain amount of material equality, in the sense that our care for one another urges us to see that everyone has what is needed not only for a decent life but even what will promote that person's ability to develop talents and gifts that in turn enrich the community. We need to notice that the respect itself is a large portion of what any person needs to liberate creativity and joy in life. No one can live happily in a social milieu that is habitually, even institutionally, demeaning. We are encouraged to share both spiritual goods and material goods. The goal of life is that we creatively arrange that we all live together in a way that expresses the divine filiation which is the deepest truth about us.

The Covenant Community

In the time of Jesus there was debate about what should be done to renew the nation and strengthen the covenant. Could it be done through the Temple, with its compromised hierarchy, or was some sort of drastic change needed? Some of us are asking the same ques-

tion with respect to our problems: Can we pass appropriate legislation to fix them, or are we experiencing such a crisis of meaning that
we need, as Michael Lerner says, "a totally different approach to reality"? Jesus seems to have been partly trying to restore old ways and
partly creating quite new extensions of the central principles. Just as
Lerner urges that we must abandon our "atomistic conceptions of the
world and learn to see ourselves as deeply interconnected with one
another and with the universe" and must construct "democratic
mechanisms to ensure that we all participate," so Jesus in his day
moved to establish a communal sharing that stressed deep interconnections and participation by all.[24]

The Gospel of Luke has Jesus announcing his mission by reading
the opening verses of chapter 61 of Deutero-Isaiah: "The Spirit of the
Lord is upon me, because he has anointed me to bring good news to
the poor. . . ." The good news is that there shall be no more poverty.
The system he confronted (and ours as well) actually requires poverty
as part of its dynamic. Wealth comes partly from profit on production; but profit is increased by reduction of costs, and the greatest cost
is labor. If people are not poor, they will not be willing to accept low-
paying jobs and will not compete against each other, which drives the
pay even lower. Cheap labor has to be protected by a margin of unemployment (at least 6 percent is desired) so as to put sufficient pressure
on the poor. We ourselves are experiencing a global free market in
cheap labor. The gospel announces that this is wrong and needs to be
replaced by an alternative arrangement that protects *people* rather
than *profits*.[25]

Any such alternative arrangement will be strenuously resisted by
the wealthy, and even by those who still hope to become wealthy. The
saying attributed to Jesus, "the poor you always have with you"
(Matt. 26:11; Mark 14:7; John 12:8), is often cited in justification of
such resistance to any attempt to change the status quo. Michael
Lerner admits that among us "many middle-income people feel
ashamed . . . that they have not been more successful . . . because they
have focused too little on looking out for number one. . . . People . . .
tell themselves that they do not really want to be" selfish, manipula-
tive, and safely slightly dishonest, but "everyone else is," so they
would "put themselves at a disadvantage" if they lived according to
"principles that no one else is willing to take seriously."

Lerner then says, "I think that these people are telling the truth:
they really would prefer to live a more moral life" but believe it is
impossible. This leads him to say that "the corporate world . . . is peo-
pled by human beings who have the same meaning-needs as everyone

else." We should all, therefore, ask, "To what extent does the economy *really* serve the common good?" and "To what extent does the economy produce spiritually, ethically, and ecologically sensitive human beings . . . capable of sustaining loving and caring relationships, who feel themselves actualized and fulfilled in the world of [their] work?"[26]

This is the sort of thinking that is easily dismissed as sentimental and unrealistic but that is regarded by (our reconstructed) Jesus as common sense. The people are in trouble; we have to help them. We have to organize life so that people won't fall into this trouble. It isn't clear that Jesus had a plan for land redistribution, but he does seem to have been highly conscious of the problem of debt. So he may have tried to find a way to help people clear themselves of debt and thus avoid losing their land. He *may* have called for something approaching the biblical "jubilee year." But that would be so complicated that it is hard to imagine it taking place, even without the Roman occupation. If he did want to hold up the value represented by that idea—the passage from Isaiah that Jesus, according to Luke's Gospel, read in Nazareth to announce his mission ends with the proclamation of a "year of the Lord's grace"—it could mean that we have to go back to the beginning, back to basics, back to the original context of the divine creation.[27]

In 1 Maccabees 14 there is a song of celebration in honor of Simon, the brother of Judas Maccabeus, who succeeded him and another brother, Jonathan, as leader of Israel. When Simon assumed the leadership, he "saw that the people were trembling with fear . . . so he encouraged them . . . [and] the spirit of the people was rekindled" (13:2, 3, 7). The song says of him that "he sought the good of his nation," and in his days "they tilled their land in peace. . . . He gave help to all the humble among his people." If this is part of the general picture of the Jesus program and movement, then practical efforts to relieve the "humble people" to the point where they can "till their land in peace" must be included. It can't be merely a moral program.

Dominic Crossan, relying on Robert Jewett, makes the suggestion that the Jesus covenant community expressed their mutual commitment by *communal* meals and perhaps *communal* sharing of possessions. The significance of this practice lies in its distinction from patronal sharing of meals and possessions. *Patronal* arrangements are made at the pleasure of a wealthy person who elects to share a meal or a field with the poor. *Communal* arrangements involve everyone in contributing to what is shared in common. Crossan says of this practice: "Communal sharing is a far more radical criticism of commercialized community than patronal sharing, because the more individual almsgiving is increased, the more systemic injustice is ignored. Patronal sharing (alms) is an act of power. Communal sharing is an act of resistance." Speaking of a time shortly after Jesus, Crossan proposes "that there was a serious attempt to establish . . . a *share-community* to which one gave, at maximum all one had or, at minimum, all one could. . . . What I see in both . . . Essene Jews and . . . Christian Jews, is a thrust toward establishing *sharing community* in reaction against *commercializing community*—an effort made, of course, to live in covenant with God."[28]

Could Jesus himself have been active in organizing communal sharings of various sorts? The Suppers may well have been affairs of this kind. Even if he and his companions proposed a supper and brought substantial amounts of food, they may have made it clear that this was to be a community experience and that everyone was expected to bring whatever they could. This is important, because the equality has to be established and celebrated. People are to experience their social equality with one another and not judge their social standing by how much each had contributed to the meal. In addition, they are to continue this practice when there is no "core group" getting it started.

There was, of course, a background for this kind of mutual assistance in peasant village life. What was needed now was a special effort because everyone was poorer. Jesus seems to have had rich friends as well as poor ones. Could he have undertaken to bring them together? Since indebtedness was the central problem, could he have tried to set up something like what we would call a "credit union," a communal share-community for the express purpose of dealing with debt? There was a Jewish custom in which the extended family usually included at least one member who was enough better off than the rest that he could afford to rescue a member who was in desperate straits, about to lose the family land to a creditor. This person was called a *goel*, and he would put up the money to save the relative from foreclosure on the understanding that the other would repay (without interest) as he could. Could Jesus have formed a "syndicate" that would act as a *goel* for members of the covenant community? Everyone would contribute to the syndicate in good times and the syndicate would protect them in bad times. If the syndicate was associated with Jesus' name and he was remembered in connection with it, perhaps he received the "surname" (in the way that others were called "the Zealot," "the Twin," "the Rock") of *goel*, which means "redeemer."

In any case, Jesus seems to have been working from the idea that people have to share with one another in order to resist the system that is being imposed upon them, and they are called to practice generosity—concentrate on how they can help their neighbors instead of how they can protect themselves. When each seeks one's own welfare, the community fragments, and each is then at the mercy of the powerful system. But if each member of the community is in *covenant* with all the others and each seeks the welfare of the others, then the community coheres. It has solidarity and strength. If you seek to save your own life, ignoring others, you will probably lose everything, but if you are willing to risk, to practice generosity, to give things away without expecting return, then—if you are in a community covenanted to live this way—you will be safe and you will in fact prosper. That's the idea.

The people's salvation is not going to come about by a supernatural miracle. It has to come from the people themselves, from their own "graciousness," that is, their free choice and action without the guarantee of a *quid pro quo*. It's a risk, but if enough people do it faithfully—with faith—then it will work. The power of united people is inestimable. Josephus records an instance in which the prefect Pontius Pilate tried to profane the Temple with Roman insignia. The Jewish protest, by its large numbers and daring offering of their lives, forced the prefect to back down. Philo of Alexandria reports a second instance. Such examples can be encouragement to people, enabling them to feel the power of the *malkuta* (the "kingdom"), the sense that "we can!"[29]

The *malkuta*, in Jesus' view, is like something that grows. It may start out small, like a mustard seed, but grow into a large bush, able to give shelter to birds (Mark 4:30). It may provoke enemies who try to inhibit its growth, but if it doesn't distract itself by attending to enemies instead of to its own growth, it will triumph in the end (Matt. 13:24). It may not prosper in every situation—that's only to be expected—but where it does take hold, it will produce an abundant harvest (Mark 4:3). It can grow secretly in some cases, without further help once the seed has been planted; in the nature of things it will come to fruition (Mark 4:26). The *malkuta* is not military, not bureaucratic, not even priestly—all associated with domination and inequality. The *malkuta* with the human face (Dan. 7:13) is the kingship of the whole people, the "holy ones of the Most High," and all the social functions that had been "dominions" shall now serve the people (Dan. 7:27).

To prepare good ground for such a *malkuta*, to plant its good seed, to help it to grow where that is needed, is not only a human possibility but the human vocation. We affirm a covenant that is dependent only on our own goodwill, our commitment to one another to seek each other's well-being and creative development. This implies that we use our intelligence and sensitivity and every talent we possess to devise ways for this *malkuta* to take form among us. The covenant community as an image of God is responsible for itself as a living, adaptive, innovative, sharing, unitary system.[30]

11

Implementing the Friendship Covenant Community

The total social program that Jesus advocated was based on communion, friendship, distribution, and partnership. This contrasts with a social organization based on domination, exploitation, accumulation, and force. His program's central principle is equality, just as the contrasting paradigm's principle is inequality.[1] The latter is vertically ordered by "power over." The former is horizontally ordered by sharing and mutual care. Even what might have been a vertical dimension—the power of God over all—is developed in a horizontal way by the distributed Spirit indwelling each social entity (individual, family, local community, the whole people). This distribution of the God-expressing Spirit implies that people must be in active partnership with God at all points.

This is the "covenant" idea: contribution, responsibility, and care work both ways, in the context of equality of mutual respect. There is no "social status." In human organization there is only functional ordering, no status ordering. All persons are respected equally, while particular gifts and expertise organize collective activity appropriately for the benefit of all. The people are committed to one another and pledge to care for the other as one cares for oneself. "Benefit of all" is a real incentive, a strong motivator. Differential benefit—more to me than to you—is experienced as a disvalue.

These ideas and their accompanying feelings (or feelings and their parallel ideas) cannot be imposed on people. They have to *emerge* in a natural and spontaneous way. The thesis is that all people *have* such feelings, at least the propensity for them, and vaguely the desire to let them surface and operate, but they are discouraged from showing and fulfilling them by the social systems into which they have been inculturated. Occasionally individuals appear who have broken free from

219

the prevailing culture and who can give opportunity to others to be free. If they can come together, they can form a community that welcomes newcomers and grows. Their cooperative lifestyle makes for stronger community unity than the selfishness, suspicion, competition, and hostility of the lifestyle they have left behind, so they have a good chance of flourishing and prevailing if they can get a good enough start, avoid interior corruption, and escape destruction by those who see them as threat.

Jesus' friendship community, in which there are no lords or servants, is like this. It was, in its original context, partly an attempt to restore old ways, and partly an intention and an effort to create new extensions of those ways. One of its images was the family and the extended kinship net. General reciprocity, giving without expectation of return, may have been an early strategy of the human species to foster family unity and to propitiate potential enemies. Various Jesus stories show this strategy being gradually extended without limit. His family of blood kin is widened to include his friends and companions who share his values: "Whoever does the will of my Father is my mother and my sister and my brother" (Mark 3:35). That includes Samaritans, who were conventionally excluded (John 4:9). By a special breakthrough, it includes Gentiles (Mark 7:28), and even enemies, the Romans of the occupying forces (Matt. 8:5-7).

There are no sexual, racial, or historical barriers to membership in this family. Its intention is to include everyone. But this does not mean that it has no structure, no principles, no operating dynamic. It has these with great clarity, especially since they are all simple and even obvious, once the basic principle of social and personal equality has been seen and accepted. There is also a kind of "method" for helping people discover themselves as members of the family.

Jesus himself would probably deny that this was some kind of special revelation or a "new dispensation." Once you see the basic truth, he might insist, that we are all God's children and therefore absolutely equal, the rest of it is just common sense. You don't need a divine teacher to spell it out for you, much less to set up a new battery of regulations and sanctions. You can make all the deductions and applications yourself and you will live by them because you see the truth and genuinely want to live that way. The reason we don't see the principles easily is that we have been brought up on falsehoods (John 8:44). Clear out the falsehoods, Jesus might say, and the reality will be apparent. Reality has a structure, and the way we ought to live has a structure; its principles have a logic. That means there is an ethic.

The Reality Ethic

The first principle in any reality ethic says that if we want to stay alive, we must have enough reverence for life to make that possible. This suggests that we ought to study the nature and needs of life. When we do that, we find that all life forms are interconnected in deep, intimate, and essential ways. Therefore, the ethic proceeds, we must cultivate these connections and nurture the life domain as a whole. While protections are in order, exploitation is not. We must constantly reexamine what constitutes exploitation, as our ethical consciousness, our conscience, continues to evolve. Necessary harvesting does not justify cruelty (calf cages, for example) or carelessness with respect to the environment (clear-cutting, overfishing, poisoning with pesticides, etc.).[2] Principles along these lines hold for life as a whole. The planet is finite, and resources are unevenly distributed. Our first priority has to be keeping life going in its diversity, in its capacity for innovation. Making profits has to take a position several steps farther to the rear, or its own existence will be threatened. This is reality.

Staying alive thus entails a realistic respect for all the levels and kinds of being that are connected and entangled with one another. A reality ethic that represents the good of the whole therefore has to say that all beings have some kind of right to exist and that, while they all do relate to one another in helpful and hurtful ways, none of them exists solely for the sake of others, but each has some right in itself to its existence. This idea deserves to be developed and its complications and problems addressed, but our topic leads us especially to human beings.

Ethical consciousness means an awareness that all human beings have in themselves and for their own sakes a right to exist. Developed, that will mean a right to exist as fully, freely, and close to fulfillment of their aspirations as is consistent with the same right exercised by others. Two capacities help us here, insight into the depths of our own being, and the power of empathy. We see the value of full existence for ourselves, and empathy enables us to realize that everyone else feels even as we do. We sense that we all feel the same inside. If I changed places with anyone, I would still have this same feeling about the value of myself and my desire to be as fully as possible. In this sense, then, we know that we are all equal, equal in our assertion that we have a right to exist and to exist well. If "God" means the unlimited power to exist, then this insight can be expressed by saying, "We are all children of God." In that sense we are all equal as persons and deserving of equal respect. Ethical consciousness means that we can *see* this by direct penetration into the reality of our situation. It is not a belief or an opinion.

Recognizing the further reality of our necessary interconnections with one another (and the rest of the world), we can see the necessity for affirming a *community of mutual care* and for working out how the viability of the community and the fulfillment of the individuals relate constructively to one another, for both values must be protected. The suggestion of the Jesus ethic, underlining the teaching of the Torah, is that this is best achieved by each person exercising concern for each other person, the famous "loving your neighbor as yourself" (Lev. 19:18). That way avoids the conflicts of each person seeking one's own good and the good of others insofar as that may contribute to oneself. The claim is made that mutual inter-concern and care are the more *realistic* way to set about the good life. This does not mean that one should undertake to tell others what is good for them—and thus simply dominate them again—but rather, one should cooperate with others in ordering the society and the world in such a way as to maximize the possibilities for everyone attaining desired fulfillment. Freedom and self-determination are prominent among the values to be attained, and concern for the integrity of the whole is also a value. The ground of existence and value is one, and the various expressions of that also constitute a oneness.

Religious Politics

In beginning to think about this, we might start from our belief in democracy as the way people can best live together for the well-being of all. Abraham Lincoln defined democracy as "the government *of* the people *by* the people and *for* the people." We originally thought of this principle as applying to the national unit. What would it mean if applied to the world unit? Would it exclude exploitation of some segments of the world for the benefit of other segments? Does democracy mean that we-the-people, qua governing, have an obligation to care for the well-being of all-the-people, qua governed? That the government of the people by the people must be *for* all the people—for, not against?

The 1993 Parliament of the World's Religions issued "A Call to our Guiding Institutions," outlining the basic ethical positions that the world religions have in common, stressing commitment to a culture of nonviolence and respect for life, of solidarity and a just economic order (with specific concern for the poor, children, disabled, refugees), of tolerance, truthfulness, and equality between men and women. The document recognizes problems and difficulties as it insists that we must find ways to build community in diversity and regulate population and life habits for sustainability. It calls on governments to make their structures of power accountable to, and serving the needs of, the people they govern, protecting their human rights, under leaders worthy of public trust. It calls similarly on international intergovernmental organizations to foster communication and cooperation to secure global harmony through universal respect for international law, rising above ethnic and cultural strife and correcting economic imbalances.[3]

Most of our religious traditions recommend that we practice forbearance, forgiveness, generosity, and even unconditional love and compassion. That is the extreme opposite of domination and exploitation and might be readily abused by those not yet fully participating in that attitude and dynamic. Perhaps there is a transitional method. The game-program called Tit-for-Tat (described in chapter 8) has been tested for efficiency in leading to mutual cooperation between two parties in repeated interactions with one another. I'll repeat how it works: Your initial move is to cooperate, to do something helpful for the other. If the other reciprocates, you continue to be friendly and helpful. If the other takes malicious or unfair advantage of your kindness, or does something hurtful, you respond in carefully measured kind—once. Then, next move, you start over again being helpful. When this behavior is repeated sufficiently, it becomes obvious to both parties that their individual and mutual advantage lies in being helpful and honest rather than deceitful and hurtful.[4]

As a particular example, perhaps we can see that these initial and repeated acts of cooperation might be recommended in the search for peace and justice in the Middle East, a part of the world especially troubled still in 2004. Where either party is in a position to offer something—anything—helpful to the other, this should be tried. Each can cease what is most hurtful to the other, seeking diplomatic means to find a harmonious solution. The key to any such dispute is that each side must listen to the other's point of view and expressed needs with a sympathetic ear and try to find a way to satisfy the legitimate desires of the other party. If this cannot at first be done with respect to the most critical issues, then let it be done with respect to nonvital, even trivial, issues in order to make a small beginning of goodwill.

Doing good to "enemies" may well be far more effective in overcoming tension and distress than taking hurtful actions against them. The latter usually merely provoke retaliations, and the cycle of violence is further energized. The "love-your-enemy" approach can probably be expected to take a generation or two to attenuate strong feelings based on good arguments (on both sides) over a long time. An initiative such as Seeds of Peace, an activities group that brings Arab and Israeli youth together for shared work and personal friendship, is a long-range effort in the right direction.

It may come about that, on the way to a full-blown covenant community of the whole planet, one nation or group of nations might emerge as a "superpower." This would be a unique moral status, having power, authority, and influence thrust upon one party, without even a single partner of equal status. Reality ethics points out that responsibility is proportionate to power, and such a political entity would hold a unique responsibility for the well-being of the entire world. How ought it to proceed? Perhaps we can propose that Tit-for-Tat would be a sound realistic base for policy, which can then be tentatively modified in the direction of trust and generosity as actual cooperation develops and remains stable. This would take into account our philosophy of democracy, that the well-being of all the people affected by the power exerted by any agent must be the goal of that agent's behavior.[5]

People who study the history of religions document how the concept of Deity tends to parallel the social organization and the value system of the community that believes in the Deity. Human nature and God nature are reflections of one another. As I said in chapter 10, the oldest religions may have worshipped gods who were rather *capricious* and careless of their effects on humans. For the last two to four thousand years we have had the *just* God who requires humans also to act justly, requiting each according to what is "deserved." This idea is gradually being invaded by the concept of the God of *unconditional love*, for whom measurement and "deserving" are meaningless, overshadowed by compassion and loving-kindness. We thus indicate an aspiration that Tit-for-Tat should move steadily in the direction of all players taking responsibility for the others out of sincere concern for their well-being.

The Hague Appeal for Peace and Justice for the 21st Century, held in 1999, was a conference planned by over a thousand nongovernmental organizations from more than one hundred nations. It addressed the question of what civil society organizations and ordinary citizens consider the challenges of the twenty-first century: war and other forms of violence, human rights and human security, and the way to engage the foundations of these problems. Its views and recommendations are expressed in The Hague Agenda for Peace and Justice. Recognizing the severity of these troubles, the Agenda nevertheless urges optimism, citing steps forward in civilization made during the twentieth century despite its dreadful conflicts and destruction. It takes the position that peace, justice, security, and well-being are the responsibility of all people, not of governments alone. It proposes that international organizations of citizens, exercising "moral imagination and courage," work "to create a 21st century culture of peace and to develop national and supranational institutions" as "guarantors of peace and justice."

The Agenda claims that "grass-roots efforts" are already having "a major impact. They are succeeding because they mobilize ordinary people" and encourage the participation of sectors of society often overlooked or excluded from registering their views when important decisions are made by governmental powers. The subscribers to the Agenda commit themselves "to listen, learn, and then to build."[6]

This is a hopeful sign. Conception of an ideal has to appear well ahead of the actual widespread practice of that ideal. We must guard against cynicism and remember that evolution works on what for us is a long time span (but, actually, in cosmic terms, it is about as quick as possible). But it doesn't go by itself. In every generation we have to give our push to the movement.

As we put compassion and cooperation together, we come more and more into sharing, into symbiosis, mutual life-promotion. The social (political, economic) dynamic is no longer a simple set of behaviors directed to the sole advantage of the agent, but something much more complex. Complexity arises from multiplicity and diversity and from complementary needs and benefits. New entities are composed by the interactions of partners. Initially each agent's behavior is governed by the fact that that agent's well-being is significantly dependent on the well-being of the partner(s). So, even if you are willing your own advantage, you have to will the advantage of the partner as well.

But because of the extraordinary capacity of human consciousness to have knowledge and feelings responsive to the experiences and feelings of others, selfish symbiosis fairly readily moves in the direction of real care for the other for the other's own sake. As we increase our capacity to care (feel) and to care (act) for others, we gradually build up a world symbiosis in which the dynamic of *agapē* has more play. It is important for us to remember at this stage of our affairs that the bottom line is human happiness; we are never entitled to use people for the sake of some other value. People are the *end* value, not a *means* value. Therefore all our political and social activities and all our economic activities must be arranged in such a way that people are valued above all other considerations.[7]

All parts of the planet are now in touch with one another. It is a small planet and its resources are not equitably distributed. They have to be deliberately shared. Clearly we need something in the way of a world government, but it must be an *elected* government, responsible and accountable to the people it governs. A coalition of transnational corporations with financial power enough to dictate domestic policy to individual nations is not a covenant-style world government.

The United Nations is a good first step in this necessary direction. We ought to support it and apply ourselves to improving and strengthening it so as to make it more beneficial to the people of the planet. Because of our experience with crisis situations in which there was significant difference between some governments and their own respective populations as to what action should be taken, we ought perhaps to consider whether referenda should be required to support votes in the Security Council. As long ago as 1972, U Thant, having served the United Nations as Secretary General, was calling for "a common global ethic" as the first thing necessary to a world order that can "assure peace, justice, and progress." By a global ethic, he said, "I have in mind a more direct connection between the U.N. and the world's peoples . . . in their hopes for a workable peace and for a safer world environment." To achieve this, he urged that we move toward a "planetary awareness" and recognize a "second allegiance" beyond that to our nation of origin or choice. We need, he said, "an allegiance to the human community as a whole and . . . eventually this allegiance must become the preeminent one."[8]

Daniel Patrick Moynihan, in his book *On the Law of Nations*, makes a strong plea for the respect all nations owe international law. Our "talk" for a long time has been that we ought to be governed according to law and not according to power. But our "walk" has very often gone in the reverse direction. Whoever "we" are who have the effective power, that party easily finds that the obstructive law doesn't apply or can be overlooked. Moynihan urges that the branch of any nation's government having the most accountability to the population has an obligation to raise the consciousness of that nation's people and government to international law as law that their nation is to obey. It is not law governing all the other nations except ourselves, and it is not optional.[9]

Recently, Walter Cronkite has brought the World Federalist Association to our attention with a renewed call ("United World Federalists" goes back to the 1940s) to participate in a "Campaign for Global Change" aimed at strengthening the United Nations. Particular points are a permanent peacekeeping force ready for rapid and effective deployment, a functioning International Criminal Court supported by all permanent members of the Security Council, a well-funded Commission for Sustainable Development to secure the environment, financial obligations of member states kept up to date, and whatever restructuring is needed to make the U.N. a fully democratic assembly representing the *peoples* of the earth, not just their governments.[10]

The point all these individuals are making is, as the International Forum on Globalization puts it, "The issue is governance. Will ordinary people have a democratic voice in deciding what rules are in the best interests of society?" Too much of the world, within nations and among nations, is presently controlled by "small ruling elites," not accountable to the people whose lives are vitally affected by the elites' decisions about government, about war, about economics, about environment. But "a better world is possible," the Forum claims, and reports on what is going on at the grass-roots level by "the hundreds of millions of extraordinary people in an emerging global civil society who . . . are forging global alliances that seek to shift the powers of governance to democratic, locally rooted, human-scale institutions that value life more than money."[11]

Local government is also important, and an old adage recommends doing everything locally that can be done that way. On the other hand, local policy has been known to disadvantage some of its citizens, in which case a higher level of organization may need to protect them. It can also happen that the local needs of a region come into conflict with conditions affecting the whole planet. An outstanding example is the destruction of the rainforests by local people trying to make a living by raising cattle. It is vital that this be stopped because of the delicate balance of Earth's atmosphere. But to do this, we must provide adequate livelihoods for the people in need.

Protection of the planet is absolutely essential, and it is a very serious matter that information on this point is not at the top of our priority list. If the planet fails, all the market shares gained, all the growth charts with rising lines, all the high percentage profits will be meaningless. Schools and television programs and politicians speaking to citizens should explain how the planetary systems of air, water, land, and living things work together to maintain an environment suitable for complex life. It is not something that we can abuse with impunity. Leaders need to say this clearly and strongly and to apply the principles to particular cases. A policy that says that caring for the planet interferes with business, constitutes a barrier to free trade and growth, or costs too much is a policy of ignorance, stupidity, and irresponsibility. Our existence depends on our keeping the tacit covenant with Earth itself.

The Covenant with Earth

"Ecology" is our recent political name for a moral conversion from domination to covenant friendship with our planet and its living creatures. Having moved from feeling at the mercy of our natural environment, to finding that we could control it to some extent and were divinely intended to have dominion over it, to becoming capable of exploiting it destructively, we are now beginning to recognize the deep ecological truth that we are all in this together. Every aspect of the planetary system enables other aspects of it and is dependent on still others.

Fortunately, there are now worldwide organizations addressing this situation, some intergovernmental based in the United Nations, some scientific, and a great many nongovernmental citizen groups. Some of these interest themselves in particular corrections and protections, such as endangered species; others deal with large-scale issues such as air and water pollution and careless use of natural resources. Probably the most important feature that needs prompt attention is the temperature. Once the planet starts overheating, that condition will set off a cascade of effects that will be almost impossible to reverse.[12]

To prevent this—and the threat is not in the far future but already here—the cooperation of all people, industries, and nations is vital. This is why steps such as the Kyoto Protocol to the United Nations Framework Convention on Climate Change are so important. Even with all the inadequacies and problems of who should participate and how the burdens should be divided, it is a historic move, one that must be pushed to find sufficient answers to its questions and difficulties.[13] In the perspective of human history, it is a quite marvelous development that so many diverse "tribes" of Earth have been willing to see this fundamental need and to commit themselves to making efforts to meet it.

But it is crucial that we all understand that this is not something that can be "balanced" against other considerations. It is an absolute demand on the part of the complex kind of life that has developed on this planet. Business and political issues are not relevant to it. Arguing that reducing pollution will cut into profits or that one country is justified in refusing to comply unless certain other countries assume similar handicaps will not cause the global warming to hold off. You can't negotiate with the conditions that make our life possible. This crisis on the biological level is obliging human beings to come together beyond their national (or transnational corporate) interests on a plane where domination is so destructive and cooperation so required that one is tempted to see it as divine providence propelling us in the direction we have to go if we are to survive.

Closely connected to the physical dimensions of the problem of temperature is the problem of population expansion and its associated problem of food production. People use energy and degrade energy to heat. Even if we could provide all the necessities of life to an ever-increasing population, our unavoidable production of waste energy would continue to overheat the planet. But, of course, we can't provide for an ever-increasing population, and the climate and land conditions won't allow us to produce food (as we have been doing on acres of land exposed to sun and rain) for such a population.

Hard on the heels of these two problems comes the problem of global health and disease control. Diseases don't stay confined to particular regions; they travel. Malnutrition and illness anywhere in the world mean distress for everybody. We have to care for one another. Supranational efforts have to be made to deal with supranational problems. Increased focus on the United Nations Health Organization, with political support and adequate funding, is indicated.

Besides these fundamental issues, there are still many others, some of nearly equal urgency, such as deforestation, loss of biodiversity, exhaustion of natural resources, overcrowding in cities, local air and water pollution, and most important of all, the consequence of all our other ills, the degradation of human life through poverty, disease, tyranny, and deprivation. We are challenged, says Christian de Duve, by a hydra. Attacking it one head at a time won't work. We have to go for the body: change humanity's behavior.[14] This inevitably entails, as Hilary French pointed out in his discussion of disputes over control of climate change, "broader insecurities about economic welfare in a global age. Until these anxieties are addressed head-on, there will be little hope" of progress on the other fronts.[15]

Economic Welfare in a Global Age

Not being stupid, we know that a place very near the top of the priority/importance list must be accorded the economy. The Jesus-covenant-supper-sharing begins with real food. That's what an "economy" (from the Greek word meaning "housekeeping") is "for." We need constantly to remind ourselves of this lest we get carried off into a world of abstractions, numbers upon numbers, and arguments about conceptual entities far removed from the real people who require real food. As the U.S. State Department's Agency for International Development declared, it is "impossible to deal effectively with [social inequities] until economic empowerment is first addressed."[16] As Michael Lerner says, once the economy has produced food and other essential goods and services, it "must also sustain human beings . . . socially" to attain a fully human style of life, and the very "process of doing this must *itself* be a part of the life" that we are seeking to create.[17] A process that treats people as means to an abstract end, rather than as the end to which all else is means, is already a failure as a human cultural enterprise.

Many nations and cultural traditions believe that freedom and self-determination are top values for the desired human life, and therefore that people must be in a position to control the economic dimension of their lives, both individually and as communities, and as limited, of course, by the similar rights of others and the rule of law. This follows from the axiom that the economic process is itself an integral component of the human lifestyle that it supports. But the so-called free-market system does not always obtain this freedom, control, and self-determination for the majority of people, and to some extent not for anyone. The more it operates as a self-determining system, with its own built-in exigencies, rewards, and punishments, the more it tends to escape control altogether.

Can the free-market system be modified in some way and to some extent without abandoning the general principle? Various creative thinkers are trying to find ways of doing this. In the first place, as John Gray points out, not all nations and cultures commit themselves to this system as a basic theory of life. "In Asian cultures market institutions are viewed instrumentally, as means to wealth-creation and social cohesion, not theologically, as ends in themselves . . . an arena of doctrinal conflict. [This] allows market institutions to be judged, and reformed, by reference to how their workings affect the values and stability of society."[18] Then, of course, one has to ask whether those "values and stability" themselves nourish the respect for people that we are urging.

Robert Kuttner proposes that functional distinctions be made between operations that ought to be left *free* under market forces and operations that need to be *regulated*. The latter include matters that affect the foundations of people's lives, absolutes that we cannot do without, such as pure water, electric power, safe food, medicines and healthcare in general. Just what should be included (communications media are now a question) and how the regulation should be handled are themselves open and readjustable issues. In some countries people have access to these decisions through their elected representatives. It is vital that these essentials not be privatized in such a way that they avoid control by the people dependent on them. Things that are necessary need to be accessible to adequate control by the people; things that are optional ought to be freely open to the market.[19]

Jeff Gates has another suggestion, which he calls the "ownership solution" to this problem. Like Kuttner's suggestions, it already has precedents in practice. We already have regulation of many industries, and we already have employee stock option plans (ESOPs). When we consider ideal ways to live, it's not too hard to dream up something that might take place in the far future, but trying to find feasible steps to take now in the near future is much more difficult. It's likely to be many, many steps to that ideal—and many "mid-course" corrections to be made along the way—but the first problem is to find the *next* step, the step to take now, from where we are. This is where an expansion of the ESOPs might be an idea.

Capitalism means ownership. Owners are people who have invested in some enterprise. Individual owners are proprietors or partners; incorporated owners are shareholders. People who are affected by the operation of the enterprise are called *stakeholders*. Gates's proposal is that just as ESOPs arrange for the people who work at the enterprise to be owners of it as shareholders, so should there be stock option plans for people who are affected by the operation of the enterprise. These would include those who provide the raw materials, those who make wholesale purchases, the ultimate customers, and those who live near (or downstream or downwind from) the plants producing the goods.

All these folks should have an arranged and encouraged way of becoming part owners of something that affects their lives. They have a stake in how that enterprise operates. So they ought to have some say about it. Shareholding is a beginning, but not a full answer. We all know that merely owning stock in a company doesn't enable you to have much say about how the company is run, unless you own a sizable block. So the next issue is how to give people whose lives are affected by an enterprise some real *voice* in what is going on. This has not yet been worked out and represents the frontier, the horizon where creativity is called for. But the general idea of starting from where we are and gradually working out from that position by stages of expansion, inclusion, and integration is an idea to be considered.[20]

David Korten also stresses ownership, urging that it and the control that needs to go with it be "locally rooted, thus increasing the likelihood that important decisions are made by those who will live with the consequences." He believes that "locally rooted, self-reliant economies create in each locality the political, economic, and cultural spaces within which people can find a path to the future consistent with their distinctive aspiration, history, culture and ecosystems."

Accountability is an important issue in this sort of idea and suggestion. Transnational corporations escape accountability, and this is the problem, so far as people are concerned. To take back their control over their own lives, Korten argues, people need to work and purchase as much as possible within a system that is on a scale they can encompass and encourage to be responsive to them.

This plan doesn't, in his view, rule out global connections and consciousness. He sees a cooperative global integration emerging from the sense of planet sharing and the intercultural communication facilitated by the new communication devices. "This process is creating a growing web of understanding, [common and complementary needs] and mutual compassion that is the proper foundation of a global community of people." What real people can share is real concerns arising on the local level where people really live, in contrast to abstract issues.

Even when harmony and compassion are least in evidence, as in warfare, we now observe the global interest and reaction and expression of opinion about the matter. This is something that has never happened before. We also observe that hard on the heels of the destructive activities of the war is supposed to come humanitarian aid to the injured people. The war itself is reported on and televised by the various parties to the activities and broadcast via satellite to everyone, so the whole world follows and hears all sides. All this is new. Even by this means global consciousness advances. Korten hopes that the consciousness will develop in the direction of "the need to act cooperatively in the global human interest through voluntary processes based on consensus and shared power."[21]

A striking example of acting cooperatively through voluntary processes based on consensus and shared power is going on in Europe, and Robert Kagan has written an important book about it. Europe, he tells us, is living by "a powerful . . . interest in building a world where military strength and hard power matter less than economic and soft power, an international order where international law and international institutions matter more than the power of individual nations, where unilateral action by powerful states is forbidden, where all nations regardless of their strength have equal rights and are equally protected by commonly agreed-upon international rules of behavior." With this philosophy, the European Union has "produced miracles . . . in the economic and political realms."

Kagan justifiably points out that this "paradise" has been made possible by the role of the United States in handling all the dirty work of policing the parts of the world that are not yet living by these peaceful and cooperative and lawful principles. But this state of affairs is not the last word. It is, in fact, the first word in a new—and so far successful—attempt to organize human life (among formerly ferocious enemies!) on altogether new principles, "freed from the laws and even the mentality of power politics."[22] Why should we not hope for, and work for, the gradual spreading of this way of life?

In many of those parts of the world that are not yet living in paradise, another new thing is happening. Small enterprises are receiving small loans and are flourishing. This is the work of the Grameen ("Village") Bank, which began in Bangladesh and has spread throughout the world. As of 1996, when David Bornstein wrote his book about it, more than two million borrowers, 94 percent of them women, had been helped. (One of the reasons that the bank is so successful is that the women have an unusually high payback rate.)

This most successful, self-sustaining anti-poverty program in the world was started by an economics professor named Muhammad Yunus, who saw that receiving billions of dollars in foreign aid did not lift his people out of poverty. The top-down method was not reaching down to where the poor live. He realized that recovery and development have to *begin* with the poor. And the poorest of the poor were landless women.

Yunus rejected the idea that poor people are not creditworthy and undertook to demonstrate respect and faith in these poor women by making loans to them. They managed their self-employment businesses well, repaid their tiny loans, and borrowed slightly larger ones. Gradually expanding, they worked their way out of poverty. Today women in thousands of villages have profited from Yunus's central idea: that the creative power and industry of poor people, liberated by these minimal loans, can build a world in which people can live properly human lives.[23]

A Properly Human Life

If we are going to implement serious neighbor-love, the first item we must attend to is health. A satisfactory human life is much harder to attain when one's health is poor. Therefore, we all ought to advocate that our societies arrange to provide basic healthcare for all members. "Our society" is an identity that we need to expand as much as possible. The health of strangers in far countries should be important to us, and we should ask that a portion of our more local (probably national) society's wealth be devoted to providing for those in need abroad. In doing this, we can remember Professor Yunus's discovery that the way to solve social problems is to *start at the bottom*: we can insist that the poorest be provided for first.

When we fail to care for others, we are defying the moral principle that points out that health is included among those "unalienable" rights to life laid down in the United States' Declaration of Independence as applying to all human beings.[24] As Hilary French says, it is "only by looking out for the health of people everywhere [that it is] now possible to promote healthy societies anywhere."[25]

Caring for the health of others is also a central responsibility of companies that manufacture items that can be dangerous. Robert Kuttner gives the examples of unsafe automobiles and products containing asbestos, and remarks, "Manufacturers shifted burdens of unsafe products to consumers as long as the courts let them get away with doing so." He goes on to say that "consumers who don't experience injuries displace the entire economic cost onto those who do. Thus, society as a whole underinvests in safe products." If we want to avoid a host of regulations and heavy traffic in court cases, Kuttner proposes that "one attractive alternative is better peer-regulation, backed by greater consumer and worker 'voice,' with the tort system and regulatory remedy on standby in the background."

A noteworthy example that might fall under the umbrella of "unsafe products" is the current crisis in malpractice insurance for physicians. Medicine is not an exact science and unwanted effects can occur, but the awards obtainable in lawsuits have now reached such levels that physicians are leaving areas with high insurance rates or are abandoning the practice of medicine altogether. In some places doctors are calling for strikes. On the other hand, there are avoidable injuries that are inadequately dealt with because physicians do not report one another's mistakes and hospitals do not discipline doctors. Again, tough peer supervision would seem the obvious thing to do; strong measures should be taken to prevent harm rather than pay for it afterward. This requires that individuals and institutions be willing to do the morally right thing rather than the locally convenient thing.

A creative initiative was taken by Harvard University in setting up a nonprofit risk insurance program that not only offered cheaper insurance but also investigated patterns of clinical practice and promoted education to prevent mistakes and injuries. Professionals themselves began to mandate procedures and standards. This program of consumer law encouraging stronger disciplinary arrangements, combined with a remaining fear of lawsuits, resulted in cutting the wrongful injury or death rate at participating hospitals by 50 percent. This is an example of the sort of steps that can be taken within the structures we already have, coupled with incentives based on higher moral motives.[26]

Health issues are involved also in industry, when economic motives dictate that costs be externalized by forcing public agencies to deal with waste products that companies decline to neutralize. Health issues are even more to the fore when the company does not invest in safe working conditions for employees. Such practices may improve profits but can hardly be considered implementation of a covenant among human beings for properly human lives. That covenant has to start from the premise that people have a right to control over the sources and conditions of their own lives. This is one of the main reasons why it would be very useful for employees and neighbors of manufacturing plants to participate in ownership and even management of the company.

If there is one thing that people certainly ought to have a right to know, it is what they are eating. Can the World Trade Organization rule that countries cannot label as such food products that contain genetically altered materials or materials treated with additional hormones? Those practices constitute a barrier to trade. The European Union, with whom this dispute arose, declared that their citizens were not willing to eat treated meat without knowing it and that they had an internal domestic right and obligation to protect their citizens.[27]

If we are to have a global-scale institution to facilitate trade and the distribution of commodities, which seems on its face to be an excellent and forward-looking thing to do, it needs to be one whose primary concern is the betterment of *people* in each part of the world, not the protection of the profits of corporations. If people begin to grasp the covenant idea, the people-are-the-bottom-line idea, we may be able to bring about such people-centered institutions. Money is one kind of power, but large numbers of organized ordinary people, especially with the support of their domestic governments, are another kind of power that may yet prevail.

Food and medicine and safe environments are all part of the health covenant. Another component is the tension of daily life. Many authorities believe that stress underlies a majority of human ills. If we didn't have so much stress we wouldn't get so sick and lose so many workdays and healthcare wouldn't cost so much. Acting on this reasoning involves passing from domination attitudes and structures to those befitting a friendship community on the smallest scales: individual, family, workplace, local communities. Genuine respect for persons in each of these situations, according equality to all regardless of sex, race, position, and so on, would go a long way toward improving the health of our populations. If we had less aggressive competition, we might expect less recourse to alcohol and other drugs to ease the pain of daily life, less crime and fewer accidents and less domestic violence. When we feel secure in our own deepest nature and release the energy to care for others, we can bring about such a state of relations in our social life. Surely it's worth trying.

One large-scale issue yet needs to be mentioned in the context of health: population control. Demographers agree that the human global population must be stabilized or there will be disaster. We need to have a global consensus on this.[28] Family planning will have to be undertaken in this context and will have to be seen as a moral obligation. Care in this area can be accorded religious status and seen as righteous and virtuous. To practice birth control will become a pious duty.

Education and the Cultures to Come

All these issues call for something global and far-reaching in the way of popular education. Those nations and those social groups that most need the relevant information, opportunity to discuss the matters freely, and access to the dietary, medical, and environmental items that can help correct some of these problems stand in need of assistance from those more favorably placed. Cultures have various attitudes toward these issues. This has to be taken into respectful and understanding consideration, but the facts nevertheless have to be (accurately ascertained and) faced, explained, and dealt with.

One statistic that seems to hold up is that countries in which education is widespread show spontaneously declining birth rates. This holds for education in general, not specifically education about reproduction. Family attitudes form one dimension of the overall culture, while general education opens many others, thus completely transforming the individual's and the community's sense of what life is about and what it can be for a person. A "liberal" education is called that because it is supposed to be a liberating experience. A liberating education feeds the spirit as material food feeds the body. Promoting this kind of educational expansion of the spirit is also part of what I have proposed as the Jesus-Supper plan for covenanted sharing of all human goods.

At the present time literacy is advancing in some countries and declining in others. Perhaps we needn't absolutely equate literacy with education. Reading and writing have certainly been a powerful means of learning and teaching, preserving knowledge and passing it on, and of creating art works that transcend utilitarian and instrumental services. But, with the coming of the electronic media, traditional writing is no longer the only way in which human beings can communicate across distances, cultures, and times. Perhaps we are to some extent in a "postliterate" world, as Marshall McLuhan suggested, and the very media we use for self-expression and communication are themselves parts of the messages we send.

But knowledge, however transmitted, is still a basic human value and must be acquired by human beings, since it cannot be inherited. Education is the reproductive means by which knowledge, values, ideas, and creations are passed from one learning generation to the next. Today much of the world is in the throes of cultural change. The United States is self-consciously assuming what it takes to be the tasks of the only remaining superpower. China is doing a makeover from communism to capitalism. Europe is enthusiastically developing its new philosophy of peace and cooperation and packaging it for export. Elements of the Muslim world are gearing up to resist having modern Western culture thrust upon them. Most of the Third World is struggling to extricate itself from the tightening toils of disease and debt, so that the various nations can participate in the goods of the industrial/information world, each in its own way. Education is vitally important in this ferment and growth.

We are inevitably growing toward a global civilization, yet each nation brings to that its own special offering. This diversity is a sign of health in an information system, and it is important that we maintain an ethic of communication that does not allow us to obliterate other-respecting differences.[29]

The new media of communication are central to these developments. Television and the Internet have put almost all of us in intimate direct touch with one another. It is sometimes thought that "technology" renders our world impersonal, but others argue that, on the contrary, through these media our sense of empathy is enhanced. When technology facilitates the way we can work together, it highlights the increasing importance of people and our interpersonal relations, in which we consciously co-create the new structures and functions of our shared world. It is people who give legitimacy to culture and who can take it away when we change our minds, change our perceptions. Therefore, access to education and to the means of learning—to all the information and training systems—is essential to a properly human life and is a foundational cultural right of every person. It is also necessary to say that people must be protected from disinformation, biased propaganda, and emotional manipulation. In the covenant, therefore, we must pledge and provide these freedoms, means of learning, and protections.[30]

When the power to learn and to control access to knowledge is securely in the hands of the people ourselves, we will form, with the help of the global communication networks, an information peerage, an unranked society in which knowledge is equally available to all. Interchange and interaction and intercare will begin to be the dynamic of the global system, undermining the foundation of the domination systems of the past. In a true network, all users participate in creating the net itself and all its various features. The lively interaction promotes constant innovation and creativity, as well as thorough testing and challenge. Peer groups render central authorities obsolete.[31]

This may well mean that the schools of the future will be very different from our present classroom/testing/grading experiences. Co-learning and development of all aspects of the full human being, including emotional, aesthetic, and spiritual faculties, in collaboration with gifted integrated teachers and models in the peer-learning context, may characterize the new cultures.

In Alfie Kohn's *The Brighter Side of Human Nature* there are a number of suggestions and examples of how this can be done. Exercises have been designed and tested for encouraging shifting of perspective and understanding others' emotions, sharing in classroom decision making and rule formulation, and co-learning as promoting prosocial attitudes and behavior.

> Having children learn from each other, rather than merely from the instructor or the texts, creates powerful bonds among them, sending a very different message than does having each child work on her own—or, worse, leading each child to assume that people must work at cross purposes, the success of each being inversely related to the other's.

Interdependence is balanced with individual accountability, and disagreement and vigorous debate are supported within a context of general cooperation, avoiding the dichotomy of hostile competition versus suppression of all conflict. Mixed ages have been useful, the older guiding the younger, experiencing helping and being responsible for a dependent, while the younger finds a role model who is not an adult.[32]

The new education will also prepare the person for a life in which appreciation (as distinguished from utilization) will play a much larger role than it presently does. Our cultures, if they go the covenant and sharing route, will open up more time for family togetherness, more time for quietness and solitude, more time for play. We will remove the sources of stress, time crowding, and frustration, and intelligently enable proper human happiness.[33]

Art, Sport, and Playfulness

A properly human life does not consist of goal-seeking behaviors alone. Play is at least as important as work, but our culture can confuse them. Fixated on work, we tend to transform even our play into work. The performing and plastic arts and the world of highly publicized sport have become big business, attended by large sums of money. Perhaps those who perform and create, those who play the games, still enjoy what they do, but it's also how they earn their living, and to that extent the activity has lost its essential character. The playful things in life are those for the sake of which the useful things are done. They are not means to a further end but ends in themselves. If we are going to confuse work and play, it is much better to make work into play, into something we enjoy, something with value in itself. Play is the Sabbath aspect of human life, when we rest from doing "in order to" gain something else and just enjoy what is.[34]

But there is another aspect to the tendency to turn play into work that is important for covenant communities. As Robert Frank has explained in *The Winner-Take-All Society,* when we can see and hear the very best on TV and CD, we tend not to go downtown for the local performance.[35] We overlook the fact that "second best" is still very, very good, worthy of our attention and appreciation. Just as a local economy strengthens the local community, so local arts and sports enliven and adorn it. They give us an opportunity to admire and enjoy one another, honoring the marvelous gifts and skills of which the human being is capable in people we live with and know familiarly. This is part of the covenant of the Jesus Supper, the sharing of the high values and experiences, the celebrating and rejoicing.

Cultivating and appreciating local talent are important from yet another point of view: they feature and promote general excellence. Our highly commercialized entertainment and automated production and service tend to reduce our culture to a marketable minimum of human spiritual excellence. This is, perhaps, the inevitable risk of democracy, as Alexis de Tocqueville pointed out. Treating all as equals leads to what we now call "dumbing-down." But it need not do so. The equality that democracy honors is an equality of personal respect. It does not require a restriction to whatever happens to be the average in taste at any given time. Taste can be cultivated. Critical intelligence can be encouraged. Even basic intelligence can often be raised. Talents can be enhanced and skill can be acquired.

Democracy means that these avenues of nurturance of the human spirit are to be equally available to all, not restricted to the elite class. In a true democracy the will of the people is that all should be enhanced. The community desires and acts so that each citizen can be lifted up, not dumbed-down. The "proper human" is not a "mindless consumer."[36]

This is where we can appropriate the motto of Alexander Dumas' *Trois Mousquetaires:* "All for one, one for all." I shall reverse it because I believe that the willingness of the one to be for all must precede the foundation of any society in which the all will be for the one. Thus "one for all" refers to our transformation from the erotic dynamic to the "agapistic," willing the well-being of all the others (as well as oneself), of the Whole (which includes oneself), instead of reducing those others to serving our needs and desires. Then can follow "all for one," which means that the community (of whatever scale) undertakes corporate efforts and responsibilities to ensure that each individual has access and assistance to self-discovery and development.

Human beings need and desire both work and play. We want to be engaged in activities in which we can learn and discover things; make things, invent, and improve things; be useful and advance health and productivity. We want to express ourselves artistically and playfully. Art is not a luxury but a human necessity, as Alfonso Montuori and Isabella Conti say.[37] A large share of our spirituality—the sense of meaningfulness and value and aspiration in life—is mediated by the arts in our cultures. This is why it is important that communities budget interest, time, and resources for promoting high-quality arts.

Buildings—offices and even factories, as well as homes, theaters, and houses of worship—should be beautiful as well as functional. Landscaped areas and parks are important. The fact that our souls require these deserves recognition and respect. The sound environment influences us greatly and merits serious attention. Noise levels from machines and traffic, and also from entertainment and music, need to be considered. The effect of music on the psyche is deep and deserves to be studied with care. A culture almost defines itself by the kind of music the people like. Are we promoting peace and fellow feeling by our popular music, or disrespect, wildness, and violence? Popular arts can express criticism and call for reform and improvement without encouraging dehumanizing emotions.

In particular, human relations ought to be lifted to higher moral levels by the arts, not debased. Pornography and cruelty have no place in a covenant community and cannot be excused by calling them freedom of speech, or art, or therapy.

Is unselfish love being promoted by this? Are we enhancing our appreciation of what the human being can be at best? These are the questions we need to ask ourselves about all our activities—in work, in sport, in art, in politics. If we focus on superficiality, grossness, violence, alienation, and depersonalization, we are "fouling our own nest," defiling our own lives.

The covenant community, therefore, will appreciate, encourage, and promote activities that advance the wonder that is the human being, looking for the good and the beautiful in each individual, and will express these values in its popular arts and sports.

Technology and Morality

Kevin Kelly, in *New Rules for the New Economy*, is worried about what is happening to our moral values in an overwhelmingly technological world. He sees no central authority, no universal belief system, and no foundational ethic. Network principles, he says, by accepting difference and plurality, with their unavoidable ambiguity, are fostering the loss of shared values. The consequent relativism leads to fragmentation rather than unity at a deeper level. Without a source of firm basic beliefs, the meaning vacuum leaves the field open for technology alone to shape the future.[38] But it's clear that there are shared foundational values in such a world: wealth is the supreme good; more wealth than one's peers is the goal—this can translate as market share; doing what is necessary to gain wealth is acceptable, approved, even obligatory; the meaning of life (if this question arises) is playing this game.

Can the cultural implementation of the covenant community meet such a challenge? My suggestion is that it meets the challenge not by going back to central authorities and rigid rules but by a network dynamic of its own, based on its own answers to what is the supreme good, how value is recognized, striven for, attained, and what is the meaning of life. Its guide is a sense of what is a "properly human" life. The argument is that we can find, in both the consequences of technological development and the methodology of the network, advantages for the properly human life.

In the first place, it isn't "technology" as such that is the threat. Everything that we have and do is the fruit of human technological enterprise. We may resist telephones answered by machines, assuring us of their concern for us and offering us a "menu" for routing our call, automated "conversations" in which we answer canned questions by pressing buttons, and waiting forever to get to speak to a real live person. But most of our technology we wouldn't dream of giving up—plumbing, electricity, transportation, surgery. These are not what we think of when we say "technology," because these are now essential features of our lives, and computers and the Internet have lately become so.

It is appropriate, therefore, for us to look for the aspects of our new technology that can support the values of the covenant community. Going back a bit to the days of the moon voyages, we can remember what astronomer Fred Hoyle said about the difference it would make, once we got off Earth and looked at it as a whole from the outside. Frank White, editor of *The Overview Effect*, collected comments from various astronauts and cosmonauts who *had* got off Earth and looked at it as a whole. One of them, Gene Cernan, said, "You don't see the barriers of color and religion and politics that divide this world. You wonder, if you could get everyone in the world up there, wouldn't they have a different feeling?"[39] This, I submit, is a moral insight growing out of the pinnacle of technology that the moon journey represents.

Robert Pollack, in *Signs of Life*, argues that the information and communication technologies reduce domination and promote community by making it possible for all people (who have access to the machines) to obtain practically all the information in the world and to be in direct communication with one another without having to go through ranking channels. This is especially appreciated by people working on common or similar projects, who are now free to concentrate on their participation in the work rather than on issues of control. If this is so, then to this extent morality has been empowered by technology and the covenant community enhanced.[40]

A spinoff of this new action-space is that we are developing a new mythology as well, one in which the individual hero is replaced by the interactive team. Robert Reich, of Harvard's Kennedy School of Government, explains and describes this in Michael Schrage's *Shared Minds*, pointing out how the new cooperative creativity—problem solving and invention by group collaboration—is (or can be) cross-cultural and global. Walls tumble and new communities emerge. But morality is not absent. Ego-promotion is not helpful in a mind-sharing work project. Acceptance of correction and improvement has to be practiced for the project to move forward as each collaborator makes an original intervention. Then trust has to enter in. The bonds of relationships in co-creativity have to arise out of faith in one another and willingness to help one do one's best.[41]

At present we are still in the midst of the culture wars, but these wars are being conducted by instruments that we have in common, fruits of our shared technology: communications; information collection and computation and storage; all sorts of weapons and protections against weapons; and background operations involving production of food, medicines, munitions, fuels. As commerce in necessary materials becomes global, the great powers—the commercial and financial corporations—are not eager for war. War is not nearly so glorious as it used to be—it interferes with business. Though some wars may still be waged for possession or control of vital resources, in general the business community as represented in the markets prefers peace.[42]

Finally, communications technology has provided us those "third places," besides work and home, where we may hobnob with all sorts of folks whom we might otherwise not meet, opportunities that used to be provided by places such as the barber/beauty shop or the pub/bar. In chatrooms, on websites, and through other forms of "virtual community," we have such "neutral ground," where we experience social equality that transcends ranking by gender, race, or money. In *Virtual Community,* Howard Rheingold gives examples of these communities formed on the Internet and of how genuinely personal they can be.[43]

Perhaps this is another way of realizing that "social equality" of which Mickey Kaus speaks in *The End of Equality.* He wants financially mixed neighborhoods in which people who otherwise would never meet people in another financial class are forced to rub shoulders in the post office, the grocery store, the dry cleaners, etc. Social equality, he insists, is what democracy is about—not necessarily money-equality, which will be difficult if not impossible to attain—and is what people really want and for the sake of which they think they want money-equality.[44] On the Net money-equality is irrelevant, it never enters into the personal relationships.

Those outside the Covenant

The hardest questions are those about what the covenant community's culture ought to do about those who do not yet participate in the covenant. Clearly, society needs protection from criminals. But is it right, in a Jesus-type covenant, to punish those who injure others? More practically, does punishing do any good? Is there a better way? Does it work? Within the ideal of the *agapē* dynamic, respect and positive feelings and actions toward all members of the community, I believe we can urge that the best thing to try is prevention. The culture needs to be such that motivations to commit crimes are minimized, and that means that a great deal of proactive thought, feeling, and action have to be devoted to this issue.

First, however, to go back to the question of punishment: I think it can be asserted that it is mostly counterproductive. Death sentences don't seem to reduce murder rates. More people who have been in prison return to prison than stay out after one sentence. No doubt some crimes are prevented by the perpetrator's fear of being caught and punished, but are such fear and such punishment covenant ways of dealing with the problem?

There is a long tradition of believing that somehow punishment "balances" crime, that the guilty party can "pay a debt to society" and the "score" can be "evened." These are basically ideas of revenge, from a time before laws and formal justice. Such vengeance often led to generations of feuding and escalation of the "punishments." Law and formal justice didn't remove them; it only codified them. Nor has religion removed them; it has incorporated them into theologies of human relations with God.

Part of my thesis is that the Jesus way denies all of this sort of thinking/feeling. God doesn't measure, doesn't balance, doesn't punish (or reward). Participation in the Divine Life, which means unconditional love, is not a reward for being obedient but is itself the very life of goodness. The teaching says that acts of injuring others (including all attitudes of disrespect) and the motives behind them are something like illnesses, not fullness of life. Therefore, the proper response to them is curing, healing, nursing, healthful feeding, and exercising—analogues of that type. Loving people into health—removing what hurts them and keeps them from enjoying the fullness of life.

Often a single individual can create a local environment in which another individual can grow into health. But when we come to the large scale, we have to create a social culture in which people have what they need to come to fullness of their potentialities. As Michael Lerner says, we can't get protection without changing our society for everyone: "No matter how many people we lock up, the spiritual repression and frustration of our meaning-needs will create more human beings ready to act [in hurting ways]. This will continue until we can sustain genuine recognition of the God-energy within each of us, and can build social institutions that are predicated on this."[45]

But the institutional dynamics we have in place at present are going to be very difficult to reorganize, even with good intentions. We have to change popular entertainment that encourages identity by social class, disrespect, and violence; jobs that leave people insecure and make family life difficult and stressful; education that doesn't connect with where children actually live and give them confident hope for their futures; the physical conditions of neighborhoods that depress people aesthetically; the way we do business by regarding only the "bottom line" and not the lives of the working people; and the whole structure of people with power over people who are powerless. Nevertheless, it is right to try and wrong to give up.

Mickey Kaus takes a stab at it with some radical and severe suggestions. His plan gives a sense of the kind of change that is required. He says the real problem is what he calls "the underclass," living by the "culture of poverty." The root of this evil he locates in cash payments to the poor. So the first thing to do is to offer government-funded jobs to all able-bodied citizens over eighteen years of age. No cash. These just-under-the-minimum-wage jobs would be subsidized—as would private-sector low-paying jobs—to bring them up to livable levels. But everybody works, men and women alike, fathers and mothers. Childcare is provided, mixing the underclass children with children from affluent families. No advantage to being unmarried.

What the government would offer would be only information on where to find a job in your locality (I hope somebody thinks about transportation); if you show up, you get paid for your work. And you get training and supervision and a letter of reference to a better job, moving you out of the poverty cycle. If you don't show up, you don't get anything—except maybe loss of your children if they are not adequately cared for (under presently existing laws). But nobody starves. The government supplements charities to provide shelter and meals, even counseling, therapy, training, but never cash. Special efforts are made to force fathers to support their children. The first generation will be the hardest, of course—and expensive for the money-making taxpayers. But the second generation of children growing up in homes in which "work, not welfare, is the norm, where the rhythms and discipline of obligation pervade daily life," will have different attitudes and different habits. It may take several generations. But, says Kaus, it will "transform the entire culture of poverty."[46]

But would it stop crime or encourage it? As long as drug dealing and robbery pay better, won't people prefer them? How will labor unions react to the provision and payment for these jobs? It is important also to say loudly that child protection and any question of separation of children from parents constitute an independent issue that needs to be treated, with full resources, in its own terms. These questions show both how difficult the transformation would be and how necessary it is to have a covenant community based on compassion, respect, generosity, and patience. Maybe this particular plan isn't the answer, but we need to develop plans that are workable, and we need to resolve to bear the difficulties for the interval required to break the patterns that produce so many ills.

In the meantime, what shall we do about the drug dealers and robbers? And the rapists and murderers? Shall we try kindness and inspiration and hope in the prisons instead of harshness and permission for the prisoners to assault one another? Will a realistic prospect of relief from frustration work better than fear of punishment? Genuine work and genuine achievement may liberate that in human nature which craves this sort of satisfaction. Could a prison—which is, after all, a controlled environment—be a different kind of culture, a more satisfying one, than the "outside"?

Those were the crimes of the poor. What about the crimes of the wealthy, usually very large-scale crimes, affecting millions of people and millions of dollars? And the perpetrators of these crimes can't claim that they have been denied opportunities or respect. White-collar crimes are probably much easier to prevent, simply by making the laws and the inspections sufficiently strict. "Creative accounting" can be outlawed and made impossible if the laws are drawn adequately and accounting education directed to keeping the laws rather than to finding loopholes and ways of getting around them. Laws can oblige employers to pay livable wages and provide safe work spaces. Something can be done to prevent ruining whole communities by withdrawing the one big business that employed most of the citizens. We need a culture that has as its primary value concern for people. This value needs to be respected and actually practiced, not faked or ignored. Total freedom for business, with accumulation of money as the highest value, is perversion of the function of the economy of a society. Our culture needs to say this loud and clear, by its behavior. A healthy culture has to create economic institutions that people can believe in and be inspired by.

So we come back to the transformation of individuals and thereby the beginning of the transformation of systems and institutions—and the willingness to believe that it can be done. Believing has, to some extent, to come first. It is very hard to act without believing that the action will be productive. But it may take a lot of acting for a long time, and the believing has to be strong enough to carry us through that time without flagging.

12

Partners with God in Creation

The central idea of the Western tradition is that human beings are partners with God in the continuing creation of the world. "Creation" isn't something that happened a long time ago in the past. It's what's going on right now, right this minute. We're in the midst of it. As Jesus said, God is God "not of the dead but of the living"(Matt. 22:32). Theologically we are living in an open universe. We have access to endless energy. Being creative is the nature of Being itself, and it is our nature. We can't identify or judge ourselves by what we have been. We must look to what we yet shall be.

This is a tremendous idea. In a historical world that had always believed in the eternal return of the seasons and the experiences of life, this idea, when it first appeared, was almost incomprehensible. This idea of *the future*. The idea of an intentional transformation of the fundamental arrangements of existence. The idea that God expects things to change, wants things to change, intends change and growth and improvement, and expects us to participate in this creative effort. God is the God of the living, is the living God. Maybe there will never be a time when it's all finished, all over. Maybe the divine creating, the human creating, will go on forever "from grace to grace," as Gregory of Nyssa said.

We look forward to "the Messianic Era." We speak of Christianity, messianism, as an outlook on life, as a meaningful worldview. On the one hand, it is positioned in the ever-receding future, and, on the other hand, it *consists of* ourselves: we are the body of the Messiah. *We* are what's coming, what's growing from grace to grace, increasing in wisdom and grace and in favor with God and one another. We are the Anointed, the commissioned, the relied on, the responsible.

What is our job? Creating the world. We are God's expanding outreach surface, God's fingertips, where the action is, where the

248

excitement and the beauty are expected to be, in human consciousness and social relations. This chapter is going to be about creating, about what it takes to exercise our innate creativity. Some conditions are external to us and social, such as ownership, political freedom, and the actual material means of creating. Some have to do with communication and the flow of information and with appreciation of our work. Some are interior, and I will discuss them as matters of faith, hope, and imagination. Arising out of that, I will express what I take to be the core of the Jesus ministry in the context of a theology of continuing creation.

When people are not prevented from fulfilling their talents and abilities by artificial and unfair classifications into social ranks, or deprived of a safe hold on their homes and livelihoods, they naturally develop their productivity and generosity. But in order to be productive and generous, people have to have some means of being productive and, generally speaking, some surplus of product. So, implied in the Holy Thursday Revolution is security in being able to produce something with which to be generous, caring, and sharing.

At this point I want to tell another story. It's both a Christian and a Jewish story, and I propose to retell it in more casual language than the New Testament usually offers. I also need to affix a preamble in which to remind us that the background of this story (in its own setting) is the Roman occupation of the Holy Land and the consequent resistance movements of the late Second Temple period. The New Testament source of the story is the Gospel of John 1:43-49.

Sitting under One's Own Fig Tree: The Nathanael Story

The setting is near where John the Baptist is preaching preparation for the coming of the Messianic Era and is baptizing people. Through John, Jesus has met Simon and his brother Andrew and another man named Philip. Partly because of John's testimony and partly from their own conversations with Jesus, these men are persuaded that Jesus has a way of ushering in the Messianic Era, when Israel will be restored to freedom and self-government and the land will enjoy peace and prosperity. They are telling this to their friends and urging them to come meet Jesus.

Philip has a friend named Nathanael, to whom he expresses his excitement: "We think we've found the one spoken of by Moses and the other prophets! It's Jesus of Nazareth, the son of Joseph."

"Nazareth?" says Nathanael skeptically, "Can anything good come out of Nazareth?" (Nazareth is a small village in Galilee; Judeans have a poor opinion of Galileans.) Philip doesn't argue or explain. He says, "Come and see," and Nathanael comes.

Now the story says that when Jesus sees Nathanael coming to him, he calls out: "Look who's coming! A true Israelite, without guile!" Nathanael, arriving, expresses suspicion: "What do you know about me?" Is this the careful, coded way people who may be involved in a resistance movement test each other? Jesus answers, "I saw you sitting under the fig tree." Whereupon, in this collapsed and condensed story, Nathanael exclaims, "Rabbi, you are the Son of God! You are the King of Israel!"

I'm going to stop the story at this point because I have the piece I want to use. The evangelist has jumped from "fig tree" to "messiahship." Why? What's the connection? If you look up "fig tree" in a concordance, you'll see.

- 1 Kings 5:5 (Jewish Publication Society): "All the days of Solomon, Judah and Israel from Dan to Beer-sheba dwelt in safety, everyone under his own vine and under his own fig tree." (In the New Revised Standard Version this is 1 Kings 4:25.)
- Micah 4, which includes the famous "swords-into-plowshares" passage, continues, "But every man shall sit under his own vine or fig tree with no one to disturb him" (v. 4).
- Zechariah 2:15 declares: "In that day many nations will attach themselves to the Lord and become His people, and He will dwell in your midst"; 3:10 continues: "In that day . . . you will be inviting each other to the shade of vines and fig trees."
- Joel 2 describes a new day of rejoicing in freedom and plenty, when enemies are driven away and threshing floors are piled high with grain, "the fig tree and vine give their full yield" (v. 22), and God promises, "You shall know that I am in the midst of Israel . . . and my people shall be shamed no more."

So, is Jesus effectively saying to Nathanael, "I see you already enjoying the fruits of the new age—the kingdom will come in our lifetime"?

Here is the question I want to develop: Is one characteristic of this kingdom of peace and plenty that each household shall have its *own* vine and fig tree? Will everyone have a secure hold on the means of livelihood and productivity and subsequent generosity in the shared Supper?

In the story, this has significance in the context of high taxes, fore-closed mortgages, lost ancestral land, people being reduced to serf-dom, perhaps on the very land that had been in their families for generations. Think of the story of the Laborers in the Vineyard (Matt. 20), waiting in the village square for some landowner to hire them. If they'd had their own vines, they would have been gathering their own fruit. But they had lost control over the means of production. They are standing there "all the day idle . . . because no one has hired" them (Matt. 20:6-7). This was the missing piece. Before you can ask people to be productive and generous, you have to see that they have the ability, the wherewithal, the means to be productive and therefore generous.

The images in these ancient stories are of land and fruit. Putting the idea more generally, we can say that every "producer"—whether of goods such as food, housing, machinery, or goods such as works of art, scientific knowledge, or religious teaching—every producer needs to have a secure hold on the means of producing whatever it is that one produces for the benefit of the community. One needs to have "creative control."

There are reasons why productivity doesn't work well when the worker doesn't have control over the production of the work. Part of it, of course, is that people don't have the incentive to care for things that don't belong to them, and part of it is that we're greedy to gar-ner all the profits for ourselves. But that's not all of it. It also has to do with the way the information moves in the system.

The agent, the one who actually does something, needs to have the information about how things are going with the work and the capability to adjust the productive action accordingly. If you're going to keep the same land for crops for a long time, you will fertilize it and protect it. If it belongs to someone else and all you get is so much money for so many hours of work on the land, you don't relate to the land itself at all, only to the clock. The worker needs to have a real relation to the work, with repetition of the productive action, modi-fied by feedback from previous cycles (remember Tit-for-Tat),[1] so that the next round of action is more productive, progressive, getting better.

The agent needs to be a real member of this cycle. That is to say, the feedback—the success of the product—has really to affect the agent. The biblical proverb says of the multitalented and hard-work-ing Valiant Woman, "Give her . . . the fruit of her hands" (Prov. 31:31), and another verse says, "He who tends a fig tree will enjoy its fruit" (27:18). If these relations do not exist, the agent stands outside the reality loop and has only an artificial, or adventitious, relation to the production/feedback cycle. The hireling agent's own real cycle has as feedback pleasing—and getting paid by—the party that hires, but this is a kind of "epicycle" to the real business of producing a successful product.

Epicycle incentives, from their adventitious feedbacks, sometimes are quite contrary to the well-being of their parent real cycles. Bureaucratic caretaking of nationally owned resources may be a case in point, the bureau operatives placing their actions in the context of matching a paper directive or using up their budget so as to be well-funded next budget year, rather than in the context of what is really good for the resource they are supposed to be protecting and/or harvesting without hurting. Healthcare operations that are controlled by for-profit business concerns make decisions inside the context of profit rather than the context of health restoration. The feedback that reaches the decision maker will concern bottom line for the business but not recovery of the patient. That's an epicycle. A real cycle has the condition of the patient come back to the physician/nurse who is actually caring for the patient and who cares about whether that patient gets well.

There is notice taken of this kind of thing in the Gospel of John (10:12-13): "He who is a hireling and not a shepherd, whose own the sheep are not, sees the wolf coming and leaves the sheep and flees." He flees because he is a hireling and cares nothing for the sheep. The "good shepherd," on the other hand, knows the sheep, and the sheep know the shepherd. The well-loved Shepherd Psalm (23), sung from the sheep's point of view, details the care the real producer takes of the means of production over which that agent has real control—usually ownership. In touch with the needs of the sheep from moment to moment, the shepherd supplies.

This explains another reason, related to the flow of information, why state socialism doesn't work. The authority for making responses to experienced needs is too delayed in reaching the people on the site, who know what ought to be done. Feedback loops have to be kept local in order to be efficient. There are difficulties with freely chosen group ownerships as well as with power-imposed nationalizations. "Commons" and communes, unless they have strong moral incentives and clear understandings about who is responsible for what, usually don't work and don't last. A strong sense of "we" and what is "ours" may enable a small group to relate positively to their work and rejoice in what each other has achieved, but it seems to cause a strain in the natural dynamic of the intrinsic information of the agent's product-response cycle.

It seems that to care for something properly, the agent needs to bond with it in some felt way. The good shepherd and the sheep "belong to" each other. Creativity arises from such bonding, from a kind of nurturing of the "means of production" by the agent, and also a respect for and gratitude to the means for its contribution to the creative product. To grow good figs, you have to have your own fig tree. As one of the psalmists says, "When you eat the fruits of your own labor, you are happy, and it is good for you" (Ps. 128:2).

The situation bears a certain resemblance to the situation that evolves to successful cooperation. It needs to be a securely held, long-term, repeated interaction. Each party needs to be appropriately responsive to the behavior of the other. The producer learns early what works and what doesn't work with the means of production and makes adjustments. Through repeated interactions, the production system evolves toward a state of maximum achievable satisfactory productivity. The reciprocal communication between the action of the producer and the effect in the product, the continuous comparison of the current state to the desired state, drives the system toward the chosen goal of the agent, which is the inherent goal of the product.[2]

Just as the evolution of cooperation is dependent on there being a fairly long series of interactions between the parties—and their knowing that they will continue in interaction for a considerable time—so the producer/product relationship needs to be close, direct, long-term, repeated, and known to be secure in this respect. This is usually achieved by ownership of the means of production, or "creative control."

Such ownership or control needs to be legally protected in order to be understood to be secure. Deeds, patents, copyrights, and such protections of the producer's sense of long-term security are thus essential to successful productivity, the productivity that has to precede the generous sharing of the Supper. "Legally protected" really means that the relationship of creative and caring productivity is guarded and itself "nurtured" by the community's commitment and guarantee.

So the orientation of neighbor-love, which is the heart of the revolution, is already present at the very foundation of the sequence of steps leading to the sharing.[3] Moreover, we see again that neighbor-love and the confidence of security are in a positive-feedback relationship. Experienced security enables neighbor-love, and community neighbor-love creates a secure environment for creative advances.

Caring creativity becomes possible, and both producer and product benefit. The human being enjoys being creative, and the creativity improves the means of production. The consequence is that the product is improved and prosperity results. From prosperity comes surplus and from surplus comes the possibility of generosity. The same (or a similar) drive that makes the human being enjoy being creative makes the human being enjoy being generous. From this background come the participants in the shared Supper, the open commensality that characterizes the kingdom of God, in which godliness itself is what is shared and found nourishing.

Human Nature: Creativity and Generosity

That the world should be imbued with godliness is the point of everything. It is the point of the Holy Thursday Revolution: Turn away from trying to dominate and devote yourselves to creating and nurturing. This will make the world grow, grow in the direction of increasing godliness. Such is the meaning of the evangelist's conjunction of the fig tree and the Messianic Age. That age is described by Rabbi Noson Gurary as "the era of universal awareness, perception, and knowledge of God. In the Messianic Age, the world will finally become what it ought to be—a receptacle for the revelation of godliness."[4]

This sense of the divine purpose for the world is central to the revolution. Many past and present religions have as their aim to enable people to escape the world, or to do their bit in the world satisfactorily in order to earn a heavenly reward and to rest in a transcendent eternal state. But suppose the divine intention itself is precisely to create—to express divine potentiality as—a world, a finite temporal structure. There is a certain fulfillment in this, doing everything that is possible. The Infinite expressing itself in the finite.

In this view, the human being, as the image of God, is also a core reality that transcends definition or limitation to particularity, yet expresses itself in particular ways—a great variety of particular ways, whose future is incalculable by us. But the intent of the human being ought to be coincident with the divine intention, namely, to create, continue to create, further create the world, the finite order, and to develop it so that it expresses and increasingly reveals the divine, more and more nearly approaching the ideal of the Messianic Age. In this context we may say that if we do not turn eagerly toward and take seriously the reality of ("believe in") this messianic ideal, then we have misunderstood the purpose of creation and the presence of human persons in the world.[5]

This is the meaning of the teaching that we are to be partners with God in making a place, indeed a home, for godliness in the finite, even in the material, which seems to be at the furthest remove from the Divine. In the story of the giving of the Torah, the revealed Teaching, the last thing said by God was "Let them make a home for me, so that I may dwell among them" (Exod. 25:81).[6] And Matthew's Gospel, in the Sermon on the Mount (5:17-18), includes the statement that the whole of the Teaching (Torah) is to be "fulfilled," filled full, brought to completion (*plērōsai*), nothing left unattained. Then, as Rabbi Gurary says, "It will be obvious . . . that the world is for God."[7] It is not an illusion or an accident or a place of trial for people. It is a work of art, and it is for God, for fulfillment of a creative intention.

The human being, God's partner in this great enterprise, can be viewed as a kind of lens that concentrates and focuses the Divine Light in the world. Creating in our world here is an ongoing joint effort. Jesus is represented as saying, "My Father is still working, and I also am working" (John 5:17). His expectations for the rest of us were framed by the fourth evangelist as, "The works that I do you also shall do, and greater works than these shall you do" (John 14:12). If we read this in the light of what we understand about cosmic evolution, what a vision opens! Creation isn't over. This isn't the peak. "What we shall be has not yet appeared" (1 John 3:2). The sense of partnership with God, of being integrated into the creative act, is a powerful insight. Insight into God, insight into human nature.

Despite our misgivings about our undoubtedly wayward behavior, the Western tradition persists in affirming that human nature is made in the "image and likeness" of God (Gen. 1:26). The stories in the Book of Genesis show human beings whose first strong desire is to be "like God," especially by being wise and knowing how to tell good from evil (Gen. 3:5-6). This encourages me to put forward the idea that the "image and likeness" consist of the human being's central urge to be like God in being creative and generous.

It may seem a bit peculiar to pick out these characters as the hereditary line, but they seem to convey what is indeed peculiar to this tradition. We may defend this choice by pointing out that "everybody knows" that the Ground of Being has to be formless, empty, infinite, eternal, and absolute. That's what it means to be the Ground. It is usually also said that it must be "unchanging," and it is often assumed that this is synonymous with "the same." But the tradition that begins with the Hebrew Bible seems to be unique in featuring God's deliberate, loving, creative act in making the world and humans.

Sometime in the early 1960s, when I was at Fordham University, Anthony Flew, the British philosopher, came to speak to the philosophy department and tell us that any consideration of life after death could not be made to make sense, because there was no way to show how it was "the same" person on either side of the "great divide." You would have to display together matching characteristics, and the two worlds were by definition so different—let alone that the other world was inaccessible to those of us on this side—that such comparison was not only unavailable but meaningless.

I felt, in a vague, "mathematiciany" sort of way, that there was some kind of mistake in this argument because of an unrecognized faulty assumption or definition, and later that evening I thought I had found it. "Sameness" was the wrong test category, dimension, or quality. "Sameness" does not work even from moment to moment in our lives now, and the notion of "change" or "unchangingness" also presents this difficulty. Both imply comparison of qualities, characteristics, descriptions, essences—"what" something is—as though you could take two still photos and superimpose them to check that there is no difference. But the unity of the person is not dependent on, or achieved by, these qualities remaining "the same" or "unchanged." The unity of our personhood is due to the *continuity* of our *existence*.

Can this not also be said of God? Especially as "God" is conceived in the Western tradition, where, in addition to the function of being Ground of Being, there is a Personal Presence, with intentionality. So we had better avoid the concepts of "change" and "changelessness," lest we become trapped in technical contradictions. The divine unity may be more safely represented by the concept of "continuity," which may already carry the sense of intentional Person-Presence. If God is to be thought of in the aspect of creating, especially creating a world that evolves and that participates in its own creation of more and more novelties, then a *dynamic continuity*, which does not answer to being either "changing" or "unchanging" (because this is an inapplicable question), may be a helpful way for us to think.

Let us say, then, that creativity is a *thrust into being*: something new appears, what did not exist now exists. There is action in this, vitality, intention, and the intention is to put personal presence, self-reality, into what is created. To extend the creator's selfhood. To radiate the creator's being. God, being by definition unchallenged, being necessarily absolutely secure in existence, intends to express unqualified joy in existence by giving existence to new beings. This is the divine generosity.

But these "new beings" cannot be thought of as either "part of" God or differentiations and complications within God's own Being, or as altogether separate and independent beings outside God. We do not have an adequate concept set and vocabulary for this relation because we are at the ground level of the ontological reality. There is nothing more primitive in terms of which to explain it.

My own favorite metaphor, as I have often said before, is a dancer's gestures and movements. No one gesture defines the Dancer—or even all of them put together—but any one gesture certainly is not anything but the Dancer's own movement, the Dancer in the act of dancing. Is that gesture something "new"? Yes. Each movement in the dance, as it appears, is new. The Dancer makes it appear. It is the Dancer's own reality. Especially it is the Dancer's expression of the Dancer's own most intimate reality, an expressed version of the Dancer's selfhood. This sort of view is the foundation for the kabbalistic mystical theologian's dictum that "there is really nothing in existence but God."[8]

In any case, this is where the human being's "image and likeness" to God are lodged. The human being is the image of God by virtue of being creative and radiative, or generous, even as God is. Indeed, we can say to some extent that the same thing is true of every aspect of the cosmic reality—stars, molecules, living organisms. But what is essential to say is that this quality of creativity/generosity is the core of human nature. Therefore, the answer to our question in the Holy Thursday Revolution of whether it is possible to change human nature from the Domination Paradigm to the Communion Paradigm can be answered by saying that it is not necessary for human nature to change, because the character of communion in friendship is already present as the core of this image of the Divine Creative Ground. It is only necessary to develop the potentiality.

The world is the carrier and expression of the divine potentiality, the possibilities for development in this cosmic order (there may be others). The human being, in our local world, is a creative partner with God in bringing these potentialities to realization. In fact, some of the novelty realization is left up to the human being. We can create our own worlds. Whenever we perform creative acts, new things come into existence that never before existed.

Probably the most awesome of these is the experience of making another human being. People *must* be aware of their partnership with God and of their own creative powers on the occasion of the birth of a child. Probably this is why the sacred story tells us that God urged people to become parents—so that they would realize what is going on. People making more people, new persons! Persons who will do no end of creative things in work and play and human relations, in art and science and philosophy, in caring for other creatures and for the world as a whole. People *caring*, as God cares and thrusts the created order forward, urging it to be ever more creative and more generous and more caring, more divine.

Faith, Hope, and Imagination

If we really "believe in" the possibility of the messianic world, then we will have a meaningful context for everything we do. If this meaning can undergird the work we do and the play we enjoy, our friendship-relations and our stranger-relations, we will be encouraging others to hope and to have some confidence that we can turn things in a good direction. Shared belief can be a very powerful force. Trying to shift the ratio of self-love to neighbor-love is not easy, even though our essential nature is set up for us to experience our deepest satisfaction from comforting and promoting the good of others just as they are sustaining and benefitting us. But when we do encourage each other and believe together, it all becomes much easier, and we discover and invent new ways to make this wonderful new life.

As we enthusiastically exhort one another not to weaken, not to give up, not to doubt that it can be done, we can remind ourselves and others that it took thirteen billion years (or so) to produce us, doing it about as fast as it can be done, starting from nothing. If you're going to create a world that is itself creative in turn, you have to let it grow on its own terms.

In the days of the bacteria, or even of the earliest land animals a billion years later, the expectation of achieving the self-consciousness and creative genius of the human being would not have appeared particularly likely, if such a thing could even have been conceived of on the basis of what then existed, yet here we are—and so are many other amazing things. The universe grows miracles, so our "messianic" expectations or intentions are not to be scoffed at as ridiculous or impossible.

If we truly want this kind of world in the future, the obvious prerequisite is that we believe that it's possible. Then, if we believe in it and understand what it takes to grow into it (which is what this book is about), and if we are willing patiently and persistently to work for it (as distinguished from expecting it to be magically and supernaturally provided by some other agency), why should we not be justified in looking for it eventually to come about? Nachmanides, in his Commentary on the Torah (Deut. 30:6), says:

> In the days of the Messiah, the choice of [our] genuine good will be natural; the heart will not desire the improper. . . . There will be no evil desire in [us] but [we] will naturally perform the proper deeds and therefore there will be neither merit nor guilt.

Had not Jeremiah said:

> See, a time is coming—declares the Lord—when I will make a new covenant with the House of Israel and the House of Judah. . . . I will put My Teaching into their inmost being and inscribe it upon their hearts. . . . No longer will they say to one another, "Heed the Lord"; for all of them, from the least of them to the greatest, shall heed Me. (31:31-34 Jewish Publication Society)

Why not? Is that harder for the universe to produce than a DNA molecule?

Here is the contemporary equivalent of Nachmanides' messianic faith in David Korten's vision of the "kingdom" that is "coming and is already here" (John 5:25):

> Let people and communities cooperate to create a good living for all. . . . People will be unified . . . by a global consciousness that we share the same planet and a common destiny. This consciousness is already emerging and has three elements unique in human history:
>
> - The formative ideas are the intellectual creations of popular movements involving millions of ordinary people . . . outside . . . elite power.
> - The participation is truly global . . . every nation, cultural and linguistic group.
> - The new consciousness is rapidly evolving [and] adapting . . . as local groups meld into global alliances . . . and con-

sensus positions are forged . . . via Internet . . . a growing web of mutual compassion . . . rooted in real-world communities of place.[9]

Webs indeed are the secret, says Kevin Kelly, "tightly interlinked entities . . . self-reinforcing feedback . . . coevolution . . . many loops of increasing returns that fill an ecosystem." The world-embracing Shared Supper, the Holy Holistic Communion. Individuals have their own various kinds of fig trees, but when the various kinds of figs are shared in the Supper, new opportunities are created for new kinds of figs: "every new species . . . co-creates a niche for yet other new species," which will supply it or will use it for further purposes of their own. Opportunity—opportunity is the key to wealth and better living. Efficiency (reducing costs and increasing profits) is only a defensive measure, protection against loss and failure. Opportunity is expansion, advance. Nets—sharing—co-create opportunities and the opportunities multiply faster than the costs add up.[10] Bias in favor of creativity and generosity. Life in the image and likeness of the Ground/Creator.

If we can conceive of such a thing as "the days of the Messiah," shall we not pause to consider what kind of being we are that we can dream so? The cosmic evolution, in our corner of the universe, has produced this strange animal that is capable of believing in love and caring for all the other creatures. Are we to write this off as nonsense, daydreaming, something to be brushed contemptuously aside as "idealistic," "utopian," and "naive"? It is a fact that we can think such an ideal, and a good many of us aspire to this ideal, and even a good number of us are willing to devote ourselves to working for the ideal. What's the matter with cosmic nature that it has produced such a ridiculous being? Why aren't we impossible? Or, putting it another way, why is it so important to some of us to cast heavy scorn on the ideal?

When nature puts forth a feeler, a new shoot of some sort, or floats a trial balloon, or strings together a new gene, it may work. It may copy, it may adapt, it may "fit" its environment—or make its environment fit it. There is no a priori call to disparage it. It may fail and then appear again. (Eyes were independently invented several times.) So it may also come to pass that what we may call the *hesed* gene will catch on at last and spread, becoming, as Louis Jacobs says in *Holy Living*, "a . . . spontaneous generation of good will in the human character which makes us delight in giving freely and joyously to others."[11] Thus Rabbi Noson Gurary says:

To believe in the coming of *Mashiach* means to believe that there will be an end to the concealment of godliness and that we will finally attain knowledge of the true existence of God. And this must be not only a belief but an *ardent hope*, for this is the purpose of our existence and of all creation.[12]

In the context of cosmic evolution, this belief and this hope can be expressed in terms of human development, of which Daisaku Ikeda says that it can "become a reality to the extent that it is based on a trust directed toward the vitality inherent in human life."[13]

Vitality, life, is always reaching out, reaching forward, striving for improvement, experimenting with novelty. If we are to move toward our improvement, we need to envision where we want to be and then design backwards to where we presently are.[14] This is the concrete, practical side of expressing faith and hope in vitality, development, improvement, perhaps even goodwill and godliness. Notice that it also implies imagination. We have to supply the "design."

Probably nothing of human significance appears in our lives without being first an idea in somebody's head. The Prologue to the Gospel according to John reminds us that everything human comes to us courtesy of the Logos—the idea, the logical connections, language, the Word. The Logos mediates the transcendence of the Ground to the finitude of the world we are making. The idea realm is not the formless absolute, but neither is it material. From it stream endlessly the forms for novel beings. It can be called the *kavod* of God, the "glory" or "radiation" from the ineffable Ground. On the horizon of this *kavod*, where it hovers over virgin matter to form new reality in it, we find another advocate, hope. Hope sustains us during the long and often difficult time of gestation as the idea gradually takes form and reality in our material circumstances. It behooves us, therefore, to pay homage to hope, God's angel at our elbow, and accept all its ministrations with humble gratitude.

It is important to recognize that hope is not a phantasm, an unreality with which we amuse or console ourselves. It is a real and powerful force, especially since it calls down on us that other great and holy Spirit, the creative imagination. We need to exercise our imaginations to offset pessimism and despair. Images of history, social organization, economic possibility, emotional commitment to one another, trust, beauty, and excellence give our lives the color and tone that we experience as contentment or cynicism. To energize our vitality we need to imagine life as expansive, purposeful, worthy of hope and effort, and cooperative with our actions on its behalf. We can make a difference, we can make something good, something lasting and meaningful. Our existence here, even in the finite, in the material, is not an illusion or an accident, but an intention; it has meaning, and no effort that we make to work with it will be wasted.[15]

The Dalai Lama urges us to remind ourselves frequently "that we have this *marvelous gift of human intelligence and a capacity to develop determination and use it in positive* ways." The realization that we have *"this great human potential* [gives us] *an underlying strength* . . . to deal with any difficulty . . . without losing hope.[16]

These are indeed great powers. In exercising them we need to study the empirical importance of positive imagery for social healing. Intelligence and will are made concretely operative by the addition of the imagination. Many of the Dalai Lama's spiritual practices include "visualizations" to cultivate understanding of how the mind works and especially to arouse compassion. Books on healing prayer emphasize using strong visualizations of the desired health, strength, and happiness of the person prayed for. In helping ourselves to gain some desired goal, imagining ourselves already in that position can be strengthening. A verse in the Gospel of Matthew (21:22) suggests that when you pray for some intention, you should believe that you already have it, and then it will be done.[17]

Peter Russell, in *The Global Brain Awakens*, calling on Fred Polak's *The Image of the Future*, develops an argument that the image we hold will often be self-fulfilling. Television provokes copycat behavior. Pessimism encourages further pessimism, and "positive visions of the future may actually help us move in a more positive direction." We ought to be optimists because our very optimism will help to justify itself. Optimism is energizing, just as pessimism is depressing and weakening. Polak found that the images of its future that a society held and publicized could be read "as a barometer, indicating the potential rise or fall of a culture."[18] Now that we are so closely connected by the Internet with so much knowledge and news of one another and so closely bound in a single economic exchange, what might be the effect of a large number of the world's people holding positive images of the world at peace through care for one another, prosperity made possible by the encouragement of creative work, friendship for one another as we respect and honor all? Would not a really new "new thing" begin to form itself? A planetary symbiosis?

The Holy Thursday Revolution, moving us from the nonreciprocal Domination Paradigm imaged as footwashing to the reciprocal, cooperative Communion Paradigm imaged as feeding one another with the goods of our own lives, is clearly *prospective* not *retrospective*. It is not concerned with how well you have behaved in the past but with getting you to behave better in the future.

The religion of Jesus is not built around death. It is not about sin and how to balance it with suffering. It is not about judgment and punishment—or even about obedience and reward. It is precisely against all such dark and fear-provoking "measuring" ideas. It is about God's unconditional love and endless creativity. It is about the unlimited potential for goodness in people, for godliness in the world, for beauty in the earth and in human souls. It is about the "kingdom," *malchut*, the union of God with people for unlimited creativity.[19]

This is the treasure hidden and buried in a field (Matt. 13:44), for which we should forsake all other pursuits, all other ways of envisioning our life and purpose in existence. Sell all your petty ambitions, says Jesus, and invest everything in this Great Work. Join the big time. Enlarge your vision. You were made for something enormous. Open your eyes and see it!

The whole of the Jesus ministry undertakes to tell us that we are beloved children of God and have nothing to fear: You belong to the realm of eternal life. You are safe, so relax and let yourselves love one another. Heal one another, feed one another. Live, love, laugh and be happy. God is in the midst of creating a wonderful world, and you're needed to make it grow properly from the inside out. Therefore be creative. Color the world with imagination. Sing new worlds into existence. Dance with joy![20]

You are children of God. You have an umbilical connection to the Divine Life, to an inexhaustible source of existence, goodness, novelty, and beauty. Draw on it. Nurse from it. How? By faith: by being convinced of it and of your own sure connection to it, by being confident in it, by trusting it, by expecting good things, by envisioning great things, by imagining new ways to express divine love in the world. We might even say that "faith" is our *capacity to draw* life and nourishment, healing and joy, from this Source. Faith is closely paralleled by our "works," our *power to give,* about which Jesus' teaching says to us: You are capable, not helpless. The divine intelligence and energy are in you. When you are productive and generous, when you send your energy *out* (*agapē*), when you don't try to accumulate and hoard it (*eros*), you thereby *draw more* into the world from that inexhaustible Source.[21]

So don't be afraid. You are very valuable to God (Matt. 10:31). You can do what needs to be done. Don't wait for something magical and supernatural to transform the world. All of us together are the

Messiah. We have to do it ourselves, it has to come from the inside out.[22]

Believe in God, and believe also in yourselves. Even a little sure confidence coupled with vision can perform miracles. Mustard-seed faith can move mountains. Understand how the divine energy works by constantly giving itself away. Tie into this energy with faith, hope, and imagination, and nothing will be impossible for you (Matt. 17:20).

Notes

Preface

1. Beatrice Bruteau, "The Whole World: A Convergence Perspective," *Anima* (Fall 1975).

2. Beatrice Bruteau, "Neo-Feminism and the Next Revolution in Consciousness," *Anima* (Spring 1977). This essay and "The Whole World" can be found in Beatrice Bruteau, *The Grand Option*, ed. Ernest Daniel Carrere, O.C.S.O. (Notre Dame, Ind.: University of Notre Dame Press, 2001). See also Beatrice Bruteau, "Neo-Feminism as Communion Consciousness," *Anima* (Fall 1978).

3. Beatrice Bruteau, "From *Dominus* to *Amicus*: Contemplative Insight and a New Social Order," *Cross Currents* 31, no. 3 (Fall 1981): 273-84.

1. The Ills of the World

1. Anthony Storr, *Human Destructiveness* (New York: Grove Weidenfeld, 1991); Ted Robert Gurr, *Why Men Rebel* (Princeton, N.J.: Princeton University Press, 1970), 3; Stephan Lackner, *Peaceable Nature: An Optimistic View of Life on Earth* (San Francisco: Harper & Row, 1984), xi; Alfie Kohn, *The Brighter Side of Human Nature: Altruism and Empathy in Everyday Life* (New York: Basic, 1990), 54, 286 n. 53; Barry M. Blechman and Stephen S. Kaplan, *Force without War: U.S. Armed Forces as a Political Instrument* (Washington: Brookings Institution, 1978); Jean Bethke Elshtain, "Savage Realities," *In These Times*, September 30, 1996, reviewing Lawrence H. Keeley, *War Before Civilization: The Myth of the Peaceful Savage* (Oxford: Oxford University Press, 1996).

2. Stephan L. Chorover, *From Genesis to Genocide: The Meaning of Human Nature and the Power of Behavior Control* (Cambridge, Mass.: MIT Press, 1979), 7-8, 80-81, 97, 101; Ashley Montagu, *The Nature of Human Aggression* (New York: Oxford University Press, 1976), 188; Dith Pran, ed., *Children of Cambodia's Killing Fields: Memoirs by Survivors* (New Haven: Yale University Press, 1997); Peter Maass, *Love Thy Neighbor: A Story of War* (New York: Knopf, 1996), about Bosnia's "ethnic cleansing"; Lyall Watson, *Dark Nature: A Natural History of Evil* (New York: HarperCollins, 1995), 62, 220, 269.

3. Associated Press, Oak Ridge, TN, "Legacy: Nuclear Age Has Cost Lives and Money," *Winston-Salem Journal*, Wednesday, August 8, 1990, W1, W6; Liz Paul, "DOE Confirms Weapons Plants Are Unsafe," *Sane World* (Summer 1987): 5-6; John Boag, "Nuclear Accidents—Lessons for the Prevention of Nuclear War," *IPPNW* [International Physicians for the Prevention of Nuclear War] *Report* (April 1987): 7-9; Victor W. Sidel, MD, and Urban Waldenström, MD, "Chemical and Biological Weapons: An IPPNW Issue?" *Vital Signs* (October 1989): 8.

4. Pierre Teilhard de Chardin, *Letters from a Traveller* (New York: Harper & Row, 1962), 219-20; Elisabet Sahtouris, *Gaia: The Human Journey from Chaos to Cosmos* (New York: Pocket Books, 1989), 142.

5. Steven T. Katz, *The Holocaust in Historical Context*, vol. 1 (New York: Oxford University Press, 1994), 175ff.; Yehudi Menuhin and Curtis W. Davis, *The Music of Man* (New York: Methuen, 1979; rept., New York: Simon & Schuster, 1986), 203-4, describing the cruelty of slavery expressed in the music of the slaves; Stephen Barlow, "A Historical Perspective on Slavery: Demeaning Institution Has Been Practiced by All Races and Most Nations," *Winston-Salem Journal*, July 12, 1997, 9; George Will, "British Society Reminds World of Shocking Truth: Slavery Still Exists," *Winston-Salem Journal*, July 3, 1990, 10; Caroline Lees, "Living: A Burgeoning Slave Trade," *Sunday Telegraph* [London], September 21, 1997; reprinted in *World Press Review* (January 1998): 40, about the present-day enslavement of children in West Africa.

6. William Greider, *Who Will Tell the People?: The Betrayal of American Democracy* (New York: Simon & Schuster, 1992), 12-14, 18.

7. Eli Sagan, *At the Dawn of Tyranny: The Origins of Individualism, Political Oppression and the State* (New York: Knopf, 1985), xvi, xx-xxii, 239-42, 286-89, 291-95, 371; see also Robert Conquest, *The Great Terror: An Assessment* (New York: Oxford University Press, 1990). Greider, "Cox on the Constitution," an interview with Archibald Cox ("the Iran-Contra affair is a larger assault on our constitutional system than Watergate"), in *Common Cause Magazine*, September/October 1987, 17-19; Lawrence E. Walsh, Independent Counsel, *Iran-Contra: The Final Report* (New York: Times Books, 1994).

8. Claire Sterling, *The Terror Network: The Secret War of International Terrorism* (New York: Holt, Rinehart and Winston, 1981).

9. Robert C. North, *The World That Could Be* (New York: Norton, 1976), 139. Consider the paradox that the development of certain technologies can lead to such dangers that many things must be kept secret and be handled by a small select group, and a democratic population cannot know what is really going on and so cannot participate in or decide on what will be done in its name and affecting its life. See, e.g., Fred Kaplan, *The Wizards of Armageddon* (New York: Simon & Schuster, 1983) on exploring possible scenarios in the event of nuclear war. Theodore J. Lowi, a political scientist at Cornell University, said, "The people are shut out at the most creative phase of policy making—where the problem is defined" ("The New Public Philosophy: Interest-Group Liberalism," in *The Political Economy: Readings in the Politics and Economics of American Public Policy*, ed. Thomas Ferguson and Joel Rogers [Armonk, N.Y.: M. E. Sharpe, 1984]). Unfortunately, in many cases the information media do not tell the people either (Greider, *Who Will Tell the People?* 74ff.). Inequality and social control can be encouraged and justified by the dissemination of falsehoods (Chorover, *From Genesis to Genocide*, 24-25). See also Cynthia Crossen, *Tainted: The Manipulation of Fact in America* (New York: Simon & Schuster, 1994), on statistical information originating from researchers in the employ of corporations or other special interests. Kathleen Hall Jamieson, *Dirty Politics: Deception, Distraction, and Democracy* (New York: Oxford University Press, 1992), analyzes ads and speeches of political campaigns.

10. Chorover, *From Genesis to Genocide*, 27. Mihaly Csikszentmihalyi states: "Oppression is a condition in which the psychic energy of one person is controlled by another against his or her will. . . . Oppressors often start their careers as pro-

tectors, and only later turn into exploiters. . . . To keep control over our own psychic energy, it becomes essential that we understand how power is being used" (*The Evolving Self* [New York: HarperCollins, 1993], 93-94); this section gives a number of good examples. Montagu relates this to the power aura of the authority figure (*Nature of Human Aggression*, 181).

11. For U.S energy use, see *Vital Signs '03*, at www.WorldWatch.org/pubs/vs/ 2003. For a sense of the difference between rich and poor countries and the conclusion of social scientists of the Third World that the dynamic of the world economy leads to greater wealth for the few and greater poverty for the many, see Gustavo Gutiérrez, *A Theology of Liberation: History, Politics, and Salvation* (Maryknoll, N.Y.: Orbis Books, 1988), 21, 24-25. On efficiency monocultures that "reflect deeply rooted dominator thinking," see Alfonso Montuori and Isabella Conti, *From Power to Partnership: Creating the Future of Love, Work, and Community* (San Francisco: HarperSanFrancisco, 1993), 243.

On the role of the World Bank and the International Monetary Fund in "laying down stringent conditions regarding the economic priorities pursued," and on money as "such a powerful facilitator of the reproduction of asymmetries of wealth and power," and on how "institutional practices and organizational principles . . . play an integral role in the perpetuation of inequality," see Nigel Dodd, *The Sociology of Money: Economics, Reason and Contemporary Society* (New York: Continuum, 1994), 99, 162-64: in the case of the "network of intolerable obligations between Third World governments, First World banks and OPEC countries . . . the decisions of creditors . . . have an inherent symbolic dimension . . . with its roots in the organization of class and power."

For general background, see Steven Solomon, *The Confidence Game: How Unelected Central Bankers Are Governing the Changed Global Economy* (New York: Simon & Schuster, 1995). For a systems explanation of how the wealthy/poor differential allows wealthy countries to become generalists, while poor countries are forced to become specialists "living from the export of one or two products only," the result being "a system" that becomes "increasingly less viable and . . . instable," see Erich Jantsch, *The Self-Organizing Universe* (New York: Pergamon, 1980), 69. On sex tourism, see Donald H. Dunson, *No Room at the Table: Earth's Most Vulnerable Children* (Maryknoll, N.Y.: Orbis Books, 2003).

12. On pollution problems, see Greider, *Who Will Tell the People?* 126-30; search on-line for Cancer Alley or Clean Air, where February 2004 websites are still posting complaints. For disparity of income and assets in the United States, see Robert H. Frank and Philip J. Cook, *The Winner-Take-All Society: How More and More Americans Compete for Ever Fewer and Bigger Prizes, Encouraging Economic Waste, Income Inequality, and an Impoverished Cultural Life* (New York: Free Press, 1995), 43, 86: "the top 1 percent of households claimed 70 percent of overall growth in personal income between 1977 and 1989. By the end of the Reagan presidency, this elite had average income nearly twenty times as large as that of the median household." On tax cuts for the wealthy, see p. 21. That this works by positive feedback, see M. Mitchell Waldrop, *Complexity: The Emerging Science at the Edge of Order and Chaos* (New York: Simon & Schuster, 1992), 34-35 and the rest of that chapter. For large farms favored over small, see Ronald D. Rotstein, *The Future* (New York: Carol, 1990), 166-67; Jantsch, *Self-Organizing Universe*, 249. On American insistence on preserving income disparities, see Daniel Yankelovich, *New Rules* (New York: Random House, 1981), 137, 139, 141ff.

13. We don't count the important costs; see Fritjof Capra, *The Web of Life: A New Scientific Understanding of Living Systems* (New York: Doubleday, Anchor, 1996), 300; Frank and Cook, *Winner-Take-All Society,* 20; Hazel Henderson, *Creating Alternative Futures* (New York: Putnam, 1978), 21-22; Josh Sugarmann, *National Rifle Association: Money, Firepower and Fear* (Washington, D.C.: National Press, 1992); Franklin E. Zimring and Gordon Hawkins, *The Citizen's Guide to Gun Control* (New York: Macmillan, 1992).

On corporations moving families, see Arthur J. Deikman, *The Wrong Way Home: Uncovering the Pattern of Cult Behavior in American Society* (Boston: Beacon, 1990), 63 (also see p. 65 on use of overwork to indoctrinate new recruits, and p. 68 for examples of companies not revealing the dangers of their products). Eknath Easwaran states: "For personal pleasure and profit we are willing to sacrifice the welfare of our families and friends, our society and environment" (*The Bhagavad Gita for Daily Living,* Vol. I [Berkeley, Calif.: Blue Mountain Center of Meditation, 1975], 41). On runaway incomes at the top, see Frank and Cook, *Winner-Take-All Society,* 61ff.; on health hazards, see 132ff.

On information politics, see Greider, *Who Will Tell the People?* 36-39, 46-48, 59, 161-62: "You want facts to support the industry's lobbying claims? It [the information industry serving Congress and government in general] pumps out facts. You want expert opinions from scholars? It has those in abundance from the think tanks corporate contributors underwrite. You want opinion polls? It hires polling firms to produce them. You want people—live voters who support the industry position? [It] delivers them. . . . [An] office has . . . three hundred phone lines. . . . Articulate young people sit in little booths every day, dialing around America [in search of] 'white hat' citizens who can be persuaded to endorse the political objectives of . . . clients . . . expensive but not difficult" (p. 38).

14. For traditional assumptions about economic growth that are killing us, see Henderson, *Creating Alternative Futures,* 2. On attitudes toward nature, see Mary Midgley, *Beast and Man: The Roots of Human Nature* (Ithaca, N.Y.: Cornell University Press, 1978), 35-36. On economics vs. ecology, see Capra, *Web of Life,* 298-304; Daniel B. Botkin, *Discordant Harmonies: A New Ecology for the Twenty-First Century* (New York: Oxford University Press, 1990), e.g., 22. For a textbook, see Andrew Goudie, *The Human Impact on the Natural Environment,* 2nd ed. (Cambridge, Mass.: MIT Press, 1986). For a contemporary view endorsed by E. O. Wilson, see Anita Gordon and David Suzuki, *It's a Matter of Survival* (Cambridge, Mass.: Harvard University Press, 1991); for an alternative view, see Stephen Budiansky, *Nature's Keepers: The New Science of Nature Management* (New York: Free Press, 1995). On attitudes toward property and ownership, see Jantsch, *Self-Organizing Universe,* 274; Henderson, *Creating Alternative Futures,* 38.

15. Peter Farb, *Humankind* (Boston: Houghton Mifflin, 1978), 368, 133-39, 128-29, 166, 163, 379; Chorover, *From Genesis to Genocide,* 30, 108-9, 124-25. On blood pressure, see Robert Ornstein and David Sobel, *The Healing Brain: Breakthrough Discoveries about How the Brain Keeps Us Healthy* (New York: Simon & Schuster, 1987), 157.

16. For the idea that each ruling class pretends to represent all, see Peter Singer, *The Expanding Circle: Ethics and Sociobiology* (New York: Oxford University Press, 1981), 117. On all the different classes wanting to be heard, see Theodore Roszak, *Person/Planet: The Creative Disintegration of Industrial Society* (Garden

City, N.Y.: Doubleday, Anchor, 1979), 13. On badges of respectability, see Yanke-lovich, *New Rules,* 132, 117, 120, 122-23. On labels supporting stereotyping and status hierarchies, see Robert Axelrod, *The Evolution of Cooperation* (New York: Basic, 1984), 148-49. On the idea that subordinates lack knowledge of themselves and what knowledge they have conflicts with what dominators say about them, see Jean Baker Miller, *Toward a New Psychology of Women* (Boston: Beacon, 1976), who points out that subordinates try to imitate dominators but still are not accepted (pp. 11-12), that what dominators do is valued, what is valued is restricted to the dominant group, and what subordinates do is devalued (pp. 21ff.); and that the dominant group creates a philosophy to justify its oppression of the subordi-nates as "normal" and "right" (p. 8).

17. Kenichi Ohmae, *The Borderless World: Power and Strategy in the Inter-linked Economy* (New York: HarperBusiness, 1990), 55.

18. Storr, *Human Destructiveness,* 115-19. On racism or some other form of demeaning intrinsically necessary to domination, see Michael Lerner, *Jewish Renewal: A Path to Healing and Transformation* (New York: Grosset/Putnam, 1994), 157ff. Kohn, *Brighter Side,* 79.

19. On the idea that men have always ruled and always will rule, see Steven Goldberg, *Why Men Rule: A Theory of Male Dominance* (Chicago: Open Court, 1993); Farb, *Humankind,* 160. See also Theodore D. Kemper, *Social Structure and Testosterone* (New Brunswick, N.J.: Rutgers University Press, 1990); Marvin Har-ris, *Cannibals and Kings: The Origins of Cultures* (New York: Random House, 1977), 41-42, 60; also Anthony Wilden, *Man and Woman, War and Peace: The Strategist's Companion* (London: Routledge & Kegan Paul, 1987), who sees "in male supremacy the most massive system of organized bullying ever to arise on earth." Wilden argues in terms of context theory, and he analyzes (among other things) the physical and mental colonization of women and children, and "shows why men beat, kill, torture, fight, and rape" (dust jacket). Male supremacy arose with agriculture and the ability to amass surplus and to hire others: Csikszentmi-halyi, *Evolving Self,* 91-92. On patriarchy, the agricultural revolution, and the invention of religion, see Diarmuid O'Murchu, M.S.C., *Quantum Theology* (New York: Crossroad, 2004). On magic and technology, see Theodore Roszak, *Unfin-ished Animal* (New York: Harper & Row, 1975), 167. On the quest, from the Renaissance on, to control nature, see Jacob Needleman, *A Sense of the Cosmos* (Garden City, N.Y.: Doubleday, 1975), 40.

On keeping women in their place by medical definition and practice, see Chorover, *From Genesis to Genocide,* 151; compare Eileen Nechas and Denise Foley, *Unequal Treatment: What You Don't Know about How Women are Mis-treated by the Medical Community* (New York: Simon & Schuster, 1994), e.g., that new medicines are tested only on men. See also Miller, *Toward a New Psychology,* 124, 24-25; Montuori and Conti, *From Power to Partnership,* 250. On women being left out of science awards, see *Science News,* February 24, 1979, 120f.; David F. Noble, *The Religion of Technology* (New York: Knopf, 1997), esp. the Appen-dix, "A Masculine Millennium: A Note on Technology and Gender," 209-28. For a case in point, see Candace B. Pert, *Molecules of Emotion* (New York: Scribner, 1997), on her scientific discoveries, for which she was expected to allow the credit and prizes to be given to men. She likens her case to that of Rosalind Franklin, "the brilliant scientist who had provided the critical link [X-ray crystallography] in the chain of reasoning that allowed Francis Crick and John Watson to [win the Nobel Prize and almost all popular mentions of the DNA structure]" (pp. 109-11). Years later, Watson acknowledged the theft of her data in *The Double Helix* (New York: Atheneum, 1968), 225. Another instance is that of Henrietta Leavitt, whose discovery of the period/luminosity relation in Cepheid variables enabled Edwin Hubble to apply it to determine the distances of galaxies. In the Larousse *Dictionary of Science and Technology*, Leavitt's name does not appear; the Cepheid variable relation is explained, but she is not mentioned; there are six entries under Hubble, crediting him with discoveries and defining various items named in his honor.

On violence, see Marilyn French, *The War Against Women* (New York: Summit, 1992). On military rapes, see Lyall Watson, *Dark Nature,* 179-80; see also George Hicks, *The Comfort Women: Japan's Brutal Regime of Enforced Prostitution in the Second World War* (New York: W. W. Norton, 1995), on forced recruitment of girls and young women to act as prostitutes for the Japanese military. That rape is considered "natural," glamorous, and acceptable, important for male identity, see Montuori and Conti, *From Power to Partnership,* 107, 91; but that it is primarily a matter of anger, see Storr, *Human Destructiveness,* 71.

20. On children as not inferior to adults, see Ashley Montagu, *Growing Young* (New York: McGraw-Hill, 1981), 134. On the prevalence and causes of child abuse, see Storr, *Human Destructiveness,* 102ff.; until recently underestimated (p. 68). See Donald G. Dutton, with Susan K. Golant, *The Batterer: A Psychological Profile* (New York: Basic, 1995); and Ann Jones, *Next Time She'll Be Dead: Battering and How to Stop It* (Boston: Beacon, 1994). For the argument that a whole complex of ills stems from lack of love for children, and a very interesting diagram of the systemic relations of these (p. 68), see Bruce Holbrook, *The Stone Monkey: An Alternative, Chinese-Scientific Reality* (New York: Morrow, 1981). On family violence, see Wilden, *Man and Woman,* 179-83: few women press charges; the police are not likely to help; the victim is blamed; for infanticide, see p. 198; for incest, p. 225. On bystander apathy and the Kitty Genovese case, see Farb, *Humankind,* 170. On the distress and confusion men feel as they are asked to change gender roles—"many fear that their rights and roles are shrinking before their eyes" (dust jacket), see Ellis Cose, *A Man's World: How Real Is Male Privilege—and How High Is Its Price?* (New York: HarperCollins, 1995).

21. On the danger of religious fanaticism, see Storr, *Human Destructiveness,* 156-57. Chorover says, "Like most hierarchically organized societies (including most nations and most parties), the Christian churches officially endorsed the idea that their own hierarchical structure reflected what Aristotle called a 'justice of proportional worth' [Aristotle believed, e.g., that some people are 'natural slaves']. . . . hierarchs reward . . . conformity . . . and punish deviance or dissent" (*From Genesis to Genocide,* 16). See Joseph Campbell, *Creative Mythology,* volume 4 of *The Masks of God* (New York: Penguin, 1968) on the crushing of Abelard by the church for his conviction that knowledge of God can be attained by reason and therefore is available also to the non-Christian world: his "fate . . . had been the announcement . . . of all the passages to follow . . . the same dreadful murder of light and life by grim power (the art of the systematic exercise of power by men over men)" (p. 398; see also preceding pages)—that is, power over people's lives, imaginations, and minds. Deikman suggests that the basic perspective of most religious groups is in terms of the superior/inferior relation. Obedience is a prime virtue. See *Wrong Way Home,* 84-85.

2. Our Basic Insecurity

1. On the complexity of human behavior, see Ashley Montagu, *The Nature of Human Aggression* (New York: Oxford University Press, 1976), 285. On the glorification of fighting, see Mary Midgley, *Beast and Man: The Roots of Human Nature* (Ithaca, N.Y.: Cornell University Press, 1978), 29. On war a sacred thing, see H. Butterfield, *The Origins of History* (New York: Basic, 1981), quoted (without page number) in Edward Harrison, *Masks of the Universe* (New York: Macmillan, 1985), 41. Many Americans believe war is human nature: see Alfie Kohn, *The Brighter Side of Human Nature: Altruism and Empathy in Everyday Life* (New York: Basic, 1990), 48 and n. 34. On the idea that people have not shown the will to forsake war, see Willis Harman, *Global Mind Change: The Promise of the Last Years of the Twentieth Century* (Indianapolis: Knowledge Systems, 1988), 154. On dehumanizing the enemy to make soldiers willing to kill, see Kohn, *Brighter Side,* 49, 57, 141, 144. On the idea that war/violence is not caused by hatred but appears when authorized, see Kohn, *Brighter Side,* 286. See also Lt. Col. Dave Grossman, *On Killing: The Psychological Cost of Learning to Kill in War and Society* (Boston: Little, Brown, 1995). It's not that we don't have an inhibition against killing our kind, but society discourages such inhibition (see Montagu, *Nature of Human Aggression,* 264). Modern war makes this easier by doing a lot of the killing at a distance, without emotional involvement (Robert C. North, *The World That Could Be* [New York: Norton, 1976], 55). Operating a killing machine is impersonal, "just doing a job" without taking responsibility for the content of the matter; those doing this are participating in the paradigm of domination not on the domination side but on the submissive side (see Montagu, *Nature of Human Aggression,* 271-72). Man invented war as an artificial challenge, to make him feel excited and alive (Colin Wilson, *Afterlife: An Investigation of the Evidence for Life after Death* [Garden City, N.Y.: Doubleday, 1987], 252). Men fight wars to support their comrades, not to dominate the enemy (Montagu, *Nature of Human Aggression,* p. 260, citing Desmond Morris, *The Naked Ape* [New York: McGraw-Hill, 1967], 176). On the same page Montagu says that Morris's teacher, Niko Tinbergen ("On War and Peace in Animals and Man," *Science* 160 [1968]: 1411-18) believed that Konrad Lorenz (*On Aggression* [New York: Harcourt, Brace & World, 1966]) was right when he claimed that the elimination, through education, of the internal urge to fight will turn out to be very difficult, if not impossible. See also Herbert Strean and Lucy Freeman, *Our Wish to Kill* (New York: St. Martin's, 1991).

2. On the fundamental value of society as power over others, see Alfonso Montuori and Isabella Conti, *From Power to Partnership: Creating the Future of Love, Work, and Community* (San Francisco: HarperSanFrancisco, 1993), 220. See William Eckhardt, *Civilization, Empires and Wars* (Jefferson, N.C.: McFarland, 1992), 206-7: civilizations, empires, and wars foster one another among primitive, civilized, and modern peoples; empirical findings support the view of Toynbee, Sorokin, and others that war and civilization are motivated by a sense of superiority and self-righteousness, which justifies destructive behavior. The trouble is structural: the authoritarian, egoistic, and compulsive nature of the way we have developed our civilizations gives them their war-making essence. We could turn this around, says Eckhardt, by restructuring civilization in a more egalitarian, altruistic, and compassionate way. However, "even the possibility of total destruction has not yet led us to make an ethical response to its challenge." On how "companyism" in

economics can lead to ill-feeling between nations, see Kenichi Ohmae, *The Border-less World: Power and Strategy in the Interlinked Economy* (New York: Harper-Business, 1990), 53. See also Arthur J. Deikman, *The Wrong Way Home: Uncovering the Pattern of Cult Behavior in American Society* (Boston: Beacon, 1990). On the idea that institutions in general order things to benefit the social class that controls them, see Edward O. Wilson, *On Human Nature* (New York: Bantam, 1979), 169. On how external domination of countries by other countries subverts the social classes within the dominated nation, see Gustavo Gutiérrez, *A Theology of Liberation: History, Politics, and Salvation* (Maryknoll, N.Y.: Orbis Books, 1973), 85, 87, 94 n. 17.

3. On Sartre and the hostile "look," see Xavier O. Monasterio, "Sartre and the Existential Approach," *International Philosophical Quarterly* 21 (1981): 80. Much apparently sexual behavior actually concerns status (Anthony Storr, *Human Destructiveness* [New York: Grove Weidenfeld, 1991], 73). Gutiérrez says that Lenin and others looked at the problem only from the point of view of capitalist nations; no one looked from the point of view of the dominated (*Theology of Liberation,* 86). It has been the same with women; there is very little literature about women or about the world from women's point of view. Almost all studies of women have been from a man's point of view. Males almost always rank higher, but females don't need rank so much, says Mary Midgley (*Beast and Man,* 337). According to Kohn, position of dominance is a better predictor of sensitivity to other people's emotional state than gender is: subordinates need to pay careful attention to dominators; as men are dominant in our culture, so women become more aware (*Brighter Side,* 307 n. 93). On the social wastefulness of rank ordering, see Robert H. Frank and Philip J. Cook, *The Winner-Take-All Society* (New York: Free Press, 1995), 127-29, with good examples.

4. On helping others = hurting oneself and hurting others = helping oneself, see Hee-Jin Kim, *Dôgen Kigen, Mystical Realist* (Tucson: University of Arizona, 1987), 200. For evidence of harm, see Kohn, *Brighter Side,* 94. On life as a zero-sum game, see Robert Axelrod, *The Evolution of Cooperation* (New York: Basic, 1984), 110, 123, 219 n. 1. On models of competition, see North, *World That Could Be,* 60-61; when people lived in small bands, competition was for status according to skill (p. 22); in tribes, skill and endurance (p. 27); in a chiefdom, competition for rank, access to goods, warfare make their first appearance (p. 31); in the state, competition for wealth, power, domination (p. 33); intense competition seen as desirable (p. 39); seen as both benefit and threat (p. 53); competition between societies (p. 47). The American culture of competitive success suggests that "excessive awareness of and concern about the feelings of others may prove counterproductive," so we bring up children to look out for themselves and not care about others "excessively" (Kohn, *Brighter Side,* 96-97). Television violence and callousness support the competitive personality, which in turn desires more products, status-symbols, and pleasure, which are purchased from the advertisers of the shows. Daniel Yankelovich points out that Americans compete vigorously in sports and education and for jobs, honors, recognition, and scientific achievement (*New Rules* [New York: Random House, 1981], 157). We honor best-sellers and admire stars. "We divide people into winners and losers, and logically so, for the system works toward such allocations." Montuori and Conti comment that the system of domination has no room for losers and yet ensures that everyone will become one ultimately (*From Power to Partnership,* 47).

5. Deikman, *Wrong Way Home,* 10.

6. Edward O. Wilson, *On Human Nature,* 192.

7. On class, success, and self-esteem, see Yankelovich, *New Rules,* 132-33; Deikman, *Wrong Way Home,* 10; see also p. 50 (status may be different in different "reference groups"), p. 71 (we have a "predilection for inequality"). On rank ordering in society as necessary for the evolution of intelligence, see Vitus B. Dröscher, *The Friendly Beast* (New York: Dutton, 1971), 199, 201. Aggressive species have more rigid domination systems (Elisabet Sahtouris, *Gaia: The Human Journey from Chaos to Cosmos* [New York: Pocket Books, 1989], 138); cf. Wilson, *On Human Nature,* 96, on role rigidity.

8. Beatrice Bruteau, "The Revelation at Sinai," *The Roll* 13 (1995): 123-31; for "new creation," see Galatians 6:15.

9. We all have a role in the paradigm of domination; it's not just the dominators: see Montuori and Conti, *From Power to Partnership,* 101-2, 183. On the attraction, for both leaders and followers, of a superior/inferior perspective, see Deikman, *Wrong Way Home,* 96. On the oppressed desiring to become oppressors, see John Dominic Crossan, *The Historical Jesus: The Life of a Mediterranean Jewish Peasant* (San Francisco: HarperSanFrancisco, 1992), 317. On the idea that losers believe they are losers, see Montagu, *Nature of Human Aggression,* 46; cf. Beatrice Bruteau, *The Psychic Grid: How We Create the World We Know* (Wheaton, Ill.: Theosophical Publishing House, 1979), 105 (positive expectations). According to Montagu, believing in ourselves as domination-programed makes totalitarian tyranny more likely (p. 295). Subordinants must avoid open conflict in order to survive (Jean Baker Miller, *Toward a New Psychology of Women* [Boston: Beacon, 1976], 9-10); they have little knowledge of their history because dominants have suppressed it (p. 11); they are so indoctrinated that they cannot tolerate the idea that their activities could be for themselves; they see themselves only in service to others (p. 62).

10. On the idea that inequality is universal, see Peter Farb, *Humankind* (Boston: Houghton Mifflin, 1978), 380-81. On different values in different cultures, see Alan Roland, "Personal Reflections II: Indian/American Encounters," *American Vedantist* 3, no. 4 (Winter 1998): 12-13. For Gandhi, cf. John 5:44. For domination learned, see Montagu, *Nature of Human Aggression,* 316-18. According to Stephan L. Chorover (*From Genesis to Genocide: The Meaning of Human Nature and the Power of Behavior Control* [Cambridge, Mass.: MIT Press, 1979], 8), great social tragedies are not to be explained simply in terms of individual psychological derangements; the intent to so explain them is itself deceptive; they are corporate and institutional derangements. On domination becoming obsessive, see North, *World That Could Be,* 136. Midgley, *Beast and Man,* 35: using certain types of other people as symbols for their own faults, men then attribute to individuals of those classes these vices. See also Montuori and Conti, *From Power to Partnership,* 191: a mentality in the domination mode has a limited range of feelings and shuts out views and feelings other than its own.

11. For men, to share means to lose; to care and serve is to be like a woman (Miller, *Toward a New Psychology,* 42, 70, 71). "Men are forced to turn off those naturally responsive parts of themselves" (ibid.). The ability of women to feel and admit these common human experiences is a strength, a closer touch with reality, but women are obliged to protect men from having these feelings (pp. 29-34). In cross-gender work, women want to do as well as men, but men expect to do better than women (Linda Asher, "Pink Collar Men and Blue Collar Women," *Psychology Today* [June 1979]: 32).

12. On males being more concerned about their relationships with other males, see Farb, *Humankind,* 315. On slavery and warfare, see Sahtouris, *Gaia,* 141. On socially cohesive activities being relegated to women, see Hazel Henderson, *Creating Alternative Futures: The End of Economics* (Berkeley: Windover, 1978), 15. On the mystery of male dominance, see Farb, 210ff.: "None of the . . . biological and psychological differences would seem to account adequately for the dominance of males in all societies. . . . The long-lived, more healthy, less accident-prone, and equally intelligent females should be the dominant sex. . . . The great paradox about male dominance is that females have allowed it to exist when they could so easily have undermined it." We are still living in a culture in which privilege, property, and power are the dominating forces (Philip Van Doren Stern, *Prehistoric Europe* [New York: Norton, 1969], 312). On dangers to life today from conflicts in the system, which are there because of the nature of the system and on characteristics inherent in large, highly stratified, intensely competitive social structures, see North, *World That Could Be,* 96-97.

On social cultivation of aggressive males and the institution of warfare, see Farb, *Humankind,* 220; cf. Marvin Harris, *Cows, Pigs, Wars, and Witches: The Riddles of Culture* (New York: Random House, 1974), who argues that males are taught to be aggressive, that "the same sort of brutalization could . . . be imposed on women." But, "if sex is to be used to energize and control aggressive behavior, then . . . both sexes cannot . . . be brutalized to an equal degree. One . . . must be trained to be dominant. . . . To make sex a reward for bravery, one of the sexes has to be taught cowardice. . . . The ultimate prospects for sexual equality depend upon the . . . elimination of military forces. . . . We should have gone little beyond the Yanomamo [tribal people of the Amazon] if the net outcome of the sexual revolution is a secure position for women . . . in the nuclear command posts" (chapter "The Savage Male," esp. 106-7).

On pleasure in war, see Montagu, *Nature of Human Aggression,* 105, where he gives a number of citations. Stern says that male deities, gods of war, appeared at the same time as the use of metal (*Prehistoric Europe,* 302) and that all the European cultures of the early Iron Age were masculine and warlike (p. 309). On "making a killing," see John N. Bleibtreu, *The Parable of the Beast* (New York: Macmillan, 1968). On small boys, see Midgley, *Beast and Man,* 341. See also Mircea Eliade, *Myths, Dreams and Mysteries: The Encounter between Contemporary Faiths and Archaic Realities,* trans. Philip Mairet (New York: Harper Torchbooks, 1967), 46-47: "song proclaims this: 'She who has not yet given birth, let her give birth; he who has not yet killed, let him kill!' It is a way of saying that the two sexes are condemned each to accept its destiny." On killing as respectable and copulation not, see Bleibtreu, 145 (nineteenth-century England). See also Midgley, 31: *"man has always been unwilling to admit his own ferocity,* and has tried to deflect attention from it by making animals out to be more ferocious than they are." (The word "ferocious" is from Latin *fera,* wild animals.) See also p. 33 for contemporary cultural events in which human cruelty is projected onto animals. See further Vitus B. Dröscher, *They Love and Kill: Sex, Sympathy and Aggression in Courtship and Mating* (New York: Dutton, 1976), 8: "The invention of the male, the luxury product of genetics, created many grave problems. In fact, we might say that the existence of the male, rather than the eating of the forbidden fruit, was what brought about the loss of Paradise." Also Lewis Thomas, *The Lives of a Cell: Notes of a Biology Watcher* (New York: Bantam, 1974), 30: "The men who run the affairs of nations today . . . have been taught that the world is an arrangement of adversary systems, that force is what counts, aggression is what drives us at the core, only the fittest can survive, and only might can make more might."

13. On androgens, see Emily Hahn, *Look Who's Talking* (New York: Crowell, 1978), 129-30. See also Theodore D. Kemper, *Social Structures and Testosterone* (New Brunswick, N.J.: Rutgers University Press, 1990); James McBride Dabbs, *Heroes, Rogues, and Lovers: Testosterone and Behavior* (New York: McGraw-Hill, 2000). On manliness, see Farb, *Humankind*, 141. On testing against peers, see Miller, *Toward a New Psychology*, 51; fear of losing manhood by developing genuine relations with people because that is "women's way" (pp. 23-24); our culture prevents men from integrating the full range of the human potential (pp. 49-51, 68, 71). For the real risk, as loss of generalized behavior, see Farb, 171ff. See also Steven Goldberg, *Why Men Rule: A Theory of Male Dominance* (Chicago: Open Court, 1993), 64-65. Dröscher (discussing fish, insects, spiders) says that only by aggression, physical strength, and domineering behavior "could males raise themselves from their lowly position as mere mating partners." He gives instances of males eaten or otherwise destroyed after serving their function of fertilization (*They Love and Kill*, 28, in a whole chapter on the creation of the male). Farb cautions against arguing from animal models to the conclusion that male dominance is inescapable; the human being can think about the issue and consider the moral values at stake (pp. 369-70).

14. Eknath Easwaran, *The Bhagavad Gita for Daily Living*, vol. 1 (Berkeley, Calif.: Blue Mountain Center of Meditation, 1975), 30; the Prayer of St. Francis includes the words, "It is in giving that we receive, it is in pardoning that we are pardoned, it is in dying [to self] that we are born to eternal life" (see Easwaran's discussion, pp. 18-19, 143, 203).

15. On the importance of contrast, note the following comments: "*even the simplest act of comparison involves emotional factors*" (J. Z. Young, *Programs of the Brain: Based on the Gifford Lectures 1975-7* [New York: Oxford University Press, 1978], 194). "There is in some quarters a naive assumption that caring for other people must be mutually exclusive with taking care of one's own needs" (Kohn, *Brighter Side*, 78). "Hurting and killing other beings is a tried and true way to prove that one's self exists and is powerful, and it is something one can learn to enjoy" (Mihaly Csikszentmihalyi, *The Evolving Self: A Psychology for the Third Millennium* [New York: HarperCollins, 1993], 247 [with examples]. "To help the poor without hurting the rich was the heart of our political philosophy" after World War II, "a political consensus shared by both rich and poor. . . . The national psychology is: Since I am getting mine, why shouldn't the other person get his? Only when people feel vulnerable themselves do they resist helping others" (Yankelovich, *New Rules*, 172).

On cultivating the sense of lack, see David Loy, "Trying to Become Real: A Buddhist Critique of Some Secular Heresies," *International Philosophical Quarterly* 32, no. 4 (December 1992): 404-5: "When we do not understand what is actually motivating us—because what we think we want is only a symptom of something else (according to Buddhism, our desire to *become* real . . .). The sense-of-self [attempts to objectify itself somehow in the world, which is impossible]. . . . The consequence of this perpetual failure is that the sense-of-self always has, as its inescapable shadow, a sense-of-*lack*." Loy quotes Ernest Becker (*The Denial of Death* [New York: Free Press, 1973], 66): "The irony of man's condition is that the deepest need is to be free of the anxiety of death and annihilation; but it is life itself which awakens it, and so we must shrink from being fully alive"; and Norman O. Brown (*Life Against Death* [New York: Vintage, 1961], 270): "The ultimate problem is not guilt but the incapacity to live. The illusion of guilt is necessary for an animal that cannot enjoy life, in order to organize a life of nonenjoyment."

Loy continues, saying that under the delusion that we are an autonomous self-consciousness, we "can never quite shake off [the] shadow feeling that 'something is wrong with me,' [so we] need to rationalize that sense of inadequacy somehow. [When we don't have a religious way of handling this], modern man usually experiences his *lack* as 'I don't have enough; I must get more.'" We attempt to fill our lacks with fame, love, wealth, and power, but all our cultural forms in these areas increase our sense of failure and lack. Loy recommends discovering that we are real already as participating members of the great interaction that is the whole world; we lack nothing, for we are everything. Compare Janine Chanteur's discussion of the roots of war in *Desire: From War to Peace*, trans. Shirley Ann Weisz (Boulder, Colo.: Westview, 1992), 24-25.

16. On the fear-based domination system kept in place by continued belief in scarcity, see Montuori and Conti, *From Power to Partnership*, 154ff. "When we suffer from . . . the fever of the ego . . . we become blind to the needs of those around us and to the unity of life" (Easwaran, *Bhagavad Gita*, 184), also p. 224: "Imprisoned in our little ego, [we are] always on the lookout to see if others are denying us things to which we entitled." We have a continual need for affirmation to support our sense of separate individual identity (Storr, *Human Destructiveness*, 12). On stress at the symbolic level, or playing within a system that produces the need to achieve in a certain way, see Ludwig von Bertalanffy, *A Systems View of Man,* ed. Paul A. LaViolette (Boulder, Colo.: Westview, 1981), 37.

3. How We Identify Ourselves

1. P. G. Wodehouse, *Something Fresh* (1915; London: Penguin, 1986), 186-87.

2. Winston L. King, Foreword to Keiji Nishitani, *Religion and Nothingness,* trans. Jan Van Bragt (Berkeley: University of California Press, 1982), xi.

3. Nishitani, *Religion and Nothingness*, 88. On contrast, see Gregory Bateson, *Mind and Nature: A Necessary Unity* (New York: Dutton, 1979), 87 *et passim.* See also Paul A. Weiss, *The Science of Life* (Mt. Kisco, N.Y.: Futura, 1973): minor disparities outshine major identities; sameness is dull. Robert Axelrod, *The Evolution of Cooperation* (New York: Basic, 1984), 111: we look for a standard of comparison. For biblical references (Isa. 46:3; 2 Cor. 10:12) urging that comparison is not an appropriate method and discussion, see B. Bruteau, "Global Spirituality and the Integration of East and West," in *The Grand Option: Personal Transformation and New Creation,* ed. Ernest Daniel Carrere, O.C.S.O. (Notre Dame, Ind.: University of Notre Dame Press, 2001), 109ff. For ego concerns based on fear, see Alfonso Montuori and Isabella Conti, *From Power to Partnership: Creating the Future of Love, Work, and Community* (San Francisco: HarperSanFrancisco, 1993), 104. Kenichi Ohmae says that nationalistic paranoia can lead to nationalistic suicide (*The Borderless World: Power and Strategy in the Interlinked Economy* [New

York: HarperBusiness, 1990], 179). Nevertheless, we tell each other: Don't try to love your neighbor; what holds society together is racism and distrust of foreigners (Ashley Montagu, *The Nature of Human Aggression* [New York: Oxford University Press, 1976], 288). On the theological and scientific idea that the human being is not part of Nature but dominates it from outside, see Ilya Prigogine and Isabelle Stengers, *Order Out Of Chaos: Man's New Dialogue with Nature* (New York: Bantam, 1984), 50. For the humanist view (challenged) that we are essentially alien to the natural world and need to subject it to us lest we become subject to it, see Rupert Sheldrake, *The Rebirth of Nature: The Greening of Science and God* (London: Century, 1990), 173-74.

4. Edward O. Wilson, *On Human Nature* (New York: Bantam, 1979), 122-23; Zev-Hayyim Feyer, "Redeeming the Holocaust: A Returnee's View," in *The Fifty-Eighth Century: A Jewish Renewal Sourcebook,* ed. Shohama Wiener (Northvale: Aronson, 1996), 28-29.

5. See Michael Lerner, *Jewish Renewal: A Path to Healing and Transformation* (New York: Putnam, 1994), 171: "The belief in selfishness [and cruelty] itself becomes one of the causes for why most people never will achieve their own good, because to do so requires living in a society based on . . . mutual connection . . . mutual recognition and . . . caring." Psychologist Harvey Hornstein suggests that we come to perception of other people already disposed to see them as alien or similar to ourselves, but *"there is nothing in any distinction between human beings that compels us to see others as they"* (*Cruelty and Kindness: A New Look at Aggression and Altruism* [Englewood Cliffs, N.J.: Prentice-Hall, 1976], 125). See also Eknath Easwaran, *The Bhagavad Gita for Daily Living,* vol. 1 (Berkeley, Calif.: Blue Mountain Center of Meditation, 1975), 338; Lerner, 196. On a sense of distance helping to overcome inhibitions against cruelty, see Anthony Storr, *Human Destructiveness* (New York: Grove Weidenfeld, 1991), 113.

On the course by which "an alienated view of life" develops in those who grow up without adequate love or sense of community bonds, see Montagu, *Nature of Human Aggression,* 323. See also Philip Kapleau, *The Three Pillars of Zen,* rev. ed. (Garden City, N.Y.: Anchor, 1980), 156: "through delusion [we believe we are estranged from one another]. It is in consequence of this alienation that we find the strong overcoming the weak and the weak accepting enslavement as an alternative to death. Yet when undeluded, human beings naturally gravitate toward one another . . . to cherish and . . . to be cherished." Eugene Linden, *Affluence and Discontent: The Anatomy of Consumer Societies* (New York: Viking, 1979), xiii: "Our [consumer] society depends on alienation for its very life." Ohmae, *Borderless World,* 201: "The press are still playing the old game. . . . They . . . cannot write a story without a fictitious 'enemy' in mind."

6. "Only political will and our basic perspective prevent us from moving constructively" (Daniel B. Botkin, *Discordant Harmonies: A New Ecology for the Twenty-First Century* (New York: Oxford University Press, 1990), 13). We need a new perception of nature as processive, inevitably changing (rather than as mechanical or divinely established). According to Ludwig von Bertalanffy, a perspective is socially learned within a symbolic framework (*A Systems View of Man* [Boulder, Colo.: Westview, 1981], xvii). On an inner map of beliefs underlying perceptions, see Willis Harman, *Global Mind Change: The Promise of the Last Years of the Twentieth Century* (Indianapolis: Knowledge Systems, 1988), 156; see also Beatrice Bruteau, *The Psychic Grid: How We Create the World We Know* (Wheaton, Ill.:

Quest, 1979). See further Arthur J. Deikman, *The Wrong Way Home: Uncovering the Pattern of Cult Behavior in American Society* (Boston: Beacon, 1990), 120 (we are apt to put a negative interpretation on others' ambiguous behaviors). Montagu, *Nature of Human Aggression,* 283 (the flaw is in the environments people have created and mistakenly identified with reality). On thinking a new way, see Gustavo Gutiérrez, *A Theology of Liberation: History, Politics, and Salvation* (Maryknoll, N.Y.: Orbis Books, 1988), 52 n. 9. Our inherited worldview (materialistic, quantitative, comparative) is obsolete—pragmatically, because it leads to greed, overgrowth, war, and pollution; intellectually, because systems theory, interactive information nets, holism, and ecology are better; and as a base for religion, because it is not believed, does not inspire, and does not lead to better relations. See Gregory Bateson, *Mind and Nature: A Necessary Unity* (New York: Dutton, 1979), 218.

7. Adin Steinsaltz, *The Thirteen Petalled Rose,* trans. Yehuda Hanegbi (Northvale, N.J.: Aronson, 1992), 20.

8. On seeing everything as separated, see Bede Griffiths, *The Marriage of East and West* (Springfield, Ill.: Templegate, 1982), 30; David Bohm, *Wholeness and the Implicate Order* (London: Routledge & Kegan Paul, 1981), xi; Easwaran, *Bhagavad Gita for Daily Living,* 326-27; Carol Ochs, *Behind the Sex of God: Toward a New Consciousness—Transcending Matriarchy and Patriarchy* (Boston: Beacon, 1977), 121. "To know something is to be connected with it completely" (interview with Adin Steinsaltz, "The Private Gate," *Parabola* 3, no. 2 [May 1978]: 25). On cherubim turning their backs on each other, see Rodger Kamenetz, *Stalking Elijah: Adventures with Today's Jewish Mystical Masters* (San Francisco: HarperSanFrancisco, 1997), 147, interviewing Judith Plaskow; he also quotes Aryeh Kaplan, who speaks of "reuniting the Holy One and His Shekhinah, which is the redemption." See also Jean Baker Miller, *Toward a New Psychology of Women* (Boston: Beacon, 1976), 9. On separating ourselves from wholeness—economically, in terms of power and authority, and in terms of our concept of wholeness, see Michael von Brück, *The Unity of Reality: God, God-Experience and Meditation in the Hindu-Christian Dialogue,* trans. James V. Zeitz (NewYork: Paulist, 1991), 207. For the idea that we don't recognize God in each other, see Lerner, *Jewish Renewal,* 29; see also p. 27 on cruelty. On the evolution of evil and the phase transition to the moral era, see Beatrice Bruteau, *God's Ecstasy: The Creation of a Self-Creating World* (New York: Crossroad, 1997), 166-74; O. W. Markley, "Human Consciousness in Transformation," in *Evolution and Consciousness: Human Systems in Transition,* ed. Erich Jantsch and Conrad H. Waddington (Reading, Mass.: Addison-Wesley, 1976), 222. On Crossan, see Catherine Keller, "The Jesus of History and the Feminism of Theology," in *Jesus and Faith: A Conversation on the Work of John Dominic Crossan,* ed. Jeffrey Carlson and Robert A. Ludwig (Maryknoll, N.Y.: Orbis Books, 1994), 75; in the same volume, see Dennis P. McCann, "Doing Business with the Historical Jesus," 141: "implicit in the social program of the historical Jesus [is] the capacity for transcending all paradigms."

9. On the power of naming, how dominant groups define subordinate ones, see Miller, *Toward a New Psychology,* 6-7. On the need for contrast, see Richard Dawkins, *The Extended Phenotype: The Gene as the Unit of Selection* (Oxford: Freeman, 1982), 15 ("X is a useless word unless there are some things that are not X"). On "binary opposition," see Menas Kafatos and Robert Nadeau, *The Conscious Universe: Part and Whole in Modern Physical Theory* (Berlin: Springer-Verlag, 1990), 131-35, discussing Noam Chomsky, Ferdinand de Saussure, Michel

Foucault, and Jacques Derrida. "What is said . . . by every significant proposition, is that things stand to each other in one way rather than in another" (Robert J. Fogelin, "Wittgenstein and Classical Scepticism," *International Philosophical Quarterly* 21, no. 1 [March 1981], 4). "Since thought works only with correlativities, a word or a concept which has no contrast has no meaning" (Thomas Silkstone, "Body and Mind," *International Philosophical Quarterly* 22, no. 3 [September 1982], 179).

On classifying and labeling, see Wilson, *On Human Nature,* 72; also p. 170: the important distinction is between the in-group and the out-group. On the idea that bad news sharpens the dividing line between the in-group and the out-group, see Alfie Kohn, *The Brighter Side of Human Nature* (New York: Basic, 1990), 37. On pseudo-speciation by cultural differences—other people of other cultures are not really people, so it is permissible to kill them, see Mary Midgley, *Beast and Man: The Roots of Human Nature* (Ithaca, N.Y.: Cornell University Press, 1978), 306. See also Lyall Watson, *Dark Nature: A Natural History of Evil* (New York: HarperCollins, 1995), 236-37: "Every society seems to need an Outsider, against which the qualities of Insiders are contrasted and confirmed. [He gives various examples.] All that we are, whatever that might be, the [Outsiders] of the world are not." Midgley says that we may not be able to get rid of the need for an "outsider" (p. 287).

But see Garina C. C. Chang, *The Buddhist Teaching of Totality: The Philosophy of Hwa Yen Buddhism* (University Park: Pennsylvania State University Press, 1989), 202: "Man's [self-nature] way of thinking, which is innate and pervasive, conditions him to regard being and nonbeing, form and emptiness and all antithetical entities, as mutually exclusive or negating. As long as he stands on this . . . side, he cannot truly think nondualistically. . . . On the other hand, all [self-nature] beings simply do not exist when viewed from the other or transcendental side." See Emile Meyerson, *Identity and Reality,* trans. K. Loewenberg (London: Allen & Unwin, 1930). For the notion of "separability," see Roland Omnès, *Understanding Quantum Mechanics* (Princeton, N.J.: Princeton University Press, 1999), 274-79; Beatrice Bruteau, "The Living One," *Cistercian Studies* 18, no. 1 (1983): 42-58.

10. Steinsaltz, *Thirteen Petalled Rose,* 133; see also p. 131: "[Repentance] is . . . a continuous going, a going after God, a going to God, day after day, year after year. . . . The very concept of the Divine as infinite implies an activity that is endless." On breaking through the ordinary mode, see, e.g., Keiji Nishitani, *Religion and Nothingness,* trans. Jan van Bragt (Berkeley: University of California Press, 1982), 2-3: "Of everything else we can ask its purpose for us, but not of religion. . . . Instead, religion poses as a starting point the question: 'For what purpose do I exist?' Is not our very existence . . . ultimately meaningless? Or, if there is a meaning where do we find it? . . . These questions and the quest they give rise to show up when the mode of looking at and thinking about everything in terms of how it relates to us is broken through." What most needs healing is our whole concept system, ideas of self, world, Absolute/God, personhood, destiny, meaning, value (ibid., 57).

Story I: The Jesus Ministry and Holy Thursday

1. On Jesus' behavior disconcerting and angering those who observed him, see, e.g., William Nicholls, *Christian Antisemitism: A History of Hate* (Northvale, N.J.:

Aronson, 1995), 74-75, 79: Jesus "imitated God" by being especially near to sinners, eating with the outcasts, not making social distinctions, touching the untouchables, associating with women, etc. "In any period and in any religion, this sort of behavior would have been considered scandalous by the devout" (p. 79). See John Dominic Crossan, *The Historical Jesus: The Life of a Mediterranean Jewish Peasant* (San Francisco: HarperSanFrancisco, 1992), 263: "Open commensality profoundly negates distinctions and hierarchies between female and male, poor and rich, Gentile and Jew. It does so, indeed, at a level that would offend the ritual laws of any civilized society. That was precisely its challenge."

The importance of the meditation is that, since knowledge about Jesus—his insight, his program—from the outside is limited, to follow his line of thought and practice we have to approach from the inside, his inside, known from the stories and by exploring our own inside deeply. See 1 Cor. 2:11: "Who knows a man's thought except the spirit of the man? So also no one comprehends the thoughts of God except the Spirit of God"; but "we have received not the spirit of the world, but the Spirit that is from God, so that we may understand" (2:12). See also Adin Steinsaltz, *The Thirteen Petalled Rose*, trans. Yehuda Hanegbi (Northvale, N.J.: Aronson, 1992), 51: "the world remains as something else than God, while the soul of man, in its depths, may be considered to be a part of God. . . . Man, by virtue of his divine soul, has the potential, and some of the actual capacity, of God Himself. This . . . expresses . . . as the ability to go beyond the limits of a given existence, to move freely." Rabbi Lawrence Kushner, *Honey from the Rock: Visions of Jewish Mystical Renewal* (Woodstock, Vt.: Jewish Lights, 1994), 137-38. "Meeting a child's needs frees him from being preoccupied with them and allows him to be open to others' needs. He feels safer, less defensive, and bolder about reaching out to people around him—even those who are different from himself" (Alfie Kohn, *The Brighter Side of Human Nature: Altruism and Empathy in Everyday Life* [New York: Basic, 1990], 87, see also 88).

2. See Beatrice Bruteau, "Global Spirituality and the Integration of East and West," *Cross Currents*, Summer/Fall, 1985, 192-93, 197, 200, 204, reprinted in Bruteau, *The Grand Option: Personal Transformation and a New Creation* (Notre Dame, Ind.: University of Notre Dame Press, 2001).

3. "Jesus attempted to shatter the boundaries [that] separate the pure from the impure and the righteous from the unrighteous" (James H. Charlesworth, *Jesus Within Judaism* [New York: Doubleday, 1988], 207). See also Crossan, *Historical Jesus*, 273. On the story of the Good Samaritan, Dr. Dorothy Remy (personal communication) has drawn attention to how the injured man feels when he finds out that he owes his life to a member of a group with whom he would have been unwilling to associate. See also Michael Lerner, *Jewish Renewal* (New York: Putnam, 1994), xxi. People naturally care for those most closely related to them; Jesus proposed expanding this sense of obligation and concern; see Peter Singer, *The Expanding Circle: Ethics and Sociobiology* (New York: Oxford University Press, 1981), e.g., 30-31; see also pp. 169, 172, on overriding genetic endowment by reason and human institutions. Albert Nolan, *Jesus before Christianity* (Maryknoll, N.Y.: Orbis Books, 1997), 78 (the whole chapter is on Jesus' expansion of family loyalty to human solidarity). See Richard J. Cassidy, *Jesus, Politics, and Society* (Maryknoll, N.Y.: Orbis Books, 1978): universalism characteristic of Jesus' social stance (p. 24 and its references); Jesus did not defer to authority (pp. 73-74); give up surplus possessions, reject violence, give new roles to women (pp. 55, 75, 164

n. 34); more on women (pp. 36ff.); on power (p. 41); against ambition and violence (p. 24); love for enemies (pp. 42, 46); social teaching tied to theology (p. 48); summary of main social principles (p. 78); teachings highly challenging to society of the day (p. 151); a threat to Rome by attacking idea of domination (p. 176).

4. On the idea that domination is nonreciprocal, see Crossan, *Historical Jesus,* 66. Jean Baker Miller supports the view that washing feet means that the activities of the servant class—concerned with life and growth—are more important than the battles for prestige that define the identities of the dominant class (*Toward a New Psychology of Women* [Boston: Beacon, 1978], 78). See Brad H. Young, *Jesus, the Jewish Theologian* (Peabody, Mass.: Hendrickson, 1995): John the Baptist is puzzled by Jesus because he is expecting a messiah (Dan. 7:13-14) who will be "given dominion and glory and kingdom" (p. 57); Jesus responds to John's inquiries by pointing to his ministry of compassion, healing, forgiveness, and encouragement (Matt. 11: 4-6; cf. Isa. 29:18-19, 35:5-6) and warning against "stumbling" over his activity, that is, misunderstanding it, missing its significance (p. 59), by continuing to think of the world order in terms of domination. Crossan urges that Jesus is announcing and *performing* a "Kingdom" in which God rules, which one enters by moral virtue, open to everyone—"nobodies and the destitute"—and which is here and now, not postponed to an indefinite (even if "soon") future (*Historical Jesus,* 292). On friendship, see Beatrice Bruteau, "From *Dominus* to *Amicus*: Contemplative Insight and a New Social Order," *Cross Currents* 31, no. 3 (Fall 1981): 280-81. The teacher's view of the teacher's role is that in the beginning reverence for the teacher is correct because the teacher guides one toward greater life; but in the end the teacher reveals that all are one and the disciple is not different from the teacher and is now also a teacher. This is the ultimate teaching that the disciple must accept from the teacher; the disciple's reverence for the teacher must be sufficient to make this acceptance possible.

5. Michael Grant, *Jesus: An Historian's Review of the Gospels* (New York: Scribner, 1977), 154. Bruce Chilton, "Origins of the Eucharist," *Bible Review* 10 (December 1994): 39; idem, *Jesus' Prayer and Jesus' Eucharist* (Valley Forge, Pa.: Trinity Press International, 1997), 52-54, 56-57, also 72-75 on a possible background of the words "This is my body, this is my blood" as said by the one presenting an animal for sacrifice in the Temple, words taken over by the Essenes when they boycotted the Temple and used bread and wine instead.

6. Crossan, *Historical Jesus,* 341-44; also p. 404. Alfonso Montuori and Isabella Conti, *From Power to Partnership: Creating the Future of Love, Work, and Community* (San Francisco: HarperSanFrancisco, 1993), 255. Peter Farb and George Armelagos, *Consuming Passions: The Anthropology of Eating* (Boston: Houghton Mifflin, 1980), 4, 211. Christian de Duve, *Vital Dust: Life as a Cosmic Imperative* (New York: Basic, 1995), 295. On the idea that to consume is to take from another, see Robert E. Birt, "The Prospects for Community in the Later Sartre," *International Philosophical Quarterly* 29, no. 2 (June 1989): 147.

7. Beatrice Bruteau, "Jesus' Suppers," *The Roll* 13, no. 3 (September 1996). Kushner, *Honey from the Rock,* 146-47.

8. Gustavo Gutiérrez, *Essential Writings,* ed. James B. Nickoloff (Maryknoll, N.Y.: Orbis Books, 1996), 185-87. Ben Witherington III gives various views of Jesus as social prophet (*The Jesus Quest* [Downers Grove, Ill.: InterVarsity, 1995]). Cassidy cites commentators who hold that Jesus did not attempt to change the prevailing social order (*Jesus, Politics, and Society,* 82ff.). On the idea that we must go

deeper than political/social reasoning, see Crossan, *Historical Jesus,* 211-12. On the idea that revolution comes by the abdication of the lord, see Margaret Mead, *Culture and Commitment* (New York: Columbia University Press, 1978), 82; Hannah Arendt, *On Revolution* (New York: Viking, 1963), 28, 22; Daniel Yankelovich, *New Rules* (New York: Random House, 1981), 250; Lerner, *Jewish Renewal,* 62-63, xx, xxviii; Steinsaltz, *Thirteen Petalled Rose,* 88-90. On implementation of Torah, see Lerner, *Jewish Renewal,* 106; Fritjof Capra, *The Web of Life: A New Scientific Understanding of Living Systems* (New York: Doubleday, 1996), 243, quoting Lynn Margolis and Dorion Sagan, *Microcosmos: Four Billion Years of Evolution from Our Microbial Ancestors* (New York: Summit, 1986), 119.

4. Person and *Perichōrēsis*

1. Daniel Walsh, *Gethsemani Archives Document 3,* 8; *Document 4, 6; Document 5,* 4, Abbey of Gethsemani, Trappist, Kentucky. For further information, see Beatrice Bruteau, Feature Review of Robert Imperato, "Merton and Walsh on the Person," *International Philosophical Quarterly* 31 (Fall 1991): 353-63 (the review contains additional material on Walsh beyond what is in the book itself). From the New Testament, see 1 John 3:9; 4:4, 6, 7; Matt. 7:24-27.

2. For the story of Nicodemus, see John 3; also Beatrice Bruteau, "Nicodemus by Night," *Sisters Today* 67, no. 1 (January 1995): 3ff.

3. Anders Nygren, *Agape and Eros,* trans. Philip S. Watson (Philadelphia: Westminster, 1953).

4. Michael Lerner, *Jewish Renewal: A Path to Healing and Transformation* (New York: Putnam, 1994), 252. On the need for a radical shift in our way of perceiving ourselves and our environment, see Robert Ornstein and Paul Ehrlich, *New World New Mind: Moving toward Conscious Evolution* (New York: Simon & Schuster, 1989), 12. On the relation of different types of logic to different types of imagination, see Matthias Neuman, O.S.B., "Toward an Integrated Theory of Imagination," *International Philosophical Quarterly* 18, no. 3 (September 1978): esp. 264 n. 43, referring to Gilbert Durand, who said that images of ascending foster logic of "either/or"; images of enclosure, of "no, but yes"; and of cycles, "both . . . and."

For argument that we are in a transitional period, moving toward a new logic, something more than a paradigm shift, see Magoroh Maruyama, "Toward Cultural Symbiosis," in *Evolution and Consciousness: Human Systems in Transition,* ed. Erich Jantsch and Conrad H. Waddington (Reading, Mass.: Addison-Wesley, 1976), 209ff. In the same volume, see O. W. Markley, "Human Consciousness in Transition," 218-20, and the table on p. 221 for stages of change as expressed in myth, culture, science, psychotherapy, and general creativity.

5. On "authenticity," see Beatrice Bruteau, "Apprenticing to Jesus the Healer," *Journal of Christian Healing* 15, no. 1 (Spring 1993): 19. On the idea that authenticity and subordination are totally incompatible, see Jean Baker Miller, *Toward a New Psychology of Women* (Boston: Beacon, 1976), 98. In the New Testament, see John 16:26-27; 4:42. On our "pervasive belief in the isolated and independent existence of objects," which Paul Teller calls "particularism," see Victor Mansfield, "Mādhyamika Buddhism and Quantum Mechanics: Beginning a Dialogue," *International Philosophical Quarterly* 19, no. 4 (December 1989): 379: if we do not insist on this belief in the "inherent existence" of "separable" beings, but admit the

"essential relatedness" of all beings, as Mādhyamika teaches, then we will understand better not only quantum mechanics but the rest of life.

On the idea that our capacity for compassion "is the true ground of all autonomous righteousness," our "genuine moral worth . . . stems [only] from this source," see Arthur Schopenhauer as quoted and cited in Joseph Campbell, *The Masks of God*, vol. 4, *Creative Mythology* (New York: Penguin, 1968), 71-73: "*another* can actually become the final concern of *my* willing. . . . I can actually participate sympathetically in [the other's experience] . . . become identified with him; [this demands that] the final distinction between me and him, which is the premise of my egoism, should, to some degree at least, be suspended."

For a comparison of "self-assertive" and "integration" thinking and values, see Fritjof Capra, *The Web of Life: A New Scientific Understanding of Living Systems* (New York: Doubleday, 1996), 10. For example, self-assertive thinking is analytic and reductionistic, whereas integrative is synthetic and holistic; self-assertive values favor competition and domination whereas integrative values stress cooperation and partnership. On the idea that verbs are better, see Mary Daly, "God Is a Verb," *Ms* (magazine), Dec. 1974. For Rabbi Zalman on God, see Zalman Schachter-Shalomi, *Paradigm Shift: From the Jewish Renewal Teachings of Reb Zalman Schachter-Shalomi*, ed. Ellen Singer (Northvale, N.J.: Aronson, 1993), 135, 141-42.

6. For Daniel Walsh's view of the "effusions" of Love, see the references in n. 1 above. Walsh has important and beautiful things to say, and there are no other sources. On persons giving grace to one another, see Beatrice Bruteau, "Trinitarian Personhood," *Cistercian Studies* 22, no. 3 (1987), 199-212; also eadem, "The One and the Many: Communitarian Nondualism," in *The Other Half of My Soul: Bede Griffiths and the Hindu-Christian Dialogue*, ed. B. Bruteau (Wheaton, Ill.: Quest, 1996), esp. 279-87.

7. On the Theotokos, see Beatrice Bruteau, "The Theotokos Project," in *Embracing Earth: Catholic Approaches to Ecology*, ed. Albert J. LaChance and John E. Carroll (Maryknoll, N.Y.: Orbis Books, 1994).

8. Pierre Teilhard de Chardin, *The Phenomenon of Man* (New York: Harper & Row, 1961). See Col. 1:24: "Corpus Christi quod est ecclesia." John 1:18 says that no one has ever seen God, but that the *monogenēs theos*, which/who is in the *kolpon* of the Father, that one has "exegeted." *Monogenēs* means singly generated, originally "born of one mother"; it can be interpreted as being the only offspring of the parent or as having only one parent, or probably said of siblings that they have a parent in common. In this text it is "singly generated God," already identified as the Logos, the creative Word. *Kolpon* means "hollow" and was used to refer to the fold in a cloth flung over one shoulder and secured by a waist belt, thus forming a pocket in which one could carry, for instance, a lamb: "he carries the lambs in his bosom." Bosom means that pocket.

The implication is that from the "emptiness" (= no-thing-ness, absolute transcendence) of the Source comes (by generation, not by creation) the expressive aspect of the Source, which exegetes the formless Origin, translating into finite forms that Reality, thus revealing the sacred mysteries. God is not "seen" because God is not see-able, cannot be an object of perception or of cognition. God can be only Subject (if we are to use such categories at all), and therefore must be approached or "realized" from the subject side, by coinherence, or con-fluence, not as subject to object ("face-to-face") but as subject in subject: "I am in the Father, and the Father is in me . . . I am in you, and you are in me."

9. Peter 1:4 says that we become (*genēsthe*) partakers/sharers (*koinōnoi* = as in "community," holding something in "common") of the divine (*theias*) nature (*physeōs*). Cf. Acts 17:28-29: "In [God] we live and move and have our being. . . . For we too are his offspring"—the apostle Paul quoting (perhaps) Epimenides and Aratus's *Phaenomena* in support of his gospel.

When the theology of the Persons of the Trinity was first forming, it was in Greek, and the word we translate as "person" was *hypostasis*. *Hypo* means "under" and *stasis* means "standing." One wonders why, when the translation into Latin was made, the word *substantia* was not used. Instead, the word *persona* was chosen, which comes from the dramatic "mask" with built-in megaphone used by actors on the stage in the theater: that "through" (*per*) which the "sound" (*sona*) comes. The mask identifies the role played by the actor, and it is not hard to see how this word was appropriated for our projection of roles and qualities that we call our "personality." But this now includes a sense of subjective presence that is not conveyed by "hypostasis."

The three hypostases in Plotinus's theology (*to hen*, the One; *nous*, the Divine Mind, home of the Platonic Forms/Ideas and the Intelligences which know them; and *psychē*, the World Soul, the Life-giver) are contemplated by, but not addressed by, the human being. From this background has developed our present ability to identify a deep subjective presence, beyond the personality with its various descriptions, which I call the *person*. Perhaps this was necessary to allow for the Jewish and Christian sense of subject–subject interaction between people and God.

5. Living inside God

1. On a new outlook in which the One manifests as many and the many realize they are One, see Ken Wilbur, *A Brief History of Everything* (Boston: Shambhala, 1996), 253-54. On a mind-set that is very different, encouraging participation, see Alfonso Montuori and Isabella Conti, *From Power to Partnership: Creating the Future of Love, Work, and Community* (San Francisco: HarperSanFrancisco, 1993), 175. On the idea that change involves images of self, society, culture, nature, body, and action, see O. W. Markley, "Human Consciousness in Transition," in *Evolution and Consciousness: Human Systems in Transition,* ed. Erich Jantsch and Conrad H. Waddington (Reading, Mass.: Addison-Wesley, 1976), 216. See also Erich Jantsch, *The Self-Organizing Universe: Scientific and Human Implications of the Emerging Paradigm of Evolution* (New York: Pergamon, 1980), 174ff., on "The Sociocultural Re-creation of the World": Sociocultural evolution turns sociobiological evolution virtually upside down (interesting diagram).

2. According to Eknath Easwaran, it is not so much that we wage a battle against ourselves as that we gain a new perspective. Once we see things differently because we have corrected a fundamental error, attitudes and actions shift of themselves. See Eknath Easwaran, *The Bhagavad Gita for Daily Living,* vol. 1 (Berkeley, Calif.: Blue Mountain Center of Meditation, 1975), 33. On living out of our own intelligence and goodwill (conscience), not from hierarchical obedience, domination/submission, or deference, see Anthony Storr, *Human Destructiveness* (New York: Grove Weidenfeld, 1991), 105ff.

Jesus' Holy Thursday Revolution is a reiteration of the liberation for new life of Sinai: the Decalogue begins with the announcement that God is the One who liberates and ends by enumerating harms from which the people are now set free—murder, stealing, adultery, deception, envy. Although selected for giving biological advantages, these behaviors (and their emotions) will now be replaced by a new life principle. We experience a shift in needs from self-esteem to self-realization. See Peter Russell, *The Global Brain Awakens: Our Next Evolutionary Leap* (Palo Alto, Calif.: Our Brain, 1995), 204-5.

3. The integration of masculine/feminine set afoot by Jesus is of extreme importance to our situation. See Bruno Barnhart, *The Good Wine: Reading John from the Center* (New York: Paulist, 1993), 406-7. Philip Slater says that the stereotypically feminine traits of sensitivity, warmth, realism, ability to communicate, mediate, cooperate, and integrate *"are precisely those most needed to successfully maintain a democratic society"* (*A Dream Deferred* [Boston: Beacon, 1991]). Therefore, they need to be developed by the whole population, not women alone (see Montuori and Conti, *From Power to Partnership*, 177).

4. On giving attention to others, see Montuori and Conti, *From Power to Partnership*, 192. On the idea that it takes a while to realize that helping others means helping oneself, see Easwaran, *Bhagavad Gita*, 310. See also Michael Lerner, *Jewish Renewal: A Path to Healing and Transformation* (New York: Putnam, 1994), 82-83: "The recognition we had at Sinai created for us an obligation. . . . Knowing that the world both can and ought to be changed gave the Jewish people a sense of being commanded. . . . Once you see things in a certain kind of way, there is no going back." You can't not know what you do know. And what we know is that when we look at anyone, we "recognize there the presence of God" and we "put ourselves unconditionally in the place of the other . . . enter into a nonerotic love of our neighbors that expects nothing in return. . . . The deepest truth of our subjectivity is not its 'being for itself,' . . . but rather its 'being for the other.' . . . [so that we see each other] as ends rather than as means, as embodiments of holiness and deserving of dignity and freedom, as infinitely precious and sacred."

Therefore, as Easwaran says, there is no point in tagging anything as "mine" (*Bhagavad Gita*, 259), no need to compete, for each person is beyond comparison with another (p. 262), and even in our occupations and professions, recognition of one another makes us rather live in poverty than work at a job that injures others (p. 312).

5. Our sense of responsibility for all makes us willing to contribute to large-scale actions (advocacy activism, charities, research) to improve the lives of many people. See Gregory Stock, *Metaman: The Merging of Humans and Machines into a Global Superorganism* (Toronto: Doubleday Canada, 1993), 139. See also Montuori and Conti, *From Power to Partnership*, 187, for an exploration of implications and applications of universal love, dating from Mo-tzu and Jesus and reappearing in Mohandas Gandhi and Martin Luther King. For an interim "competition-welfare model," see Robert C. North, *The World That Could Be* (New York: Norton, 1976), 65-66. See also Andrew Cline, "Flawed Concept: Living-wage laws are beginning to take root in North Carolina," *Winston-Salem Journal*, March 11, 1998, A-13; also Reb Zalman Schachter-Shalomi on "Interpeacing," in *Paradigm Shift: From the Jewish Renewal Teachings of Reb Zalman Schachter-Shalomi*, ed. Ellen Singer (Northvale, N.J.: Aronson, 1993), 267; and Rabbi Robert N. Levine, *There Is No Messiah and You're It: The Stunning Transformation of Judaism's Most Provocative Idea* (Woodstock, Vt.: Jewish Lights, 2003).

6. Richard Dawkins, *The Selfish Gene* (New York: Oxford University Press, 1976), 99-100. Frans de Waal, *Good Natured: The Origins of Right and Wrong in Humans and Other Animals* (Cambridge, Mass.: Harvard University Press, 1996), 14-17, 5. On reciprocal altruism, see Dawkins, 197-202; Lyall Watson, *Dark Nature: A Natural History of Evil* (New York: HarperCollins, 1995), 255. On Tit-for-Tat, see Robert Axelrod, *The Evolution of Cooperation* (New York: Basic, 1984), 53 and passim; Paul Gilbert, *Human Nature and Suffering* (New York: Guilford, 1992), 211, 219. On empathy, see Adrian Desmond, *The Ape's Reflexion* (London: Blond & Briggs, 1979), 195. On the idea that at birth we already have "a rudimentary empathic distress reaction," see Alfie Kohn, *The Brighter Side of Human Nature: Altruism and Empathy in Everyday Life* (New York: Basic, 1990), 66, citing A. Sagi and M. L. Hoffman. Subsequent pages in Kohn show development, which is also discussed in Gilbert, 207.

7. On Ramakrishna, see *The Gospel of Sri Ramakrishna*, recorded by Mahendranath Gupta, originally published in five volumes over the years 1897-1932, trans. Swami Nikhilananda (New York: Ramakrishna-Vivekananda Center, 1942). On the love beyond the justice response, see Beatrice Bruteau, *The Grand Option: Personal Transformation and a New Creation* (Notre Dame, Ind.: University of Notre Dame Press, 2001), 165-69. Brad H. Young, *Jesus the Jewish Theologian* (Peabody, Mass.: Hendrickson, 1995), 169. See *The Dhammapada: The Sayings of the Buddha,* a new rendering by Thomas Byrom (New York: Vintage, 1976), 4 (sayings probably gathered in northern India in the third century B.C.E. and written down in Ceylon in the first century B.C.E.). *Dhamma* means law, justice, righteousness, discipline, truth; *pada* means path, step, foot, foundation. On the Dalai Lama, see Rodger Kamenetz, *The Jew in the Lotus* (Northvale, N.J.: Aronson, 1994), 185-86. Compare Axelrod, *Evolution of Cooperation,* 40: In computer tournaments for the study of effective rules/programs for scoring well in the iterated Prisoner's Dilemma, rules that were very forgiving (cooperated again after other player defected) and that began with trust fared much better than rules that defected at every opportunity in distrust of the other.

8. On reorientation of basic ideas, see Hazel Henderson, *Creating Alternative Futures: The End of Economics* (New York: Berkley, 1978), 25, discussing Karen Horney, fundamental conflicts in American values, and the need to develop new ideas/values/feelings to go with the new globally interdependent economy. On feeling good, see Kohn, *Brighter Side,* 73, 292 n. 27; see also 307 n. 89 on energy available to care for others.

On how feelings relate to health, see Robert Ornstein and David Sobel, *The Healing Brain: Breakthrough Discoveries about How the Brain Keeps Us Healthy* (New York: Simon & Schuster, 1989), 149: "Harvard psychologist David McClelland and colleagues . . . suggested that the need to exercise power over others is related to differences in immune function and susceptibility to disease." See also Joseph LeDoux, *The Emotional Brain* (New York: Simon & Schuster, 1996), 132 (physiology of insecurity), and 240-42 (stress pathways in the brain and hormones, shriveling of cells under stress). See also Candace B. Pert, *Molecules of Emotion* (New York: Scribner, 1997), on the interrelations of the nervous, endocrine, and immune systems through a common communication network of peptides; on the immune system in particular, see pp. 159-64, 181-84; on psychoneuroimmunology, pp. 172-73, 176-77; on the benefits of forgiveness, pp. 240, 304, 306.

On being transparent to the divine light, see Schachter-Shalomi, *Paradigm*

Shift, 187: Habad Hasidism (*Habad* is an acronym for *hokhmah, binah, da'at*—wisdom, understanding, knowledge.) Hasidism is a Jewish charismatic renewal movement of the eighteenth century, literally meaning "piety, devotion." It teaches that thoughts produce feelings, attitudes, behavior. "Hasidic masters taught their disciples how to fill their hearts and minds" with content that would make them transparent to the power and the light of the soul.

The Habad lineage derives from Rabbi Shneur Zalman (1745-1813): "He taught [his disciples] to love each other as brothers, share their joys and sorrows, meet . . . for mutual encouragement and exhortation. The goal was selfless service, but . . . one also attained faith in God's absolute goodness and the joy of dedicating one's life to Him amid the fellowship of a like-minded brotherhood." This was a "fusion of the intellectual, emotional, social, and spiritual facets of Judaism," which provided its practitioners with "the fortitude to withstand the perennial persecution to which . . . Jewry was subject." Habad also taught that the human being is "God's corporealized reflection, and . . . that the moving force behind a Jew's desire and ability to serve God was his divine soul" (Roman A. Foxbrunner, *Habad: The Hasidism of R. Shneur Zalman of Lyady* (Northvale, N.J.: Aronson, 1993), 198-99. See also Easwaran, *Bhagavad Gita,* 290.

9. Andrew Greeley and William C. McCready, "Are We a Nation of Mystics?" *New York Times Magazine,* January 18, 1975. Andrew Bard Schmooker, *Out of Weakness: Healing the Wounds That Drive Us to War* (New York: Bantam, 1988), 294. Compare my "multilevel Eucharist" with Rabbi Schachter-Shalomi's's ascending order of attunement according to the deep structure of the Kabbalah: We attune "1) our bodies to God in action, 2) our emotions—in devotion, 3) our intellect to reality maps based on our understanding of God's plan, harmonizing the value complexes of our traditions with the clearest view we have of how what-is works, and 4) our spirit as an organic part of the 'body of God' and 5) [we] ground this attunement in our being as a prelude to 'know Him/Her in all your ways.' Action directives received as a result of this grounding have the flavor and urgency of divine commandments" (*Paradigm Shift,* 184).

10. Kamenetz, *Jew in the Lotus,* 182. Having "meaning" means being situated in a larger context. We need mysticism because it supplies the largest context. Lawrence Kushner, *The River of Light: Spirituality, Judaism, Consciousness* (Woodstock, Vt.: Jewish Lights, 1995), 67-68; David Aaron, *Endless Light: The Ancient Path of the Kabbalah to Love, Spiritual Growth, and Personal Power* (New York: Simon & Schuster, 1997), 18, 168-69, 172-73. Cf. Kamenetz, p. 189: We have a stake in it.

11. On *minyan,* see Schachter-Shalomi, *Paradigm Shift,* 258. On community of minds, see G. W. F. Hegel, *The Phenomenology of Spirit,* section 69, 43 (various translations and editions). On heightened awareness and communication, see Walter Pankow, "Openness as Self-Transcendence," in *Evolution and Consciousness: Human Systems in Transition,* ed. Erich Jantsch and Conrad H. Waddington (Reading, Mass.: Addison-Wesley, 1976), 20. If you see yourself as wide enough to embrace another, you don't need a moral exhortation to care about your neighbor (Fritjof Capra, *The Web of Life: A New Scientific Understanding of Living Systems* [New York: Doubleday, 1996], 12).

We tend to think of energy in terms of either possession or destruction, but there are other energies that we have not developed so well, energies of insight, understanding, and creativity. See Chögyam Trungpa, *Cutting Through Spiritual*

Materialism (Boulder, Colo.: Shambhala, 1973), 181. "We don't realize what tremendous energy for selfless living we have lying dormant within us" (Easwaran, *Bhagavad Gita,* 44).

Group sharing can lead to "demonic collective in-group ego," which excludes and despises those outside; it is vital to guard against this by identifying basically as simply Human, not siding with one label so as to reject others. The sense of community must explicitly say by its experience that the reality of every other enriches one's own. See Frederick Franck, *Fingers Pointing Toward the Sacred: A Twentieth Century Pilgrimage on the Eastern and Western Way* (Junction City, Ore.: Beacon Point, 1994), 219.

We can also learn that "it is good for you when other people love other people besides you." You have a stake in their love for each other, for there is more love loose in the system, circulating among all the participants. If we cling to our good, it loses its value; if we give it to others and they share it still further, it multiplies and we are all filled with goodness. See Lawrence Kushner, *Honey from the Rock: Visions of Jewish Mystical Renewal* (Woodstock, Vt.: Jewish Lights, 1994), 140-41.

6. "In the Days of the Messiah"

1. See Gustavo Gutiérrez, *A Theology of Liberation* (Maryknoll, N.Y.: Orbis Books, 1988), 91: The oppressed change their consciousness and acquire a new way of seeing themselves and their relation to the world, become creative of new modes of life, become active in transformation. Theodore Roszak says, "Nothing less than a revolution of the sensibilities will serve our purpose, whatever social revolutions we may also have to undertake. The way forward is inevitably the way inward" (*Unfinished Animal* [New York: Harper & Row, 1975], 239). Gutiérrez adds that development is a total social process and only for methodological convenience or in a partial sense can one speak of economic, political, cultural, or social development (*Theology of Liberation,* 38 n. 9). Robert C. North warns that "even a revolution that . . . alters some social, economic, and political institutions in obvious ways may not, in the long run, make . . . much difference. . . . Often such a revolution does little more than substitute a new ruling elite for the old" (*The World That Could Be* [New York: Norton, 1976]). He cites the French Revolution. We might also cite the Christian church, from which Jesus' radical egalitarianism disappeared very shortly and in which a new structure of domination was erected. What is needed is "real social learning," says North. Gutiérrez says that we need a scientific and structural knowledge of social-economic dynamics (p. 49). I am saying that we need a mystical transformation in which we become capable of recognizing the divine image in every other human being and thereby become capable of acting accordingly in terms of equality and generosity.

2. Gutiérrez, *Theology of Liberation,* 91; Sir John Eccles and Daniel N. Robinson, *The Wonder of Being Human: Our Brain and Our Mind* (Boston: Shambhala, 1985), 3; Hannah Arendt, *On Revolution* (New York: Viking, 1963), 222. See also Daniel Yankelovich, *New Rules* (New York: Random House, 1981), 220-21; also see the chapter entitled "Rewriting the Giving/Getting Compact." Margaret Mead, *Culture and Commitment* (New York: Columbia University Press, 1978), 5: "The voiceless and the oppressed in every part of the world have begun to demand more power. . . . A profound disturbance is occurring in the relationships between the

strong and the weak, the possessors and the dispossessed." Jean Baker Miller, *Toward a New Psychology of Women* (Boston: Beacon, 1976), 88: Women's sense of human community is the absolutely essential next step in Western history if we are to survive.

3. Michael Lerner believes that we are in the midst of "a worldwide religious and spiritual revival," because secularism does not satisfy human needs. We are reacting against "an economic/political system focused on production and accumulation, power and control," to which human beings have become "appendages." "Human beings," he says, "need to be embedded in communities of meaning," to see their lives "as part of some larger framework of meaning . . . that connects them to . . . values in which they can believe" (*Jewish Renewal: A Path to Healing and Transformation* [New York: Putnam, 1994], 265).

For the role of technology, see North, *World That Could Be,* 14ff.: "the world's great revolutionaries have been inventors and innovators rather than . . . politicians or soldiers." Innovations break the equilibrium of the system, says Gutiérrez, *Theology of Liberation,* 23. They are directly technological and economic, but they are also indirectly political and social, because they imply contradictions and they overcome the prevailing system. Social change lags behind technological change, says Peter Farb (*Humankind* [Boston: Houghton Mifflin, 1978], 366), and this tension also causes social change.

On computer-aided manufacturing being taught to Third World countries so that they also may become producers (and thus rich enough to be markets), see Kenichi Ohmae, *The Borderless World: Power and Strategy in the Interlinked Economy* (New York: HarperBusiness, 1990). On computer-aided collaboration bringing people together to create a product by meeting in a shared creative space, see Michael Schrage, *Shared Minds: The New Technologies of Collaboration* (New York: Random House, 1990).

4. North, *World That Could Be,* 71; Mead, *Culture and Commitment*, 155, 148.

5. Rodger Kamenetz, *The Jew in the Lotus* (Northvale, N.J.: Aronson, 1994), 181-82. The Source of Being makes possible transformation (Lerner, *Jewish Renewal*, 127).

6. On Haywood, see Alfonso Montuori and Isabella Conti, *From Power to Partnership: Creating the Future of Love, Work, and Community* (San Francisco: HarperSanFrancisco, 1993), 137. On the Jesus Supper, see Beatrice Bruteau, "The Eucharist of Everyday Life," *Spirit and Life* 93 (January-February 1997): 12ff. On Jesus as Democriton, see Leon Lederman with Dick Teresil, *The God Particle* (Boston: Houghton Mifflin, 1993), 56. The particle in question is actually the Higgs particle, said to interact with all other particles; Lederman is having a fictional conversation with Democritus, the original particle man, who proposes that this particle from the foundation of the universe (hence "God" particle) be named after him; I have appropriated the neologism "democriton" for Jesus—Lederman doesn't say anything like this. For Schachter-Shalomi on "interpeacing," see *Paradigm Shift: From the Jewish Renewal Teachings of Reb Zalman Schachter-Shalomi,* ed. Ellen Singer (Northvale, N.J.: Aronson, 1993), 267; on "share-flow," 274-75. For the idea that all of us are Messiah, see Robert N. Levine, *There Is No Messiah and You're It: The Stunning Transformation of Judaism's Most Provocative Idea* (Woodstock, Vt.: Jewish Lights, 2003). See also Barbara Marx Hubbard, *Conscious Evolution: Awakening the Power of Our Social Potential* (Novato, Calif.: New

World, 1998), 127-29, 130, 136, 141; Lewis Thomas, *The Lives of a Cell: Notes of a Biology Watcher* (New York: Bantam, 1974), 167-68, 131-33, 151; Joseph A. Bracken, S.J., *Society and Spirit: A Trinitarian Cosmology* (Toronto: Associated University Presses, 1991), 43-44, 114.

7. W. Daniel Hillis, "Close to the Singularity," in John Brockman, *The Third Culture* (New York: Simon & Schuster, 1995), 383. Thomas, *Lives of a Cell,* 167 (the old notion of an autonomous self is now a myth), 147-48 (nature is not for separateness, rather things tend to live with and in one another). Fred Hapgood, *Up the Infinite Corridor: MIT and the Technical Imagination* (Reading, Mass.: Addison-Wesley, 1993), 182; see further pp. 180-91. Gregory Stock, *Metaman: The Merging of Humans and Machines into a Global Superorganism* (Toronto: Doubleday Canada, 1993), 49. Hazel Henderson speaks of a decentralized communitarian society based on human organic technology, not recreating factionalism and parochial views; she relates this to female social wisdom (*Creating Alternative Futures: The End of Economies* [New York: Berkley, 1978], 19-20). See also Magoroh Maruyama, "Toward Cultural Symbiosis," in *Evolution and Consciousness: Human Systems in Transition,* ed. Erich Jantsch and Conrad H. Waddington (Reading, Mass.: Addison-Wesley, 1976), 204, for different types of interaction among social parties—separatism, symbiosis, parasitism, antibiosis, mutual antibiosis—as to who gains, who loses.

8. Hazel Henderson, *The Politics of the Solar Age: Alternatives to Economics* (Garden City, N.Y.: Doubleday, Anchor, 1981), 115-19.

9. Lerner, *Jewish Renewal,* 257, 259. See also Norman Cousins, *Celebration of Life* (New York: Harper & Row, 1974), 20-21, 43-44: human nature has need of being loving just as much as of being competitive; when blocked from identifying with others, it becomes neurotic. See further Frank White, *The Overview Effect* (Boston: Houghton Mifflin, 1987), reports of astronauts and cosmonauts, on the effects of the lunar voyage—setting eye on small Earth and seeing the moral implications.

10. See Hazel Henderson, *Building a Win-Win World* (San Francisco: Berrett-Koehler, 1996). Implicit is the idea that economic justice requires a communicative process whose central element is the reciprocal recognition of free persons. On the idea that economic systems evolve together, see Erich Jantsch, *The Self-Organizing Universe: Scientific and Human Implications of the Emerging Paradigm of Evolution* (New York: Pergamon, 1980), 196. Fritjof Capra, *The Web of Life: A New Scientific Understanding of Living Systems* (New York: Doubleday, Anchor, 1996), 301: economics encourages competition, expansion, and domination; ecology encourages cooperation, conservation, and partership. For the Ohmae material, see his *Borderless World,* xii, 208, 93ff., 57.

11. On man as dominating the animals, see Mircea Eliade, *Myths, Dreams, and Mysteries: The Encounter between Contemporary Faiths and Archaic Realities,* trans. Philip Mairet (New York: Harper Torchbook, 1960), 67, 63, 71. See also Swami Vivekananda, *What Religion Is,* ed. John Yale (New York: Julian, 1962), 97: seeing the world as holy, not as unconscious, lifeless, mechanistic, here for our convenience, tempting, hostile, etc., but as the expression of God. Vivekananda (d. 1902), disciple of Ramakrishna (d. 1886), represented a universalized Vedanta at the Parliament of the World's Religions in Chicago, 1893. See also Connie Barlow, *Green Space, Green Time: The Way of Science* (New York: Springer-Verlag, 1997); and Stephen H. Schneider, *Laboratory Earth* (New York: Basic, 1997).

12. Both males and females can have high empathy responses (Alfie Kohn, *The Brighter Side of Human Nature: Altruism and Empathy in Everyday Life* [New York: Basic, 1990], 124). On birth without fear, see Joseph Chilton Pearce, *Magical Child: Rediscovering Nature's Plan for Our Children* (New York: Dutton, 1977). On education, see Gerald Mische and Patricia Mische, *Toward a Human World Order* (New York: Paulist, 1977), chapter 8, "Human/Religious Values are 'Subversive.'" See also Robert Ornstein and Paul Ehrlich, *New World, New Mind: Moving toward Conscious Evolution* (New York: Simon & Schuster, 1989), chapter 9, "A Curriculum About Humanity"; David E. Purpel, *The Moral and Spiritual Crisis in Education: A Curriculum for Justice and Compassion in Education* (New York: Bergin & Garvey, 1989). On art, see Yehudi Menuhin and Curtis W. Davis, *The Music of Man* (New York: Simon & Schuster, 1987), 294: "The listener becomes something more than a consumer, he becomes a participant." On architecture, Conservative Rabbi Leonard Gordon says, "The move from an architecture in which the rabbi is up on a bimah and the congregation below, to one in which the Torah is at the center of a circle, implies a whole new theology," in Rodger Kamenetz, *Stalking Elijah: Adventures with Today's Jewish Mystical Masters* (San Francisco: HarperSanFrancisco, 1997), 247. For details on self-realization, see my *Easter Mysteries* (New York: Crossroad, 1995), esp. the chapter on baptism; and Lex Hixon, *Coming Home* (Burkett, N.Y.: Larson, 1995), esp. the chapter on the ox-herding pictures. See also Jacob Bronowski, *A Sense of the Future: Essays in Natural Philosophy* (Cambridge, Mass.: MIT Press, 1977), 209 (from the single obligation to work together for the truth, all the human values can be deduced), 210 (mutual affection, mutual indwelling, each giving life to each; science, truth-seeking, grows by the work of each meeting each and "grafting each on each"), 258ff. (continuing research, dissent, creativity in science, social thought, ethics, etc.), 202-3 (the impossibility of being good without being wise—there is no substitute for intelligence; no amount of love makes up for ignorance and hiding from the truth).

13. M. Mitchell Waldrop, *Complexity: The Emerging Science at the Edge of Order and Chaos* (New York: Simon & Schuster, 1992), 67: Once the whole intellectual fabric was seamless. Maybe it can be that way again. See also Edward O. Wilson, *Consilience: The Unity of Knowledge* (New York: Knopf, 1998). "The morning star . . . " (2 Pet. 1:19).

7. "You Can't Change Human Nature!"

1. Ben Bova, *Immortality: How Science Is Extending Your Life Span—and Changing the World* (New York: Avon, 1998), 240. Scientific backup can be found in Theodore D. Kemper, *Social Structure and Testosterone: Explorations of the Socio-Bio-Social Chain* (New Brunswick, N.J.: Rutgers University Press, 1990), esp. chapter 2, p. 27 (diagrams relations among testosterone, dominance, social structure, aggression, sexual activity, and norepinephine); 30-35, 71-76 (aggression). A briefer treatment is available in Robert J. Russell, *The Lemur's Legacy: The Evolution of Power, Sex, and Love* (New York: Tarcher, 1993), 64-68. If serotonin is low, there is insufficient inhibition of aggression (Anthony Storr, *Human Destructiveness* [New York: Grove Weidenfeld, 1991], 40).

2. Jared Diamond, *Guns, Germs, and Steel: The Fates of Human Societies* (New York: Norton, 1997), 172-73.

3. Edward O. Wilson, *Consilience: The Unity of Knowledge* (New York: Knopf, 1998), 259-60.

4. Carl Sagan, *The Dragons of Eden: Speculations on the Evolution of Human Intelligence* (New York: Random House, 1977), 53-54. See also Storr, *Human Destructiveness*, 74-75: "the gesture of presentation becomes a means of indicating friendliness or submission, since it has the effect of suppressing aggression in the animal to which it is addressed. . . . In human beings . . . bowing, curtsying, kow-towing, and kneeling . . . all make the submissive person appear smaller. . . . Just as presentation, a female action, may be performed by either sex, so mounting, a male action, is performed by both sexes when dominance rather than coitus is in question."

5. Wilson, *Consilience*, 260.

6. Russell, *Lemur's Legacy*, 153.

7. Ibid., 155-57. We may ask, Why do people do some of these things? E. O. Wilson's answer is, Because they represent good reproductive strategies (*On Human Nature* [New York: Bantam, 1979], 42).

8. Carl Sagan and Ann Druyan, "How Much Are We Like the Chimps? What They Tell Us About Ourselves," adapted from *Shadows of Forgotten Ancestors* (New York: Random House, 1992), in *Parade Magazine*, June 7, 1992, 12. However, see also Aaron Lynch, *Thought Contagion: How Belief Spreads Through Society* (New York: Basic, 1996), 66: "Yet great physical ability to dominate might not entirely explain the historically prevalent belief that men should dominate. Indeed, our closest primate relative, the bonono, has a social structure in which smaller, weaker females dominate bigger, stronger males. Their females simply gang up on any male who tries to dominate by force."

9. See Adrian Desmond, *The Ape's Reflexion* (London: Blond & Briggs, 1979), 230: "The chimpanzee hunt . . . is evidence for incipient dominance breakdown, both during the hunt—when the leadership switches in a flash—and especially during the ensuing begging phase." William F. Allman, *The Stone Age Present: How Evolution Has Shaped Modern Life—From Sex, Violence, and Language to Emotions, Morals, and Communities* (New York: Simon & Schuster, 1994), 155: "The reason that human warfare is more lethal than the fights among chimpanzee groups is not that humans are more violent than chimps, but that humans are more cooperative and so are capable of unleashing more power."

Allman has an interesting explanation for how the cooperation gets started. It depends on whether males or females leave home to seek mates. If the males depart, the females form strong cooperative alliances, and then they fight for resources in group-against-group encounters. But chimpanzee and human males stay home and females migrate to their mates' groups. Thus these males form intense alliances—"old boy networks"—which they use to attack comparable groups of males. He relates this differential to the fact that "nowhere in the world have women formed armies to fight other groups of women for access to men."

Russell, *Lemur's Legacy*, 151; see also 152: "The creation of an outside enemy is crucial to successful male bonding and coexistence. Chimpanzees, like humans, divide the world into 'us' versus 'them.' It matters not that the enemy poses no genuine threat. . . . It matters that the coalition's survival is impossible without an enemy." War is "the ultimate male bonding ritual," which male humans have carried "to heights undreamt by our ancestors." "The need for war is little understood by human females. . . . [It] seems a terrible . . . inefficient way to settle disputes. . . . But war did not evolve to settle disputes. War evolved to displace in-group male aggression. . . . More than any other social institution, [warfare] clearly separates and clarifies the distinctly different goals of men and women. . . . It is only recently, through the rationalizations . . . and deceptions made possible by human language, that male coalitions have convinced a majority of citizens that war is broadly beneficial or necessary."

10. Ilya Prigogine and Isabelle Stengers, *Order Out of Chaos: Man's New Dialogue with Nature* (New York: Bantam, 1984), 163, 231.

11. Fred Hoyle and Chandra Wickramasinghe, *Lifecloud: The Origin of Life in the Universe* (New York: Harper & Row, 1978), 183.

12. On the Pauli Exclusion Principle, see Harald Fritzsch, *Quarks: The Stuff of Matter* (New York: Basic, 1981), 25. On the idea that defense mechanisms are needed to produce form, otherwise there is a general flow of life, and thus the usefulness of inflammation, whose opposite is symbiosis, see L. Thomas, "Adaptive Aspects of Inflammation," in *Immunopathology of Inflammation,* ed. B. K. Forsher and J. C. Houck (Amsterdam: Excerpta Medica, n.d.), 1-10. Compare John D. Barrow and Frank J. Tipler, *The Anthropic Cosmological Principle* (New York: Oxford University Press, 1988), 596, for a biological exclusion principle: two species cannot occupy the same niche in the same territory.

One of the first stages in the morphogenesis of the embryo is the formation of a gradient in the system (Prigogine and Stengers, *Order Out of Chaos,* 150). On the importance of getting away from symmetry, and on the need for differentials, see Werner R. Loewenstein, *The Touchstone of Life: Molecular Information, Cell Communication, and the Foundations of Life* (New York: Oxford University Press, 1999), 33-34. It is nonequilibrium that brings order out of chaos (Prigogine and Stengers, 287), and far from equilibrium there is no more leveling out or equal probability of this or that happening (p. 143). Things can be reordered only by expenditure of more energy (Michael Shallis, *On Time: An Investigation into Scientific Knowledge and Human Experience* [New York: Schocken, 1983], 69). On dissipative systems and the idea that input needs to exceed output, see Jeff Gates, *The Ownership Solution: Toward a Shared Capitalism for the Twentieth-First Century* (Reading Mass.: Addison-Wesley, 1998), 82. Eating other living things has been selected for because it saves the metabolic cost of production (Erich Jantsch, *The Self-Organizing Universe: Scientific and Human Implications of the Emerging Paradigm of Evolution* [New York: Pergamon, 1980], 107).

13. David P. Barash, *Sociobiology and Behavior* (New York: Elsevier, 1977), 63: "The Central Theorem of Sociobiology . . . states: When any behavior under study reflects some component of genotype, animals should behave so as to maximize their inclusive fitness." Wilson, *Consilience,* 154, 139 (definition of "heritable" in mathematical terms—too long and complicated to quote here), 259 (dominance hierarchy), 191-93 (sociobiology as a broad perspective on human social behavior). His concern is how to unite social studies with natural science and make them real sciences with predictive power.

14. Derek Bickerton, *Language and Human Behavior* (Seattle: University of Washington Press, 1995), 4-5: "sociobiologists . . . have not been cautious in their predictions of what such an approach might achieve." He interprets sociobiology as claiming that "biological imperatives that govern animals in general . . . continue

to manifest themselves in our species despite . . . culture," and he cites M. Ridley, *The Red Queen: Sex and the Evolution of Human Nature* (New York: Macmillan, 1993), 4, saying, "there is nothing in our natures that was not carefully 'chosen' . . . for its ability to contribute to eventual reproductive success." He does not find this approach helpful, because "what is . . . most essential, if we are to understand our true nature . . . is precisely the part of it that we do *not* share with other creatures." Alfie Kohn (*The Brighter Side of Human Nature: Altruism and Empathy in Everyday Life* [New York: Basic, 1990], 24) says that "sociobiology is unfalsifiable . . . set up in such a way that no fact could ever refute it," and he cites Barry Schwartz, *The Battle for Human Nature: Science, Morality and Modern Life* (New York: Norton, 1986), 190-91, giving examples of precisely opposite behavioral strategies each being a maximalization of fitness where it occurs, and concluding that "theories with this much flexibility . . . explain nothing."

Some misapprehensions are pointed out by Peter Singer, *The Expanding Circle: Ethics and Sociobiology* (New York: Farrar, Straus & Giroux, 1981), 44-45, who stresses (p. 53) that "the suggestion that an aspect of human ethics is universal . . . in no way justifies that aspect. . . . Nor does the suggestion that a particular aspect of human ethics has a biological basis do anything to justify it." He feels there is "much misunderstanding." E. O. Wilson challenges traditional belief, etc. ("The Ethical Implications of Human Sociobiology," *Hastings Center Report* 10 [1994]: 29; idem, *Sociobiology: The New Synthesis* [Cambridge, Mass.: Harvard University Press, 1975], 3-4, 129). See also Howard L. Kaye, *The Social Meaning of Modern Biology: From Social Darwinism to Sociobiology* (New Haven: Yale University Press, 1986), 99-101, 106-7.

15. On human nature and epigenetic rules, see Wilson, *Consilience*, 216, 193; on p. 147 he lists sixty-seven universals of culture, citing George P. Murdock; on p. 217 he discusses variation. Niles Eldredge, *Dominion* (New York: Holt, 1995), xiii-xv, 176. Richard Brodie, *Virus of the Mind: The New Science of the Meme* (Seattle: Integral, 1996), 217. Inherited nature may threaten survival, says Storr (*Human Destructiveness,* 112); he quotes Stanley Milgram, *Obedience to Authority* (New York: Harper & Row, 1974), 188: "[Man's subordination of his individuality to an institutional structure] is a fatal flaw nature has designed into us, and which in the long run gives our species only a modest chance of survival. [Ironically] loyalty, discipline and self-sacrifice . . . are the very properties that create . . . organizational . . . war and bind men to malevolent systems of authority." Kohn, *Brighter Side,* 214-15. Marshall Sahlins, *The Use and Abuse of Biology: An Anthropological Critique of Sociobiology* (Ann Arbor: University of Michigan Press, 1976), 57. No one knows the total potentiality: see *Evolution and Consciousness: Human Systems in Transition,* ed. Erich Jantsch and Conrad H. Waddington (Reading, Mass.: Addison-Wesley, 1976), 214.

16. Eli Sagan, *At the Dawn of Tyranny: The Origins of Individualism, Political Oppression, and the State* (New York: Knopf, 1985), 249. Wilson, *Consilience,* 253; idem, *On Human Nature,* 93. A meme is "something out in the world that, by its existence, alters people's behavior so that more copies of the thing get created" (Brodie, *Virus of the Mind,* 176). Aaron Lynch lists seven general patterns that he calls "modes of thought contagion," qualities that help a meme get copied: quantity parental (having many children to whom the meme is passed), efficiency parental, proselytic, preservational, adversative, cognitive, and motivational

(*Thought Contagion,* 3); ensuing pages discuss these in detail; for how these apply, e.g., to Christianity, see 107ff.

On dominance hierarchies and wanting power, see Brodie, *Virus of the Mind,* 110-11: "Why are men so obsessed with dominance relationships, with who's above and below them on the power ladder? The best theory is that it was an adaptation to establish which males had sexual rights to which women without constantly fighting about it . . . business, government, military, . . . church . . . on the surface . . . [have] little to do with access to females, but the behavior and feelings men have in them are still the same." Storr says that "for many natures, the pleasures of exercising power are more compelling than those of sex . . . human violence and cruelty are predominantly concerned with power relationships" (*Human Destructiveness,* 99; cf. p. 85 on sadomasochism).

J. M. Fritzman, "Escaping Hegel," *International Philosophical Quarterly* 33, no. 1 (March 1993): 61-62. Teresa Amabile presented a hundred subjects with two book reviews, one very positive . . . other very negative (written by the same reviewer so style would be the same). Subjects were asked to rate the reviewer: "the negative reviewer was seen as more intelligent and competent, with higher literary expertise than the positive reviewer" ("Brilliant But Cruel: Perceptions of Negative Evaluators," *Journal of Experimental Social Psychology* 19 [1983]: 151). See further Kohn, *Brighter Side,* 39-40.

17. Stephan L. Chorover, *From Genesis to Genocide: The Meaning of Human Nature and the Power of Behavior Control* (Cambridge, Mass.: MIT Press, 1979), 22; see also 87: Charles Darwin believed in social hierarchies; Alfred Russel Wallace did not. On the idea that natural differences, measured, are genetic, see R. C. Lewontin, Steven Rose, and Leon J. Kamin, *Not in Our Genes: Biology, Ideology, and Human Nature* (New York: Pantheon, 1984), 84, in a chapter entitled "I.Q.: The Rank Ordering of the World." Brodie, *Virus of the Mind,* 158, 162, 88; pp. 194-95 list "push buttons": security, crisis, food, sex, problem-solving/learning, dominance, belonging. Compare Lynch's modes and examples in general. On gender equality, see Lynch, *Thought Contagion,* 62-67. Lynch's chapter 5 studies the success of various Western religions in terms of "natural selection" of memes and details advantageous traits.

18. Wilson predicts that "future generations will be genetically conservative . . . will resist hereditary change . . . to save the emotions and epigenetic rules" (*Consilience,* 277). Alteration might make us "better" in some way, but "why should a species give up the defining core of its existence, built by millions of years of biological trial and error?" Communism reduces incentive to produce (Lynch, *Thought Contagion,* 20). It leaves people disconnected from the means of production (Gates, *Ownership Solution,* 19). Allocation of talent by bureaucrats is disastrous (Robert H. Frank and Philip J. Cook, *The Winner-Take-All Society* [New York: Free Press, 1995], 7). Mickey Kaus says that "socialism has its virtues . . . and relative material equality may be one of them. . . . But there are consequences attached . . . those who choose socialism must be prepared to give up the sort of material prosperity that only captialist nations seem able to achieve" (*The End of Equality* [New York: Basic, 1992], 11). Various combinations can be tried, but "the natural dynamics of capitalism" will eventually win. Kaus argues that equality in money can't be attained together with other values, but that what we really want, anyway, is social equality, and that can be attained in ways that he discusses. Jeff

Gates, who is one of those who want to try some adjustments to capitalism to achieve more equality, has some "horror stories" to tell about elite groups practicing capitalism even under Communist government (*Ownership Solution*, 247).

Mary Midgley (*Beast and Man: The Roots of Human Nature* [Ithaca, N.Y.: Cornell University Press, 1978], 81) makes the remark about Konrad Lorenz, apparently in reference to his *On Aggression* (New York: Harcourt, Brace, World, 1963).

19. Kohn gives some examples of how people may judge that loving your neighbor too much is not a good idea (*Brighter Side*, 96-97) and cites Mark Barnett, "Empathy and Related Responses in Children," in *Empathy and Its Development,* ed. Nancy Eisenberg and Janet Strayer (Cambridge: Cambridge University Press, 1987), 158: "In structured interpersonal competitions, such as an athletic contest or a classroom exam, excessive awareness of and concern about the feelings of others may prove counterproductive." Kohn comments: "instead of taking this as evidence of the destructiveness of competition, . . . we try to discourage children from caring 'excessively.'" Christian de Duve points out that "evolution tends to stagnate if not prodded" (*Vital Dust: Life as a Cosmic Imperative* [New York: Basic, 1995], 231). Midgley says, "Beings who would love everybody equally and unfailingly . . . would land us in the mess we always reach if we ignore the central structure of our feelings" (*Beast and Man,* 81). A comic strip panel shows a TV psychologist holding up a picture of the strip's hero and saying, "Anyone who risks his life daily for no reward needs psychological help!"

Ashley Montagu (*The Nature of Human Aggression* [New York: Oxford University Press, 1976], 46-47) rehearses Herbert Spencer's ideas and social Darwinism, social approval of "ambition, greed, self-aggrandizement, competitiveness, exploitation of others and indifference to their plights" and the view that "losers are inferior to winners . . . failures themselves were persuaded by it . . . believed in their own inferiority, and . . . supported the system that degraded them." He then tells about Dr. John Rowan Wilson, an English physician, who reviewed Robert Ardrey's *Territorial Imperative* (New York: Dell, 1966) with approval and admiration, suggested that immigrants of "different culture and . . . appearance" should be discouraged, racial prejudice is a good idea, and "we should stop aiming at the impossible task of trying to love and understand our neighbours."

Michael Lerner gives examples of similar opinions, that "liberalism" can undermine self-interest and that the market proves that "selfishness works" (*Jewish Renewal: A Path to Healing and Transformation* [New York: Putnam, 1994], 19-20). Those who feel that way urge minorities at risk not to trust others but to take care of their own first. Lerner listens and appreciates where those feelings are coming from, then undertakes to lay out another way.

Wilson distinguishes "hard-core altruism" (willingness to sacrifice unconditionally for close kin) from "soft-core," extended to almost anyone from whom reciprocation can be expected (*On Human Nature*, 162, 171). He says, "True selfishness, if obedient to the other constraints of mammalian biology, is the key to a more nearly perfect social contract" (p. 164). Roger Lewin (*Complexity: Life at the Edge of Order and Chaos* [New York: Macmillan, 1992], 58-59) tells about Stuart Kauffman's computer simulations of the interaction of species in an ecosystem, each behaving selfishly but having to adjust to what the others are doing. The conclusion is that "collective adaptation to selfish ends produces the maximum average fitness, each species in the context of others . . . collective good is ensured."

Interested readers can go to Kauffman himself in the masterwork, *The Origins of Order: Self Organization and Selection in Evolution* (New York: Oxford University Press, 1993) or the popular, but still very instructive, *At Home in the Universe: The Search for Laws of Self-organization and Complexity* (New York: Oxford University Press, 1995). About creating a new set of victims, see Gil Bailie, *Violence Unveiled: Humanity at the Crossroads* (New York: Crossroad, 1997), 18.

20. On rewards and punishments, see David Bohm and F. David Peat, *Science, Order, and Creativity* (New York: Bantam, 1987), 231-33: they bemoan this fact and urge that such outside pressures and ulterior motives inhibit creativity, which must find its satisfaction in its own process. Kaus continues his argument that we can't have both capitalism and money equality: "Capitalism depends on money inequality as the spur to work—if you work more you get paid more. It depends on vast inequality as the spur to risk-taking—people will gamble their money on a project because they will get rich if it succeeds. Capitalism is a *system* . . . you cannot . . . change one part . . . without affecting the others . . . cannot . . . keep all the nice parts . . . and get rid of all the nasty ones. [Selfishness and greed] are what make the system work. You can't have capitalism and material equality because capitalism is constantly generating extremes of *inequality*" (*End of Equality*, 9).

This is the result of positive feedback: possession of the trait (money in this case) enables the trait to increase: money makes money. One consequence is that we rack up huge inequalities and polarities. Unless some form of negative feedback is introduced, we become a "winner-take-all" society, as Frank and Cook explain. If we did have equal incomes, they say, "few would work hard and take risks. We thus confront an agonizing trade-off, the economists tell us, between equality and economic prosperity" and reluctantly agree to "reward people in rough proportion to the market value of the things they produce" (*Winner-Take-All Society*, vii).

21. See J. Z. Young, *Programs of the Brain: Based on the Gifford Lectures, 1975-7* (New York: Oxford University Press, 1978), 140-41, on the discovery of the pleasure centers in the brain: "It is not possible any longer to consider that human aims and values are set by some transcendent, intuitive process . . . they are basically regulated by . . . certain parts of the brain. . . . The great question is then, can we find a basis for prescriptive statements in descriptive ones? . . . We can now say something about the origins of human beliefs just as we can about the origins of our desires and fears. They are all the products of our human nature and the complicated cultural conditions that this nature has brought about. I am claiming that we are more likely to reach useful and satisfactory conclusions by considering this knowledge about origins than by assuming that our values are set by a divinely endowed inner imperative."

Freeman Dyson, *Weapons and Hope* (New York: Harper & Row, 1984), 15. Stewart Brand, *The Media Lab: Inventing the Future at MIT* (New York: Viking, 1987), 235. On paradise in the South Pacific, see Alfonso Montuori and Isabella Conti, *From Power to Partnership: Creating the Future of Love, Work, and Community* (San Francisco: HarperSanFrancisco, 1993), 129, 131. Joseph H. Berke speaks for the "salutary psychic and social effects" of "even pernicious impulses" as a "necessary stimulus to action . . . a modicum of envy is a necessary impetus for change. If everyone had as much as they needed and wanted, there would be little incentive to do anything" (*The Tyranny of Malice: Exploring the Dark Side of Character and Culture* [New York: Summit, 1988], 276).

22. Bova, *Immortality*, 187.

8. It's the Nature of Nature to Change

1. On a "point of inflection," see Jonas Salk, *The Survival of the Wisest* (New York: Harper & Row, 1973), 21. Barbara Marx Hubbard, *Conscious Evolution: Awakening the Power of Our Social Potential* (Novato, Calif.: New World Library, 1998), 150-51. Jeff Gates, *The Ownership Solution: Toward a Shared Capitalism for the Twenty-First Century* (Reading, Mass.: Addison-Wesley, 1998), 130, 349. Magoroh Maruyama, "Toward Cultural Symbiosis," in *Evolution and Consciousness: Human Systems in Transition,* ed. Erich Jantsch and Conrad H. Waddington (Reading, Mass.: Addison-Wesley, 1976), 207. Michio Kaku, *Visions: How Science Will Revolutionize the 21st Century* (New York: Doubleday, Anchor, 1997), 19. Michael Lerner, *The Politics of Meaning: Restoring Hope and Possibility in an Age of Cynicism* (Reading, Mass.: Addison-Wesley, 1996), 248. Hazel Henderson, *Creating Alternative Futures: The End of Economics* (New York: Berkley, 1978), 25. Robert C. North, *The World That Could Be* (New York: Norton, 1976). O. W. Markley, "Human Consciousness in Transformation," in *Evolution and Consciousness,* ed. Jantsch and Waddington, 227. Niles Eldredge, *Dominion* (New York: Holt, 1995), 125-26, 130-32 (the difference between human-caused loss of habitat and mass extinctions of the past is that we continue to cause such loss, there is no chance to recover, evolution to adapt is not triggered). Robert Ornstein and Paul Ehrlich, *New World, New Mind: Moving Toward Conscious Evolution* (New York: Simon & Schuster, 1989), 3. David Bohm and F. David Peat, *Science, Order, and Creativity* (New York: Bantam, 1987), 206-7. Peter Russell, *The Global Brain Awakens: Our Next Evolutionary Leap* (Palo Alto, Calif.: Global Brain, 1995), 22.

Additional material can be found in Michael Lerner, *Jewish Renewal: A Path to Healing and Transformation* (New York: Putnam, 1994), 335: systemic change is needed at the corporate level. Gates, *Ownership Solution,* 132: immoral corporate activity must be stopped; p. 165: we need to reconceive the role of government, because what the public needs is institutions that guide rather than dominate; p. xx: if free enterprise democracy is not generating the results its citizens intend, then we need to reengineer it. See also in Henderson, *Creating Alternative Futures,* 28: we need to remap our economy, to redesign its models; p. 39: the problems we have with inflation, pollution, depletion of resources, human alienation, unemployment, maldistribution, and so on, should force us to reassess our theories of value; pp. 41-42: we need new concepts in economics, need to reexamine profit, productivity, efficiency, utility, and so on.

2. On global commerce, see William Greider, *One World, Ready or Not: The Manic Logic of Global Capitalism* (New York: Touchstone, 1997), 470-72. On the dichotomy of individual and society collapse, see Alfonso Montuori and Isabella Conti, *From Power to Partnership: Creating the Future of Love, Work, and Community* (San Francisco: HarperSanFrancisco, 1993), 253. Alfie Kohn, *No Contest: The Case Against Competition,* rev. ed. (Boston: Houghton Mifflin, 1986), 144-45, 149-155, 270 n. 42, detailing cross-cultural studies, including a massive study of 110 nations.

3. Hazel Henderson, *Building a Win-Win World: Life Beyond Global Economic Warfare* (San Francisco: Berrett-Koehler, 1996), 131-37; eadem, *Creating Alternative Futures,* 16-18, 24. Kenichi Ohmae, *The Borderless World: Power and*

Strategy in the Interlinked Economy (New York: HarperBusiness, 1990), 120-21. Robert Axelrod, *The Evolution of Cooperation* (New York: Basic, 1984), 177; see also 178-79; further literature on altruism, 220. On predisposition to empathy, see Alfie Kohn, *The Brighter Side of Human Nature: Altruism and Empathy in Every-day Life* (New York: Basic, 1990), 118. See also "To Love When Others Hate," interview with Beyers Naude, *Sojourners*, February 1988, 17. Gil Bailie, *Violence Unveiled: Humanity at the Crossroads* (New York: Crossroad, 1995), 21.

4. Robert A. Baron, *Human Aggression* (New York: Plenum, 1977), 269. Also Kohn, *No Contest*, 144 and 270 n. 42: aggression is learned. The Seville Statement is reprinted as an appendix in Kohn, *Brighter Side*, 269-70. On workers becoming owners, see Gates, *Ownership Solution*, 100. On no more pyramids, see Ohmae, *Borderless World*, 99-100. See also Gerald Ross and Michael Kay, *Toppling the Pyramids: Redefining the Way Companies Are Run* (New York: Random House, 1994), e.g., 15-16. In addition, see Peter Block, *Stewardship: Choosing Service over Self-Interest* (San Francisco: Berrett-Koehler, 1993): "Stewardship is the willingness to be accountable for the well-being of the larger organization by operating in ser-vice, rather than in control, of those around us." See Gates, *Ownership Solution*, 146-47, for an example.

5. De Boer is cited as personal communication in Anthony Storr, *Human Destructiveness* (New York: Grove Weidenfeld, 1991), 147. De Boer thinks there may be some connection between this behavior and the Eskimo practice of "extero-gestational" care of infants, providing the newborn with an environment closely resembling that of the womb by keeping the baby in constant contact with the mother's body. He says that such a culture produced "adults from whom it was impossible or difficult to elicit inter-personal aggressive responses" (p. 146 in Storr). Edward T. Hall, *Beyond Culture* (Garden City, N.Y.: Doubleday, Anchor, 1976), 35. Lerner, *Politics*, 49. Bob Thaves, *Frank and Ernest*, October 6, 1999 (distributed by NEA, Inc.).

6. Kohn, *Brighter Side*, 12-13.

7. Joseph Needham, *The Grand Titration: Science and Society in East and West* (London: Allen & Unwin, 1979), 36. *Titration* is a term borrowed from chem-istry: it means "the determination of the quantity of a given compound in a solu-tion by observing the amount of a solution of another compound at known strength required to convert the first completely into a third, the end-point being ascertained by a change of color or other means." By analogy one can "'titrate' the great civi-lizations against one another . . . and so . . . analyse the various constituents, social or intellectual, to see why one combination could far excel" in one age of the world "while another could catch up later" (p. 12).

"We are children of God" (1 John 3:1-2); "God is still working" (John 5:17). On not expecting to finish, see Gregory of Nyssa's vision of a redeemed life that simply goes on growing and expanding and learning "from glory to glory" (*From Glory to Glory: Texts from Gregory of Nyssa's Mystical Writings*, selected and introduced by J. Danielou, trans. H. Musurillo [Crestwood, N.Y.: St. Vladimir's Seminary Press, 1979]). See also Bernard Glassman and Rick Fields, *Instructions to the Cook: A Zen Master's Lessons in Living a Life That Matters* (New York: Bell Tower/Crown, 1996), 160: "In Buddhism, the bodhisattva makes a vow not to enter nirvana in order to enjoy his or her own enlightenment until *all* sentient beings have attained enlightenment. Since new beings are born every second, this will obviously take a very long time, possibly forever." Also, p. 163: "When we really do something completely, nothing is left." Compare Matthew 5:17, where Jesus "vows" to *implement* the Torah (divine teaching) *completely* (*plērōsai*).

8. Fritjof Capra, *The Web of Life: A New Scientific Understanding of Living Systems* (New York: Doubleday, Anchor, 1996), 294. J. Z. Young, *Programs of the Brain: Based on the Gifford Lectures, 1975-7* (New York: Oxford University Press, 1978), 270. For "unsimulatable," see Heinz R. Pagels, *The Dreams of Reason: The Computer and the Rise of the Sciences of Complexity* (New York: Simon & Schuster, 1988), 227-30.

9. Eknath Easwaran, "What Makes Me a Human Being?" *Blue Mountain* 10, no. 5 (September-October 1999): 1. Leon R. Kass, "Beyond Biology," *New York Times Book Review*, August 23, 1998.

10. On the idea that all nature is changing, see Ilya Prigogine and Isabelle Stengers, *Order Out of Chaos* (New York: Bantam, 1984), 92. Evolution produces increasingly flexible phenotypes of social systems and cultures (Erich Jantsch, "Evolution: Self-Realization through Self-Transcendence," in *Evolution and Consciousness,* ed. Jantsch and Waddington, 58). On the origin of the eukaryotic cell, see Lynn Margulis, *Symbiosis in Cell Evolution* (San Francisco: Freeman, 1981), or Beatrice Bruteau, *God's Ecstasy: The Creation of a Self-Creating World* (New York: Crossroad, 1997), 118-20.

11. On symbiosis, see Bruteau, *God's Ecstasy,* 89; consult index for various applications.

12. Kohn does not give a reference to the quotation from Cooley. On the thought of goodness as threatening, see Kohn, *Brighter Side,* 41; and on believing that we are helplessly "evil," p. 42; on ordinary people doing good deeds in high percentages, p. 64. For stories of good deeds, see Faith Middleton, *The Goodness of Ordinary People: True Stories from Real Americans* (New York: Crown, 1996).

13. Kohn, *Brighter Side,* 290 nn. 8, 10, 11, 12; see also p. 66: "One study of preschoolers during free play discovered that sixty-seven of the seventy-seven children shared with, helped, or comforted another child at least once during only forty minutes of observation."

14. David C. Korten, *When Corporations Rule the World* (San Francisco: Kumarian/Berrett-Koehler, 2001), 249-50, 260. There is a chapter entitled "Good Living," beginning on p. 249.

15. Genes must cooperate with other genes: see Richard Dawkins, *Unweaving the Rainbow: Science, Delusion and the Appetite for Wonder* (Boston: Houghton Mifflin, 1998), 217, 219, 221-22.

16. Axelrod, *Evolution of Cooperation,* 20-21. This is a foundational book, referred to by many other authors; see also his *Harnessing Complexity: Organizational Implications of a Scientific Frontier,* co-authored by Michael D. Cohen (New York: Free Press, 1999).

17. Charles Darwin, *The Descent of Man, and Selection in Relation to Sex,* facsimile ed. (Princeton, N.J.: Princeton University Press, 1981), 1:163-64. George C. Williams, *Adaptation and Natural Selection* (Princeton, N.J.: Princeton University Press, 1974), 94. Robert Trivers, "The Evolution of Reciprocal Altruism," *Quarterly Review of Biology* 46 (1971): 35-56. Robert Wright makes use of game theory (*The Moral Animal: Evolutionary Psychology and Everyday Life* [New York: Vintage, 1994], 191ff.). See also Steven Kelman, *Regulating America, Regulating Sweden: A Comparative Study of Occupational Safety and Health Policy* (Cambridge, Mass.: MIT Press, 1981), 142-44: "Accommodationist institutions [as

distinguished from "adversarial"] encourage achieving agreement . . . by negotiations. . . . Agreements are encouraged because of psychological processes that tend to occur in [small, ongoing] groups and provide normative inducements toward agreements . . . promote . . . preferences and perceptions that would not have existed without the ongoing relationship." Robert Kuttner quotes Kelman and then asks us to "note how diametrically opposed this is to the market model of man, in which relationships are arm's-length, contingent, and transitory, and motivations are purely instrumental and self-interested rather than collective and empathic" (*Everything for Sale: The Virtues and Limits of Markets* [New York: Knopf, 1997], 298). Hazel Henderson also remarks that the history of the twentieth century has been exceptional in its use of "hierarchical, competitive, conflict models," whereas "over 95 percent of the experience of human societies is in managing small, homogeneous populations in long-settled habitats" (*Building a Win-Win World*, 22 -23). Robert Wright thinks that our normal history shows "how steadfastly, even unconsciously, human nature pursues non–zero-sum gain [win-win, not win-lose or zero-sum], shaping social structure to that end" (*Nonzero: The Logic of Human Destiny* [New York: Pantheon, 2000], 34-35).

18. On the idea that "greedy and bully" strategies are the worst, see Lynn Margulis and Dorion Sagan, *Microcosmos: Four Billion Years of Evolution from Our Microbial Ancestors* (New York: Summit, 1986), 125, using Axelrod's work; see also pp. 130 ("eventually only cooperators were left") and 190 (on co-evolution). On the rich getting richer, see James Lardner, "The Rich Get Richer: What Happens to American Society When the Gap in Wealth and Income Grows Larger?" *U.S. News & World Report*, February 21, 2000, 39-43. This balanced article offers statistics and charts as well as color photographs of the rich, traces some history. Alexis de Tocqueville was "struck" by "the general equality of position among the people," and "then something happened," starting in 1979 when the wealth ratio of the top to the bottom suddenly became 10; by 1989, 16; and by 1999, 19 to 1.

Most economists think it's all right, but Alan Greenspan, chairman of the Federal Reserve Board, allows that "inequality" could pose a "major threat to our security," and Lardner reports a Harris Poll showing that "some 75 percent of Americans believe that the rewards of the new economy have been unevenly distributed," and he displays a pie chart showing that one-fifth of the population gets 50 percent of the income. And this is just within America, the wealthiest country. When the gap is considered on a world scale, the disparity is much greater. Economists don't talk much about this sort of thing causing trouble. That, Lardner concludes, "could be a big mistake." On the destructive effects of wealth inequality, see John Gray, *False Dawn: The Delusions of Global Capitalism* (New York: New Press, 1998), e.g., 114ff.; David Korten, n. 14 above; Timothy Gorringe, *Fair Shares: Ethics and the Global Economy* (New York: Thames & Hudson, 1999); Tom Athanasiou, *Divided Planet: The Ecology of Rich and Poor* (Boston: Little, Brown, 1996).

19. The market culture, with its values and its logic, acts as a self-fulfilling prophecy, creating preferences that are then claimed as natural. See Kuttner, *Everything for Sale*, 57; Herman E. Daly and John B. Cobb, Jr., *For the Common Good: Redirecting the Economy toward Community, the Environment, and a Sustainable Future*, 2nd ed. (Boston: Beacon, 1994), 50-51, 138ff. John O'Neil, *Five Bodies: The Human Shape of Modern Society* (Ithaca, N.Y./London: Cornell University Press, 1985). Daly and Cobb, quoting Charles L. Schultze, former economic advi-

sor to the president of the U.S. and in 1994 senior fellow at the Brookings Institution (pp. 138-39). Schultze says further: "Harnessing the . . . motive of . . . self-interest to promote the common good is perhaps the most important social invention mankind has achieved" (reported in Barry Schwartz, *The Battle for Human Nature: Science, Morality, and Modern Life* [New York: Norton, 1986], 247). This is what we are being taught to believe.

20. Lerner, *Jewish Renewal*, 172-73; Gates, *Ownership Solution*, 154-55, referring to Louis O. Kelso and Mortimer J. Adler, *The Capitalist Manifesto* (New York: Random House, 1958; emphasis added). For facts and figures on the effect on families, communities, unemployment, homelessness, crime rate, marriage and divorce, single parenting, etc., of a forced free-market system, see Gray, *False Dawn*, 29-32 (Britain), 39ff. (New Zealand), 44ff. (Mexico).

9. Memes, Mysticism, and Phase Transitions

1. Bernard Glassman, *Bearing Witness: A Zen Master's Lessons in Making Peace* (New York: Bell Tower/Crown, 1998), 112, 168. Charles A. Reich also speaks of "opposition to the System as a whole" and of "a restored social contract" (*Opposing the System* [New York: Crown, 1995], book jacket).

2. Socrates, as well as Jesus, saw that ill-doers needed healing: it is worse for your own soul to commit injustice than to suffer it, because the unjust act contradicts your own nature. Socrates saw his own philosophical work as therapeutic, awakening perception of moral values and urging people to "care for their souls." Alfonso Montuori and Isabella Conti, *From Power to Partnership: Creating the Future of Love, Work, and Community* (San Francisco: HarperSanFrancisco, 1993), 168 (interviewing Krippner).

3. Edward O. Wilson, *Consilience: The Unity of Knowledge* (New York: Knopf, 1998), 43, quoting George Scialabba, "The Tormented Quest of Michel Foucault," a review of *The Passion of Michel Foucault*, by James Miller, in the *Boston Sunday Globe*, January 3, 1993, A-12.

4. Michael Lerner, *The Politics of Meaning: Restoring Hope and Possibility in an Age of Cynicism* (Reading Mass.: Addison-Wesley, 1996), 27-29; idem, *Jewish Renewal: A Path to Healing and Transformation* (New York: Grosset/Putnam, 1994), 420-21.

5. On internalized market memes, see Lerner, *Politics*, 210; Robert Kuttner, *Everything for Sale: The Virtues and Limits of Markets* (New York: Knopf, 1997), 40-41.

6. On the danger meme, see Richard Brodie, *Virus of the Mind: The New Science of the Meme* (Seattle: Integral, 1996), 88. On employee well-being in Japan, see Timothy Gorringe, *Fair Shares: Ethics and the Global Economy* (New York: Thames & Hudson, 1999), 229-30. Robert Axelrod and Michael D. Cohen, *Harnessing Complexity: Organizational Implications of a Scientific Frontier* (New York: Free Press, 1999), 124, 126, 157.

7. Aaron Lynch, *Thought Contagion: How Belief Spreads Through Society* (New York: Basic, 1996), 3-9. See also Brodie, *Virus of the Mind*.

8. Gorringe, *Fair Shares*, 81 (maximization of profit by cheap labor). Frank Lloyd Wright, *The Living City* (New York: Horizon, 1959), 21 (the context is different, but the remark makes a significant point). Mitch Albom, *Tuesdays with*

Morrie (New York: Doubleday, 1997), 33; "Morrie" is Morrie Schwartz, professor at Brandeis University, who died in 1995. The book records his last days. See also Lerner, *Politics,* 238; David C. Korten, *When Corporations Rule the World,* 2nd ed. (San Francisco: Kumarian/Berrett-Koehler, 2001), 258, 260-61.

9. For the mystical transmission or initiation through "closed lips," see Plato's Seventh Letter, 340c-341d: "One must . . . explain what preliminary steps and how much hard work it will require." A person who "is genuinely devoted to philosophy," pious, and with a "natural affinity and fitness for the work," will see this as "a path of enchantment" and will enter on it prepared to "strain every nerve . . . or die in the attempt." It is not the sort of thing that can be written down. "I certainly have composed no work in regard to it, nor shall I ever do so . . . for there is no way of putting it in words like other studies. Acquaintance with it must come rather after a long period of attendance on instruction in the subject itself and of close companionship, when, *suddenly, like a blaze kindled by a leaping spark, it is generated in the soul and at once becomes self-sustaining*" [emphasis added]. Section 344e adds that anyone who has attained to this will feel "the same reverence for the subject that I do" and therefore not write about it. Nor is there any need to write it for one's own memory, "for there is no danger of anyone forgetting it, once [the] mind grasps it." On the human being's quest for the self, see, e.g., D. M. Dooling, "Focus," *Parabola* II.3.1; Beatrice Bruteau, *The Psychic Grid: How We Create the World We Know* (Wheaton, Ill.: Quest, 1979), chapter entitled "The Gridmaker" (a work on epistemology, in which the metaphor is a triode tube: the world being the cathode, the knowing consciousness the anode, and the community's conviction system the grid, which modifies the signal passing from cathode to anode; the conscious self, however, can modify the signal structure of the grid); Hazel Henderson, *Building a Win-Win World: Life Beyond Global Economic Warfare* (San Francisco: Berrett-Koehler, 1996), 15.

10. Eknath Easwaran, *The Bhagavad Gita for Daily Living,* vol. 1 (Berkeley, Calif.: Blue Mountain Center of Meditation, 1975), 336, 360-61, 324. The way to healing lies through doubt (Keiji Nishitani, *Religion and Nothingness,* trans. Jan Van Bragt [Berkeley: University of California, 1982], 18). See also Bernard Glassman and Rick Fields, *Instructions to the Cook: A Zen Master's Lessons in Living a Life That Matters* (New York: Bell Tower/Crown, 1996), 51. On "work-practice," see p. 72, but the whole book is about the relation between work-practice and sitting-practice, with the examples of the Zen community's foundation of businesses and renovation of apartment buildings in a depressed area of Yonkers. This is an excellent instance of the sort of thing Holy Thursday is about. Antoine de Saint-Exupéry, *Wind, Sand and Stars,* chapter 3, "The Tool," ¶2 (many editions; I have the translation by Lewis Galantière, bound together with *Night Flight* and *Flight to Arras* and published as *Airman's Odyssey* [New York: Reynal & Hitchcock, 1942], 39). On the "naked self," see, e.g., *The Book of Privy Counseling,* chapter 1 (many editions; I have it edited and introduced by William Johnston, bound together with the same [unknown] author's *The Cloud of Unknowing* [Garden City: Doubleday Image, 1973], 149-51; the idea recurs throughout both books).

11. Rachel Naomi Remen, *My Grandfather's Blessings: Stories of Strength, Refuge, and Belonging* (New York: Riverhead, 2000), 23; see also 44 ("I thought I was empty because I did not have enough"), 10 ("our only refuge is in the goodness in each other," 6 ("the place"), 12 ("altars"), 2 ("when we remember we can bless life, we can repair the world"), 72-73 (the prayer; the last line, Gen. 28:16).

Some readers may enjoy Lawrence Kushner, *God Was in This Place & I, i Did Not Know It: Finding Self, Spirituality, and Ultimate Meaning* (Woodstock, Vt.: Jewish Lights, 1994). Compare Kahlil Gibran, *The Prophet,* The Departure: "That which is you dwells above the mountain and roves with the wind. It is not a thing that crawls into the sun for warmth or digs holes into darkness for safety, but a thing free, a spirit" (various editions, e.g., London: Heinemann, first published 1926, this reprint 1971, p. 108). Gelek Rinpoche is quoted in Remen, *My Grandfather's Blessings,* 81.

Easwaran, "dazzling beauty" (*Bhagavad Gita,* 363). Eckhart on "God-seed" is from Easwaran, "What Makes Me a Human Being?" *Blue Mountain* 10, no. 5 (September-October, 1999): 5, without reference. But see Nishitani's deep discussion of Eckhart on self-discovery in the desert of the godhead, beyond all egoity, in pure subjectivity, as the "uncreated I AM" (*Religion and Nothingness,* 61ff.). The "union" of the soul with God is not a matter of two beings approaching one another and then joining. Rather, it means "that from ever deeper within the soul itself, the element of self is broken through again and again . . . the depths of God breaking its way up from the soul's innermost recesses . . . the birth of God in the soul . . . in so doing the soul returns . . . more deeply to itself and becomes . . . more truly itself . . . the final ground of the soul, its *bottomless ground* . . . [where] the soul can for the first time return to be itself" (p. 62).

12. Thomas Keating, *Open Mind, Open Heart: The Contemplative Dimension of the Gospel.* The organization making this way of prayer available is Contemplative Outreach (9 William St., P.O. Box 737, Butler, N.J. 07405). It offers information on local centering prayer support groups, frequent retreats and training sessions, and so on.

A simple outline of the general instruction for any meditative practice (where, when, posture, clothing, etc.) is given in Glassman and Fields, *Instructions to the Cook,* 29-30, including how to focus on and count the breath, a widely used method. Easwaran's way is a little different. He recommends repetition of the mantram outside the meditation period (while walking, waiting, doing simple tasks). The meditation itself consists of slow mental recitation of memorized passages from the world's spiritual literature that appeal to the meditator. A favorite is the Prayer of St. Francis, which begins, "O Lord, make me an instrument of your peace." Years of repetition of this tend to produce real peacefulness in the meditator, which can also be shared with those the meditator meets. The current kabbalistic revival has produced a good number of books on Jewish meditation practices. There are also Sufi and Taoist methods. For Glassman on the effect of meditation, see *Instructions to the Cook,* 36-37.

13. See, e.g., Carl Rogers, "The Necessary and Sufficient Conditions of Therapeutic Personality Change," *Journal of Consulting Psychology* 21 (1957): 95-103, where the phrase was first used. See also Rogers, *On Becoming a Person* (Boston: Houghton-Mifflin, 1961), passim. The "transcendentals" in metaphysics are being, unity, truth, goodness, and beauty. They are absolutely universal predicates, attaching to everything that is insofar as it exists, transcending any other quality it may have. On "first action" rather than "re-action," see the section on "Transcendent Freedom" in Beatrice Bruteau, *The Grand Option: Personal Transformation and a New Creation* (Notre Dame, Ind.: University of Notre Dame Press, 2001), 162-63. David Aaron, *Endless Light: The Ancient Path of the Kabbalah to Love, Spiritual Growth, and Personal Power* (New York: Simon & Schuster, 1997), 24. For Joseph

Jaworski on synchronicity, see *The Inner Path of Leadership* (San Francisco: Berrett-Koehler, 1996), 182.

Mach's Principle says that in order to give a thorough account of the dynamic state of any body, its relations to all other bodies and forces in the whole universe would have to be taken into consideration. Bell's Theorem has to do with correlated states, which maintain their relation to one another even if one is changed at a distance too great for a signal to reach the other (at the speed of light); the implication suggested here is that somehow the correlated states are a single system.

Lerner, *Politics,* 18-19. Gorringe, *Fair Shares,* 84. Mickey Kaus, *The End of Equality* (New York: Basic, 1992), 104. Jeff Gates, *The Ownership Solution: Toward a Shared Capitalism for the Twenty-First Century* (Reading, Mass.: Addison-Wesley, 1998), 172. Michael Lerner says that the new movement is trying to figure out just how the teaching about turning to God as the energy for transformation can be applied *collectively* (*Jewish Renewal,* 181). Robert Kuttner says that the market model of human nature has great difficulty regarding altruism as something worth cultivating, but economic theory is wrong about human motivation and behavior (*Everything for Sale,* 61).

14. Lerner, *Jewish Renewal,* 74-75.

Story II: The Revelation at Sinai

1. Avigdor Bonchek, *Studying the Torah: A Guide to In-Depth Interpretations* (Northvale, N.J.: Aronson, 1996), 21. See also *Zohar: The Book of Splendor,* selected and edited by Gershom Scholem (New York: Schocken, 1963), 121-22.

2. See Schmuel Boteach, *Wisdom, Understanding, and Knowledge: Basic Concepts of Hasidic Thought* (Northvale, N.J.: Aronson, 1996), 248.

3. See Moshe Braun, *The Jewish Holy Days: Their Spiritual Significance* (Northvale, N.J.: Aronson, 1996), 391.

4. Ibid., 398-400. Cf. Beatrice Bruteau, *What We Can Learn from the East* (New York: Crossroad, 1995), 103ff. (chapter entitled "The Immaculate Conception, Our Original Face").

5. Braun, *Jewish Holy Days,* 382, 288, 370. See also Lawrence Kushner, *The River of Light: Spirituality, Judaism, Consciousness* (Woodstock, Vt.: Jewish Lights, 1990), 51-52.

6. Boteach, *Wisdom,* 23, 123; Braun, *Jewish Holy Days,* 401.

7. Gershom Scholem, *Kabbalah* (Jerusalem: Keter, 1974; repr., New York: Meridian/New York Times Books, 1978), 147.

8. Braun, *Jewish Holy Days,* 397, 372-73, 403. On the light "shining from one end of the universe to the other," see Matt. 24:27; Luke 13:21. On the kingdom being "hidden" in the natural world, see Matt. 13:33; Luke 13:21; some translations have "mixed" but the Greek is "hid." On the impossibility of sin, see 1 John 3:9b. See also *Gospel of Thomas,* logion 112: "The kingdom of the Father is spread throughout the earth, but people do not see it."

9. Quoted in Braun, *Jewish Holy Days,* 169-70.

10. See, e.g., Richard Dawkins, *The Selfish Gene* (New York: Oxford University Press, 1976), and its sequents. Also Christopher Wills, *The Wisdom of the Genes* (New York: Basic, 1989); and Lyall Watson, *Dark Nature: A Natural History of Evil* (New York: HarperCollins, 1995).

11. Braun, *Jewish Holy Days,* 391.

12. Boteach, *Wisdom,* 184-85.

13. Ibid., 99-100.

14. Abraham Joshua Heschel, *I Asked for Wonder: A Spiritual Anthology,* ed. and with an introduction by Samuel N. Dresner (New York: Crossroad, 1992), xii, x. Perhaps God's question is, "Can we make humanity in our image?" (cf. Gen. 1:26).

15. These points were brought out in a lecture by Professor Andrew Ettin, Temple Emanuel, Winston-Salem, North Carolina, Fall, 2000.

10. Jesus and the Covenant Community

1. For a complete layout of the scholarly method, see, e.g., John Dominic Crossan, *The Historical Jesus: The Life of a Mediterranean Jewish Peasant* (San Francisco: HarperSanFrancisco, 1992), xxvii-xxxiv.

2. The stories about children reinforce this reading. As Jose Ignacio Lopez Vigil and Maria Lopez Vigil say, "In Jesus' milieu, children mattered very little . . . the young were often grouped with the deaf-mutes and idiots. . . . In the same manner that Jesus had an authentically revolutionary attitude toward women, his actions toward children—very much related to how he related with women—were surprising during his time. He made children privileged heirs of the Kingdom of God. This means that children . . . already have their own worth, and not just for what they will be when they grow up. Jesus' position had no precedent in the traditions of his ancestors. It was absolutely original" (*Just Jesus,* vol. 1, *A People Starving for Love,* trans. Trinidad Ongtangco-Regala [New York: Crossroad, 2000], 251).

A derivative of this method says that any parts of the storytelling that are not consistent with this sense of the *character* of the hero can be questioned as inauthentic, whereas those that are consistent with the character may be regarded as possibly true—at least not seriously misleading, even if not factual.

For an example of the Church's official view of women, which endured for centuries and has not entirely changed even now, see Thomas Aquinas, *Summa Theologiae*: "The woman is subject to the man on account of the weakness of her nature, both of mind and of body. . . . Man is the beginning of woman and her end." The passage is cited in Mark Gerzon, *A Choice of Heroes: The Changing Face of American Manhood* (Boston: Houghton Mifflin, 1982), 226, in the middle of a chapter on whether manhood has to imply lordship.

3. Howard Thurman, *Jesus and the Disinherited* (Boston: Beacon, 1976), 43: Discussing the experience of black Americans, he says, "Most of the accepted social behavior-patterns assume segregation to be normal—if normal, then correct; if correct, then moral; if moral, then religious. Religion is thus made a defender and guarantor of the presumptions."

4. Douglas E. Oakman, *Jesus and the Economic Questions of His Day* (Lewiston/Queenston: Edwin Mellen Press, n.d.), 12 n. 14, 21-25, 17-18. Richard A. Horsley, with John S. Hanson, *Bandits, Prophets, and Messiahs: Popular Movements at the Time of Jesus* (San Francisco: Harper & Row, 1985), 2-4.

5. Oakman, *Jesus and the Economic Questions,* 25-26, 23.

6. Ibid., 46-47, 49ff., 38ff., 23. On the commodification of labor, see Robert Kuttner, *Everything for Sale: The Virtues and Limits of Markets* (New York: Knopf, 1997), 77.

7. Oakman, *Jesus and the Economic Questions,* 72, 70-71 (Herod's wealth was about 20 percent of the Galilee's production), 68, 62.

8. Ibid., 52ff., esp. 55 (on land tenancy and losses through debt), 73. Robert Redfield, *Peasant Society and Culture: An Anthropological Approach to Civilization* (Chicago: University of Chicago Press, 1956), 64. Oakman, *Jesus and the Economic Questions,* 73ff., 41, 78-79. See also Richard A. Horsley and Neil Asher Silberman, *The Message and the Kingdom: How Jesus and Paul Ignited a Revolution and Transformed the Ancient World* (New York: Grosset/Putnam, 1997), 101. Compare Kuttner, *Everything for Sale,* 75-76. Oakman, 79.

9. Oakman, *Jesus and the Economic Questions,* 75-76. The Greek word in the NT usually translated "thief" is *lēstēs,* which describes especially group activity, "plundering," as by pirates, by those who operate in "bands," hence "bandits." The Markan passage indicates that there was a bandit insurrection in progress at the time Jesus was captured. See also John 18:12: the detachment of (Roman) soldiers responsible for the capture was a *speira,* a company of two hundred to six hundred men, under a *chiliarchos,* commander of a thousand men, appropriate for dealing with a small-scale insurrection. As was the usual Roman practice, those captured were crucified—a public spectacle intended to discourage further insurrection. Crucifixion was a punishment reserved for insurrectionists, not common thieves. That Jesus was not himself a bandit is indicated by the Matthean texts, but he was somehow confused with them. The gospels do not tell us how many bandits were crucified on this occasion, only that Jesus was crucified among them.

10. Horsley (*Bandits,* 65) describes bandit activity and Herod's efforts to eradicate it; he quotes Josephus, who says that whole families were inhabiting the bandit caves.

11. Horsley, *Bandits,* 69-70.

12. Ibid., 234. Roy W. Hoover, "The Problem of an Incredible Creed and the Promise of a Credible Faith," in *The Once & Future Faith,* Spring 2001 Meeting, Westar Institute (Jesus Seminar) (Santa Rosa, Calif.: Polebridge Press, 2001), 8.

13. Horsley, *Bandits,* 234, citing Matt. 22:1-14; Luke 14:15-24; 6:20-26; Mark 10:23-31, and recommending Elisabeth Schüssler Fiorenza, *In Memory of Her: A Feminist Theological Reconstruction of Christian Origins* (New York: Crossroad, 1983), 140-53. On debt, see Horsley, p. 59, citing Exod. 21:2; Deut. 15:1-18; Lev. 25:35-42. See also Crossan, *Historical Jesus,* 222-23, on loans, interest, and fines for nonrepayment.

14. Rabbi Milton Steinberg, *Basic Judaism* (San Diego: Harcourt Brace, 1975), 5.

15. The word I have rendered as "implement" is *plērōsai,* usually translated "fulfill," with the connotation of vindicating a foretold future. But the meaning of the word is simply to "complete," as in hiring all the hands needed to make up a crew. "Implement" comes from the Latin *implere,* also meaning to "fill up." The dictionary gives "carry out" as the meaning.

16. Neil Douglas-Klotz, *The Hidden Gospel: Decoding the Spiritual Message of the Aramaic Jesus* (Wheaton, Ill.: Quest, 1999), 84. *Gospel of Thomas,* logion 113, says: "The Kingdom of the Father is spread out on the earth and people do not see it."

17. Michael Samuel, *The Lord Is My Shepherd: The Theology of a Caring God* (Northvale, N.J.: Aronson, 1996), 173, 182, 185.

18. For a "Radical Mini-Catechism" tracing these teachings to the basic doc-

uments in the *Didache,* Luke, Matthew, and the *Gospel of Thomas,* see John Dominic Crossan, *The Birth of Christianity: Discovering What Happened in the Years Immediately after the Execution of Jesus* (San Francisco: HarperSanFrancisco, 1998), 387ff. For an analysis of artificial-distinction-memes of human ideas and concepts, see Richard Brodie, *Virus of the Mind: The New Science of the Meme* (Seattle: Integral, 1996), 218ff.

19. On the need for critical mass, see Jeff Gates, *The Ownership Solution: Toward a Shared Capitalism for the Twenty-First Century* (Reading, Mass.: Addison-Wesley, 1998), 213. For a contemporary Jewish teaching on the need for the entire community to be active in bringing about the ideal social order, see Arthur Hertzberg, with Aron Hirt-Manheimer, *Jews: The Essence and Character of a People* (San Francisco: HarperSanFrancisco, 1998), 160, recounting the doctrine of R. Shneur Zalman, the first Lubavitcher Rebbe, author of the *Tanya.* This view is dependent on that of Isaac Luria, sixteenth-century kabbalist, and contends that we need not wait patiently for the Messianic Era, but can hasten that day. Everyone has a role to play, "from the most ignorant and the most alienated to the most learned and most pious," in bringing about the "perfection" of the time of "the resurrection of the dead, meaning the revelation of Ein [no] Sof [end]-light [the infinite] in this physical world." The destiny of the world as a whole is "in everybody's hands; it [is] not a matter for elites. . . . Each individual [has] an indispensable and active share in bringing about the cosmic redemption."

20. Oakman, *Jesus and the Economic Questions,* 166. Parallels can be seen among the following:

religion—capriciousness, justice, unconditionality
physics—chance, determinism, quantum mechanics
philosophy—chaos [*apeiron,* without boundary, lacking form], form [finite], the Absolute [infinite, transcending form].

The apostle Paul, although he spoke of the free graciousness of God and the removal of class barriers among believers, still held that the penalty for the universal sin of the world had to be paid. Unconditionality is a concept difficult to get used to. The feeling of a need to "balance" things, to give or withhold according to what is "deserved," to "judge," persists.

21. *Mishnah Sanhedrin* 4:5. David M. Elcott, *A Sacred Journey: The Jewish Quest for a Perfect World* (Northvale, N.J.: Aronson, 1995), 13.

22. David Aaron, *Endless Light: The Ancient Path of the Kabbalah to Love, Spiritual Growth, and Personal Power* (New York: Simon & Schuster, 1997), 24.

23. Mickey Kaus, *The End of Equality* (New York: Basic, 1992), 162.

24. Ben Witherington III, *The Jesus Quest: The Third Search for the Jew of Nazareth* (Downers Grove, Ill.: InterVarsity, 1995), 221. Michael Lerner, *The Politics of Meaning: Restoring Hope and Possibility in an Age of Cynicism* (Reading, Mass.: Addison-Wesley, 1996), 252-53. See also Barbara Marx Hubbard, *Conscious Evolution: Awakening the Power of Our Social Potential* (Novato, Calif.: New World, 1998), 124, on "A New Social Architecture," which presents our society as "a whole system in transition."

25. Lopez Vigil and Lopez Vigil, *Just Jesus,* 1:109. David C. Korten, *When Corporations Rule the World,* 2nd ed. (San Francisco: Kumarian, 2001), 217 and *passim.* Jerry Mander, "Economic Globalization and the Environment," *Tikkun* 16, no. 5 (September–October 2001), 33-40.

26. Lerner, *Politics,* 140-41, 234-35. Of course, this program will not work if

the present poor want to become rich and take their turn at oppressing. See Lopez Vigil and Lopez Vigil, *Just Jesus,* 1:17.

27. See Lopez Vigil and Lopez Vigil, *Just Jesus,* 1:21. Oakman, *Jesus and the Economic Questions,* 43. The "jubilee year" calls not only for all debts to be canceled but for the land to be restored to the family who originally held it when the Promised Land was first divided among the invading Israelites.

28. Crossan, *Birth of Christianity,* 472, 427; Robert Jewett, "Tenement Churches and Communal Meals in the Early Church: The Implications of a Form-critical Analysis of 2 Thessalonians 3:10,11," *Biblical Research* 38 (1993): 23-43. See Josephus, *Jewish War* 2.127: "each gives what he has to any in need and receives from him in exchange something useful to himself" (describing the economic arrangements of the Essenes; see Crossan, *Birth of Christianity,* 449). For an interesting contemporary application of "sharing" as distinct from "exchanging," see Michael Schrage, *Shared Minds: The New Technologies of Collaboration* (New York: Random House, 1990), 144. Gates, *Ownership Solution,* 231: there are some goods whose value increases when they are shared, for instance, information and means of communication.

29. Oakman, *Jesus and the Economic Questions,* 166: generosity is the aim of the new social order. Horsley gives the text from Josephus and some other references (*Bandits,* 38-39).

30. Elcott, *Sacred Journey,* 60; for our human responsibility, see 9.

11. Implementing the Friendship Covenant Community

1. It is important to remember that "equality" does not inhibit creative diversity. It does not translate to "same." What we have to watch out for is letting diversity inhibit equality: for example, the idea that sexes are not the same, therefore not equal; different races are not equal, etc.

2. Although not treated explicitly here, the question of animal rights falls under this principle.

3. To obtain the full document and to comment on it, reach the Council for a Parliament of the World's Religions, P.O. Box 1630, Chicago IL 60690-1630; telephone 312-629-2990, e-mail 99info@cpwr.org, website www.cpwv.org.

4. Robert Axelrod, *The Evolution of Cooperation* (New York: Basic, 1984).

5. Thomas Friedman, *Longitudes and Attitudes* (New York: Farrar, Straus, Giroux, 2002), 77. See also *The Jeruslem Report* of February 10, 2003, 12-17, "Six Key Challenges for the Next Government . . . and how it should meet them," by Leslie Susser, with Hanan Sher and Isabel Kershner, which makes some important remarks that can serve as examples of the recommendations made above and be applicable in comparable situations elsewhere: "What [the Israeli (Sharon) government] hasn't tried [in order to stop terrorism] is reducing the Palestinian motivation to attack." They quote Boaz Ganor, director of the Herzliyah-based International Policy Center for Counterterrorism: "We should carry out humanitarian relief and disseminate propaganda in Arabic. . . . Top politicians, even the prime minister, should appeal to the Palestinians over the heads of their leaders, and explain . . . what they could achieve in negotiations. . . . None of this has been done and it should all be tried. . . . "

The article further recommends "reaching out to Israel's Arabs, . . . at the bottom of Israel's social and economic heap . . . [after] years of being shortchanged on funding from the state. . . . There are still large discrepancies in state funding . . . in some cases . . . getting worse. . . . Along with the Arab community's feeling of discrimination and neglect, built up over 50 years, is a growing sense of delegitimization. . . . Above all, the Arab minority chafes at its powerlessness and exclusion from decision-making. . . . Experts recommend affirmative action for Arabs in government posts." They also speak of change coming "from the bottom up, through Jewish-Arab grass-roots civic action."

This is representative of the suggestion that parties to dispute and tension should try looking through the other's eyes as sympathetically as possible. There have been for some time voices from the Palestinians expressing willingness to live in peace with Israel. Ordinary people can understand and appreciate one another's desires to live their ordinary lives in friendship rather than violence.

See also B. Bruteau, "Sharing a Sacred Supper: The Moral Role of a 'Superpower,'" in *Spiritual Perspectives on America's Role as Superpower,* created by the editors at Skylight Paths (Woodstock, Vt., 2003), 196-203.

6. The Hague Agenda for Peace and Justice for the 21st Century, http://www.haguepeace.org/appeals/ english.html. As a UN document, the Hague Agenda is available in all the United Nations languages: Arabic, Chinese, English, French, Russian, and Spanish. The reference number is A/54/98. To obtain the Agenda in any of these languages, access the above URL or the United Nations website: http://www.un.org.

7. Compassionate concern must also be extended to other sentient beings so that all (most? selected species?) may live together in some suitable way. How to arrange this is a problem on the frontier of our learning. Some topics, particularly affecting farm animals, and some affecting wild animals, are fairly clear. What to do about creatures that reproduce in great numbers and become afflictions to others is not yet clear. We cannot yet focus properly on the right-to-life of all these other species. It must exist in some way, but there are many contradictions. Protection of the interlocking contributions of microbes, plants, light, soil, water, climate, and so on to keep the planet poised in this miraculous balance that makes complex life possible here, is fairly well understood scientifically but is failing to be implemented politically and economically to such an extent that our complex life forms may be at serious risk. Consult Peter D. Ward and Donald Brownlee, *Rare Earth: Why Complex Life Is Uncommon in the Universe* (New York: Springer, 2000).

8. U Thant, "Reflections of a Mediator," *World,* July 4, 1972, 38-39.

9. Daniel Patrick Moynihan, *On the Law of Nations* (Cambridge, Mass.: Harvard University Press, 1990), 176-77.

10. World Federalist Association, 418 7th St. SE, Washington, DC 20003-2796: promotional material for "Campaign for Global Change," circulated in late winter of 2003.

11. "Alternatives to Economic Globalization," by Jerry Mander and eighteen other board members and associates of the International Forum on Globalization. This article, published in *Tikkun,* January-February 2003, 39ff., is an adaptation of the Introduction to *Alternatives to Economic Globalization: A Better World Is Possible,* a consensus report by the same authors and published by Berrett-Koehler in 2002.

12. See Ward and Brownlee, *Rare Earth,* 168-69, 206-12. For ways in which democratic means can be employed at local and national levels to curb injury to the

ecology, see, e.g., Michael Lerner, *The Politics of Meaning* (Reading Mass.: Addison-Wesley, 1997), 133; and Hazel Henderson, *Building a Win-Win World: Life Beyond Global Economic Warfare* (San Francisco: Berrett-Koehler, 1996), 41, which also indicates the growing markets for pollution control products. For the present status of biodiversity, see Richard Leakey and Roger Lewin, *The Sixth Extinction* (London: Weidenfeld and Nicolson, 1996); and Connie Barlow, *Green Space, Green Time: The Way of Science* (New York: Springer, 1997), which brings together many of the most prominent voices on this matter.

13. The Clinton administration did not submit the Kyoto Protocol to the Senate, which would have defeated it (Robert Kagan, *Of Paradise and Power* [New York: Knopf, 2003], 45). See also Hilary French, *Vanishing Borders: Protecting the Planet in the Age of Globalization* (A Worldwatch Book; New York: Norton, 2000), 94ff., 105ff., 208-9. See also the website www.unfccc.org/resources/docs/convkp/kpeng.html.

14. Christian de Duve, *Vital Dust: Life as a Cosmic Imperative* (New York: Basic, 1995), 273-74.

15. French, *Vanishing Borders*, 99.

16. Jeff Gates, *The Ownership Solution: Toward a Shared Capitalism of the 21st Century* (Reading Mass.: Addison-Wesley, 1998), 276.

17. Lerner, *Politics*, 238ff.

18. John Gray, *False Dawn: The Delusions of Global Capitalism* (New York: New Press, 1998), 192.

19. Robert Kuttner, *Everything for Sale: The Virtues and Limits of Markets* (New York: Knopf, 1997).

20. Gates, *Ownership Solution, passim.*

21. David C. Korten, *When Corporations Rule the World* (San Francisco: Kumarian/Berrett-Koehler, 2001), 245, 241, 243.

22. Kagan, *Of Paradise and Power*, 37, 21, 72-73, 57; see also p. 55.

23. David Bornstein, *The Price of a Dream: The Story of the Grameen Bank and the Idea That Is Helping the Poor to Change Their Lives* (New York: Simon & Schuster, 1996).

24. Philip Kitcher, *The Lives to Come* (New York: Simon & Schuster, 1996), 133-36, 138, 141-42, 308ff.

25. French, *Vanishing Borders*, 42.

26. Kuttner, *Everything for Sale*, 314, 315, 316-17.

27. French, *Vanishing Borders*, 111, 114-15; cf. Korten, *When Corporations Rule the World*, 295. Marilyn Berlin Snell reports that "the Like-Minded Group—made up of most developing nations plus China—[have been active] in protocol negotiations and at WTO meetings. Two of the most important issues debated at these meetings have been whether a country has a right to know what it is importing, and whether a government has a right to refuse an import it believes endangers its population. As drafted, the Biosafety Protocol now states that nations have such rights. The next step is ratification by at least 50 nations and ensuring that the WTO or other international bodies cannot overrule the protocol" ("Against the Grain," *Sierra* [July-August 2001]: 30). Update as of February 27, 2004: The eighty-seven member states of the Catagena Protocol on Biosafety, which entered into force in September 2003, have adopted documentation requirements and other procedures for promoting the safety of international trade in living (or genetically) modified organisms (LMOs or GMOs). The United States has refused to sign the

treaty, has lobbied heavily against it, and warned the nations signing that their action may "have consequences." The treaty protects nations against the illegal entry of unapproved genetically engineered organisms into their farm fields, environment, and food supply. The European Union, which has strict regulations for GE foods, announced that "we are firm to make this protocol work" (European Environment Commission). For more information, see www.biodiv.org and www. unep.ch. The above was still being posted on December 6, 2004.

28. See de Duve, *Vital Dust,* 280ff.; Michio Kaku, *Visions: How Science Will Revolutionize the 21st Century* (New York: Doubleday, Anchor, 1997), 331-32; Gray, *False Dawn,* 200. Consult references such as Ben Zuckerman and David Jefferson, *Human Population and the Environmental Crisis* (Sudbury, Mass.: Jones & Bartlett, 1996).

29. But see John Kenneth Galbraith, *The Good Society* (Boston: Houghton Mifflin, 1996), 134: "In this world there is no literate population that is poor, no illiterate population that is not." Robert Kagan (*Of Paradise and Power*) speaks to these issues, as does Hazel Henderson (*Building a Win-Win World,* 30). On protecting differences, see Karl A. Plank, "The Eclipse of Difference" and subsequent discussion in *Merton and Judaism: Recognition, Repentance, and Renewal,* ed. Beatrice Bruteau (Louisville, Ky.: Fons Vitae, 2003).

30. Michael Schrage, *Shared Minds: The New Technologies of Collaboration* (New York: Random House, 1990), perhaps esp. chapter 12. Willis Harman, *Global Mind Change: The Promise of the Last Years of the Twentieth Century* (Indianapolis: Knowledge Systems, 1988), 155-56, on people giving legitimacy. For access to the media, see Charles A. Reich, *Opposing the System* (New York: Crown, 1995), 144. Hilary French speaks of democratizing global politics by emphasizing the role of citizen groups and by making information freely and widely available (*Vanishing Borders,* 170).

31. On information peerage, see Kevin Kelly, *New Rules for the New Economy: Ten Radical Strategies for a Connected World* (New York: Viking, 1998): in a system, providers are also consumers and information flows symmetrically to all nodes (p. 128). "In hierarchies, members are ranked in privilege relative to one another; in networks, members relate as peers. . . . Rank is a . . . substitute for ubiquitous real-time information. . . . When information is plentiful, peers take over" (p. 119). "The net tends to dismantle authority and shift to peer groups" (pp. 132, 103). Neil Gershenfeld, *When Things Start to Think* (New York: Holt, 1999), 89: The reason why the net is so successful, so reliable, and so innovative is that all users can participate in creating it. (It can serve as a structural and dynamic model for the JESUS program for a Just Egalitarian [or Empathetic] Social Unity System.) See also T. Irene Sanders, *Strategic Thinking and the New Science* (New York: Free Press, 1998), 8: the new knowing has to do with how to work with patterns of interaction, locally and globally.

32. Alfie Kohn, *The Brighter Side of Human Nature: Altruism and Empathy in Everyday Life* (New York: Basic, 1990), 168-71. Consult Shinichi Suzuki, *Nurtured by Love* (New York: Exposition, 1969); and J. Cummins and D. Sayers, *Brave New Schools: Challenging Cultural Illiteracy Through Global Learning Networks* (New York: St. Martin's, 1995).

33. Kuttner, *Everything for Sale,* 356: "increased time pressure . . . squeezes out . . . the aspect of life built around neither work nor family, but around life-affirming sociability." Also see James Gleick, *Faster* (New York: Pantheon, 1999).

34. Abraham Joshua Heschel, *The Sabbath: Its Meaning for Modern Man* (New York: Farrar, Straus, Giroux, 1951), 5: "The Sabbath is not for the sake of the weekdays; the weekdays are for the sake of the Sabbath" (referring to *Zohar*, I, 75). Its meaning is not merely rest from labor but provision of delight.

35. Robert H. Frank and Philip J. Cook, *The Winner-Take-All Society* (New York: Free Press, 1995), in general; see p. 12 for a recommendation that we encourage our brightest students to study in our state universities instead of applying to the Ivy League institutions. This is another instance of trying to increase the significance of local life, a more distributed system.

36. Morris Berman, *The Twilight of American Culture* (New York: Norton, 2000), 61-62, 47.

37. Alfonso Montuori and Isabella Conti, *From Power to Partnership: Creating the Future of Love, Work, and Community* (San Francisco: HarperSanFrancisco, 1993), 212.

38. Kelly, *New Rules*, 159-60.

39. Frank White, *The Overview Effect* (Boston: Houghton Mifflin, 1987), 39.

40. Robert Pollack, *Signs of Life: The Language and Meanings of DNA* (Boston: Houghton Mifflin, 1994).

41. Schrage, *Shared Minds*, 57-58, 139-40; Kelly, *New Rules*, 132ff.

42. See the optimistic words of Gregory Stock (not too well supported by the current rash of terrorist activity and "preemptive" but highly disruptive strikes by U.S.-led coalitions) in *Metaman: The Merging of Humans and Machines into a Global Superorganism* (Toronto: Doubleday Canada, 1993), 115-16; but in the long run he may be right.

43. Howard Rheingold, *The Virtual Community: Homesteading on the Electronic Frontier* (Reading Mass.: Addison-Wesley, 1993), 25, commenting on and quoting from Ray Oldenburg, *The Great Good Place: Cafés, Coffee Shops, Bookstores, Bars, Hair Salons, and Other Hangouts at the Heart of a Community* (New York: Marlowe, 1999).

44. Mickey Kaus, *The End of Equality* (New York: Basic, 1992), 23. The ambiguous title doesn't mean that equality should come to an end (though Kaus thinks that the quest for *money*-equality is probably a lost cause), but that the desirable goal, the end to which other strivings are the means, is *social* equality, which ought to be sought by a variety of means.

45. Lerner, *Politics*, 147-48.

46. Kaus, *End of Equality*, 124-35.

12. Partners with God in Creation

1. See the conditions for long-term repeated interaction leading to cooperation in Robert Axelrod, *The Evolution of Cooperation* (New York: Basic, 1984), 59ff.

2. James R. Beniger, *The Control Revolution: Technological and Economic Origins of the Information Society* (Cambridge, Mass.: Harvard University Press, 1986), 434.

3. Tom Bethell, *The Noblest Triumph: Property and Prosperity through the Ages* (New York: St. Martin's, 1998), 197.

4. Noson Gurary, *The Thirteen Principles of Faith: A Chasidic Viewpoint*, compiled and edited by Moshe Miller (Northvale, N.J.: Aronson, 1996), 205. The

book is arranged as commentaries on Maimonides' Thirteen Principles of Faith. The relevant principle here is no. 12: "I believe with complete faith in the coming of the Messiah. Even though he tarry, I will eagerly await his coming every day." Rabbi Gurary holds that the task of the Messiah is to reveal God, whose purpose in creating is to make a material place where godliness is totally revealed, where God dwells in a totally revealed way. When the Messiah comes, we will see how the world was created for the sake of the Torah (the Truth about God). The world is for *God*. Looked at this way, says Gurary, you can see that if you don't "believe in the coming of the Messiah," you've missed the whole point. You've failed to understand the purpose of the creation, the giving of the Torah, and the descent of human souls into the world (p. 203).

5. Ibid., 203, 213.

6. Both the Jewish Publication Society translation and the New Revised Standard Version give "sanctuary," but I wanted to try the effect of something more intimate, "home." After all, it is intended as a "dwelling."

7. Gurary, *Thirteen Principles*, 203.

8. E.g., Rabbi Shneur Zalman of Liadi (eighteenth century) taught: "Everyone who has insight into the matter will understand clearly that everything created and having being is [the expression of] the Force of God which . . . flows through it from its divine source. . . . There is really nothing in existence besides God." Reported by Alan Unterman in *The Way of the Jewish Mystics,* compiled and edited by Perle Besserman (Boston: Shambhala, 1994), 232-33. See also Rabbi Rami Shapiro, *Hasidic Tales: Annotated and Explained* (Woodstock, Vt.: Jewish Lights, 2004), 46, commenting on Ps. 16:8: "I have placed the Divine Presence before me always": "Living with the awareness of God's Presence is . . . seeing the nonduality that is God manifest as the duality that is creation. There is nothing other than God." Compare John 1:18, p. 283n8, above.

9. David Korten, *When Corporations Rule the World,* 2nd ed. (San Francisco: Kumarian/Berrett-Koehler, 2001), 242-43.

10. Kevin Kelly, *New Rules for the New Economy: 10 Radical Strategies for a Connected World* (New York: Viking, Penguin, 1998), 141-42.

11. Louis Jacobs, *Holy Living: Saints and Saintliness in Judaism* (Northvale, N.J.: Aronson, 1990), 2-3. For typical usage of *hesed* in the Bible, see Exod. 34:6; Jer. 2:2; 31:2; Hos. 2:21; 6:6; 10:12-13; 12:7-8; Joel 2:13; Jonah 4:2; Micah 6:8.

12. Gurary, *Thirteen Principles*, 206 (emphasis added).

13. Daisaku Ikeda is the founder of the Boston Research Center for the 21st Century. The quotation is taken from his foreword to *Subverting Greed: Religious Perspectives on the Global Economy,* ed. Paul F. Knitter and Chandra Muzaffar (Maryknoll, N.Y.: Orbis Books, 2002), xiv.

14. See Jeff Gates, *The Ownership Solution: Toward a Shared Capitalism for the Twenty-First Century* (Reading, Mass.: Addison-Wesley, 1998), 176.

15. For an interesting discussion of hope and imagery in the context of popular scientific views, see Eric J. Lerner, *The Big Bang Never Happened: A Startling Refutation of the Dominant Theory of the Origin of the Universe* (New York: Times [Random House], 1991), 414ff. His point is that our images of the origin— and therefore the destiny—of the universe form a remote background for our present attitudes of hope or meaninglessness. The physical theory concerns electromagnetic vortices in a matter/antimatter plasma for which the question of origin does not arise and from which can be derived alternatives to conventional

accounts of galaxy clusters, quasars, and black holes, as well as the cosmic expansion (see esp. pp. 218ff.). Scientific *models*, in their domain of idea orderliness, fulfill the same functions as do *myths* in theirs.

16. Dalai Lama and Howard C. Cutler, *The Art of Happiness: A Handbook for Living* (New York: Riverhead [Penguin Putnam], 1998), 288-89.

17. Ibid., 125: To cultivate a certain value, "first . . . thoroughly understand the value . . . this gives you a feeling of conviction and determination. Then . . . using your imagination, your creativity . . . visualize yourself in [the] situation . . ."; see also pp. 43 (positive conditioning), 55 (imagination), 176 (persistent training). See Agnes Sanford, *The Healing Light* (New York: Ballantine, 1947), basic to many such practices, still valuable today. Another old book by Neville (Neville Lancelot Goddard) is *Awakened Imagination* (Los Angeles: G. & J., 1954). He follows William Blake in asserting that "imagination is the very gateway of reality . . . [our] Eternal Body, The Divine Body. . . . By imagination we have the power to be anything we desire to be. Through imagination we disarm and transform the violence of the world" (p. 20); he gives examples of imagining being *in* the desired state, as distinguished from merely thinking *about* how good it would be if "Thinking *from* the end, from the feeling of my wish fulfilled, was the source of everything that happened as outer cause" (p. 48). "Controlled inner talking" is part of this practice, by which we "construct and inwardly affirm that we are what we want to be . . . by frequently occupying the feeling of our wish fulfilled . . . the frequency . . . is the secret of success" (pp. 104-5).

18. Peter Russell, *The Global Brain Awakens: Our Next Evolutionary Leap* (Palo Alto, Calif.: Global Brain, 1995), 306ff.; see also 221-23.

19. Hebrew *malchut* ("kingdom") is the tenth emanation from the Infinite in the kabbalistic Tree of Life, the levels, or successive qualities, through which the act of creation communicates divinity to materiality. It means, says Rabbi Wayne Dosick (*Dancing with God* [San Francisco: HarperSanFrancisco, 1997], 73), the union between God and People, "the place of the climax of creation, where God and God's children meet . . . where the transcendent Infinite God—the *keter*, the crown, the highest of all [divine expressions]—comes into communion and relationship with the finite human beings who are the 'crowning' work of creation" in which all polarizations are resolved and integrated. This happens here, in our physical world, in our daily reality. Compare my "Trinitarian Life Cycle" in, e.g., Beatrice Bruteau, *God's Ecstasy: The Creation of a Self-Creating World* (New York: Crossroad, 1997), 176, 178.

Neil Douglas-Klotz, in *The Hidden Gospel: Decoding the Spiritual Message of the Aramaic Jesus* (Wheaton, Ill.: Quest, 1999), 83-96, discusses the cluster of meanings around the Aramaic word *malkuta*. Remarking at the outset that Jesus uses the word over a hundred times in the Gospels (mostly in Matthew and Luke) and that it is linguistically feminine and related to Canaanite *malkatu*, an epithet of the Great Goddess, and therefore should be translated "Queendom," he directs attention to its root, *MLK*, "the sign of the creative word, the empowering vision, the counsel that rules by its ability to express the most obvious next step for a group" and has the personal force of "I can!"

It is associated in the Gospel with two other words. The first of these, usually translated "repentance," is *teshuva* (Hebrew), meaning to turn, or return, to "come again, flow back . . . to its origin, or original rhythm." It has the sense of uniting "with something by affinity, because it feels like going home" (see Jesus' saying in

Matt. 19:8 that divorce was allowed only on account of hardheartedness, but that "it was not so in the beginning," and the repeated pleas of God through the prophets [e.g., Hosea 11; 14] to the people to "return" to the One who loves them).

The second word associated with *malchut* is *qereb*, meaning "near." The kingdom is said to be "at hand," here now, something you can touch. "The time is fulfilled" (Mark 1:15). It is time to come back to the beginning, to the original intention of the Creator. We are "ripe"; it is "harvest" time. This is associated with the "I can" aspect, the "we can" meaning of *malchut*: empowerment from deep inside that can rouse a whole nation, move it to make the great "return." Douglas-Klotz offers as examples of the rare historical case of an entire community suddenly changing its whole way of life, "the fall of the Berlin Wall and the ending of apartheid in South Africa."

We can pray that our sense of "can" will be strengthened and aligned with the Creator's original intention, that the kingdom will come and God's will be done, and if we do not achieve the full-blown effect at once, we can at least plant seeds and set bread to rise.

20. Color the world with imagination: Robert Fulghum, *All I Really Need to Know I Learned in Kindergarten* (New York: Villard [Random House], 1988), 50. See also his exercise of the "musical chairs" to enable people to experience physically their fear and frustration when they compete for too few seats and then the comfort of mutual support with places for everybody by sitting on the floor in a front-to-back ring (Robert Fulghum, *Maybe [Maybe Not]: Second Thoughts from a Secret Life* [New York: Villard Books, 1993], 122ff.). Aslan the Lion, the Christ symbol in C. S. Lewis's *Chronicles of Narnia*, sings a world into existence. On worshipping God by dancing, see Dosick, *Dancing with God*, 61-64, 251-52.

21. The Aramaic word for "faith" is *haimanuta*, confidence, firmness, integrity of being in sacred unity, a sense of certainty or rootedness that keeps one unshaken by outer events (Douglas-Klotz, *Hidden Gospel*, 33-34). In the Gospels, Jesus customarily tells people who have experienced healing that it is their own faith (Greek *pistis*) that has made them whole. He also warns strongly against *doubt*, *doubling* one's imagination ("I can walk on water," "I can't walk on water!" Matt. 14:31; cf. Jas. 1:8 and 4:8).

22. Rabbi Robert Levine says that God is waiting for the Messiah—ourselves—to take seriously the transformative task of creating the world. It's not that *we* are waiting; *God* is waiting for us to realize how this thing works (*There Is No Messiah—and You're It: The Stunning Transformation of Judaism's Most Provocative Idea* [Woodstock,Vt.: Jewish Lights, 2003), 157; see also p. 80).

Rabbi Tarfon says in an oft-quoted text: "The day is short and the work is great, and the laborers are sluggish and the wages are high and the householder is urgent. . . . The work is not on you to finish, but neither are you free to desist from it" (*Avot* [The Teachings of] the Fathers II, 20-21, cited in David Hartman, *Joy and Responsibility* [Jerusalem: Ben-Zvi-Posher, 1978], 2). Compare the parable of the Workers in the Vineyard (Matt. 20).

Bibliography

Aaron, David. *Endless Light: The Ancient Path of the Kabbalah to Love, Spiritual Growth, and Personal Power.* New York: Simon & Schuster, 1997.

Albom, Mitch. *Tuesdays with Morrie.* New York: Doubleday, 1997.

Allman, William F. *The Stone Age Present: How Evolution Has Shaped Modern Life—From Sex, Violence, and Language to Emotions, Morals, and Communities.* New York: Simon & Schuster, 1994.

Arendt, Hannah. *On Revolution.* New York: Viking, 1963.

Athanasiou, Tom. *Divided Planet: The Ecology of Rich and Poor.* Boston: Little, Brown, 1996.

Axelrod, Robert. *The Evolution of Cooperation.* New York: Basic, 1984.

Axelrod, Robert, and Michael D. Cohen. *Harnessing Complexity: Organizational Implications of a Scientific Frontier.* New York: Free Press, 1999.

Bailie, Gil. *Violence Unveiled: Humanity at the Crossroads.* New York: Crossroad, 1997.

Barash, David P. *Sociobiology and Behavior.* New York: Elsevier, 1977.

Barlow, Connie. *Green Space, Green Time: The Way of Science.* New York: Springer-Verlag, 1997.

Barlow, Stephen. "A Historical Perspective on Slavery: Demeaning Institution Has Been Practiced By All Races and Most Nations," *Winston-Salem Journal,* July 12, 1997.

Barnhart, Bruno. *The Good Wine: Reading John from the Center.* New York: Paulist Press, 1993.

Baron, Robert A. *Human Aggression.* New York: Plenum, 1977.

Barrow, John D., and Frank J. Tipler. *The Anthropic Cosmological Principle.* New York: Oxford University Press, 1988.

Beerman, Morris. *The Twilight of American Culture.* New York: Norton, 2000.

Beniger, James R. *The Control Revolution: Technological and Economic Origins of the Information Society.* Cambridge, Mass.: Harvard University Press, 1986.

Berke, Joseph H. *The Tyranny of Malice: Exploring the Dark Side of Character and Culture.* New York: Summit, 1988.

Bethell, Tom. *The Noblest Triumph: Property and Prosperity through the Ages.* New York: St. Martin's, 1998.

Bickerton, Derek. *Language and Human Behavior.* Seattle: University of Washington Press, 1995.

Blechman, Barry M., and Stephen S. Kaplan: *Force without War: U.S. Armed Forces as a Political Instrument.* Washington: Brookings Institution, 1978.

Block, Peter. *Stewardship: Choosing Service over Self-Interest.* San Francisco: Berrett-Koehler, 1993.

Boag, John. "Nuclear Accidents—Lessons for the Prevention of Nuclear War,"

IPPNW [International Physicians for the Prevention of Nuclear War] *Report,* April 1987.

Botkin, Daniel B. *Discordant Harmonies: A New Ecology for the Twenty-First Century.* New York: Oxford University Press, 1990.

Bohm, David, and F. David Peat. *Science, Order, and Creativity.* New York: Bantam, 1987.

Bonchek, Avigdor. *Studying the Torah: A Guide to In-Depth Interpretations.* Northvale, N.J.: Aronson, 1996.

Bornstein, David. *The Price of a Dream: The Story of the Grameen Bank and the Idea That Is Helping the Poor to Change Their Lives.* New York: Simon & Schuster, 1996.

Boteach, Schmuel. *Wisdom, Understanding, and Knowledge: Basic Concepts of Hasidic Thought.* Northvale, N.J.: Aronson, 1996.

Bova, Ben. *Immortality: How Science Is Extending Your Life Span—and Changing the World.* New York: Avon, 1998.

Bracken, Joseph A., S.J. *Society and Spirit: A Trinitarian Cosmology.* Toronto: Associated University Presses, 1991.

Brand, Stewart. *The Media Lab: Inventing the Future at MIT.* New York: Viking, 1987.

Braun, Moshe. *The Jewish Holidays: Their Spiritual Significance.* Northvale, N.J.: Aronson, 1996.

Brockman, John. *The Third Culture.* New York: Simon & Schuster, 1995.

Brodie, Richard. *Virus of the Mind: The New Science of the Meme.* Seattle: Integral, 1996.

Bruteau, Beatrice. "Apprenticing to Jesus the Healer." *Journal of Christian Healing* 15, no. 1 (Spring 1993).

———. "The Eucharist of Everyday Life." *Spirit and Life* 92 (January-February 1997).

———. "From *Dominus* to *Amicus:* Contemplative Insight and a New Social Order." *Cross Currents* 31, no. 3 (Fall 1981).

———. *God's Ecstasy: The Creation of a Self-Creating World.* New York: Crossroad, 1997.

———. *The Grand Option: Personal Transformation and a New Creation.* Notre Dame, Ind.: University of Notre Dame Press, 2001.

———. *Merton and Judaism: Recognition, Repentance, and Renewal.* Louisville, Ky.: Fons Vitae, 2003.

———. "Merton and Walsh on the Person." *International Philosophical Quarterly* 31 (Fall 1991).

———. "Neo-Feminism as Communion Consciousness." *Anima* 5 (Fall 1978).

———. "Nicodemus by Night." *Sisters Today* 67, no. 1 (January 1995).

———. *The Psychic Grid: How We Create the World We Know.* Wheaton, Ill.: Quest, 1979.

———. "The Theotokos Project." In *Embracing Earth: Catholic Approaches to Ecology,* edited by Albert LaChance and John E. Carroll. Maryknoll, N.Y.: Orbis Books, 1994.

———. "Trinitarian Personhood," *Cistercian Studies* 22, no. 3 (1987).

Bruteau, Beatrice, ed. *The Other Half of My Soul: Bede Griffiths and the Hindu-Christian Dialogue.* Wheaton, Ill.: Theosophical Publishing House, 1996.

Budiansky, Stephen. *Nature's Keepers: The New Science of Nature Management.* New York: Free Press, 1995.

Byron, Thomas. *The Dhammapada: Sayings of the Buddha: A New Rendering.* New York: Vintage, 1976.

Campbell, Joseph. *The Masks of God:* volume 4, *Creative Mythology.* New York: Penguin, 1968.

Capra, Fritjof. *The Web of Life: A New Scientific Understanding of Living Systems.* New York: Doubleday, Anchor, 1996.

Chorover, Stephan L. *From Genesis to Genocide: The Meaning of Human Nature and the Power of Behavior Control.* Cambridge, Mass.: MIT Press, 1979.

Conquest, Robert. *The Great Terror: A Reassessment.* New York: Oxford University Press, 1990.

Cook, Philip J., and Robert H. Frank. *The Winner-Take-All Society.* New York: Free Press, 1995.

Cox, Archibald. "Cox on the Constitution." Interview. *Common Cause Magazine* 13 (September/October 1987).

Crossan, John Dominic. *The Birth of Christianity: Discovering What Happened in the Years Immediately after the Execution of Jesus.* San Francisco: HarperSanFrancisco, 1998.

————. *The Historical Jesus: The Life of a Mediterranean Jewish Peasant.* San Francisco: HarperSanFrancisco, 1992.

Crossen, Cynthia. *Tainted: The Manipulation of Facts in America.* New York: Simon & Schuster, 1994.

Csikszentmihalyi, Mihaly. *The Evolving Self.* New York: HarperCollins, 1993.

Dabbs, James McBride. *Heroes, Rogues, and Lovers: Testosterone and Behavior.* New York: McGraw-Hill, 2000.

Dalai Lama and Howard Cutler, *The Art of Happiness: A Handbook for Living.* New York: Riverhead, 1998.

Daly, Herman E., and John B. Cobb, Jr. *For the Common Good: Redirecting the Economy Toward Community, the Environment, and a Sustainable Future.* 2nd ed. Boston: Beacon, 1994.

Danielou, Jean. *From Glory to Glory: Texts from Gregory of Nyssa's Mystical Writings, Selected and Introduced.* Translated by H. Musurillo. Crestwood, N.Y.: St. Vladimir's Seminary Press, 1979.

Danson, Donald H. *No Room at the Table: Earth's Most Vulnerable Children.* Maryknoll, N.Y.: Orbis Books, 2003.

Darwin, Charles. *The Descent of Man, and Selection in Relation to Sex.* Princeton, N.J.: Princeton University Press, 1974.

Dawkins, Richard. *The Selfish Gene.* New York: Oxford University Press, 1976.

————. *Unweaving the Rainbow: Science, Delusion and the Appetite for Wonder.* Boston: Houghton Mifflin, 1998.

de Duve, Christian. *Vital Dust: Life as a Cosmic Imperative.* New York: Basic, 1995.

Deikman, Arthur J. *The Wrong Way Home: Uncovering the Pattern of Cult Behavior in American Society.* Boston: Beacon, 1990.

De Waal, Frans. *Good Natured: The Origins of Right and Wrong in Humans and Other Animals.* Cambridge, Mass.: Harvard University Press, 1996.

Desmond, Adrian. *The Ape's Reflexion.* London: Blond & Briggs, 1979.

Diamond, Jared. *Guns, Germs, and Steel: The Fates of Human Societies.* New York: Norton, 1997.

Dodd, Nigel. *The Sociology of Money: Economics, Reason & Contemporary Society.* New York: Continuum, 1994.

Dosick, Rabbi Wayne. *Dancing with God.* San Francisco: HarperSanFrancisco, 1997.

Douglas-Klotz, Neil. *The Hidden Gospel: Decoding the Spiritual Message of the Aramaic Jesus.* Wheaton, Ill.: Quest, 1999.

Dyson, Freeman. *Weapons and Hope.* New York: Harper & Row, 1984.

Easwaran, Eknath. *The Bhagavad Gita for Daily Living,* volume 1. Berkeley: Blue Mountain Center of Meditation, 1975.

Eccles, Sir John, and Daniel N. Robinson. *The Wonder of Being Human: Our Brain and Our Mind.* Boston: New Science Library, 1985.

Ehrlich, Paul. *New World, New Mind: Moving Toward Conscious Evolution.* New York: Simon & Schuster, 1989.

Eisenberg, Nancy, and Janet Strayer, eds. *Empathy and Its Development.* Cambridge, Mass.: Cambridge University Press, 1987.

Elcott, David M. *A Sacred Journey: The Jewish Quest for a Perfect World.* Northvale, N.J.: Aronson, 1995.

Eldredge, Niles. *Dominion.* New York: Holt, 1995.

Eliade, Mircea. *Myths, Dreams, and Mysteries: The Encounter between Contemporary Faiths and Archaic Realities.* Translated by Philip Mairet. New York: Harper Torchbook, 1960.

Farb, Peter. *Humankind.* Boston: Houghton Mifflin, 1978.

Foley, Denise, and Eileen Nechas. *Unequal Treatment: What Do You Know about How Women Are Mistreated by the Medical Community?* New York: Simon & Schuster, 1994.

Foxbrunner, Roman A. *Habad: The Hasidism of R. Shneur Zalman of Lyady.* Northvale, N.J.: Aronson, 1993.

Franck, Frederick. *Fingers Pointing Toward the Sacred: A Twentieth Century Pilgrimage on the Eastern and Western Way.* Junction City, Ore.: Beacon Point, 1994.

Frank, Robert H., and Philip J. Cook. *The Winner-Take-All Society.* New York: Free Press, 1995. Original: Garden City, N.Y.: Anchor, 1979.

French, Hilary. *Vanishing Borders: Protecting the Planet in the Age of Globalization.* New York: Norton, 2000.

Friedman, Thomas. *Longitudes and Attitudes.* New York: Farrar, Straus, Giroux, 2002.

Fritzsch, Harald. *Quarks: The Stuff of Matter.* New York: Basic, 1981.

Fulghum, Robert. *All I Really Need to Know I Learned in Kindergarten.* New York: Villard, 1998.

Galbraith, John Kenneth. *The Good Society.* Boston: Houghton Mifflin, 1996.

Gates, Jeff. *The Ownership Solution: Toward a Shared Capitalism for the Twenty-First Century.* Reading, Mass.: Addison-Wesley, 1998.

Gerzon, Mark. *A Choice of Heroes: The Changing Face of American Manhood.* Boston: Houghton Mifflin, 1982.

Gilbert, Paul. *Human Nature and Suffering.* New York: Guilford, 1992.

Glassman, Bernard. *Bearing Witness: A Zen Master's Lessons in Making Peace.* New York: Bell Tower/Crown, 1998.

Glassman, Bernard, and Rick Fields. *Instructions to the Cook: A Zen Master's Lessons in Living a Life That Matters.* New York: Bell Tower/Crown, 1996.

Goldberg, Steven. *Why Men Rule: A Theory of Male Dominance.* Chicago: Open Court, 1993.

Gordon, Anita, and David Suzuki. *It's a Matter of Survival.* Cambridge, Mass.: Harvard University Press, 1991.

Gorringe, Timothy. *Fair Shares: Ethics and the Global Economy.* New York: Thames & Hudson, 1999.

Goudie, Andrew. *The Human Impact on the Natural Environment.* 2nd ed. Cambridge, Mass.: MIT Press, 1995.

Gray, John. *False Dawn: The Delusions of Global Capitalism.* New York: New Press, 1998.

Greeley, Andrew, and William C. McCready. "Are We a Nation of Mystics?" *New York Times Magazine,* January 18, 1975.

Greider, William. *One World, Ready or Not: The Manic Logic of Global Capitalism.* New York: Touchstone, 1997.

———. *Who Will Tell the People? The Betrayal of American Democracy.* New York: Simon & Schuster, 1992.

Gupta, Mahendranath. *The Gospel of Sri Ramakrishna,* recorded by Mahendranath Gupta. Originally published in five volumes (1897-1932). Translated by Swami Nikhilananda. New York: Ramakrishna-Vivekananda Center, 1942.

Gurary, Noson. *The Thirteen Principles of Faith: A Chasidic Viewpoint, compiled and edited by Moshe Miller.* Northvale, N.J.: Aronson, 1996.

Gurr, Ted Robert. *Why Men Rebel.* Princeton, N.J.: Princeton University Press, 1970.

Gutiérrez, Gustavo. *A Theology of Liberation: History, Politics, and Salvation.* Maryknoll, N.Y.: Orbis Books, 1988.

Hall, Edward T. *Beyond Culture.* New York: Doubleday, Anchor, 1976.

Hapgood. *Up the Infinite Corridor: MIT and the Technical Imagination.* Reading, Mass.: Addison-Wesley, 1993.

Harman, Willis. *Global Mind Change: The Promise of the Last Years of the Twentieth Century.* Indianapolis: Knowledge Systems, 1988.

Harris, Marvin. *Cannibals and Kings: The Origin of Cultures.* New York: Random House, 1977.

Hawkins, Gordon, and Franklin E. Zimring. *The Citizen's Guide to Gun Control.* New York: Macmillan, 1992.

Henderson, Hazel. *Building a Win-Win World: Life Beyond Global Economic Warfare.* San Francisco: Berrett-Koehler, 1996.

———. *Creating Alternative Futures: The End of Economics.* New York: Berkley, 1978.

Hertzberg, Arthur, with Aaron Hirt-Manheimer. *Jews: The Essence and Character of a People.* San Francisco: HarperSanFrancisco, 1998.

Heschel, Abraham Joshua. *I Asked for Wonder: A Spiritual Anthology.* Edited with an Introduction by Samuel N. Dresner. New York: Crossroad, 1992.

———. *The Sabbath: Its Meaning for Modern Man.* New York: Farrar, Straus, Giroux, 1951.

Hicks, George. *The Comfort Women: Japan's Brutal Regime of Enforced Prostitution in the Second World War.* New York: W. W. Norton, 1995.

Horsley, Richard A., and Neil Asher Silberman. *The Message and the Kingdom: How Jesus and Paul Ignited a Revolution and Transformed the Ancient World.* New York: Grosset/Putnam, 1997.

Horsley, Richard A., with John S. Hanson. *Bandits, Prophets, and Messiahs: Popular Movements at the Time of Jesus.* San Francisco: Harper & Row, 1985.

Hoyle, Fred, and Chandra Wickramasinghe. *Lifecloud: The Origin of Life in the Universe.* New York: Harper & Row, 1978.

Hubbard, Barbara Marx. *Conscious Evolution: Awakening the Power of Our Social Potential.* Novato, Calif.: New World, 1998.

Jacobs, Louis. *Holy Living: Saints and Saintliness in Judaism.* Northvale, N.J.: Aronson, 1990.

Jamieson, Kathleen Hall. *Dirty Politics: Deception, Distraction, and Democracy.* New York: Oxford University Press, 1992.

Jantsch, Erich. *The Self-Organizing Universe: Scientific and Human Implications of the Emerging Paradigm of Evolution.* New York: Pergamon, 1980.

Jantsch, Erich, and Conrad H. Waddington, eds. *Evolution and Consciousness: Human Systems in Transition.* Reading, Mass.: Addison-Wesley, 1976.

Johnson, William, ed. *The Cloud of Unknowing.* Garden City: Doubleday Image, 1973.

Kagan, Robert. *Of Paradise and Power.* New York: Knopf, 2003.

Kaku, Michio. *Visions: How Science Will Revolutionize the 21st Century.* New York: Doubleday, Anchor, 1997.

Kamenetz, Rodger. *The Jew in the Lotus.* Northvale, N.J.: Aronson, 1994.

———. *Stalking Elijah: Adventures with Today's Jewish Mystical Masters.* San Francisco: HarperSanFrancisco, 1997.

Katz, Steven T. *The Holocaust in Historical Context.* New York: Oxford University Press, 1994.

Kaus, Mickey. *The End of Equality.* New York: Basic, 1992.

Kaye, Howard L. *The Social Meaning of Modern Biology: From Social Darwinism to Sociobiology.* New Haven: Yale University Press, 1986.

Keating, Thomas. *Open Mind, Open Heart: The Contemplative Dimension of the Gospel.* Butler, N.J.: Contemplative Outreach. 1992.

Keeley, Lawrence H. *Before Civilization: The Myth of the Peaceful Savage.* New York: Oxford University Press, 1996.

Kelman, Steven. *Regulating America, Regulating Sweden: A Comparative Study of Occupational Safety and Health Policy.* Cambridge, Mass.: MIT Press, 1981.

Kemper, Theodore D. *Social Structure and Testosterone: Explorations of the Socio-Bio-Social Chain.* New Brunswick, N.J.: Rutgers University Press, 1990.

Kitcher, Philip. *The Lives to Come.* New York: Simon & Schuster, 1996.

Knitter, Paul F., and Chandra Muzaffar, eds. *Subverting Greed: Religious Perspectives on the Global Economy.* Maryknoll, N.Y.: Orbis Books, 2002.

Kohn, Alfie. *The Brighter Side of Human Nature: Altruism and Empathy in Everyday Life.* New York: Basic, 1993.

Korten, David C. *When Corporations Rule the World.* San Francisco: Kumarian/Berrett-Koehler, 2001.

Kushner, Lawrence. *God Was in This Place & I, i Did Not Know It: Finding Self, Spirituality and Ultimate Meaning.* Woodstock, Vt.: Jewish Lights, 1994.

———. *Honey from the Rock: Visions of Jewish Mystical Renewal.* Woodstock, Vt.: Jewish Lights, 1994.

———. *The River of Light: Spirituality, Judaism, Consciousness.* Woodstock, Vt.: Jewish Lights, 1995.

Kuttner, Robert. *Everything for Sale: The Virtues and Limits of Markets.* New York: Knopf, 1997.

Lackner, Stephan. *Peaceable Nature: An Optimistic View of Life on Earth.* San Francisco: Harper & Row, 1984.

Leakey, Richard, and Roger Lewin. *The Sixth Extinction.* London: Weidenfeld & Nicolson, 1996.

Lederman, Leon, with Dick Teresil. *The God Particle.* Boston: Houghton Mifflin, 1993.

LeDoux, Joseph. *The Emotional Brain.* New York: Simon & Schuster, 1996.

Lerner, Eric J. *The Big Bang Never Happened: A Startling Refutation of the Dominant Theory of the Origin of the Universe.* New York: Times [Random House], 1991.

Lerner, Michael. *Jewish Renewal: A Path to Healing and Transformation.* New York: Grosset/Putnam, 1994.

Levine, Robert N. *There Is No Messiah and You're It: The Stunning Transformation of Judaism's Most Provocative Idea.* Woodstock, Vt.: Jewish Lights, 2003.

Lewin, Roger. *Complexity: Life at the Edge of Order and Chaos.* New York: Macmillan, 1992.

Lewontin, R. C., Steven Rose, and Leon J. Kamin. *Not in Our Genes: Biology, Ideology, and Human Nature.* New York: Pantheon, 1984.

Loewenstein, Werner R. *The Touchstone of Life: Molecular Information, Cell Communication, and the Foundations of Life.* New York: Oxford University Press, 1999.

Lopez Vigil, Jose Ignatio, and Maria Lopez Vigil. *Just Jesus:* volume 1, *A People Starving for Love.* Translated by Trinidad Ongtangco-Regala. New York: Crossroad, 2000.

Lynch, Aaron. *Thought Contagion: How Belief Spreads through Society.* New York: Basic, 1996.

Maass, Peter. *Love Thy Neighbor: A Story of War.* New York: Knopf, 1996.

Mansfield, Victor. "Mādyamika Buddhism and Quantum Mechanics: Beginning a Dialogue." *International Philosophical Quarterly* 19, no. 4 (December 1989*)*.

Margulis, Lynn. *Symbiosis in Cell Evolution.* San Francisco: Freeman, 1981.

Margulis, Lynn, and Dorion Sagan. *Microcosmos: Four Billion Years of Evolution from Our Microbial Ancestors.* New York: Summit, 1986.

Markley, O. W. "Human Consciousness in Transformation." In *Evolution and Consciousness: Human Systems in Transition,* edited by Erich Jantsch and Conrad H. Waddington. Reading, Mass.: Addison-Wesley, 1976.

Maruyama, Magoroh."Toward Cultural Symbiosis." In *Evolution and Consciousness: Human Systems in Transition,* edited by Erich Jantsch and Conrad H. Waddington. Reading, Mass.: Addison-Wesley, 1976.

Mead, Margaret. *Culture and Commitment.* New York: Columbia University Press, 1978.

Menuhin, Yehudi, and Curtis W. Davis. *The Music of Man.* New York: Simon & Schuster, 1986.

Middleton, Faith. *The Goodness of Ordinary People: True Stories from Real Americans.* New York: Crown, 1996.

Midgley, Mary. *Beast and Man: The Roots of Human Nature.* Ithaca, N.Y.: Cornell University Press, 1978.

Milgram, Stanley. *Obedience to Authority.* New York: Harper & Row, 1974.

Miller, Jean Baker. *Toward a New Psychology of Women*. Boston: Beacon, 1978.

Mische, Gerald, and Patricia Mische. *Toward a Human World Order*. New York: Paulist Press, 1977.

Montagu, Ashley. *The Nature of Human Aggression*. New York: Oxford University Press, 1976.

Montuori, Alfonso, and Isabella Conti. *From Power to Partnership: Creating the Future of Love, Work, and Community*. San Francisco: HarperSanFrancisco, 1993.

Moynihan, Daniel Patrick. *On the Laws of Nations*. Cambridge, Mass.: Harvard University Press, 1990.

Needham, Joseph. *The Grand Titration: Science and Society in East and West*. London: Allen & Unwin, 1979.

Needleman, Jacob, *A Sense of the Cosmos*. Garden City, N.Y.: Doubleday, 1975.

Neuman, Matthias, O.S.B. "Toward an Integrated Theory of Imagination." *International Philosophical Quarterly* 18, no. 3 (September 1978).

Nishitani, Keiji. *Religion and Nothingness*. Translated by Jan Van Bragt. Berkeley: University of California Press, 1982.

Noble, David F. *The Religion of Technology*. New York: Knopf, 1997.

North, Robert C. *The World That Could Be*. New York: Norton, 1976.

Nygren, Anders. *Agape and Eros*. Translated by Philip S. Watson. Philadelphia: Westminster, 1953.

Oakman, Douglas E. *Jesus and the Economic Questions of His Day*. Lewiston/Queenston: Edwin Mellen Press, n.d.

Ohmae, Kenichi. *The Borderless World: Power and Strategy in the Interlinked Economy*. New York: HarperBusiness, 1990.

O'Murchu, Diarmuid. *Quantum Theology*. New York: Crossroad, 2004.

O'Neil, John. *Five Bodies: The Human Shape of Modern Society*. Ithaca, N.Y./London: Cornell University Press, 1985.

Ornstein, Robert, and David Sobel. *The Healing Brain: Breakthrough Discoveries about How the Brain Keeps Us Healthy*. New York: Simon & Schuster, 1989.

Ornstein, Robert, and Paul Ehrlich, *New World New Mind: Moving toward Conscious Evolution*. New York: Simon & Schuster, 1989.

Pagels, Heinz R. *The Dreams of Reason: The Computer and the Rise of the Sciences of Complexity*. New York: Simon & Schuster, 1998.

Pankow, Walter. "Openness as Self-Transcendence." In *Evolution and Consciousness: Human Systems in Transition*, edited by Erich Jantsch and Conrad H. Waddington. Reading, Mass.: Addison-Wesley, 1976.

Paul, Liz. "DOE Confirms Weapon Plants Are Unsafe," *SaneWorld* (Summer 1987).

Pearce, Joseph Chilton. *Magical Child: Rediscovering Nature's Plan for Our Children*. New York: E. P. Dutton, 1977.

Pert, Candace B. *Molecules of Emotion*. New York: Scribner, 1997.

Plank, Karl A. "The Eclipse of Difference." In *Merton and Judaism: Recognition, Repentance, and Renewal*, edited by Beatrice Bruteau. Louisville, Ky.: Fons Vitae, 2003.

Pollack, Robert. *Signs of Life: The Language and Meaning of DNA*. Boston: Houghton Mifflin, 1994.

Pran, Dith, ed. *Children of Cambodia's Killing Fields: Memoirs by Survivers*. New Haven: Yale University Press, 1997 .

Prigogine, Ilya, and Isabelle Stengers. *Order Out of Chaos: Man's New Dialogue with Nature.* New York: Bantam, 1984.

Purpel, David E. *The Moral and Spiritual Crisis in Education: A Curriculum for Justice & Compassion in Education.* New York: Bergin & Garvey, 1989.

Redfield, Robert. *Peasant Society and Culture: An Anthropological Approach to Civilization.* Chicago: University of Chicago Press, 1956.

Reich, Charles A. *Opposing the System.* New York: Crown, 1995.

Remen, Rachel Naomi, *My Grandfather's Blessings: Stories of Strength, Refuge, and Belonging.* New York: Riverhead, 2000.

Rheingold, Howard. *The Virtual Community: Homesteading on the Electronic Frontier.* Reading, Mass.: Addison-Wesley, 1993.

Ridley, M. *The Red Queen: Sex and the Evolution of Human Nature.* New York: Macmillan, 1993.

Rogers, Carl. *On Becoming a Person.* Boston: Houghton Mifflin, 1961.

Ross, Gerald, and Michael Kay. *Toppling the Pyramids: Redefining the Way Companies Are Run.* New York: Random House, 1994.

Roszak, Theodore. *Person/Planet: The Creative Disintegration of Industrial Society.* Garden City, N.Y.: Doubleday, Anchor, 1979.

———. *Unfinished Animal.* New York: Harper & Row, 1975.

Rotstein, Ronald D. *The Future.* New York: Carol, 1990.

Russell, Peter. *The Global Brain Awakens: Our Next Evolutionary Leap.* Palo Alto, Calif.: Global Brain, 1995.

Russell, Robert J. *The Lemur's Legacy: The Evolution of Power, Sex, and Love.* New York: Tarcher, 1993.

Sagan, Carl. *The Dragons of Eden: Speculations on the Evolution of Human Intelligence.* New York: Random House, 1977.

Sagan, Eli. *At the Dawn of Tyranny: The Origins of Individualism, Political Oppression, and the State.* New York: Knopf, 1985.

Sahlins, Marshall. *The Use and Abuse of Biology: An Anthropological Critique of Sociobiology.* Ann Arbor: University of Michigan Press, 1976.

Sahtouris, Elisabet. *Gaia: The Human Journey from Chaos to Cosmos.* New York: Pocket Books, 1989.

Saint-Exupéry, Antoine de. *Airman's Odyssey.* New York: Reynal & Hitchcock, 1942.

Salk, Jonas. *The Survival of the Wisest.* New York: Harper & Row, 1973.

Samuel, Michael. *The Lord Is My Shepherd: The Theology of a Caring God.* Northvale, N.J.: Aronson, 1996.

Sanford, Agnes. *The Healing Light.* New York: Ballantine, 1947.

Schachter-Shalomi, Reb Zalman. *Paradigm Shift: From the Jewish Renewal Teachings of Reb Zalman Schachter-Shalomi,* edited by Ellen Singer. Northvale, N.J.: Aronson, 1993.

Schmooker, Andrew Bard. *Out of Weakness: Healing the Wounds That Drive Us to War.* New York: Bantam, 1988.

Schneider, Stephen H. *Laboratory Earth.* New York: Basic, 1997.

Scholem, Gershom. *Kabbalah.* Jerusalem: Keter, 1974; reprint, New York: Meridian/New York Times Books, 1978.

Schrage, Michael. *Shared Minds: The New Technologies of Collaboration.* New York: Random House, 1990.

Schüssler Fiorenza, Elisabeth. *In Memory of Her: A Feminist Theological Reconstruction of Christian Origins.* New York: Crossroad, 1983.

Schwartz, Barry. *The Battle for Human Nature: Science, Morality, and Modern Life.* New York: Norton, 1986.

Shapiro, Rabbi Rami. *Hasidic Tales: Annotated and Explained.* Woodstock, Vt.: Jewish Lights, 2004.

Singer, Ellen, ed. *Paradigm Shift: From the Jewish Renewal Teachings of Reb Zalman Schachter-Shalomi.* Northvale, N.J.: Aronson, 1993.

Singer, Peter. *The Expanding Circle: Ethics and Sociobiology.* New York: Oxford University Press, 1981.

Slater, Philip. *A Dream Deferred.* Boston: Beacon, 1991.

Sobol, David, and Robert Ornstein. *The Human Brain.* New York: Simon & Schuster, 1987.

Solomon, Steven. *The Confidence Game: How Unelected Central Bankers Are Governing the Changed Global Economy.* New York: Simon & Schuster, 1995.

Steinberg, Rabbi Milton. *Basic Judaism.* San Diego: Harcourt Brace, 1975.

Sterling, Claire. *The Terror Network: The Secret War of International Terrorism.* New York: Holt, Rinehart, and Winston, 1981.

Stock, Gregory. *Metaman: The Merging of Humans and Machines into a Global Superorganism.* Toronto: Doubleday Canada, 1993.

Storr, Anthony. *Human Destructiveness.* New York: Grove Weidenfeld, 1991.

Sugarman, Josh. *National Rifle Association: Money, Firepower and Fear.* Washington: National Press, 1992.

Suzuki, David, and Anita Gordon. *It's a Matter of Survival.* Cambridge, Mass.: Harvard University Press, 1991.

Teilhard de Chardin, Pierre. *Letters from a Traveller.* New York: Harper & Row, 1962.

———. *The Phenomenon of Man.* New York: Harper & Row, 1956.

Thomas, Lewis. *The Lives of a Cell.* New York: Bantam, 1974.

Thurman, Howard. *Jesus and the Disinherited.* Boston: Beacon, 1976.

Trungpa, Chögyam. *Cutting through Spiritual Materialism.* Boulder, Colo.: Shambhala, 1973.

Vivekananda, Swami. *What Religion Is.* Edited by John Yale. New York: Julian, 1960.

Waldrop, M. Mitchell. *Complexity: The Emerging Science at the Edge of Order and Chaos.* New York: Simon & Schuster, 1992.

Ward, Peter D., and Donald Brownlee. *Rare Earth: Why Complex Life Is Uncommon in the Universe.* New York: Springer, 2000.

Watson, Lyall. *Dark Nature: A Natural History of Evil.* New York: HarperCollins, 1995.

White, Frank. *The Overview Effect.* Boston: Houghton Mifflin, 1987.

Wilbur, Ken. *A Brief History of Everything.* Boston: Shambhala, 1996.

Wilden, Anthony. *Man and Woman, War and Peace: The Strategist's Companion.* London: Routledge & Kegan Paul, 1987.

Williams, George C. *Adaptation and Natural Selection.* Princeton, N.J.: Princeton University Press, 1981.

Wills, Christopher. *The Wisdom of the Genes.* New York: Basic, 1989.

Wilson, Edward O. *Consilience: The Unity of Knowledge.* New York: Knopf, 1998.

Wright, Frank Lloyd. *The Living City.* New York: Horizon, 1959.

Wright, Robert. *The Moral Animal: Evolutionary Psychology and Everyday Life.* New York: Vintage, 1994.

———. *Nonzero: The Logic of Human Destiny.* New York: Pantheon, 2000.

Yankelovich, Daniel. *New Rules.* New York: Random House, 1981.

Young, Brad H. *Jesus the Jewish Theologian.* Peabody, Mass.: Hendrickson, 1995.

Young, J. Z. *Programs of the Brain: Based on the Gifford Lectures, 1975-7.* New York: Oxford University Press, 1978.

Zuckerman, Ben, and David Jefferson. *Human Population and the Environmental Crisis.* Sudbury, Mass.: Jones & Bartlett, 1996.

Subject Index

Name Index

Flew, A., 256
Fogelin, R. J., 279n9
Foxbrunner, R. J., 287n8
Francis of Assisi, 176
Franck, F., 288n11
Frank, R., 240
Franklin, R., 269n19
Freeman, L., 176
French, H., 229, 234
French, M., 21
Fritzman, J. M., 135
Fulbright, W., 115
Fulghum, W., 316n20
Fuller, B., 112

Gandhi, M., 31
Gates, J., 141, 159, 178, 231, 296n18, 298n1
Gelek Rimpoche, 175
Gilbert, P., 90
Glassman, B., 161-62, 176, 299n7, 303n10, 304n12
Goldberg, S., 34
Gordon, L, 291n12
Gorringe, T., 156-57, 178
Grant, M., 60
Gray, J., 230
Greeley, A., 98
Gregory of Nyssa, 248
Greider, W., 12, 17, 269n13
Gurary, N., 254-55, 260, 314n5
Guttiérrez, G., 64, 104, 272n3, 288n1

Hall, E. T., 147
Hanson, J., 203, 205
Hapgood, F., 113
Harris, M., 20, 274n12
Havel, V., 141
Haywood, R., 110
Henderson, H., 113-14, 141, 144, 171, 290n7&n10, 301n17
Hertzberg, A., 308n19
Heschel, A. J., 192-93, 298n1
Hillel, 188
Hillis, D., 113
Hoover, R., 204
Hornstein, H., 277n5
Horsley, R., 203, 205
Hoyle, F., 242
Hubbard, B. M, 112, 119, 140.

Ikeda, D., 261

Jacobs, L., 260
Jantsch, E., 267n11
Jaworski, J., 178
Jewett, R., 21
Josephus, 217

Kagan, R., 233
Kaku, M., 141
Kamenetz, R., 99, 108
Kapleau, P., 277n5
Kass, L. R., 149
Kauffman, S., 296-97n19
Kaus, M., 178, 213, 244-45, 295n18, 297n20
Keating, T., 175
Kelly, K., 241, 260
Kelman, S., 300n17
King, M. L., Jr., 93
King, W., 42
Kohn, A., 91, 133, 143, 147, 151, 238, 272n3, 280n1, 296n19, 300n13
Korten, D. C., 152, 168, 232, 259
Krippner, S., 163
Kushner, L., 54, 63, 99, 288n11
Kuttner, R., 164, 231, 234, 301n17

Leach, M., xii
Leavitt, H., 270n19
Lerner, M., 43, 46, 56, 65, 76, 115, 141, 147, 158, 163, 168, 178, 181, 214, 230, 245, 277n5, 285n4, 289n3, 296n19
Levine, R., 316n22
Lewin, R., 296n19
Linden, K., 277n5
Lopez Vigil, J. and M., 306n2
Lorenz, K., 137
Lowi, T. J., 266n9
Loy, D., 275n15
Luria, I., 308n19
Lynch, A., 136, 166, 292n8, 294n16.

Main, J., 176
Margulis, L., 66, 154
Markley, O. W., 46, 141
Maruyama, M., 141
May, G., 46
McClelland, D., 286n8
McLuhan, M., 106, 237
Mead, M., 107, 288n2
Meyerson, E., 48